Internationalization of Emerging Economies and Firms

Also by Marin Marinov

FOREIGN DIRECT INVESTMENT IN CENTRAL AND EASTERN EUROPE (*with Svetla Marinova*)

INTERNATIONAL BUSINESS (*with Michael Czinkota, Ilkka Ronkainen, Michael Moffett and Svetla Marinova*)

INTERNATIONALIZATION IN CENTRAL AND EASTERN EUROPE

MARKETING IN THE EMERGING MARKETS OF CENTRAL AND EASTERN EUROPE: The Balkans

MARKETING IN THE EMERGING MARKETS OF ISLAMIC COUNTRIES

MARKETING IN THE EMERGING MARKETS OF LATIN AMERICA

THE CHANGING NATURE OF DOING BUSINESS IN TRANSITION ECONOMIES (*with Svetla Marinova*)

Also by Svetla Marinova

FOREIGN DIRECT INVESTMENT IN CENTRAL AND EASTERN EUROPE (*with Marin Marinov*)

INTERNATIONAL BUSINESS (*with Michael Czinkota, Ilkka Ronkainen, Michael Moffett and Marin Marinov*)

THE CHANGING NATURE OF DOING BUSINESS IN TRANSITION ECONOMIES (*with Marin Marinov*)

Internationalization of Emerging Economies and Firms

Edited by

Marin Marinov
Professor, University of Gloucestershire

and

Svetla Marinova
Professor, Aalborg University

palgrave
macmillan

First published 2012 by
PALGRAVE MACMILLAN

Palgrave Macmillan in the UK is an imprint of Macmillan Publishers Limited, registered in England, company number 785998, of Houndmills, Basingstoke, Hampshire RG21 6XS.

Palgrave Macmillan in the US is a division of St Martin's Press LLC, 175 Fifth Avenue, New York, NY 10010.

Palgrave Macmillan is the global academic imprint of the above companies and has companies and representatives throughout the world.

ISBN: 978–0–230–34833–2

This book is printed on paper suitable for recycling and made from fully managed and sustained forest sources. Logging, pulping and manufacturing processes are expected to conform to the environmental regulations of the country of origin.

A catalogue record for this book is available from the British Library.

A catalog record for this book is available from the Library of Congress.

10 9 8 7 6 5 4 3 2 1
21 20 19 18 17 16 15 14 13 12

Printed and bound in the United States of America

To our beloved parents with everlasting gratitude,

To all devoted colleagues and friends with respect

Marin and Svetla

Contents

Tables

Figures

Boxes

Contributors

Claude Chailan is Professor of Marketing at the International University of Monaco and visiting professor at ITESM, Puebla campus, in Mexico. He is also a guest lecturer at a number of business schools, such as Escuela de Administracón de Negocios in Lima and Ecole Supérieure des Affaires in Beirut, and French universities. Previously Chailan held high-level positions in international management, including senior positions at Danon, Sara Lee and L'Oréal. He was actively involved in the development of international brands in France, Mexico and Venezuela. Chailan received his Master's from ESSEC Business School in Paris and diploma in Political Science from IEP, Aix-en-Provence. He holds a doctorate in marketing management from the University of Nice Sophia-Antipolis. His articles have been published in journals such as *Euromed Journal of Business*, the *Journal of Product and Brand Management*, the *Journal of Marketing Management* and the *Journal of Technology Management in China*.

Elaine Y. T. Chew is Lecturer in the School of Business at Monash University, Malaysia. She obtained her BA in Business at Monash University, Australia, MBA at Otaru University of Commerce and PhD at Nagoya University, Japan. Her research interests include international business, organizational behaviour and human resource management. Previously she worked on a government-funded project examining the pattern internationalization processes of Malaysian business ventures and the determinants of foreign direct investment by Malaysian companies.

Enrique Claver is Professor and Head of the Department of Management at the University of Alicante, Spain. He received his PhD from the University of Valencia, Spain. His primary research interests are strategic management, knowledge management and international management. He has published research papers in international journals including *Information & Management*, *Total Quality Management & Business Excellence*, *International Business Review*, the *Asia Pacific Journal of Management*, *Emerging Markets Finance and Trade*, the *Journal of Asia Business Studies*, *Family Business Review*, the *Journal of General Management*, *Chinese Management Studies*, *Cross Cultural Management: An International Journal*, the *International Journal of Tourism Research* and the *International Journal of Contemporary Hospitality Management*.

Bruno Henrique Rocha Fernandes is Senior Lecturer of the Master's and Doctorate Management Program and Dean of Graduate Studies at Universidade Positivo, Curitiba, Brazil. He is a visiting researcher at the University of Plymouth, UK. He obtained his PhD at Universidade de São

Paulo-USP, and his Master's at Universidade Federal do Paraná. He was a visiting researcher at the University of Cambridge, UK, in 2003. Fernandes has authored numerous books and articles. His research on organizational strategy is mainly focused on the resource based view and addresses organizational capabilities and competences, strategic performance measurement systems and people engagement in strategy. He has consulted for foreign companies operating in Brazil.

Marian Gorynia is Professor of International Business at the Faculty of International Business and Economics, Department of Strategy and Policy of International Competitiveness at the Poznan University of Economics in Poland, where he is also Rector. His main research areas include international business (strategy of the firm in international business, international competitiveness of firms and industries, foreign direct investment), strategic management and industrial organization. Gorynia has published extensively in Polish and international scholarly journals, including *Eastern European Economics*, *Russian and East European Finance and Trade*, the *Journal of Transnational Management Development*, the *Journal of Transnational Management*, the *Journal of East–West Business*, the *Eastern Journal of European Studies*, the *Journal for East European Management Studies*, *Competitiveness Review*, the *Journal of Euro-Asian Management*, *Mondes en Developpement* and the *Czech Sociological Review*. He has also authored or co-authored 15 books. He has served on the editorial boards of the *Journal of Transnational Management Development*, the *Journal of Transnational Management* and *Ekonomista*. He is a member of the Board of the European International Business Academy and of the Board of the International Management Development Association.

Michael W. Hansen is Associate Professor and Head of the Center for Business and Development Studies, Copenhagen Business School. Hansen's research is focused on multinational corporation (MNC) strategy in developing countries (Asia in general and India in particular) and emerging economies, internationalization of Danish industry towards developing countries, linkages between MNCs and local firms in developing countries, outward foreign direct investment from developing countries, and foreign direct investment and the environment.

Francis Ille is Associate Professor of International Business at the International University of Monaco. He has been a visiting professor at Ocean University of China in Qingdao and at IILM, Delhi, India, and guest lecturer at several Western European universities. His business career, extending over 30 years, took him from Procter & Gamble to IBM where he held marketing and sales management positions in Africa, the Middle East, Asia and the United States. He has also participated in several consulting missions as an expert for TACIS programmes of the European Commission in the fields of development of the private sector in the Commonwealth of Independent

States and Africa. He has published in the *Journal of Chinese Economic and Foreign Trade Studies*.

Siv Marina Flø Karlsen is Associate Professor at Oslo University College in the Faculty of Social Sciences. Her research interests include international marketing, internationalization of small- and medium-sized enterprises, global firms and corporate social responsibility.

Chin Kian Low is Lecturer and Head of the Department of International Business at the Faculty of Accountancy and Management at the University of Tunku Abdul Rahman, Malaysia. He obtained his BA and MBA at the University of South Alabama, USA. He is currently pursuing his PhD in International Business at the University of Tunku Abdul Rahman, Malaysia. His research interests include international business, international entrepreneurship and organizational behaviour. He has previously been involved in projects funded by the Malaysian government that are related to Malaysian foreign direct investment in China.

Randi Lunnan is Professor of Strategy at BI Norwegian School of Management in Oslo, Norway. She is currently a visiting professor at Temple University, Philadelphia, USA. Her research interests include international management and strategic alliances. She has been concerned with how alliances evolve over time and specifically what affects the sharing of knowledge and the rejuvenation of alliances. Lunnan has also looked into the structuring of businesses across national boundaries, both in terms of localization of head office functions and standardization versus adaptation of strategy and work practices.

Marin Marinov is Professor of International Business and Management at the University of Gloucestershire, UK. He has held a number of professorial appointments worldwide, including universities in Germany, Sweden, Denmark, Bulgaria, USA, Finland, France, Portugal, China and Spain. His research encompasses internationalization of businesses, multinational corporations, business development in emerging markets, business policy and strategy, and research in curricula development for business education. Marinov has consulted for multinational firms and national governments on topics related to strategies in the process of internationalization, mostly via foreign direct investment. He has published eight books, including three on marketing in emerging markets; he has also written numerous book chapters and articles published in refereed academic journals.

Svetla Marinova is Associate Professor of International Business at Aalborg University, Denmark. She has an MBA from the University of Warwick, UK, and a PhD from Copenhagen Business School, Denmark. She has taught and conducted extensive research in many countries on both sides of the Atlantic and in Asia. Her research interests include business internationalization and the role of institutions, strategy of multinational firms from emerging markets, and changes in management and marketing of firms undergoing intensive internationalization. Marinova has published four books, numerous book chapters and papers in refereed academic journals including *International Marketing Review, Research in Marketing, European Journal of Marketing* and *Advances in International Marketing.*

Lee Peng Ng is Lecturer at the Faculty of Business and Finance in the University Tunku Abdul Rahman, Malaysia. She obtained her BA and MBA from the Northern University of Malaysia (University Utara in Malaysia). She is currently pursuing her PhD at the Northern University of Malaysia. Her research interests include work–life balance, work engagement, stress or burnout, and international business. She has recently been involved in a government-funded collaborative research project of the Ministry of Science, Technology & Innovation that examines the patterns of the internationalization of Malaysian business ventures and the determinants of foreign direct investment by Malaysian companies.

Jan Nowak is Professor of Marketing at the Business School of Central European University in Budapest, Hungary. He has previously taught and administered academic and executive training programmes at the University of New Brunswick, Canada, and the University of the South Pacific, Fiji. Nowak holds a Master's in Management and a PhD in Business Administration from Warsaw University. He specializes in marketing and international business, consults for a number of companies, and develops and delivers professional training courses. He has published five books, more than 50 papers in international refereed periodicals and conference proceedings, numerous reports, working papers, book chapters, case studies and other research outputs. His articles have appeared in the *Journal of International Consumer Marketing,* the *International Review of Retail, Distribution and Consumer Research,* the *Journal of Transnational Management Development,* the *Journal for East European Management Studies, Eastern European Economics, The Electronic Journal on Information Systems in Developing Countries,* the *Journal of Euro-marketing,* the *Journal of East–West Business* and the *Journal of International Food and Agribusiness Marketing.* Nowak is a member of the editorial boards of the *Journal of East–West Business* and the *Journal of Transnational Management.*

Niina Nummela is Professor of International Business at Turku School of Economics at the University of Turku, Finland. Her areas of expertise include international entrepreneurship, cross-border acquisitions, interfirm cooperation and research methods. She has published widely in academic journals, including the *Journal of World Business, Management International Review,* the *European Journal of Marketing, International Small Business Journal* and the *Journal of Engineering and Technology Management,* among others. Additionally, she has contributed to several books. She has edited *International Growth of SMEs* (2010).

Andrei Panibratov is Associate Professor at the Graduate School of Management, Saint Petersburg University, Russia. He obtained his MBA from the University of Wales and a PhD in Economics from Saint Petersburg State University. He has attended professorial training programmes at the Haas School of Business, University of California at Berkeley, Texas A&M University, HEC-Paris, Aalto University School of Management (Finland) and Fundação Dom Cabral (Brazil). He has participated in consulting and research projects for the World Bank, UMIST (UK), Lappeenranta University of Technology School of Business (Finland), Tampere University of Technology (Finland), and in a number of European and Russian firms. His research interests include strategy of Western multinational enterprises in Russia, internationalization of Russian firms, marketing decisions when moving abroad and outward foreign direct investment from Russia.

Bent Petersen is Professor of International Business at the Copenhagen Business School (CBS) and Head of Department of Strategic Management and Globalization. Previously he was Director of the Doctoral School in Economics and Management at CBS, where he received his PhD and Master's in Business Economics. For five years he worked as an economist at the Carlsberg Research Center, Department of Biotechnology and Business Diversification (Denmark). His primary research interests are in internationalization of emerging economy firms, global value chains, and dynamics of global sourcing. He has published in the *Journal of International Business Studies*, the *Journal of Business Research*, *Managerial Decisions and Economics*, the *Journal of International Marketing*, *Management International Review*, *Long Range Planning*, *International Studies of Management & Organization*, *International Business Review*, *World Development* and the *Journal of International Management*, among others. He is a member of the Academy of International Business, the European International Business Academy and the Strategic Management Society. He has been a visiting scholar in France (HEC), Australia (University of Queensland) and Sweden (University of Gothenburg).

Song-Hanh Pham is Senior Lecturer at Sheffield Business School, UK, where she is a fellow of the Higher Education Association and module leader for Global Supply Chain Management. She is also a consultant for medium-size manufacturers and service organizations that seek to expand their markets abroad, especially into emerging markets. Earlier in her career, she worked as lecturer and vice dean of the International Economic and Business Faculty at the Foreign Trade University in Vietnam. She earned her Master's in International Economics from the University of Birmingham, UK, and her PhD from the Copenhagen Business School, Denmark, with a major in international business.

Daniela Buzzulini Prioste is currently an MBA candidate in the International Management Program at Fundação Instituto de Administração at the University of São Paulo. She has a degree in business administration from the Catholic University of São Paulo. She works as an IT consultant and graduate lecturer at Serviço Nacional de Aprendizagem Comercial, Brazil. She has 15 years experience in banking automation. Prioste has also worked for the two main private Brazilian banks, Bradesco and Itaú Unibanco. Her work experience includes management of international projects and the exploration and technical analysis of international companies. Her main research interests are in corporate diplomacy and the internationalization of companies.

Diego Quer is Associate Professor in the Department of Management, University of Alicante, Spain, where he obtained his PhD. His primary research interests include several topics of international management, such as entry modes in internationalization with a special focus on the Chinese context. He has published research papers in, among other journals, *Asia Pacific Journal of Management, International Business Review, Emerging Markets Finance and Trade, Chinese Management Studies, Family Business Review, Cross Cultural Management: An International Journal,* the *International Journal of Tourism Research,* the *International Journal of Contemporary Hospitality Management,* the *Journal of General Management,* the *Journal of Asia Business Studies,* the *Asia Pacific Journal of Business Administration* and the *Journal of China Tourism Research.*

Mélanie Raukko is a post-doctoral researcher in international business at Turku School of Economics, University of Turku, Finland. Currently she is a visiting researcher at Manchester Business School. Raukko's research interests are in cross-border mergers and acquisitions, performance after mergers and acquisitions, value creation in acquisitions, human resource and cultural integration.

Laura Rienda is Associate Professor in the Department of Management, University of Alicante, Spain, where she obtained her PhD. Her main research interests include family business management, international management, and business and management in India. She has published research papers in international journals including the *Asia Pacific Journal of Management, Family Business Review, Chinese Management Studies, Cross Cultural Management: An International Journal,* the *Journal of General Management,* the *Journal of Small Business and Enterprise Development,* the *Asia Pacific Journal of Business Administration* and *La Revue des Sciences de Gestion.*

Karl Sauvant is the founding executive director of the Vale Columbia Center on Sustainable International Investment, Senior Research Scholar and Lecturer in Law at Columbia Law School, Co-Director of the Millennium Cities Initiative, and Guest Professor at Nankai University, China. Until July 2005, Sauvant was director of the United Nations Conference on Trade and Development Division on Investment, Technology and Enterprise Development, the focal point in the UN system for matters related to foreign direct investment (FDI) and technology, as well as a major interface with the private sector. While at the UN, he created, in 1991, the prestigious annual *World Investment Report*, of which he was the lead author until 2004. He is the author of, or responsible for, a substantial number of publications on issues related to economic development, FDI and services. In 2006, he was elected an Honorary Fellow of the European International Business Academy, and in 2011 he was elected Fellow of the Academy of International Business. He received his PhD from the University of Pennsylvania in 1975.

Henrik Schaumburg-Müller has recently retired as professor at the Center for Business and Development Studies at the Copenhagen Business School. He has been working with business and development related issues for almost 40 years. In recent years, he worked mainly on strategies of developing country firms, their positions and upgrading in global value chains, and their linkages to multinational corporations.

René Eugenio Seifert is Assistant Professor in Management at Universidade Positivo, Curitiba, Brazil. He obtained his PhD at the University of Birmingham, UK, and BA and Master's in Business Administration from the Universidade Federal do Paraná, Brazil. His research interests are mainly in the relationship of interpretation and strategic choice, organizational growth, small business development, management and sustainability. He has worked extensively in the area of international trade of Brazilian firms. Seifert is a co-founder of the Instituto Brasileiro de Estudos e Pesquisa Social, the Brazilian institute for social research, and is an active member of Casa da Videira, an NGO working on alternative solutions for urban sustainability.

Marjan Svetličič is Professor at the Faculty of Social Sciences, University of Ljubljana, where he was awarded Ambassador of Science of the Republic of Slovenia. He is Fellow of the European Academy of International Business (EIBA), a member of the board of the Trans European Policy Study Association, Vice Chair of the COST project 'The Emergence of Southern Multinationals' and a member of the FP7 Advisory Group for International Scientific Cooperation. Svetličič was also President of the EIBA. His areas of research interest and expertise are foreign direct investments, transnational firms, European Union integration, internationalization of small countries, globalisation, and internationalization. He has authored more than 300 articles and many books, including *Enhanced Transition by Outward Internationalization: Outward FDI by Slovene Firms* (co-authored with A. Jaklič), *Small Countries in a Global Economy* (co-edited with D. Salvatore and J. P. Damijan) and *The World Economy: Challenges of Globalization and Regionalization* (co-edited with H. Singer).

Piotr Tarka works at the Faculty of International Business and Economics, Department of Strategy and Policy of International Competitiveness at Poznan University of Economics in Poland. His research interests are in methods of statistical measurement, multivariate data analysis, marketing research effectiveness analysis, customer data and computer-aided statistics. He worked for a few years as data analyst and consultant at Research International and Imas International. He is the author of 60 articles and numerous research publications. As an active member of the Polish Statistical Association and the International Classification and Data Analysis, he participates in many academic workshops and scientific meetings.

Jens Erik Torp is a research associate at the Center for Business and Development Studies, Copenhagen Business School. He has for more than 30 years worked with private sector development related issues as a researcher and consultant. Recently, his research has focused on the implications of foreign direct investment from Asian countries.

Tiia Vissak is Senior Researcher in International Economics and Business at the Faculty of Economics and Business Administration, University of Tartu, Estonia, where she obtained her PhD. Her main research interests are different forms of linear and non-linear internationalization, international entrepreneurship issues, networks and strategic alliances, transition economies and case studies as a research methodology. Vissak is a reviewer for several journals, including the *International Business Review* and the *Journal of East–West Business*.

Witold Wilinski is Lecturer at the World Economy Faculty in the Warsaw School of Economics, Poland. His current research focuses on internationalization and outward foreign direct investment from post-communist countries, strategies of multinational companies and corporate finance. He received his PhD from the Warsaw School of Economics and his Post-Master Diploma from the University Paris Dauphine, France. He has 12 years of professional experience in corporate finance, including a CFO position.

Radoslaw Wolniak is Senior Lecturer at the Faculty of Economic Sciences, University of Warsaw, Poland, where he received his Master's and PhD in Economics. He also completed postgraduate studies at Harvard University Graduate School of Business Administration and at Kellogg Graduate School of Management, Northwestern University in the USA. Wolniak has conducted research on foreign direct investment and on the strategy of multinational firms. He has published articles in international refereed journals and books on these subject areas. He has over 30 years teaching experience in international business, the strategy of multinational firms and international marketing. He has held positions on management and supervisory boards of companies in Poland and is engaged in business consulting for foreign firms. He is also a member of the International Management Development Association and the European International Business Academy.

Cesar Akira Yokomizo is a PhD candidate at the São Paulo Business Administration School, Fundação Getulio Vargas (FGV), Brazil, and at the School of Economics, Business Administration and Accountancy, University of São Paulo (USP), Brazil. Currently he is a graduate lecturer at Fundação Instituto de Administração (Brazil) and Serviço Nacional de Aprendizagem Comercial (Senac, Brazil), and conducts research in Brazil for FGV. He holds a Master's in Business, has a specialist degree in network engineering and telecommunications systems from the National Institute of Telecommunications (Inatel, Brazil) and degrees in both computing engineering and economics from USP. His main research interests include international strategy and innovation, innovation management, knowledge management, information and communication technologies, and information technology.

Xiaotian Zhang is a PhD student at the Faculty of Economics and Business Administration, University of Tartu, Estonia. He holds a Master's from Belarus State Economic University and has also studied architecture in China. His main research interests are on forms of internationalization, entry mode and target country selection in internationalization. He is the founder and CEO of the firm OÜ Raatuse International Trade.

Youzhen Zhao is Associate Professor of International Business and Strategy at the School of Management, Fudan University, China, where she obtained her PhD in Management. She has been a visiting scholar at Bocconi University, Italy (2010), the Massachusetts Institute of Technology (2005), the University of Oregon (2004) and Washington University in St Louis (2000). Her recent research interests include regional headquarters and R&D centres of multinational enterprises in China, cross-border mergers and acquisitions of Chinese firms, and the creation of international new ventures.

1
Internationalization of Emerging Economies and Firms

Marin A. Marinov and Svetla T. Marinova

Introduction

After the First World War international business became an integral part of the activities of firms in economically advanced economies. The internationalization process intensified under the impact of the growing national economic activities, the international movement of capital, the demand for raw materials and food, the introduction of international property laws, and the development of technology and infrastructure. Consequently, multinational corporations (MNCs) experienced accelerated growth and became dominant players in the world marketplace. MNCs entered overseas markets via exporting and foreign direct investment (FDI).

The Second World War acted as an external shock, reconfiguring the world marketplace. Consequently, US, UK and Dutch MNCs became the largest and most significant foreign direct investors from 1945 until the end of the 1970s, with their FDI accounting for more than two-thirds of the world's FDI. In the early post-war period the volume of the world FDI flows was negatively impacted upon by the decline of the colonial empires, the development of communist states and the considerable government intervention in economic activities, including widespread nationalization.

The introduction of the Open Door Policy in China at the end of the 1970s, the fall of the Berlin Wall in 1989, the development of regional economic blocs, reduced government interference in business activities, worldwide implementation of privatization programmes and the globalization of capital flows have all led to a boost of the internationalization of national economies and of their firms, initially in the developed world alone, then in both the developed and developing parts of the world. Those changes acted as triggers for the rise of firms from emerging markets that had high aspirations for a significant international presence. The process of liberalization and democratization in former communist and authoritarian countries; the transfer of know-how, marketing and management expertise; technological development; and the emergence of business support structures have all facilitated the rapid internationalization of MNCs from emerging economies.

Theoretical foundation for the internationalization of emerging economies and firms

The conceptualization of internationalization theories has been embedded in industrial organization and economics. Until the end of the 1980s internationalization theory drew on the internationalization experience of US and West European firms before and after the Second World War (see for example Coase, 1937; Bain, 1956; Williamson, 1971; Rugman, 1981; Buckley and Michie, 1996). The contemporary internationalization of economies and firms from the developing parts of the world, such as China, India, Russia, Brazil, Malaysia and many others, have posed serious questions as to the viability and applicability of extant theoretical paradigms dealing with firm internationalization (Mathews, 2002b, 2006).

The resource-based view concerning internationalization asserts that foreign expansion strategy depends on exclusive endowments of the home economy, which provide opportunities for building competitive advantages (Tan and Vertinsky, 1996; Prien and Butler, 2001) at the country or firm level. Wernerfelt (1984) distinguishes resources as tangible and intangible as well as having a time dimension. Resources provide opportunities for the appearance and strengthening of competitive advantages (Barney, 1991; Peteraf, 1993), depending on the specifics of any particular competitive environment (Tallman, 1992; Brush and Artz, 1999).

In the process of their internationalization, economies and firms may also have resources that are disadvantageous and account for country-specific and firm-specific disadvantages when entering new markets (Child and Rodrigues, 2005). Compensation for existing disadvantages of emerging economies and their firms can be done in the process of their internationalization via acquiring new assets (Deng, 2004). Beneficial resources are unique and hard to replicate. They can give an economy and its firms competitive advantages in the long run (Barney, 1991; Amit and Schoemaker, 1993). Penrose (1959) argues that the most important and long lasting assets shape specific advantages that can sustain the internationalization process. At any specific period of time an economy or a firm can possess superior strength, considering its advantages, and certainly it may own resources that restrain value creation and are disadvantageous for entering foreign markets (see for example Leonard-Barton, 1992; Hu, 1995; Rangan and Drummond, 2004). Rugman (1981) developed and introduced a matrix relating country- and firm-specific advantages and their role in internationalization. The matrix has been explored in relation to internationalizing emerging economies and their firms (Rugman, 2007; Rugman and Li, 2007).

A key competitive advantage on country and firm level is entrepreneurship. It may be especially significant in creating and utilizing other advantages into dynamic capabilities, as well as creating strategic opportunities at country and firm level. Most significant country-specific advantages stem from natural resource endowments, labour force characteristics, cultural and economic factors as well as sometimes an appealing country brand.

The set of country and firm advantages and disadvantages can evolve over time (Amit and Schoemaker, 1993) as well as their impact on institutional development (Child and Tse, 2001). Cuervo-Cazurra et al. (2007) argue that resources that are advantages in the home market can become disadvantageous abroad. Taking an integrative perspective it is clear that firm internationalization should be viewed through an economic, social and political lens (Child and Rodrigues, 2005) considering the characteristics of the home and host context.

The institution-based view relating to internationalization activities argues that institutions are a set of formal and informal rules and their enforcement arrangements (Schmoller, 1990 [1900]). Institutions simultaneously define, facilitate and restrain strategic choices (Peng and Delios, 2006) as they shape institutional embeddedness of business activities (North, 1990) in a specific context. Institutions set the rules and norms for the functioning of firms and industries (Ring et al., 2005; Peng et al., 2008). In developed countries institutions are considered beneficial if they uphold conditions for the effective execution of market mechanisms (Meyer et al., 2009). In emerging economies institutions are demoted as detrimental, as in general they are less developed and do not guarantee effective markets. Makino et al. (2002) found that institutional differences in emerging economies are more salient and that both formal and informal institutions impact strongly on business development.

The internationalizing firms from emerging economies are referred to as latecomer firms. Debatably they do not possess numerous sturdy competitive advantages when compared to their global rivals (Rui and Yip, 2008). This is generally applicable to all firms from emerging economies at the initiation of their internationalization. Consequently, emerging economies and their firms originally display severe disadvantages in terms of their international competitiveness (Hennart, 2009). The latecomer perspective provides an insight of how internationalization could be used to compensate for initial competitive disadvantages of national economies and firms (Mathews, 2002a).

The critical latecomer advantages are in labour intensive production, cost leadership, flexibility and speed of adaptation in terms of production processes and products (Makino et al., 2002). Some latecomer economies and their firms are embedded in a culture, such as Confucianism, that encourages incessant learning and self-development vis-à-vis rivals. Disadvantages of latecomer economies and firms could range from lack of knowledge of the market dynamics to lack of technological or management know-how. Innovations, know-how, technology, production process, marketing and managerial expertise are readily obtainable in developed country contexts from where they could be accessed. Consequently, supported in a number of cases by their governments, latecomer firms go into developed markets with a clear cut strategic intent to obtain assets providing them with potentials to create competitive advantages.

When latecomer firms penetrate other emerging economies' contexts, they mostly seek markets and resources while possessing certain advantages vis-à-vis MNCs from developed countries. Such advantages, added to government support (Child and Rodrigues, 2005), enable latecomer firms to compete successfully against MNCs from the developed world (Dawar and Frost, 1999) in contexts with underdeveloped institutional environment and market mechanisms (Khanna and Palepu, 1997, 2000; Cuervo-Cazurra and Genc, 2008). The internationalization of latecomer economies and firms presents a challenge to international business theory to focus on the potential relevance of domestic institutional factors in transitional contexts. It also presents an opportunity to explore the evolution of country- and firm-specific advantages in contexts where formal institutions appear immature from a Western perspective.

Accelerated internationalization of emerging economies and firms

Fast internationalization also referred to as accelerated internationalization is a new phenomenon of the world economy, which is observed in developed and emerging economies (Schrader et al., 2001). Leading latecomer economies and firms internationalize especially fast. Thus accelerated internationalization represents an idiosyncratic characteristic of such entities. When attaining it, latecomer emerging economies and firms need to overcome a number of disadvantages such as the need for advanced technology. Most importantly the key success factors in applying accelerated internationalization have been managerial, organizational novelties well suited to the evolving new conditions of the global economy. These new moves towards overseas operations have been possible via strategic novelties that allowed latecomers to exploit their statuses to attain successful fast internationalization. Successful accelerated internationalization is facilitated by accelerated international entrepreneurship (Oviatt and McDougall, 1999) for born global firms (Weerawardena et al., 2007).

Schrader et al. (2001:1228) point out that 'there is little theory about managing international risk for firms experiencing the accelerated internationalization'. Miller (1992) puts forward five types of strategic deeds to reduce international risks, namely imitation, risk avoidance, flexibility, cooperation and control. It seems that some firms from emerging economies engaging in accelerated internationalization engage in imitation. Flexibility as a strategic approach has helped latecomers decrease the expenditure associated with inner organizational adjustment to varying international conditions. The strategic approaches linked to cooperation with other businesses, from both advanced and emerging economies and which are striving for a high level of control, are also applied by rapidly internationalizing firms from emerging economies. There is evidence that risk avoidance is the least applied strategy for risk reduction by such firms (see for example Deng, 2004; Luo et al., 2010). Carving market niches as suggested by Kohn (1997) has been a successful strategy for risk reduction applied by emerging economy firms, with traditional low-tech products, internationalizing in developed economies (Liu and Li, 2002).

Inward foreign direct investment in emerging economies

Inward foreign direct investment (IFDI) into emerging economies has been increasing significantly in recent years in spite of the global economic downturn. Thus in 2010 emerging economies received for the first time more than half of the world FDI (see Figure 1.1) amounting to US$525 billion, which is 53 per cent of a total of US$1,122 billion (*The Hindu*, 2011). IFDI was on the rise in mainland China, Hong Kong (PR of China), Indonesia, Malaysia, Singapore and Vietnam among many other emerging economies. Main regional winners have been South East Asia and to a lesser extent Latin America. In the meantime there was a 14 per cent decrease in IFDI into South Asia in 2010. This downward trend has been most significantly felt in India. The country had a 31.5 per cent decrease in IFDI.

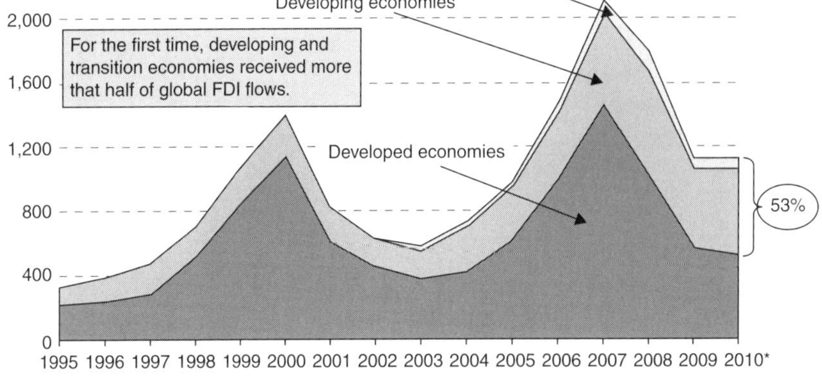

Figure 1.1 FDI inflows: global and by group of economies, 1995–2010 (US$ billion)

Source: UNCTAD, Global Investment Trends Monitor, 2011, www.unctad.org/en/docs//webdiaeia 20111_en.pdf.

While global FDI in 2010 rose by 1 per cent, IFDI in emerging economies increased by about 10 per cent in comparison with 2009. This has been mostly due to the sustained economic performance of the majority of the emerging economies and the rising South–South FDI flows.

Outward foreign direct investment from emerging economies

Outward foreign direct investment (OFDI) from emerging economies has risen considerably during the past decade, amounting to US$220 billion in 2008 (see Figure 1.2). OFDI flows are strongly concentrated. Just four of them, Russia, China, Brazil and India accounted for almost 70 per cent of the bulk of OFDI from emerging economies, and seven of them were responsible for 89 per cent in 2008.

In most of the emerging economies, insignificant attention is paid to OFDI by the home government. Exceptions are countries such as Singapore. The strategy of its government is to develop 'an external wing' of the national economy through OFDI (Sauvant et al., 2010). China, which has developed an institutional OFDI system (Luo et al., 2010), and recently Russia are in the process of developing such a system. In the meantime countries such as Brazil (Fleury and Fleury, 2011) and India (Sauvant et al., 2011) do not have national policy and institutional support systems for OFDI.

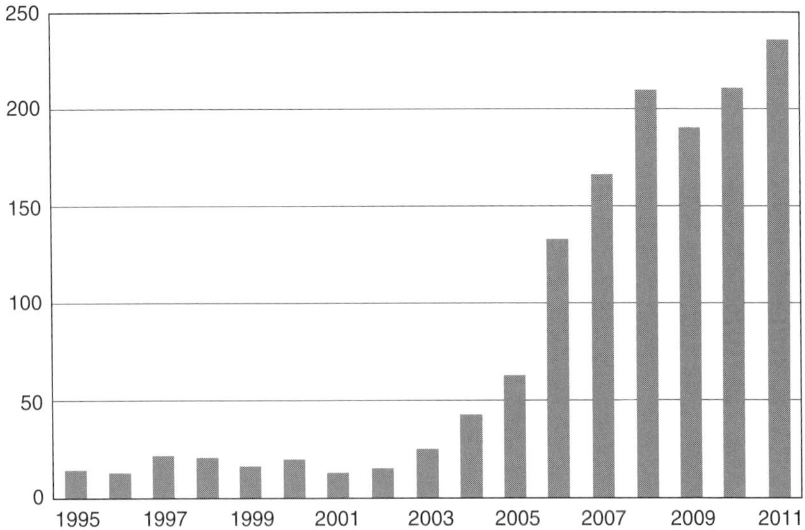

Figure 1.2 OFDI from emerging economies, 1995–2011 (US$ billion)

Source: IMF statistics (2010), www.efic.gov.au/country/mwrd/worldriskdevelopmentsbackissues/Pages/WorldRiskDevelopmentsOctober2010.aspx.

The motives for OFDI from emerging economies vary significantly depending on home and host country characteristics. Considering OFDI motives of Asian emerging economies (Rasiah et al., 2010) claim that they can be arranged in terms of significance throughout the process of their international expansion as follows: market seeking, followed by labour seeking with progressively increasing importance, natural resource seeking, value chain control seeking, financial incentive seeking and technology seeking. Panibratov (2010) as well as Kalotay and Sulstarova (2010) argue that the motives for Russian OFDI fluctuate considerably, with key ones being market seeking, resource seeking, strategic asset seeking and efficiency seeking. Moreover it has been claimed that a serious motive in the 1990s for Russian OFDI has been alleviating political and economic risk at home via 'capital flight' strongly linked to 'system escape' (see for example Panibratov, 2010). In the paper by Böwer et al. (2009) 2,645 cases of outward mergers and acquisitions (M&As) from emerging economies, in the period January 1999 to March 2008, have been evaluated. The major motives for these investments were the seeking of natural resources, technology and markets.

Overview of the book

Chapter 2 by Karl Sauvant deals with issues concerning governments worldwide seeking to attract FDI and who, for that purpose, have liberalized their national regulatory frameworks for FDI and established a strong international investment regime. Nevertheless, there is evidence that, as a result of a number of important documents, discussed in the chapter, national governments re-evaluate their stance towards FDI, or at least some of its types. The re-evaluation has demonstrated itself in a number of regulatory changes that may eventually lead to a regime balancing the rights of investors and host countries in a manner that would place more emphasis on maintaining policy space for host country governments while still providing protections for foreign investors.

Chapter 3, by Witold Wilinski, investigates and assesses the level of internationalization of economies and their firms originating from former communist countries. The investigation makes the analysis using the internationalization of developed economies and their firms as a benchmark. Thus differences in the process have been used to compare and contrast internationalization in two dissimilar contexts. More specifically the focus is on the regions of Central and Eastern Europe, south-eastern Europe, as well as the Commonwealth of Independent States (CIS), excluding the Asian former Soviet Union republics. The chapter analyses the proactive internationalization of economies and firms from those regions using official data on outward FDI. Ultimately a detailed comparative analysis of MNEs from the emerging economies from the three regions is conducted, evaluating the role of the factors impacting on the internationalization process at the country and firm level.

Chapter 4 by Marian Gorynia, Jan Nowak, Piotr Tarka and Radosław Wolniak studies the role of contextual specifics on the Investment Development Path (IDP) model of ten countries of Central and Eastern Europe (CEE), all members of the European Union. The aim of the chapter is to investigate the timing and explore the factors that have influenced the movement of the ten CEE economies through their IDP stages. The authors have identified the current positioning of these countries on their IDP journey using a graph depicting the relationship between net outward investment position (NOIP) per capita and GDP per capita, as well as a complete data analysis of inward and outward FDI stock and the absolute values of the NOIP. The analysis shows different positions of the economies studied. Reasons for differences in IDP experiences are investigated on the basis of which new theoretical considerations to the original IDP model are suggested.

Chapter 5 by Marjan Svetličič uses empirical studies and our own survey conducted in various regions of the European Union. The evidence demonstrates that FDI can contribute to the sustainable development of countries and regions, provided that it is integrated in national and regional development policies. Differences have been identified in the role and promotion of FDI between transition emerging and Western developed economies. Most importantly transition economies see FDI as a more important instrument for enhancing country and firm competitiveness than Western countries. Further evidence holds that emphasis on policies attracting FDI is different in the two contexts. It has been demonstrated that FDI incentives work better in developed regions of the European Union while, in less developed regions, economic fundamentals are critical. Enhancing long-lasting FDI implies emphasis on preserving existing FDI and its upgrading along the international value chain. Policies for promoting FDI should also include supporting and promoting local multinationals in their engagement in outward FDI to enhance restructuring of the home economy.

In Chapter 6, Siv Marina Flø Karlsen, Youzhen Zhao and Randi Lunnan investigate the development of rapidly internationalizing Chinese and Norwegian small and medium-sized firms. The commonality among cases was the way these born-global firms considered and implemented the speed of their globalization. Although firms varied in size and rate of expansion they all turned global quite rapidly after their start-ups. A key cause for the speedy international development of the Chinese firms has been the fact that they have a much larger export share than expected for a born-global small or medium-sized firm. In the process the Chinese government has played an active role by facilitating and funding local firm development and internalization. The research findings raise the question, Is a new theory to explain the globalization of Chinese firms needed? Even if extant theories on born-global firms may be suitable for this purpose, the roles played by the central and provincial governments needs to be taken into consideration and studied in depth.

In Chapter 7 Tiia Vissak and Xiaotian Zhang conduct an investigation on firms becoming born global, that is starting their internationalization after establishment and entering markets in other continents and, in some cases, also using more advanced market entry modes. They study how three Chinese firms have become truly born global without having any previous market experience or knowledge. They bring evidence that throughout their internationalization the investigated firms acquired necessary knowledge mainly through participating in trade fairs and learning from friends and long-term cooperation partners, as well as via hiring highly experienced staff.

In Chapter 8 by Andrei Panibratov the internationalization of Russian high-tech multinational enterprises (MNEs) is analysed. Firms from the telecommunications and IT sectors growing overseas have been investigated. The preference Russian MNEs have when considering entry choices, environmental constraints and investment alternatives have been evaluated. Due to the rapid development of the Russian high-tech sector, there has been a considerable rise of sophisticated technologies in the sector. Consequently, when internationalizing Russian MNEs have mostly applied acquisition of strategic assets than advanced technologies. Escalating OFDI diversification presents Russian MNEs with capabilities to match the internationalization attempts of their global rivals. Home sustainable economic development, low cost prospects for international expansion, Russian government assistance, and a large high quality cheap labour force are expected to continue to drive the extension of Russian firms abroad.

Chapter 9 by Niina Nummela and Mélanie Raukko sheds light on conceptual issues related to the role of culture in cross-border acquisitions and makes suggestions how best to analyse such acquisitions in future studies when cultures of advanced and emerging economies blend. The investigation links the key culture-related constructs, such as cultural awareness, fit and distance, as well as acculturation, with the acquisition process. A longitudinal real-time case study of an Indian–Finnish acquisition in the IT field is studied. The key findings support the following. First, successful cultural integration requires not only cultural fit and awareness, but also understanding. Second, in a cross-border acquisition the perceived cultural differences vary during the process. Hence, cultural learning occurs and enhances cultural integration and increases the cultural awareness of both parties involved in an acquisition. Third, acculturation may lead to a negative outcome, if the expectations concerning the integration process are not met.

Chapter 10 by Bent Petersen and Song-Hanh Pham addresses the issue of whether manufacturers from emerging economies should engage in the downstream activities of marketing and sales. They examine how manufacturers taking export marketing and sales responsibility experience better export performance than those who leave these downstream activities more or less in the hands of global intermediaries or buyers. Hypotheses are formulated in relation to responsibility of specific marketing and sales activities covering the core marketing mix. The hypotheses are tested on a large sample of firms from the wood furniture industry of Vietnam. The results suggest that engagement in marketing and sales generally has a positive payoff in terms of higher export growth and profitability.

Chapter 11, by Elaine Chew, Lee Peng Ng and Chin Kian Low, brings evidence that international business activities are no longer dominated by well-established large multinational firms. They claim that the traditional view that the internationalization of firms is a sequential and incremental learning process has also been seriously challenged. They aim at contributing to filling the gap of the investigation of the internationalization process of Malaysian firms. To do this, they examine the approaches and processes adopted by Malaysian firms when venturing abroad. Five case studies are presented. The findings support the view that internationalization activities of firms from emerging economies are not necessarily conducted in a sequential mode. The patterns and speed of firm internationalization have been influenced by firm characteristics prior to internationalization, management expertise and capabilities, technological level and the ability to create and maintain business networks.

In Chapter 12, the study of Chinese multinationals conducted by Diego Quer, Enrique Claver and Laura Rienda outlines the distinctive characteristics of the internationalization process. They analyse the influence of various host country factors on the location of Chinese OFDI. From a sample of 189 OFDI decisions made by 35 mainland Chinese firms in 63 countries in various parts of the world, the study results show that host market size and the existence of an overseas Chinese presence in the host country are positively associated with the number of Chinese FDIs. Surprisingly, the study conveys that greater difficulties associated with doing business overseas and the high level of host country political risk have no effect on Chinese FDI abroad.

In Chapter 13 by Rene Eugenio Seifert and Bruno Henrique Rocha Fernandes the case of a born-global Brazilian firm, Trikke Tech Inc., is presented. In their study the authors have considered how particular meanings and understandings have informed international entrepreneurship. The research findings imply that the inception of the firm Trikke as a born-global venture has been enlightened by the entrepreneurs' perception that the firm's pioneering product had an inherent value and probable opportunities for commercialization and entrepreneurial success for which persistence and risk taking was required. These entrepreneurial understandings have been vital in orienting international actions of the firm. Their analysis also suggests that meanings and understandings – oriented to the use of alternative governance structures and action in multiple countries – were not antecedents to the firm's inception but emerged in the course of entrepreneurs' attempts to venture internationally.

In Chapter 14, Daniela Prioste and Cesar Yokomizo researched the internationalization specifics of a firm from Brazil operating in the software industry. Their research results show two distinct internationalization paths pursued by the firm. The first one is via creation of their own office in Canada and another via establishing a partnership with a Portuguese firm. The firm's Canadian experience in internationalization developed slowly but more consistently, while the Portuguese experience was fast, but, by not considering some aspects critical for internationalization, ended with the partnership breaking down.

In Chapter 15, Claude Chailan and Francis Ille investigate the grounds guiding an emerging economy firm in developing a particular approach to branding. They also bring evidence about the role of brand strategy in creating a sustainable competitive advantage. The applied case-study investigation demonstrates that the creating brand policy is mostly the result of an initial managerial selection supplemented by increasing knowledge and expertise, with particular 'triggering' occasions playing the role of catalysts. The research findings propose important considerations concerning branding by firms from emerging economies that are expanding overseas.

In Chapter 16, Michael Hansen, Jens Erik Torp and Henrik Schaumburg-Müller present an outline of Chinese and Indian investments in Denmark, reflecting on whether these investments are a new or conventional type of investment. Analysing the blueprints of Chinese and Indian FDI in Denmark using two theoretical positions, new insights concerning the motives behind Asian investments have been identified, taking the perspective on a relatively small open economy. They show that the Asian investors in Denmark are truly unconventional in a number of aspects. Instead of being identified as market-seeking entries in mature industries, many actual investments have been found to be strategic asset-seeking in technological frontier industries, obviously aimed at increasing capabilities upstream or downstream, regarding the value chain of investing firms. Considering the conventional approach, many seemed to fall into the category of traditional trade support investments in industries where emerging economies habitually have their comparative advantages, namely in: largely low cost IT and software; textiles and garments; and electronics. It has furthermore been confirmed that the strategic ambitions of Chinese and Indian investors in certain cases have been jeopardized by problems of integrating the Danish acquisitions and consequently harvesting the strategic rents of the investment.

References

Amit, R. and Schoemaker, P.J.H. (1993). Strategic assets and organisational rents. *Strategic Management Journal*, 14(1), 33–46.

Bain, J. (1956). *Barriers to New Competition*. Boston, MA: Harvard University Press.

Barney, J. (1991). Firm resources and sustained competitive advantage. *Journal of Management*, 17(1), 99–120.

Böwer, U., Fernandez, D. and Thimann, C. (2009). Outward FDI from emerging markets: evidence from firm-level M&A data. (www.eea-esem.com/files/papers/EEA-ESEM/2009/1137/2009-02-12-OFDI-paper-Boewer.pdf).

Brush, T., and Artz, K. (1999). Toward a contingent resource-based theory: The impact of information asymmetry on the value of capabilities in veterinary medicine. *Strategic Management Journal*, 20(3), 223–50.

Buckley, P. and Michie, J. (1996). *Firms, Organizations and Contracts: A Reader in Industrial Organization*. Oxford: Oxford University Press.

Child, J. and Rodrigues, S. (2005). The internationalisation of Chinese firms: a case for theoretical expansion? *Management and Organization Review*, 1(3), 381–410.

Child, J. and Tse, D.K. (2001). China's transition and its implications for international business. *Journal of International Business Studies*, 32(1), 5–21.

Coase, R. (1937). The nature of the firm. *Economica*, 5, 386–405.

Cuervo-Cazurra, A. and Genc, M. (2008). Transforming disadvantages into advantages: developing-country MNEs in the least developed countries. *Journal of International Business Studies*, 39(6), 957–79.

Cuervo-Cazurra, A., Maloney, M. and Manrakhan, S. (2007). Causes of the difficulties in internationalization. *Journal of International Business Studies*, 38(5), 709–25.

Dawar, N. and Frost, T. (1999). Competing with giants: survival strategies for local companies in emerging markets. *Harvard Business Review*, 77(2), 119–29.

Deng, P. (2004). Outward investment by Chinese MNCs: motivations and implications. *Business Horizons*, 47, 8–16.

Fleury, A. And Fleury, M.T.L. (2011) *Brazilian Multinationals: Competences for Internationalization*, Cambridge: Cambridge University Press.

Hennart, J.-F. (2009). Down with MNE-centric theories! Market entry and expansion as the bundling of MNE and local assets. *Journal of International Business Studies*, 40, 1432–54.

Hindu, The (2011). Emerging economies get more FDI for the first time, 19 January. (www.thehindu.com/business/Economy/article1102477.ece).

Hu, Y. (1995). The international transferability of the firm's advantages. *California Management Review*, 37(4), 73–88.

Kalotay, K. and Sulstarova, A. (2010). Modelling Russian outward FDI. *Journal of International Management*, 16(2), 131–42.

Khanna, T. and Palepu, K. (1997). Why focused strategies may be wrong for emerging markets. *Harvard Business Review*, 75(4), 41–51.

Khanna, T. and Palepu, K. (2000). The future of business groups in emerging markets: long-run evidence from Chile. *Academy of Management Journal*, 43(3), 268–85.

Kohn, T.O. (1997). Small firms as international players. *Small Business Economics*, 9, 45–51.

Leonard-Barton, D. (1992). Core capabilities and core rigidities: A paradox in managing new product development. *Strategic Management Journal*. 13(S1), 111–26.

Liu, H. and Li, K. (2002). Strategic implications of emerging Chinese multinationals: the Haier case study. *European Management Journal*, 20(6), 699–706.

Luo, Y., Xue, Q. and Han, B. (2010). How emerging market governments promote outward FDI: experience from China. *Journal of World Business*, 45(1), 68–79.

Makino, S., Lau, C. and Yeh, R. (2002). Asset-exploitation versus asset-seeking: implications for location choice of foreign direct investment from newly industrialised economies. *Journal of International Business Studies*, 33(3), 403–21.

Mathews, J. (2002a). Competitive advantages of the latecomer firm: A resource-based account of industrial catch-up strategies. *Asia–Pacific Journal of Management*, 19(4), 467–88.

Matthews, J. (2002b). *Dragon Multinational: Towards a New Model of Global Growth*. New York, NY: Oxford University Press.

Matthews, J. (2006). Dragon multinationals: New players in the 21st century globalization. *Asia–Pacific Journal of Management*, 25(1), 5–27.

Meyer, K., Estrin, S., Bhaumik, S. and Peng, M. (2009). Institutions, resources and entry strategies in emerging economies. *Strategic Management Journal*, 30(1), 61–80.

Miller, K.D. (1992). A framework for integrated risk management in international business. *Journal of International Business Studies*, 23, 311–31.

North, D. (1990). *Institutions, Institutional Change and Economic Performance*. Cambridge: Cambridge University Press.

Oviatt, B.M. and McDougall, P.P. (1999). A framework for understanding accelerated international entrepreneurship, in R. Wright (ed.), *Research in Global Strategic Management*. Stamford, CT: JAI Press, 23–40.

Panibratov, A. (2010). Russian multinationals: entry strategies and post-entry operations. Electronic Publications of Pan-European Institute, 15/2010. (www.tse.fi/FI/yksikot/erillislaitokset/pei/Documents/Julkaisut/Panibratov_netti_final2.pdf). Peng, M. and Delios, A. (2006). What determines the scope of the firm over time and around the world? An Asia Pacific perspective. *Asia–Pacific Journal of Management*, 23(4), 385–405.

Peng, M., Wang, D. and Jiang, Y. (2008). An institution-based view of international business strategy: A focus on emerging economies. *Journal of International Business Studies*, 39(5), 920–36.

Penrose, E. (1959). *The Theory of the Growth of the Firm*. Oxford: Oxford University Press.

Peteraf, M. (1993). The cornerstones of competitive advantage: A resource-based view. *Strategic Management Journal*, 14(3), 179–91.

Prien, R. and Butler, J. (2001). Is the resource based view a useful perspective for strategic management research? *Academy of Management Review*, 26(1), 22–40.

Rangan, S. and Drummond, A. (2004). Explaining outcomes in competition among foreign multinationals in a focal host market. *Strategic Management Journal*, 25(3), 285–93.

Rasiah, R., Gammeltoft, P. and Jiang, Y. (2010). Home government policies for outward FDI from emerging economies: lessons from Asia, *International Journal of Emerging Markets*, 5(3/4), 333–57.

Ring, P., Bigley, G., D'Aunno, T. and Khanna, T. (2005). Perspectives on how governments matter. *Academy of Management Review*, 30(2), 308–20.

Rugman, A. (1981). *Inside the Multinationals: Economics of Internal Markets*. New York, NY: Columbia University Press.

Rugman, A. (2007). Multinational enterprises from emerging markets. Paper presented at the Berlin Roundtable Meeting on 'The Role of the G8 in an Endangered Global Economic and Political Climate', Berlin, June 1–2.

Rugman, A. and Li, J. (2007). Will China's multinationals succeed globally or regionally? *European Management Journal*, 25(5), 333–43.

Rui, H. and Yip, G. (2008). Foreign acquisitions by Chinese firms: A strategic intent perspective. *Journal of World Business*, 43(2), 213–26.

Sauvant, K.P., Maschek, W.A. and McAllister, G.A. (eds) (2010). *Foreign Direct Investments from Emerging Markets: The Challenges Ahead*. New York, NY: Palgrave Macmillan.

Sauvant, K.P., Pradhan, J.P., Chatterjee, A. and Harley, B. (eds) (2011). *The Rise of Indian Multinationals: Perspectives on Indian Outward Foreign Direct Investment*. New York, NY: Palgrave Macmillan.
Schmoller, G. (1990 [1900]). *Simmels Philosophie des Geldes*, ed. P.U. Hein. Frankfurt: Peter Lang.
Shrader, R.C., Oviatt, B.M. and McDougall, P.P. (2001). How new ventures exploit tradeoffs among international risk factors: lessons for the accelerated internationalization of the 21st century. *Academy of Management Journal*, 43(6), 1227–47.
Tallman, S. (1992). A strategic management perspective on host country structure of multinational enterprises. *Journal of Management*, 18(3), 455–71.
Tan, B. and Vertinsky, I. (1996). Foreign direct investment by Japanese electronic firms in the United States and Canada: modeling the timing of entry. *Journal of International Business Studies*, 27(4), 655–81.
Weerawardena, J., Mort, G., Liesch, P. and Knight, G. (2007). Conceptualizing accelerated internationalization in the born global firm: a dynamic capabilities perspective. *Journal of World Business*, 42(3), 294–306.
Wernerfelt, B. (1984). A resource-based view of the firm. *Strategic Management Journal*, 5(2), 171–80.
Williamson, O. (1971). The vertical integration of production: Market failure considerations. *American Economic Review*, 61, 112–23.

2

The Regulatory Framework for Investment: Where Are We Headed?

Karl P. Sauvant

Introduction

As Yair Aharoni (2010) has pointed out, 'globalization compels almost all firms to organize all value-added activities in a global manner'. Globalization has, in no small measure, been driven by foreign direct investment (FDI). While world FDI flows averaged US$50 billion during the first half of the 1980s, they had reached US$2.1 trillion in 2007 (before declining, I would say temporarily, to US$1.1 trillion in 2009, on account of the financial crisis and recession) (UNCTAD, 2010) (Table 2.1).[1]

These flows, undertaken by more than 80,000 multinational enterprises (MNEs), had accumulated to a stock of some US$19 trillion in 2009. The FDI stock generated in this manner, via 800,000 plus foreign affiliates, produces estimated sales of goods and services of some US$30 trillion, a figure that compares with world exports of US$16 trillion (one-third of which consists of intrafirm trade). These figures refer only to control exercised by parent companies through FDI. Control over firms abroad can, of course, also be exercised through various non-equity forms (e.g. management contracts, technology and franchising agreements), in this manner (probably considerably[2]) expanding the scope of international production falling under the common governance of MNEs.

Be that as it may, FDI has become more important than trade in delivering goods and services to foreign markets, integrating not only markets but also national production systems through an internal international division of labour of MNEs. This creates an integrated international production system – the productive core of the globalizing world economy. Moreover, since FDI consists of a bundle of tangible and intangible assets (including capital, employment, technology, skills, access to markets), it can play an important role in a country's development effort.[3]

At the same time, the landscape of the world FDI market is changing. In particular, firms headquartered in emerging markets are becoming important players, with, among them, state-controlled entities (especially

Table 2.1 Selected indicators of FDI and international production, 1990–2009

	Value at current prices (billions of US$)				Annual growth rate (per cent)				
Item	**1990**	**2005**	**2008**	**2009**	**1991–95**	**1996–2000**	**2001–05**	**2008**	**2009**
FDI inflows	208	966	1,771	1,114	22.5	40.0	5.2	–15.7	–37.1
FDI outflows	241	893	1,929	1,101	16.8	36.1	9.2	–14.9	–42.9
FDI inward stock	2,082	11,525	15,491	17,743	9.3	18.7	13.3	–13.9	14.5
FDI outward stock	2,087	12,417	16,207	18,982	11.9	18.4	14.6	–16.1	17.1
Income on inward FDI	74	791	1,113	941	35.1	13.4	31.9	–7.3	–15.5
Income on OFDI	120	902	1,182	1,008	20.2	10.3	31.3	–7.7	–14.8
Cross-border M&As[a]	99	462	707	250	49.1	64.0	0.6	–30.9	–64.7
Sales of foreign affiliates	6,026	21,721	31,069[b]	29,294[c]	8.8	8.2	18.1	–4.5[b]	–5.7[c]
Gross product of foreign affiliates	1,477	4,327	6,183[d]	5,812[c]	6.8	7.0	13.9	–4.3[d]	–5.7[c]
Total assets of foreign affiliates	5,936	49,252	71,694[f]	77,057[f]	13.7	19.0	20.9	–4.9[f]	7.5[f]
Export of foreign affiliates	1,498	4,319	6,663[g]	5,186[g]	8.6	3.6	14.8	15.4	–22.2[g]
Employment by foreign affiliates (thousands)	24,476	57,799	78,957[b]	79,825[i]	5.5	9.8	6.7	–3.7[h]	1.1[i]
Memorandum									
GDP (in current prices)	22,121	45,273	60,766	55,005	5.9	1.3	10.0	10.3	–9.5
Gross fixed capital formation	5,099	9,833	13,822	12,404[i]	5.4	1.1	11.0	11.5	–10.3
Royalties and licence fee receipts	29	129	177	–	14.6	8.1	14.6	8.6	–
Export of goods and services	4,414	12,954	19,986	15,716	7.9	3.1	14.8	15.4	–21.4

[a] Data are available only from 1987 onwards (M&As: mergers and acquisitions).

[b] Data for 2007 and 2008 are based on the following regression result of sales against inward FDI stock (in millions of US$) for the period 1980–2006: sales1 471.6211 + 1.9343 * inward FDI stock.

[c] Data for 2009 based on the observed year-over change of the sales of 3,659 TNCs' foreign operations between 2008 and 2009.

[d] Data for 2007 and 2008 are based on the following regression result of gross product against inward FDI stock (in millions of US$) for the period 1982–2006; gross product = 566.7633 + 0.3658 * inward FDI stock.

[e] Decline in gross product of foreign affiliates assumed to be the same as the decline in sales.

[f] Data for 2007 and 2008 are based on the following regression result of assets against inward FDI stock (in millions of US$) for the period 1980–2006: assets = –3,387.7138 + 4.9069 * inward FDI stock.

[g] Data for 1995–97 are based on the following regression result of exports of foreign affiliates against inward FDI stock (in millions of US$) for the period 1982–94: exports = 139.1489 + 0.6413 * FDI inward stock. For 1998–2009, the share of exports of foreign affiliates in world export in 1998 (33.3%) was applied to obtain the values.

[h] Based on the following regression result of employment (in thousands) against inward FDI stock (in millions of US$) for the period 1980–2006: employment = 17,642.5861 + 4.0071 * inward FDI stock.

[i] Data for 2009 based on the observed year-over change of the estimated employment of 3,659 TNCs' foreign operations between 2008 and 2009.

[j] Based on data from IMF, World Economic Outlook, April 2010.

Note: Not included in this table are the values of worldwide sales by foreign affiliates associated with their parent firms through non-equity relationships and of the value of sales of the parent firms themselves. Worldwide sales, gross product, local assets, exports and employment of foreign affiliates are estimated by extrapolating the worldwide data of the foreign affiliates of TNCs from Austria, Canada, the Czech Republic, Finland, France, Germany, Italy, Japan, Luxembourg, Portugal, Sweden and the United States for sales; those from the Czech Republic, Portugal, Sweden, and the United States for gross product; those from Austria, Germany, Japan and the United States for assets; those from Austria, the Czech Republic, Japan, Portugal, Sweden and the United states for exports; and those from Austria, Germany, Japan, Switzerland and the United States for employment, on the basis of the shares of those countries in worldwide outward FDI stock.

Source: UNCTAD, based on its FDI/TNC database (www.unctad.org/fdi statistics); UNCTAD, GlobStat; and IMF, International Financial Statistics, June 2010.

state-owned enterprises and sovereign wealth funds (SWFs)) rising in importance. This, in turn, contributes to a reassessment of the costs and benefits of FDI in general, considering that such investment is, after all (from the perspective of governments), just a tool to advance their growth and development.

Given the role that FDI plays in the world economy and can play in national development, it is important to understand how this investment is regulated, both at the national and international levels. And since the international regulatory framework for investment has become an important parameter for national policy and rule making in this area, the following discussion focuses on the characteristics and development of the international investment regime.

The national regulatory framework

At the national level, many host countries, and especially emerging markets,[4] have special laws and regulations in place that govern FDI, typically complemented by provisions in other laws and regulations (e.g. concerning taxation). The story of national FDI regulation, at least since the mid-1980s, is one of creating a favourable climate for this investment: countries have progressively liberalized the conditions for the entry of MNEs into their markets (e.g. by opening sectors to foreign investors); facilitated the operations of these enterprises (e.g. by abolishing performance requirements); and provided various protections to MNEs and their foreign affiliates (e.g. against arbitrary nationalizations). The data compiled by UNCTAD since 1992 document this story convincingly: out of a total of 2,748 regulatory FDI changes made by countries across the world during the period 1992–2009, 89 per cent were in the direction of making the investment climate more favourable to foreign investors (Table 2.2).

These regulatory changes have been accompanied by active efforts to attract FDI. Virtually all countries have an investment promotion agency at the national level, and many have such agencies also at the provincial and even city levels. There may be some 8,000 agencies in existence today worldwide,[5] making the world market for FDI highly competitive. Typically, these agencies seek to attract as much FDI as possible to their shores, although an increasing number also have become more focused by targeting investors that can make a particular contribution to the host economy, in line with its overall development objectives. Financial, fiscal, regulatory and other incentives are an important tool for this purpose, even though the effectiveness of such incentives is often questionable (see UNCTAD, 1996).

In addition, a rising number of home countries of MNEs (including virtually all developed countries, but also more and more emerging markets) facilitate the internationalization of their firms and even provide support to their MNEs to expand abroad (see Buckley et al., 2010; De Beule and Van

Table 2.2 National regulatory changes, 1992–2009[a]

Item	1992	1993	1994	1995	1996	1997	1998	1999	2000	2001	2002	2003	2004	2005	2006	2007	2008	2009
Number of countries that introduced changes	43	56	49	69	66	76	60	65	70	71	72	82	103	92	91	58	54	50
Number of regulatory changes	77	100	110	112	114	150	145	139	150	207	246	242	270	203	177	98	106	102
Liberalization/ promotion	77	99	108	106	98	134	136	130	147	193	234	218	234	162	142	74	83	71
Regulations/ restrictions	–	1	2	6	16	16	9	9	3	14	12	24	36	41	35	24	23	31

[a] Compared with reporting on these numbers in previous World Investment Reports, the wording in the table has changed from 'more favorable' to 'liberalization/promotion' and from 'less favorable' to 'regulations/restrictions'.

Source: UNCTAD (2010:77).

Den Bulcke, 2010), ranging from the provision of information about investment opportunities abroad, to the financing of feasibility studies, to the offering of insurance of investments against political risk.[6] This reflects the expectation of governments that, to remain internationally competitive in an open world economy, their firms increasingly need to acquire a portfolio of locational assets that provides them with better access to markets and resources of various kinds.

All in all, the national regulatory regime for FDI in host and home countries is today very favourable to foreign investors – probably more favourable than at any time in history. In particular, the manufacturing and natural resources[7] sectors are largely open to such investment, although the liberalization process in the services sector has not gone equally far. In addition, countries actively seek to attract FDI, and home countries support the internationalization process of their firms through various means. One of these means is the establishment of a strong international investment law regime.

The international regulatory framework

As the principal capital exporting countries and homes to most MNEs, the developed countries have been the principal advocates and drivers of the establishment of a strong international investment law regime. Reflecting their interests, they sought rules that protect the investments made by their firms abroad and, beyond that, facilitate their operations in foreign markets, both in terms of market entry and managing their foreign affiliates on a day-to-day basis. At the same time, it was expected that such a regime would encourage the flow of investment to countries that were seen as lacking a strong rule of law in the investment area, especially the developing countries (and, later, the economies in transition).

As in the trade area, the construction of this investment regime began with bilateral treaties, in particular friendship, commerce and navigation treaties and, since 1959, bilateral investment treaties (BITs);[8] by the end of 2009, there were about 2,750 BITs and some 250 free trade agreements with substantial investment chapters (UNCTAD, 2010:81). The international investment law regime also consists of various regional,[9] interregional[10] and partial multilateral[11] agreements (collectively 'international investment agreements' –(IIAs)). In the absence of a comprehensive multilateral agreement on investment, the international investment law regime today consists therefore of a patchwork of rules, including voluntary instruments,[12] that is multilayered and multifaceted.

Not surprisingly, furthermore, most IIAs reflect the interest and priorities of the developed countries as the traditional home countries of MNEs. In particular, they typically provide distinct protections for the post-entry treatment of foreign investors, including fair and equitable treatment, full protection and security, treatment otherwise in accordance with the international minimum standard, and prompt, adequate and effective compensation in case of expropriation. Most modern investment agreements also provide investors with a direct right to enforce these protections through investor–state arbitration. More recently, a growing number of these instruments also seek to facilitate the entry and operations of investors, most importantly by granting national treatment at the pre-establishment phase and most-favoured-nation treatment.[13]

In other words, the international investment law regime focuses largely on the rights of investors and the responsibilities of host countries, enforceable under international law. From that perspective, the regime today is open, stable and predictable, provides for transparent rules for the treatment of foreign investors and their foreign affiliates and can be enforced if need be. In fact, one could argue that the international investment law regime is stronger than the international trade regime, as it can be enforced directly by investors, as opposed to investors having to go through their governments in order to settle claims if and when they feel aggrieved. To quote Thomas Waelde (2009:514):

> Investment treaties ... have built, indubitably, one of the most effective and truly legal regimes within the fragmented and mostly quite rudimentary institutional frameworks for the global economy. Comparable in terms of legal character and effectiveness to the WTO regime, the international investment regime is arguably more advanced, as it fully incorporates the most important and directly affected non-state actors. In a longer-term perspective, claimants (and their lawyers), who are essentially driven by private interests, help ensure greater compliance and effectiveness for the treaties and their underlying objectives than can or is achieved by exclusively inter-state implementation procedures. It also goes beyond the prospective-remedy-only sanction available under the WTO.

Factors driving change

These are the characteristics of the *current* international regulatory framework for FDI. However, a number of developments are underway that have an impact on the nature of this framework. Six are particularly noteworthy.

A changing appreciation of the quality of FDI

While all governments continue to seek FDI as it can make a contribution to growth and development, a number of them are paying more attention to the *quality* of the investment they seek to attract, in terms of both the mode of entry of investment and the extent to which it has sustainable development characteristics.

As to the first consideration, relatively little attention was paid in the recent past to whether foreign investors entered a market through greenfield projects (i.e. the establishment of new production facilities) or through mergers and acquisitions (M&As)[14] – both were seen as bringing the bundle of tangible and intangible assets associated with FDI that are important for development (see UNCTAD, 2000; Globerman and Shapiro, 2010). In a number of countries, however, certain M&As are increasingly regarded with reservation. The principal reason is that M&As merely represent a change in ownership and are often accompanied by restructuring (and hence frequently involve a reduction in employment if not the closing down of some production capacities), while greenfield investments create new productive capacity and hence employment.[15] More importantly, when cross-border M&As target firms in sensitive sectors (which can range from military hardware to critical infrastructure and sectors central to economic development) or national champions (in any industry), the political reaction can be particularly strong.[16] This changing attitude towards M&As is important as they are the principal form of market entry for foreign investors in developed countries and an increasingly important form in emerging markets.

As to the extent to which FDI has sustainable development characteristics, the objective of a number of governments is no longer just to obtain more such investment, but rather sustainable FDI. 'Sustainable FDI' is defined here as FDI that contributes as much as possible to economic, social and environmental development and good governance (especially in terms of a mutually beneficial distribution of benefits associated with an investment[17]), while remaining profitable for the investing firms. While a number of governments have traditionally targeted investment that contributes particularly to economic development, the other dimensions of this concept have typically received less attention.[18] This seems to be changing, especially as regards the social dimension of the concept but also the environmental one (see in this context also UNCTAD, 2010).

The broader implication of this development is that some types of FDI are no longer being considered as equally welcome, i.e. that a number of governments are taking a more differentiated attitude towards the characteristics that incoming FDI takes[19] – a fact (as will be discussed below) that is reflected in changes in the regulatory framework for foreign investment.

The rise of emerging market MNEs

Adverse reactions to incoming M&As can be even stronger when the acquirer is a firm headquartered in an emerging market.[20] While traditionally the developed countries as a group have always been the most important host countries (absorbing by far more than half of all investment flows), the bulk of this investment came from other developed countries and was easily accepted.[21] But with the rise of emerging market MNEs,[22] this picture is changing. FDI flows from emerging markets have become important, having reached US$351 billion in 2008, around seven times the average of world FDI outflows during the first half of the 1980s. On average, emerging markets accounted for 11 per cent of global FDI outflows during 1995–2000; that share rose to 14 per cent during 2003–08. Even during the crisis year of 2008, when outflows from developed countries declined by almost 20 per cent, those from emerging markets rose by 4 per cent; in 2009, while outflows from developed countries plummeted by nearly half, those from emerging markets declined only by a bit more than one-fifth. As a result, the share of emerging markets in world FDI flows rose to 16 per cent in 2008 and 25 per cent in 2009.[23]

These aggregate data mirror, of course, the growth in foreign assets of MNEs headquartered in emerging markets (of which there are over 20,000 (UNCTAD, 2010:17)), and whose value has risen faster than the assets of their competitors headquartered in the industrialized world. In 2008 (the latest year for which these data are available), the foreign assets of the 100 largest MNEs from developing countries rose by 12 per cent over the previous year, while the corresponding growth rate for the world's 100 biggest MNEs (overwhelmingly from industrialized countries) was only 1 per cent.[24]

This rise of MNEs headquartered in emerging markets changes the global FDI landscape. It remains to be seen how long it will take for the developed countries to accept these new competitors on equal terms (as investment treaties demand), or whether they will seek to impose new restrictions on entry, particularly when it takes the form of M&As in high profile sectors. The integration of these new global players in the world FDI market is a difficult process, especially when they are different (or operate differently) from established MNEs.

One of these differences is that, in the case of a number of the new home countries, the most important players include state-controlled entities – in particular state-owned enterprises and, increasingly, sovereign wealth funds. In the case of China (an extreme case), some 80–90 per cent of outward FDI flows and stock are controlled by state-run enterprises.[25] This aspect has given rise to special concerns (justified or not) about, for example, whether state-controlled entities pursue non-commercial objectives when investing abroad, benefit from non-transparent favourable government treatment, or lack proper governance and accountability structures. As a result, some countries, such as Australia, Canada, Germany and the United States, have become more cautious about sovereign FDI (see the discussion below).

The broader implication of the rise of emerging market MNEs is that a growing number of emerging markets – among them Brazil, China, India and Russia (the BRIC countries), but also such countries as Chile, Mexico, Egypt, South Africa, Malaysia, the Republic of Korea, Singapore and Thailand – see themselves no longer only as host countries but also as home countries, with implications for the international investment policies that they are pursuing. At the same time, host countries may exhibit some scepticism when it comes to the growing importance of emerging market MNEs, especially when these are state-controlled entities.

Rising attention to national interest

Another implication of the rise of emerging market MNEs and the more differentiated attitude of governments to the form that incoming FDI takes is that considerations of 'national interest' (and related concepts, such as 'national security' and 'essential security interests') have become more important in recent years, with these concepts not always clearly distinguishable from each other, and individual countries focusing on different aspects of them.

This is particularly true for a number of developed countries, but it also is beginning to extend to a number of emerging markets. For example, in the post-9/11 United States, essential security concerns related to FDI have achieved greater saliency, as have concerns over foreign control over critical infrastructure. Such concerns are particularly evident when, in the case of M&As, the prospective acquirer is headquartered in a country that may be considered a strategic competitor of the United States (as is China), or is based in a country whose political allegiances are viewed with some suspicion (e.g. some Islamic states) and/or is a state-controlled entity. For Western and Central European countries, 'national security' concerns may reflect political fears of domination by investors from some countries (e.g. Russia and increasingly China) or concerns of threats to the 'national interest' posed by foreign takeovers of national champions in key industries. For Russia, in turn, 'national interest' or 'security' concerns may emerge from investments related to the exploitation of natural resources or investment in firms controlling military technology. For some emerging markets, such as China, 'national security' is being defined primarily in terms of economic development and hence focuses on strategic industries seen as crucial to continuing growth. And in yet other contexts, such as Argentina in the wake of its 2001–02 economic crisis, 'essential security' concerns have come to be associated with that nation's right to take emergency actions in the wake of domestic turmoil.[26] What is common to all these approaches is that the underlying security threat to the nation is intentionally left undefined. This is not surprising, as governments want to have the flexibility to define 'national interest' and similar concepts in relation to specific circumstances, without being straight jacketed by pre-established definitions and commitments.

The broader implication of this development is that a number of developed countries that, in the past, sought strict international investment disciplines are now seeking greater flexibility and more policy space for themselves (an approach championed in the past principally by developing countries), in order to be able to pursue policies and take actions that they consider necessary – and enshrine this approach in their national regulatory frameworks and IIAs.

The rise of investment disputes

Since the international investment law regime allows for investor–state disputes, it is not surprising that the number of cases in which investors feel aggrieved by actions taken by host countries is rising. (In fact, it is surprising that this has not occurred earlier and that there are not more such disputes, considering the number of MNEs and foreign affiliates that exist.[27]) The number of treaty-based international investment disputes has risen dramatically in recent years, with more than half of the 357 known arbitration cases having arisen between the beginning of 2004 and the end of 2009 (Figure 2.1). Crucially, these disputes involve not only emerging markets as respondents (as was perhaps originally thought), but also developed countries, including the United States,[28] as host countries. These disputes can lead to substantial awards against respondent countries.[29]

Both the number of disputes as well as the types of claims being made in them are giving rise to second thoughts on the part of IIA signatories, many of which did not expect the types of challenges to government regulation or even judicial actions that are emerging in the course of treaty-based arbitrations. Complaints that state parties to investment treaties are increasingly put on the defensive in investor–state claims and that, even when states win the underlying disputes, the threat of litigation produces an untoward regulatory chill have become a common refrain among a number of non-governmental organizations, including in developed countries. There is also a perception that, although the goal of the investment regime was to promote harmonious and predictable rules, investor–state arbitral decisions have not led to consistent international investment law, even producing inconsistent

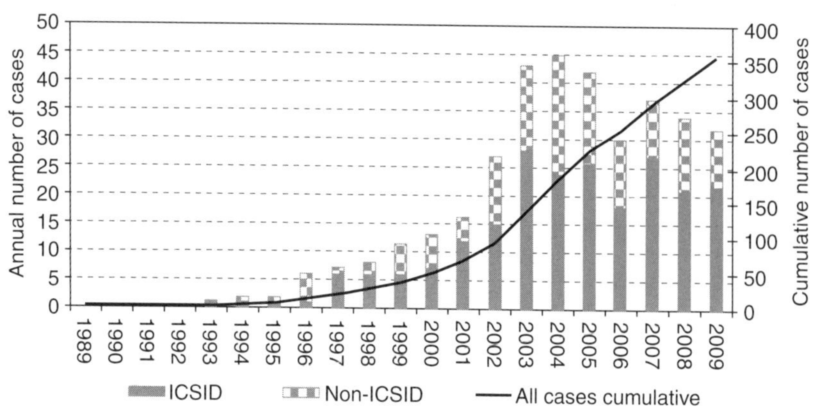

Figure 2.1 Known investment treaty arbitrations (cumulative and newly instituted cases), 1989–2009

Note: ICSID:

Source: UNCTAD (2010:84).

rulings arising under strikingly similar facts (for a discussion of Argentine cases, see Alvarez and Khamsi, 2009). The high profile of some investor–state decisions and the adverse attention drawn to a number of them that implicate policy questions have also undermined the contention that international arbitrations will successfully depoliticize such matters.

The broader implication of these developments is that governments of developed countries, led by the United States, are becoming more conscious of their status as host countries[30] and, in that position, potentially subject to claims against them. As a result, governments are becoming more sceptical of their decisions to delegate the right to initiate investment disputes to private third-party beneficiaries and more concerned about the consequences of such delegation on their continuing right to regulate in the public interest. This, in turn, further influences the attitude that countries take to the content of international investment obligations.

Doubts about whether IIAs lead to more FDI

There are also growing questions as to whether one of the principal purposes of IIAs is being achieved, namely the goal of increasing FDI flows, especially to emerging markets, with the help of investment treaties. Empirical research to date has not established a clear relationship between such agreements and FDI flows.[31] This is not surprising, as factors relating to host countries' economies (especially market size and growth, the quality of the infrastructure, skills, innovatory capacity) are by far the most important FDI determinants, and it is therefore difficult to isolate any IIA-specific effects.[32] It is also not surprising given the fact that most IIAs are premised on the assumption that a good regulatory framework (as established by IIAs) is sufficient to encourage MNEs to go forward with their investments; this ignores the fact that, at best, the (national and international) regulatory framework can only be enabling – but unless the economic determinants allow for profitable investments, it is very unlikely that FDI will take place.[33] Moreover, IIAs, as a rule, do not provide for active measures by the home country to encourage their firms to invest abroad (and especially in emerging markets or in the least developed countries) or to help institutions in host countries to acquire the capacity to attract foreign investors. In fact, although IIAs presume that the protection of investment and the removal of governmental barriers to free capital flows would enhance such flows, the treaties themselves were not necessarily intended to promote such flows, at least as far as some capital exporting countries are concerned.[34] They were, at best, signalling devices to encourage investors to seek out those host countries with a favourable investment climate.

The broader implication of this development is that, if IIAs do not necessarily lead to more investment flows, governments may become less inclined to make investor-protection and liberalization commitments – or even to conclude such agreements in the first place.

Doubts about whether OFDI is a good thing for home countries

As mentioned earlier, all developed countries and a growing number of developing countries facilitate or even support the outward investment of their firms. However, doubts have occasionally arisen in a number of developed countries as to whether OFDI is indeed beneficial for home countries.[35] Trade unions in particular are concerned about the export of jobs being seen as associated with OFDI; and such concerns are particularly potent during times of economic crisis and high levels of unemployment. While a number of studies have shown that OFDI is beneficial to home countries, at least on balance and for developed home countries (see Moran, forthcoming: sect. 7; Globerman and Shapiro, 2008; Visser, 2006), the public debate in the United States and Europe at times assumes differently. Most recently, for example, offshoring has led to calls in the United States to restrict this kind of activity (see Politi, 2010; Cohen, 2010). There have also been threats by some in the United States Congress to block the approval of BITs and free trade agreements (or even to withdraw from existing agreements, including the North American Free Trade Agreement (NAFTA); see Palmer, 2010). In Western Europe, outward investment in general has occasionally come under fire in some countries, under the heading of 'delocalization'; in at least one instance, the president of one country is reported to have linked the provision of aid to some firms to these firms repatriating from abroad some production facilities or keeping the production of certain products at home (see Hall, 2010).

In the case of emerging markets that have become important outward investors, doubts of this kind do not seem to have become prominent so far, although it would not be surprising if they should become so at a point in the future. After all, most emerging markets do not have all the production capacities they need to provide their citizens with an advanced standard of living. Hence, investment abroad to create production capacities there could easily lead, at some point, to a backlash against OFDI in emerging markets, even though such investment is in the interest of the firms involved as they need (as mentioned earlier) a portfolio of locational assets to remain internationally competitive.

The broader implication of this situation is that there is a tension between the objective of MNEs to maximize their global (or at least regional[36]) competitiveness, on the one hand, and the objective of governments to maximize the performance of their territorially bound economies, on the other hand. The establishment of regulatory frameworks for FDI in light of a sometimes somewhat fragile consensus about the benefits of OFDI for home countries needs to take this tension into account.

These are all developments that, in various ways, influence national and international FDI rule making. They show that governments look at FDI with fresh eyes as regards the costs and benefits that it brings to them, not only in terms of its contribution to economic development, but also in terms of serving broader national objectives. The following section shows that this revaluation of at least certain types of FDI is beginning to find its expression in national and international regulatory frameworks and their implementation.

The changing regulatory regime for FDI

As a result of these developments, a number of countries have introduced changes or 'clarifications' in their national regulatory regime that provide them with more leeway to deal with incoming investments, especially when these are undertaken by state-controlled entities and are taking the form of M&As. Significantly, the erstwhile strongest supporter of open national rules and a strong international investment law regime is leading this change.[37] In the United States, the Foreign Investment and National Security Act of 2007 and its subsequent implementing regulations strengthened the role of the Committee on Foreign Investment in the United States (CFIUS) as a screening mechanism for IFDI under national security aspects. CFIUS has the authority to review and investigate covered transactions and to negotiate, impose and enforce conditions necessary to mitigate any threat to national security presented by any such transaction. A transaction will be investigated if, among other things, it involves a foreign government-controlled entity and if it would result in control of any critical infrastructure and could impair national security. Neither 'national security' nor 'critical infrastructure' is defined precisely. Germany, too, changed its law on foreign investment in 2009, to allow the government to review certain takeovers by firms from outside the European Economic Area. Australia and Canada tightened or 'clarified' their regulations in 2008 and 2009, respectively, emphasizing that M&As by foreign state-controlled entities will receive special attention. France identified at the end of 2005 a number of sectors in which FDI is restricted. The Commission of the European Community, for its part, initiated in 2008 a process of consultations, with a view towards arriving at a common approach about SWFs. The OECD, too, undertook a similar process and arrived in 2008 at 'Guidelines for Recipient Country Investment Policies Related to National Security'.[38] Outside the OECD area, Russia adopted in 2008 a law that established procedures for foreign investments in companies of strategic importance for national defence and security, and China (which always had a list of encouraged, restricted and prohibited projects for foreign investors) introduced during 2006–08 a review process in light of national economic security considerations. Finally, the IMF decided in 2007, prodded by developed countries, to identify best practices for SWFs; as a result, and with the participation of representatives of SWFs, 'Generally Accepted Principles and Practices' (the 'Santiago Principles') were adopted in 2008, reflecting 'appropriate governance and accountability arrangements as well as the conduct of investment practices by SWFs on a prudent and sound basis' (IWG, 2008:4).

As can be seen from the dates of these various initiatives, the great majority of them were started before the world financial crisis and recession struck in late 2008. In fact, during the crisis, state-controlled entities were often regarded as 'white knights' that bailed out particular financial institutions in distress, and countries heeded the calls of the Group of 20 to refrain from FDI protectionism (G8, 2009). However, once countries have emerged fully from the crisis while, on the other hand, SWFs and state-owned enterprises amass even higher foreign exchange earnings and seek to invest them in equities,[39] it is likely that the fears related to them will reassert themselves and will be reflected in national and international regulatory instruments.

More broadly, during the crisis and recession, countries sought more capital to help them emerge from the recession; in other words, IFDI was particularly welcome. At the same time, as long as unemployment remains high in key home countries, the question of the offshoring of services is likely to remain a topic for discussion; in other words, OFDI could potentially be restricted or at least discouraged. However, once countries have emerged from the recession and once unemployment has declined, some of the other considerations discussed earlier, as they relate to the cost–benefit calculation of governments regarding FDI, are likely to reassert themselves, especially when it comes to M&As targeting national champions or other enterprises considered important to the national economy (e.g. in natural resources[40]). For the same reason, it may also well be that further liberalization, especially in sensitive services sectors, may slow down.

Partly as a result of legislative changes, countries – especially (but not only) developed ones, but including all those mentioned earlier – have also strengthened their capacity to screen FDI projects, typically focused on M&As. In the case of the United States, for example, the number of filings with the CFIUS rose, between 2001 and 2008, from 55 to 155, and the number of investigations grew from 1 to 23 (Figure 2.2).

In 2008, 15 per cent of CFIUS filings led to investigations. While the number of notifications declined in 2009 to 65,[41] the number of investigations rose to 25, representing about 40 per cent of the filings – a substantial increase. It should be noted that these types of examinations of M&As, in the United States and elsewhere, are typically not subject to judicial review but rather take place within the 'black box' of discussions within the relevant government agencies, thereby reducing the transparency of the decision-making process and regulatory framework.

The change towards a more circumscribed treatment of foreign investors and more policy space for governments in light of a changed cost–benefit calculation on the part of governments is also beginning to be reflected in international investment agreements and, with that, is bound to influence the international investment law regime in general. In particular, leading countries such as Canada and the United States are now concluding IIAs with more limited protections for investors and greater scope for governmental

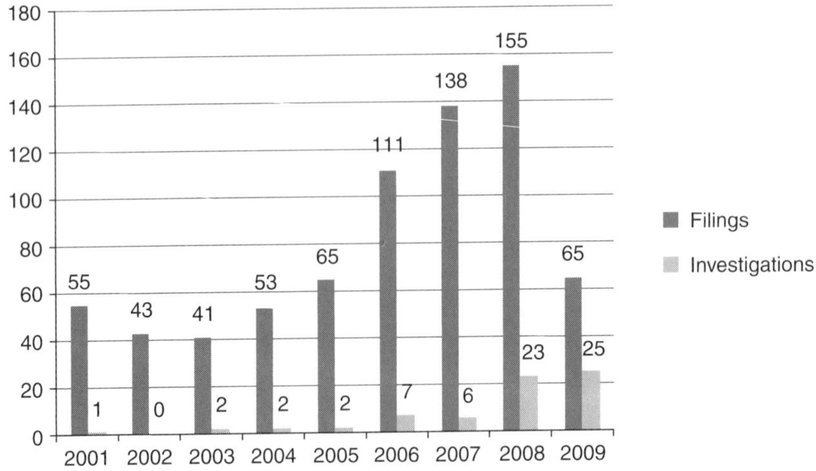

Figure 2.2 CFIUS filings and investigations, 2001–09

Source: US Treasury Department (www.ustreas.gov).

action, including through broad exceptions. Changes to United States' IIAs include a narrower definition of fair and equitable treatment and reduced scope for investors to claim that they have been the victims of a regulatory taking.[42] Canada has opted for an ample list of general exceptions from IIA protections inspired by those contained in Article XX of the General Agreement on Tariffs and Trade (GATT).[43] These changes lessen the risk of unpredictably broad interpretations of investment protections by investor–state arbitrators. Most importantly, some countries, such as the United States, are turning to a 'self-judging' essential security exception intended to oust certain disputes, at the option of the respondent state, from investor–state arbitration altogether. Given the fact that 'essential security' is left undefined, such an exception from arbitrability potentially undermines the entire edifice of international investment law. More generally, the countries worldwide that introduced during 2006–07 at least one change making their investment climate less welcoming for foreign investors accounted for 40 per cent of world FDI flows (Sauvant, 2009:240).

While the policy changes in China and Russia concerned all FDI, those in most developed countries paid special heed to state-controlled entities as a class of investors, introducing differential treatment for them. The latter also applies to the initiatives by the European Commission, the OECD and the IMF, even if they remain voluntary. They are justified largely on the basis of national security considerations, in particular the fear that the FDI activities of state-controlled entities, especially in the case of M&As, are driven not so much by commercial but rather by political considerations. This may well be the case, but to date there is no systematic evidence to show that (be it for sovereign wealth funds and state-owned enterprises from emerging markets or developed countries); that is, it is difficult to show that a substantial number of investment decisions would not have been undertaken by private firms in the same situation on the basis of commercial considerations alone.

In any event, the changes in the national and international regulatory frameworks for FDI go beyond specific considerations regarding state-controlled entities. They show that governments are searching for a new balance between the rights and responsibilities of governments and foreign investors at both the national and international levels, driven by the various developments discussed earlier.

Among these developments, probably none is more important than the blurring of the traditional distinction between developed 'capital exporting' and developing 'capital importing' countries. To be sure, developed countries have always been (and still remain) the principal host countries for FDI – but this FDI originated overwhelmingly in other developed countries; any issues that arose in connection with this investment could be discussed and settled in the framework of the OECD, on the basis of the instruments of that organization. What is new for developed countries is the rising influx of FDI from emerging markets. While emerging markets continue to remain primarily host countries,[44] the rise of their own MNEs is likely to bear on their perspective on the international investment law regime as governments in a growing number of emerging markets are now paying more attention to their status as capital exporters, as their firms, some of which have become major international players,[45] invest abroad.

Both developed countries and emerging markets now need to balance their positions as home and host countries, and hence their objectives: as home countries, they seek a strong international regulatory regime that protects foreign investors and facilitates their operations; as host countries, they seek an international regulatory regime that leaves them sufficient policy space for their right to regulate in the public interest. It is a tension that finds its expression in the negotiation of IIAs.

This tension is exemplified by changes in the model BITs and actual investment treaties of the United States and China, as both are today simultaneously the leading capital exporting (home) and capital importing (host) countries among, respectively, the developed countries and the emerging markets (see for example Alvarez, 2009). United States IIAs began as very strong investor protection devices, as laid out in their clearest form in the 1984 US model BIT and the IIAs based on it.[46] Once the United States became a respondent in treaty-based international investment claims after the conclusion of NAFTA, it gradually circumscribed or even dropped various protections in order to maintain the regulatory space it needed to pursue its own policy objectives and limit the possibility that claims could be brought against it; this evolution is captured in the 2004 United States model BIT and the IIAs based on it (Alvarez, 2008; Vandevelde, 2009b). Chinese IIAs, for their part, began as relatively weak investor protection devices, but then moved in the direction of the strongly investor-protective United States model of 1984 (as the Chinese invested in significant numbers and amounts abroad) – only to move, in their latest BITs, toward the United States' position of less expansive formulations on such a key protection standard as fair and equitable treatment (ibid.).

The extent to which two leading capital exporters and importers of the world, China and the United States, are now groping to find the right balance that reflects their positions as both host and home countries, are concluding separate investment agreements with increasingly similar provisions and are even negotiating one as between themselves, gives rise to the hope that, eventually, and despite the proliferation of IIAs, the 'spaghetti bowl' of agreements will eventually coalesce around agreed terms that respect the need of investors for the rule of law and fairness of process and the right of governments to regulate in the public interest. Perhaps this will occur in the framework of a multilateral agreement on investment that enshrines a new balance of the rights and responsibilities of the various stakeholders in the regime and promotes sustainable FDI, and, thereby, as Aharoni put it, attempts to 'determine the optimum balance between the incentives necessary to attract FDI and the regulation required to defend the pubic interest' (Aharoni, 2010:56).

Notes

This chapter draws partly on Sauvant and Alvarez (2011). I gratefully acknowledge helpful comments by Seev Hirsch, Ucheora Onwuamaegbu, Srilal Perera and Ravi Ramamurti, as well as the help of Wouter Schmit Jongbloed in the finalization of this manuscript.

1. This source, or earlier editions of it, has also been used for the following data, unless otherwise indicated.
2. No systematic data exist on the importance of such non-equity forms; but in some industries (e.g. hotels) they are widespread.
3. See for example UNCTAD (1999); Moran (2006, forthcoming); Dunning (1994); Dunning and Lundan (2008). However, it should be noted that national policies are important to maximize the positive effects of FDI and minimize any negative ones.
4. 'Developed countries' are all members of the Organisation for Economic Co-operation and Development (OECD), minus Chile, Mexico, the Republic of Korea and Turkey. 'Emerging markets' are all economies that are not members of the OECD, plus Chile, Mexico, the Republic of Korea and Turkey. 'Developing countries' are all emerging markets that do not belong to the Commonwealth of Independent States and south-east Europe. See UNCTAD (2010) for individual members of these groups.
5. MCI (2009:1). For a review of the performance of these agencies at the national level, see IFC (2009).

6. On political risk, see MIGA (2009). For an example of how the institution of one country, the United States, has handled political risk, see Kantor et al. (2011).
7. In the natural resources sector, the involvement of MNEs often takes forms other than FDI (e.g. production sharing agreements, management contracts); however, in either case, control over the assets involved is typically in the hands of foreign investors.
8. The year 1959 was when the first BIT, between the Federal Republic of Germany and Pakistan, was concluded.
9. Most important among them, the North American Free Trade Agreement, Chapter Eleven (www.ustr.gov/trade-agreements/free-trade-agreements/north-american-free-trade-agreement-nafta).
10. Most important among them various OECD instruments, including OECD (1961, 1976) and the Energy Charter Treaty (ECT), Part III, Articles 10–17 (www.encharter.org).
11. Especially the Agreement on Trade-related Investment Measures (TRIMs) and the General Agreement on Trade in Services (GATS), concluded in the framework of the WTO. The latter is particularly important as some two-thirds of FDI consists of services FDI. See also the Multilateral Investment Guarantee Agency, established in 1988 in the framework of The World Bank Group.
12. For example, the OECD 'Guidelines for Multinational Enterprises' (which are part of the OECD Declaration, OECD, 1976).
13. For a discussion of international investment law, see, for example, Salacuse (2010); Muchlinski et al. (2008); Muchlinski (2007); Dolzer and Schreuer (2008); and Reinisch (2009). For critical views, see for example Harten (2007); Alvarez (2008, 2011); Sornarajah (2004, 2008, 2010).
14. Although some countries, like Australia and Canada, have since long screened large M&As.
15. The advantages and disadvantages of M&As vs greenfield FDI are discussed, in great detail, in UNCTAD (2000) and Globerman and Shapiro (2010).
16. See, for example, the attempted acquisition of Unocal (United States) by CNOOC (China) or the rumoured acquisition attempt of Danone (France) by PepsiCo (United States).
17. This is particularly relevant in the natural resources sector, especially in light of swings in the prices of such resources and the distribution of the resulting revenues.
18. Indicative of this are the results of a survey of investment-promotion agencies undertaken in 2010 by the Vale Columbia Center on Sustainable International Investment regarding the extent to which these agencies pay attention to sustainable FDI; see VCC (2010).
19. It may be indicative of this that arbitral tribunals have weighted in on the definition of 'investment' for Investment Center for Settlement of Investment Disputes (ICSID) jurisdiction purposes, including discussing whether contribution to development is an essential element; see e.g. MHS v Malaysia and the annulment decision.
20. See, for example, the discussions surrounding the acquisition of Arcelor by Mittal, Lenovo's acquisition of the PC division of IBM, and Tata's bid for Corus; see Sauvant (2009).
21. Developed countries continue to attract most FDI, although in 2009 emerging markets attracted almost half of the world's FDI inflows as the economies of these countries remained more resilient in the wake of the financial crisis and recession.

22. See UNCTAD (2009); Sauvant (2008); Sauvant and McAllister (2010). In fact, in 2008, outward FDI flows from China were higher than the average of world FDI flows during the first half of the 1980s.
23. Calculated on the basis of data from UNCTAD (2010).
24. UNCTAD (2010:18). To a certain extent, of course, this reflects the lower level of assets from which the former started as outward investors, compared with the latter.
25. See Cheng and Ma (2007:15). It should be noted that a number of developed country state-owned entities undertake FDI as well. For a discussion of China's outward FDI, see Davies (2010).
26. On Argentina, see for example Alvarez and Khamsi (2009). The lessons of Argentina have apparently been taken to heart by others; see for example the latest Canadian Model BIT (permitting 'prudential' measures with respect to the banking sector) and the United States latest BIT (including a self-judging essential security clause). For discussion, see Mendenhall (2011).
27. Depending on the applicable IIA, foreign affiliates and, indeed, individual investors in affiliates may be able to initiate disputes.
28. By the end of 2009, at least 81 governments (49 of developing countries, 17 of developed countries, 15 of economies in transition) had been or were involved in treaty-based arbitrations; investors from developed countries had initiated the overwhelming number of claims. See ibid.
29. See for example *CME Czech Republic B.V.* v. *Czech Republic*, (2003) UNCITRAL (http://ita.law.uvic.ca/documents/CME-2003-Final_001.pdf), which awarded CME Czech Republic B.V. US$ 269,814,000 in damages for breach of an investment treaty.
30. As is suggested by the United States' divisive debates over the content of its United States' Model BIT. See the Report of the Subcommittee on Investment of the Advisory Committee on International Economic Policy regarding the Model Bilateral Investment Treaty, (www.state.gov/e/eeb/ris/othr/2009/131098.htm).
31. The most important studies are contained in Sauvant and Sachs (2009). As a recent study observed: 'the literature on BITs is stalemated on whether they actually increase FDI' (Tobin and Busch, 2010). The same study observed, however, that BITs might make free trade agreements more likely and, in this manner, indirectly influence FDI flows. Perhaps one of the reasons for this finding is that corporate counsels seem to be relatively unfamiliar about the existence of BITs – at least this is the result of a survey of United States MNEs; see Yackee (forthcoming).
32. For a discussion of the FDI determinants, see UNCTAD (1998:ch. 4) and Dunning and Lundan (2008). Some countries, like Brazil, attract considerable amounts of FDI, even though it has not ratified any of the BITs it had negotiated.
33. Conversely, even when the regulatory framework is not very good, FDI will take place if profitable investment opportunities exist. For example, investments in the mining sector took place in the Congo even during the country's civil war.
34. As Vandevelde (2009a:45) observed for the United States: 'When the BIT program was inaugurated in the Carter Administration, the United States had seen the BITs as a means of building a body of state practice consistent with its view of customary international law while protecting existing stocks of investment. In part because of concerns that labor otherwise would oppose the agreements, United States BIT negotiators initially had made clear not only to potential United

States BIT partners but to Congress as well that there was no evidence that BITs would lead to increased outward investment flows. By the early 1990s, however, the promotion of democracy and market economics in the transitional economies was a major foreign policy objective and BITs were regarded as a means of promoting outward investment'. As this observation suggests, the promotion of FDI was not a goal when the United States' BITs programme began in the 1970s. However, over time, the argumentation changed, and eventually BITs were justified in the United States as a means of investment promotion.

35. See for example O'Murchu and Cienski (2010), who, in their article entitled 'Twinings to move tea plant to Poland', report that the move 'has drawn sharp criticism from both workers and members of the European parliament'.
36. As Alan Rugman (2005) shows, most MNEs are primarily regional in their operations.
37. The developments discussed in this paragraph are documented in Sauvant (2009) and are therefore not individually referenced here.
38. Recommendation adopted by the OECD Council on 25 May 2009, (www.oecd.org/dataoecd/11/35/43384486.pdf).
39. SWFs are estimated to control about US$4 trillion dollars (Sovereign Wealth Fund Institute, October 2010, www.swfinstitute.org), an amount that is estimated to go up to US$12 trillion by 2015, given certain assumptions; see Jen (2007).
40. See for example the preliminary decision of the Government of Canada to block the acquisition of PotashCorp (Canada) by BHP Billiton (Australia) in November 2010 (Beattie and Simon, 2010).
41. The decline may have been the result of the lower number of cross-border M&As into the United States on account of the crisis and the decline of FDI inflows; that number fell from 1,297 in 2007 to 1,117 in 2008, to 710 in 2009, and 293 during January to May 2010; in terms of value, cross-border M&As into the United States declined from US$165 billion in 2007 to US$40 billion in 2009 (see www.unctad.org/Templates/Page.asp?intItemID=5545&lang=1); FDI flows into the United States declined from US$324 billion in 2008 to US$130 billion in 2009 (UNCTAD, 2010:167). It is not known how many cross-border M&As that were intended or initiated but did not go forwards because of the new regulatory framework in the United States.
42. United States' Model BIT 2004 (www.state.gov/documents/organization/117601.pdf).
43. Canadian Model BIT 2004 (www.international.gc.ca/trade-agreements-accords-commerciaux/assets/pdfs/2004-FIPA-model-en.pdf); GATT (www.wto.org/english/docs_e/legal_e/06-gatt_e.htm).
44. The IFDI flows of emerging markets were roughly an average of US$650 billion during 2007–09, while their outward flows during the same period were an average of US$310 billion; the IFDI stock of emerging markets was US$5.4 trillion in 2009, compared with an outward stock of US$3 trillion (UNCTAD, 2010: Annex Tables 1 and 2).
45. The four BRICs (Brazil, Russia, India and China) alone accounted for more than a third of FDI outflows from emerging markets during 2007–09 (UNCTAD, 2008: Annex Tables 1 and 2). For rankings of the largest MNEs based in the BRICs, see www.vcc.columbia.edu.
46. See Alvarez (2008) and Vandevelde (2009b). The full text of the 1984 United States Model BIT can be found in Vandevelde (1992).

References

Aharoni, Yair (2010). Reflections on multinational enterprises in a globally interdependent world economy, in Karl P. Sauvant and Geraldine McAllister, with Wolfgang A. Maschek (eds), *Foreign Direct Investment from Emerging Markets: The Challenges Ahead*. New York: Palgrave Macmillan, p. 42.

Alvarez, José E. (2008). The evolving foreign investment regime. *American Society of International Law*. (www.asil.org/ilpost/president/pres080229.html).

Alvarez, Jose E. (2009). Contemporary foreign investment law: An 'empire of law' or the 'law of empire'? *Alabama Law Review*, 60, 943–75.

Alvarez, José E. (2011). The once and future foreign investment regime, in Mahnoush Arsanjani, Jacob Katz Cogan, Robert D. Sloane and Siegfried Wiessner (eds), *Looking to the Future: Essays on International Law in Honor of W. Michael Reisman*. Leiden and Boston, MA: Brill Martinus Nijhoft.

Alvarez, José E. and Khamsi, Kathryn (2009). The Argentina crisis and foreign investors: A glimpse into the heart of the investment regime, in Karl P. Sauvant (ed.), *Yearbook on International Investment Law and Policy, 2008/2009*. New York: Oxford University Press, pp. 379–478.

Beattie, Alan and Simon, Bernard (2010). Race for resources tests trade openness. *Financial Times*, 6–7 November.

Buckley, Peter J. (2010). What can emerging markets learn from the outward direct investment policies of advanced countries?, in Karl P. Sauvant and Geraldine McAllister, with Wolfgang A. Maschek (eds), *Foreign Direct Investment from Emerging Markets: The Challenges Ahead*. New York: Palgrave Macmillan, pp. 243–76.

Cheng, Leonard K. and Ma, Zihui (2007). China's outward FDI: Past and future. (www.nber.org/books_in_progress/china07/cwt07/cheng.pdf).

Cohen, William S. (2010). Obama and the politics of outsourcing. *Wall Street Journal*, 12 October.

Davies, Ken (2010). Outward FDI from China and its policy context. Columbia FDI Profiles, 18 October. (www.vcc.columbia.edu).

De Beule, Filip and Van Den Bulcke, Daniel (2010). Changing policy regimes in outward foreign direct investment from emerging markets: from control to promotion", in Karl P. Sauvant and Geraldine McAllister, with Wolfgang A. Maschek (eds), *Foreign Direct Investment from Emerging Markets: The Challenges Ahead*. New York: Palgrave Macmillan, pp. 277–304.

Dolzer, Rudolf and Schreuer, Christoph (2008). *Principles of International Investment Law*. New York: Oxford University Press.

Dunning, John H. (1994). Re-evaluating the benefits of foreign direct investment. *Transnational Corporations*, 2(1), 23–51.

Dunning, John H. and Lundan, Sarianna M. (2008). *Multinational Enterprises and the Global Economy*. Cheltenham: Edward Elgar.

G8 Leaders' Declaration (2009). Responsible Leadership for a Sustainable Future. *L'Aquila*, G8 Summit 2009. (www.g8italia2009.it/static/G8_Allegato/G8_Declaration_08_07_09_final,0.pdf).

Globerman, Steven and Shapiro, Daniel (2008). Outward FDI and the economic performance of emerging markets, in Karl P. Sauvant, with Krisitn Mendoza and Irmak Ince (eds), *The Rise of Transnational Corporations from Emerging Markets: Threat or Opportunity?* Cheltenham: Edward Elgar, pp. 229–71.

Globerman, Steven and Shapiro, Daniel (2010). Modes of entry by Chinese firms in the United States: Economic and political issues, in Karl P. Sauvant (ed.), *Investing in the United States: Is the US Ready for FDI from China?* Cheltenham: Edward Elgar, pp. 22–44.

Hall, Ben (2010). France to rein in state-backed groups. *Financial Times*, 4 August.

Harten, Gus van (2007). *Investment Treaty Arbitration and Public Law*. New York: Oxford University Press.

IFC (International Finance Corporation) (2009). *Global Investment Promotion Benchmarking 2009: Summary Report*. Washington, DC: World Bank).

IWG (International Working Group of Sovereign Wealth Funds) (2008). Sovereign wealth funds: Generally accepted principles and practices, 'Santiago Principles'. (www.iwg-swf.org/pubs/gapplist.htm).

Jen, Stephen (2007). How big could sovereign wealth funds be by 2015? Morgan Stanley Global Economic Forum, 4 May. (www.morganstanley.com).

Kantor, Mark, Nolan, Michael D. and Sauvant, Karl P. (eds) (2011). *Reports of Overseas Private Investment Corporation Determinations*. New York: Oxford University Press.

MCI (Millennium Cities Initiative and Vale Columbia Center on Sustainable International Investment) (2009). *Handbook for Promoting Foreign Direct Investment in Medium-size, Low-budget Cities in Emerging Markets*. New York: MCI and VCC, p. 1. (www.vcc.columbia.edu).

Mendenhall, James (2011). The evolution of the essential security exception in U.S. trade and investment agreements, in Karl P. Sauvant, Lisa E. Sachs and Wouter P.F. Schmit Jongbloed (eds), *Sovereign Investment: Concerns and Policy Reactions*. New York: Oxford University Press.

MIGA (Multilateral Investment Guarantee Agency) (2009). *World Investment and Political Risk 2009*. Washington, DC: MIGA.

Moran, Theodore H. (2006). *Harnessing Foreign Direct Investment for Development: Policies for Developed and Developing Countries*. Washington: Center for Global Development.

Moran, Theodore H. (forthcoming). *Foreign Direct Investment and Development: Launching a Second Generation of Policy Research. Avoiding the Mistakes of the First, Re-evaluating Policies for Development and Developing Countries*. Washington: Peterson Institute for International Economics.

Muchlinski, Peter (2007). *Multinational Enterprises and the Law*, 2nd edn. New York: Oxford University Press.

Muchlinski, Peter, Ortino, Federico and Schreuer, Christoph (eds) (2008). *The Oxford Handbook of International Investment Law*. New York: Oxford University Press.

OECD (1961). *Code of Liberalisation of Capital Movements*. Paris: OECD.

OECD (1976). *Declaration on International Investment and Multinational Enterprises*. Paris: OECD.

O'Murchu, Cynthia and Cienski, Jan (2010). Twinings to move tea plant to Poland. *Financial Times*, 9 November.

Palmer, Doug (2010). U.S. lawmakers launch push to repeal NAFTA. *Washington Post*, 4 March. (www.reuters.com/article/dUSTRE6233MS20100301).

Politi, James (2010). Bill on overseas jobs raises hopes and fears in US. *Financial Times*, 27 September.

Reinisch, Auguest (2010). *Recent Developments in International Investment Law*. Paris: A. Pedone.

Rugman, Alan (2005). *The Regional Multinationals*. Cambridge, UK: Cambridge University Press.

Salacuse, Jeswald W. (2010). *The Law of Investment Treaties*. New York: Oxford University Press.

Sauvant, Karl P. with Mendoza, Kristin and Ince, Irmak (eds) (2008). *The Rise of Transnational Corporations from Emerging Markets: Threat or Opportunity?* Cheltenham: Edward Elgar.

Sauvant, Karl P. (2009). Driving and countervailing forces: A rebalancing of national FDI policies, in Karl P. Sauvant (ed.), *Yearbook on International Investment Law and Policy, 2008/2009*. New York: Oxford University Press, pp. 215–72.

Sauvant, Karl P. and Alvarez, Jose E. (2011). Introduction: international investment law in transition, in Jose E. Alvarez and Karl P. Sauvant, with Kamil Ahmed and Gabriela del P. Vizcaino (eds), *The Evolving International Investment Regime: Expectations, Realities, Options*. New York: Oxford University Press.

Sauvant, Karl P. and McAllister, Geraldine with Maschek, Wolfgang A. (2010) (eds), *Foreign Direct Investment from Emerging Markets: The Challenges Ahead*. New York: Palgrave Macmillan.

Sauvant, Karl P. and Sachs, Lisa E. (eds) (2009). *The Effect of Treaties on Foreign Direct Investment: Bilateral Investment Treaties, Double Taxation Treaties and Investment Flows*. New York: Oxford University Press.

Sornarajah, M. (2004). *The International Law of Foreign Investment*, 2nd edn. Cambridge: Cambridge University Press.

Sornarajah, M. (2008). A coming crisis: expansionary trends in investment treaty arbitration, in Karl P. Sauvant with Michael Chiswick-Patterson (eds), *Appeals Mechanism in International Investment Disputes*. New York: Oxford University Press, pp. 39–80.

Sornarajah, M. (2010). Toward normlessness: The ravages and retreat of neo-liberalism in international investment law, in Karl P. Sauvant (ed.), *Yearbook on International Investment Law and Policy 2009/2010*. New York: Oxford University Press, ch. 16.

Tobin, Jennifer L. and Busch, Marc L. (2010). A bit is better than a lot: Bilateral investment treaties and preferential trade agreements. *World Politics*, 62, 1–42.

UNCTAD (1996). *Incentives and Foreign Direct Investment*. Geneva: UNCTAD.

UNCTAD (1998) *World Investment Report 1998: Trends and Determinants*. Geneva: UNCTAD.

UNCTAD (1999). *World Investment Report 1999: Foreign Direct Investment and the Challenge of Development*. Geneva: UNCTAD.

UNCTAD (2000). *World Investment Report 2000: Cross-border Mergers and Acquisitions and Development*. New York and Geneva: UNCTAD.

UNCTAD (2009). *World Investment Report 2006: FDI from Developing and Transition Economies. Implications for Development*. Geneva: UNCTAD.

UNCTAD (2010). *World Investment Report 2010: Investing in a Low-carbon Economy*. Geneva: UNCTAD.

Vandevelde, Kenneth J. (1992). *United States Investment Treaties Policy and Practice*. Boston: Kluwer.

Vandevelde, Kenneth J. (2009a). *U.S. International Investment Agreements*. New York: Oxford University Press.

Vandevelde, Kenneth J. (2009b). A comparison of the 2004 and 1994 U.S. Model BITs: Rebalancing investor and host country interests, in Karl P. Sauvant (ed.), *Yearbook on International Investment Law and Policy, 2008/2009*. New York: Oxford University Press, pp. 283–316.

VCC (Vale Columbia Center on Sustainable International Investment) (2010). Investment promotion agencies and sustainable FDI: Moving toward the fourth generation of investment promotion. Report of the findings of the Survey on Foreign Direct Investment and Sustainable Development undertaken by the Vale

Columbia Center on Sustainable International Investment (VCC) and the World Association of Investment Promotion Agencies (WAIPA), 25 June 25. (www.vcc.columbia.edu).

Visser, Hans (2006). Outward foreign direct investment: Is it a good thing?, in G. Meijer, W.J.M. Heijman, J.A.C. van Ophem and B.H.J. Verstegen (eds), *Heterodox Views on Economics and the Economy of the Global Society*. Wageningen: Wageningen Academic, pp. 343–58.

Waelde, Thomas W. (2009) Improving the mechanisms for treaty negotiation and investment disputes: competition and choice as the path to quality and legitimacy, in Karl P. Sauvant (ed.), *Yearbook on International Investment Law and Policy, 2008/2009*. New York: Oxford University Press, p. 514.

Yackee, Jason Webb (forthcoming). How much do U.S. corporations know (and care) about bilateral investment treaties? Some hints from new survey evidence. *Columbia FDI Perspective*.

3

Internationalization of Companies from Former Communist Countries: Outward Foreign Direct Investment from Central, East and South Europe, and the Commonwealth of Independent States

Witold Wilinski

Introduction

Most of the publications concerning internationalization of multinational enterprises (MNEs) focus on companies originating from the countries of the triad including North America, the European Union and Japan. The largest trade exchange in the world as well as investment capital flows in the form of foreign direct investment (FDI) take place between these regions.

However, since the early 1980s, new MNEs originating from developing economies have entered the world business arena. Among them, most new MNEs come from Asian countries and Latin America. Consequently, most publications concerning the issues related to the reasons for their growth and the application of strategy to international markets concerns mostly the companies coming from these two regions. Undoubtedly, the region which was politically dominated by the Soviet Union before 1990 did not have companies operating at an international level. The lack of market mechanisms, as well as dependency on political decisions and lack of private independent companies, hindered companies from this region from entering global competition. Most companies operating in the conditions of centrally planned economies were not only ineffective economically, but were also unable to compete efficiently with companies operating in market economies.

Thus, at the time of market transformation in the early 1990s, the economies of Central and Eastern European countries (CEECs) and those formed as a result of the disintegration of the USSR were not only characterized by a significantly lower GDP per capita when compared to highly developed countries, but they were also disadvantaged technologically, except for some branches of industry. Moreover, the low level of internationalization of their economies, as measured by the level of export to GDP, coupled with the lack of liquid exchange rates and their insignificant share in global investment flows, represented fundamental barriers to the creation of MNEs. This however does not mean that at the beginning of the 1990s MNEs did not exist in these economies. A good example is the group of states formed after the disintegration of Czechoslovakia and Yugoslavia. In those contexts MNEs were born from the disintegration process as overnight the companies which had subsidiaries in the ex-federal republics became international. This was only the beginning of the process of internationalization of companies from the Central and Eastern Europe (CEE) region.

The years 1990–2010 were a period of sudden political and economic changes in the transition economies. The changes in the political systems were coupled with economic restructuring. There were major differences between the transition in CEE and the economic development of South Korea, Taiwan or Chile, where economical reforms were implemented and the resulting gradual increase of wealth of the population led to political changes. From the 20-year perspective, one must assess that the system transformation did not bring about uniform results. On the one hand, the pace of economical reforms was not the same in all countries; on the other hand, the political changes, including geopolitical ones, were not always undisturbed. Examples include, but are not limited to: the process of gaining independence by the Baltic states of Estonia, Latvia and Lithuania; Yanayev's attempted putsch in Russia; the disintegration of and wars in ex-Yugoslavia; the war in Moldova and Transnistria; and the disintegration of Czechoslovakia. Ultimately, the above mentioned factors account for the present diversity in economic achievements and performance of transition economies. When assessing the changes related to system transformation, transition economies may be grouped as follows:

- Democratic states with a market economy and a large contribution from the private sector;
- Democratic states with a market economy and a relatively large contribution from state-owned companies;
- States with an authoritarian political system with a relatively large contribution from state-owned companies.

The first group includes the new EU member states (Bulgaria, the Czech Republic, Estonia, Lithuania, Latvia, Poland, Romania, Hungary, Slovenia and Slovakia) and the countries of Albania, Bosnia and Herzegovina, Croatia, Georgia, Montenegro, the Former Yugoslav Republic of Macedonia, Moldova and Serbia. The second group includes Russia. The third group includes countries such as Belarus, Kazakhstan and other Asian former USSR republics. From the point of view of this study, the process of creation of MNEs and the strategy adopted by them depends to a large extent on the group of countries which the company belongs to. The analysis excludes Kyrgyzstan, Turkmenistan, Uzbekistan, Tajikistan, Armenia and Azerbaijan due to the comparatively low level of internationalization of companies from these Asian states.

Main streams of foreign direct investment theory

FDI is the most advanced form of business internationalization. As a rule, companies start their expansion into foreign markets by means of exporting. Subsequently, they set up foreign branches and only at the final phase of the internationalization of their activities do they commit to greenfield investment or purchase shares in existing locally operating companies. The main task of the theories addressing FDI is to answer the questions: Who makes foreign investment? Why and where is it made? What is the impact of the investment on the investing and recipient economies? From the point of view of this study, it is a serious drawback of the existing FDI theories that none of them takes into consideration market transformation processes in the CEECs, including first of all the new European Union member states. Thus there is no uniform FDI theory describing the process of the internationalization of the activities of the companies in post-socialist countries.

One of the earlier theories, considered as a landmark, is the product life cycle theory (Vernon, 1966). Vernon made a theoretical generalization of Posner's theory, which interprets structure and streams of international exchange. Buckley and Casson (1976) applied transaction cost analysis to an international context for their internalization theory, which is concerned with imperfections in markets for intermediate products, including technology, organizational know-how and marketing skills. At present, the most encompassing theory which describes the mechanisms of making FDI is Dunning's (1980, 1993, 1996) eclectic paradigm of international production, also known as the ownership, location and internalization (OLI) paradigm. Other frequently used theories are the development paradigm of Kojima and Ozawa (1984) and Ozawa (1992), and the theory developed by Luostarinen and Welch (Luostarinen, 1970; Welch and Luostarinen, 1988). The first cross-sectional analysis of the outward foreign direct investment (OFDI) concerning selected states of CEE was carried out in 1999–2002, which was related to a small group of states that comprised of the Czech Republic, Estonia, Poland, Slovenia and Hungary (Svetličič and Rojec, 2003). At present, the rate of outward investment from Russia and CEE is continuously increasing. This growth is related mainly to companies from the new member states of the European Union (EU).

The three advantages defined in Dunning's eclectic theory, namely ownership, location and internationalization, have an impact on the decisions of companies associated with foreign investment. The theory is supplemented by the Investment Development Path (IDP), which shows the dependence between the level of economic development and the investment position of a state, i.e. the relation between inward and outward investment. Goldstein (2009:82) concludes that the IDP model has indeed proven very useful for smaller European economies. Some emerging economies, despite their large size and potential, may suffer from an unwelcoming investment climate and therefore register relatively low inflows at the same time as their companies invest abroad. In other words, multinationalization may emerge as a defensive strategy to escape a harsh home business environment.

According to the IDP model, the states pass through five development stages depending on their economic development level, which in turn has an influence on the net outward investment (NOI) level. The assessment, of which stage a given state is at, depends on the relation between outward and inward investment. Based on the economic development level of the state (in this case measured by means of GDP per capita), foreign investors willing to make investment are motivated by reasons different than those affecting the decisions made by local entrepreneurs willing to invest abroad (with unchanged GDP per capita at the time of making the decision by local and foreign investors).

In the IDP model, when the states are at the same stage of economic development but have a differentiated structure for their level of international investment engagement, the difference is explained using the advantages introduced by Dunning in the OLI paradigm. At present, the economic structure of developed economies becomes more and more alike as they have a similar structure for their assets. Some economies with a higher level of economic development, measured by GDP per capita, pass on to subsequent, higher stages of the IDP model. More and more frequently, particularly in integration groupings such as the EU, we note an increase in reciprocal FDI, characterized by a similar value of outflows and inflows of FDI between particular states.

From a macroeconomic point of view, inward and outward investments depend on the level of economic development of the state receiving the investment as well as the country-of-origin of the investment. According to Dunning's eclectic theory of international production, this dependence is presented by means of the IDP model, the application of which leads to the conclusion that both inward and outward investments increase as a result of the economic development of a country. At the early stages of development, a state achieves higher levels of attractiveness to foreign investors through the development of location advantages (local market, cheap labour force, various types of tax incentives). Consequently, inward investment grows rapidly, whereas outward investment remains at a very low level or simply does not exist. When GDP per capita increases, the inward investment growth rate gradually drops, whereby the outward investment growth rate accelerates. This is due to the fact that, as a result of economic growth, some companies can increase their revenues and become more and more focused on activities in international markets because the rate of return on the capital invested in the local market (both its relative value and absolute value) is gradually decreasing as a result of the increase of the ratio of capital cost to labour cost. As a result of the higher level of income per capita, the value of outward foreign investment becomes equal to or higher than the value of inward foreign investment. At this development stage, dominant forms of outward investment are the transactions carried out by large transnational corporations creating international networks of production. This type of gradual growth and evolution of OFDI was also outlined partially in the Scandinavian sequential internationalization model and partially in the product life-cycle theory.

The analysis of the NOI index should consider the fact that a so-called 'bulk privatization' took place in CEE transition economies in the period of 1990–2010. This was an unprecedented scale of privatization of entire branches of national economies, which were state-owned before 1989. Therefore, if one could eliminate this factor (i.e. the inflow of capital related to privatization processes), the value of NOI would probably be different. However, it is doubtful whether it would be positive, as in the 1990s the FDI outflow from this group of states was actually negligible. The inflow of FDI was also related to the need for market liberalization and deregulation, which was discussed, for instance, by Cuyvers and de Beule (2005:2).

It is important to remember that the IDP paradigm is not always a suitable tool for the analysis of OFDI. As correctly observed by Kalotay (2004:11–12), one of the relative weaknesses of the IDP may be due to the fact that, on the side of GDP per capita, it does not consider differences in income distribution. In other words, it is tacitly assumed either that national income is evenly distributed among the population or that, at least at a given level of development, the income distribution of countries is fairly equal. Kalotay concluded that clearly there are two different worlds: one of the 'small' countries where there are signs of the applicability of the IDP and other standard analyses; and another one for the Russian Federation, where a combination of 'system-escape' factors (capital flight) and global corporate strategic aspirations result in a major capital exporting world, without having the necessary GDP per capita usually assumed for that.

Main methodological problems

One of the main problems concerning the analysis of MNEs from developing countries is that there is no comparable and consistent statistical data concerning foreign investments (FDI) made by companies. There are of course published data concerning particular countries or regions; however, there are no edited financial data at the global level. Until today, the main source of statistical data concerning global investment flows is the World Investment Report published annually by UNCTAD.

Currently, a relatively large methodological problem in analysing MNEs is the impossibility of being able to define unequivocally the 'nationality' of the company. UNCTAD's statistical data, on which most publications on global FDI are based, do not contain information concerning the shareholders' structure within the company. Therefore, quite often the investments of a company with headquarters in a certain country, which are reported as investments of that country, may be in fact investments related to another entity (company) originating from a different country. A further problem exists with determining the country-of-origin of the shareholders. This may in some cases be obvious if the firm is listed on the stock exchanges, but in other cases this may be rather difficult to identify, especially in cases of quite a large fragmentation of the shareholders' structure. However, not all authors omit the issue related to a company's country-of origin. For instance Rugraff (2010) in his work on four CEECs (the Czech Republic, Hungary, Poland and Slovakia) analyses OFDI with respect to the shareholders' structure of the MNEs that invested abroad, dividing the companies into those with and without home capital, i.e. that originating from these four countries and companies, which are subsidiaries of international corporations that engage in OFDI.

More extensively, problems with determining corporate nationality have been described by Goldstein (2009:7–10) who analyses four types of situations:

- Companies established in developed countries by non-resident entrepreneurs;
- Companies that move their primary listing to an advanced country's financial market in order to benefit from lower currency risk and higher liquidity;
- Companies incorporated in developing countries that are in turn subsidiaries of OECD MNCs;
- Companies from developing countries that are owned by financial investors based in OECD countries.

Apart from these four types, where the differentiation of the nationality of MNEs is undoubtedly difficult, the so-called 'round-trip' FDI must be mentioned. This is OFDI by MNEs seeking to reinvest these same funds into the home country as IFDI. This is very much the case with Chinese and Russian companies, which make investments through entities based in Cyprus, the Virgin Islands, Hong Kong and the Cayman Islands among others. Due to the difficulties mentioned above when determining the country-of-origin, in this study I will consider only the country where the investing company has its registered seat (whatever the structure and origin of the shareholders).

Rugman and Doh's (2008:154) approach to dividing companies operating on foreign markets will be adopted for methodological purposes. The authors divide the companies with respect to their geographic structure of sales into four types:

- Home region firms (generate over 50 per cent of their sales in the home region);
- Biregional firms (generate less than 50 per cent of their sales in the home region and over 20 per cent in another triad region);
- Host region firms (generate over 50 per cent of their sales in another triad region, outside their home region);
- Global firms (generate less than 50 per cent of their sales in the home region and over 20 per cent in each region of the triad).

In the above division, Rugman and Doh understand a region as one of the triad regions. This means that, according to this definition, a company could be considered global if it operates in Northern America, Asia and Europe. The authors (2008:150) have also concluded that the theoretical literature indicates that MNEs expand abroad based on a complex interaction between firm specific advantages (FSAs) and country specific advantages(CSAs). The successful MNEs from these three regions in general expand abroad to exploit FSAs that they have developed in their home markets. The activities of their foreign subsidiaries, to an overwhelming degree, tend to replicate for local distribution the FSAs developed in the home market. Initial investments are usually made in the closest region, and only later on is the activity expanded to more distant regions. The essential question is whether global MNEs will be formed in the transition economies of CEE and whether CSAs will be based on knowledge, highly educated workers and an advanced infrastructure, which could guarantee the creation of companies operating outside the European region.

Outward foreign direct investment from transition economies in the global context

Despite a capital and technological advantage, the gap separating the developed economies from developing economies is gradually closing. The economic advantage of Europe and Northern America over the other economic areas (which to a large extent was started as early as the 19th century in the industrial revolution era) has begun gradually to decrease. This thesis is confirmed by the fact that the group of economically advanced countries has been joined by Japan, South Korea and, with their rapidly advancing internationalization, the BRIC (Brazil, Russia, India and China) countries. The percentage share of the level of investments (FDI inward stock) in developing economies with relation to the total of global investments between 1990 and 2008 increased insignificantly from 27.3 to 29.5 per cent. Meanwhile, the share of developing economies in FDI outward stock in the same period increased from 8.1 to 14.7 per cent (see Table 3.1). This means that the rate of outflow of FDI from developing economies is much faster than the rate of inflow of FDI to these countries. In effect, the process of internationalization of these economies is advancing rapidly and they can efficiently compete with entities from developed economies.

In the opinion of Narula (2010:12–13), the evolution of the 'first wave' MNEs towards the 'second wave' MNEs was initially enhanced by the fundamental but gradual change in the structure of the world economy, much of which is often generalized as being a direct result of globalization. These changes can be considered from the developing country perspective as being of two kinds. First, there are those that have been largely exogenous to these countries but which have affected their economic structure, both as members of the world economic order and as individual economies. Globalization, in the sense of greater cross-border economic interdependence between firms, markets and countries, has impacted on firms by creating broader and more competitive markets across countries. There have also been structural changes within individual countries in direct response to these exogenous changes, and as such they may be considered as endogenous to most developing economies. Second, the endogenous changes are primarily associated with the actions and policies of governments. One of the most important of these changes over the past decade or so has been a fundamental shift in the policy orientation of developing countries from an import-substituting role (or a centrally planned one) to an export-oriented, outward looking one.

Table 3.1 Inward and outward FDI stock in developed and developing economies in 1990 and 2008

	Inward FDI stock (US$ billion)		Outward FDI stock (US$ billion)		Inward FDI stock (percentage of world total)		Outward FDI stock (percentage of world total)	
	1990	2008	1990	2008	1990	2008	1990	2008
Developed economies	1413	10213	1640	13624	72.7	70.5	91.9	85.3
Developing economies	530	4276	145	2357	27.3	29.5	8.1	14.7
World	1942	14489	1786	15980	100.0	100.0	100.0	100.0

Source: UNCTAD (2009).

Table 3.2 Regional breakdown of inward and outward FDI stock in 1990 and 2008

	FDI inward stock (US$ billion)		FDI outward stock (US$ billion)		FDI inward stock (percentage of total)		FDI outward stock (percentage of total)	
	1990	2008	1990	2008	1990	2008	1990	2008
Developed Europe	809	6933	888	8997	41.7	47.8	49.7	56.3
New EU member states	4	471	1	78	0.3	4.6	0.1	0.6
North America	508	2691	515	3682	26.1	18.6	28.9	23.0
Asia and Oceania	358	2584	68	1697	18.5	17.8	3.8	10.6
Other developed economies	96	589	238	944	4.9	4.1	13.3	5.9
Latin America	111	1182	58	561	5.7	8.2	3.2	3.5
Africa	61	511	20	98	3.1	3.5	1.1	0.6
South-East Europe & CIS	0	420	0	225	0.0	2.9	0.0	1.4
New EU, South-East Europe and CIS	4	892	1	304	0.3	7.5	0.1	2.0

Source: UNCTAD (2009).

In terms of regional breakdown, the largest percentage share in the global FDI outward stock is held by the developed European countries (an increase from 49.7 to 56.3 per cent between 1990 and 2008) (see Table 3.2). North America comes second with a decrease from 28.9 to 23.0 per cent. Asia and Oceania rank third with an increase from 3.8 to 10.6 per cent. In the years 1990–2008, the countries from the ex-Soviet bloc noted an increase from 0.2 to 2.0 per cent of total global OFDI stock. The more than tenfold increase of FDI outward stock value from countries of this region is a result of a very low level of investment before 1990, which in turn is the result of a former economic restrictive system that discouraged internationalization processes. Out of the 2.0 per cent of FDI outward stock of the former communist countries, 1.3 per cent are Russian investments, 0.6 per cent are investments of new EU member states, while only 0.1 per cent are investments from other CIS countries (see Table 3.2). Value-wise, the FDI outward stock from CIS countries amounts to US$216 billion (of which most are Russian investments of US$203 billion), while that from the new EU member states is US$68 billion, and from South and Eastern European countries it is US$3.8 billion. In 2008, the total value of OFDI stock from transition economies was US$288 billion, of which the first five countries had 90 per cent of the total investments with respect to OFDI stock value. These countries are Russia, Poland, Hungary, the Czech Republic and Slovenia. One must however remember that before 1999 most FDI outflows from Russia were of an informal nature and it is highly possible that before this date the outward investment position of the country was largely underreported (see for example Bulatov, 1998; Kalotay and Sulstarova, 2010). This may well be the reason why data published by the Bank of Russia and UNCTAD concerning the stock of OFDI for 2008 were not identical (see for example UNCTAD, 2009; Kalotay and Sulstarova, 2010).

The values of FDI outward stock in relation to GDP are provided in Table 3.3. For Russia itself, the OFDI stock to GDP equals 16.2 per cent, which visibly exceeds the value of this index for CIS and for the new EU member states from CEE. Undoubtedly, the value of Russian FDI exceeds the average value of both OFDI stock per capita and OFDI stock to GDP in CIS countries. Detailed data concerning the value of both indices for the analysed group of countries is provided in Table 3.4.

The average value of the OFDI stock as a percentage of GDP for developed economies in 2008 amounted to 33 per cent. While this value for the European countries was 46.7 per cent, in North America it amounted to 23.4 per cent and in Asia and Oceania to 15.3 per cent. Apparently, despite some increase, the level of internationalization of the new EU member states, CIS and South and Eastern Europe remains at a relatively low level (see Table 3.5).

When analysing the process of creation of MNEs in developing countries, one must stress that it is based on the following factors:

- Protection of the internal market using tariff and paratariff barriers against foreign competition;
- Capital support from the national financial institutions;
- Government support for the oligopolies operating in the internal market;
- Access to relatively cheap labour;

Table 3.3 Outward FDI stock to GDP (OFDI to GDP) and outward FDI stock per capita in 2008

	Population million	GDP (US$ million)	Outward FDI stock (US$ million)	Outward FDI stock per capita (US$)	Outward FDI stock to GDP (percent)
CIS	217	1569930	215864	996	13.7
New EU members from CEE	102	1158394	68359	671	5.9
South and Eastern Europe	25	167989	3832	155	2.3

Sources: Own calculations, data for outward FDI from UNCTAD (2009); data for population and for GDP from IMF (2010).

- Lack of patent protection and, thanks to that, quick access to foreign technologies;
- A relatively large internal market;
- Utilization of natural resources.

The above mentioned factors indicate that the process of creation of MNEs in developing economies has been supported to a large extent by the governments of the respective countries. This means that the conscious formation of institutional regime has played a large role in reducing the economic gap between developed and transition economies. Currently, from among the former communist countries, the governments of countries which became EU members will not be able to support the creation of their MNEs in such an active way. This results from the fact that one of the objectives of the common economic area of the EU is to create conditions for free competition

Table 3.4 Outward FDI stock as a percent of GDP for CEE and CIS in 2008.

Country	OFDI stock	Population (million)	GDP per capita (US$)	OFDI stock to capita (US$)	GDP (US$ million)	OFDI stock to GDP (percent)
Estonia	6686	1.3	13509	5004	18048	37.0
Slovenia	8650	2.0	24583	4291	49560	17.5
Russia	202837	141.4	8874	1434	1254784	16.2
Hungary	14179	10.0	12386	1414	124241	11.4
Czech Republic	9913	10.4	18194	951	189669	5.2
Croatia	3635	4.4	14243	826	62669	5.8
Lithuania	1990	3.3	10775	596	35966	5.5
Poland	21814	38.1	11098	572	422962	5.2
Latvia	1066	2.3	10701	471	24195	4.4
Kazakhstan	5842	15.6	8715	374	135954	4.3
Slovak Republic	1901	5.4	16315	351	88299	2.2
Bulgaria	1248	7.6	5916	165	44780	2.8
Ukraine	7005	45.7	2542	153	116169	6.0
Albania	147	3.2	3825	46	12240	1.2
Romania	912	21.4	7503	43	160675	0.6
Georgia	130	4.4	2937	30	12923	1.0
Bosnia & Herzegovina.	29	4.0	4636	7	18544	0.2
Belarus	50	9.7	5165	5	50101	0.1
Serbia	0	7.4	5808	0	42979	0.0

Source: UNCTAD (2009).

Table 3.5 FDI stock as a percentage of GDP in 1990 and 2008

Region	Type of FDI	1990	2008
World	inward	9.1	24.5
	outward	8.5	26.9
Developed economies	inward	8.1	24.7
	outward	9.5	33.0
Europe	inward	10.7	36.0
	outward	11.8	46.7
North America	inward	8.0	17.1
	outward	8.1	23.4
Other developed economies	inward	2.8	9.5
	outward	6.9	15.1
Developing economies	inward	13.8	24.8
	outward	4.1	14.0
Africa	inward	12.5	33.2
	outward	4.8	7.2
Latin America and the Caribbean	inward	9.9	27.3
	outward	5.4	12.9
Asia and Oceania	inward	16.1	22.8
	outward	3.3	15.3
South-East Europe and CIS	inward	–	17.9
	outward	–	10.0

Source: UNCTAD (2009).

and to counteract oligopoly and monopolistic behaviours. Moreover, the direct public aid for companies has been limited to a large extent. These factors show that the tools used by emerging economies such as China and Russia for the last decades in the creation of MNEs cannot and will not be used by new EU member states. Therefore, a fundamental question arises – what competitive advantages can be used by companies from the new EU member states in developing activities in international markets?

MNEs from transition economies

The governments of countries such as Russia and Kazakhstan have influenced the formation of key enterprises by actively pursuing geopolitical and economical objectives. Initially this was done by the creation of a favourable oligopolistic or monopolistic system in the respective home markets. Such a system limited competition both domestically and internationally, enabling the creation of companies with an originally strong national or international regional position, which gave such companies a good starting position to compete at a global scale. Kalotay and Sulstarova (2010:138) estimate that the role of the state is of crucial importance in explaining the evolution of OFDI from the Russian Federation. During the presidency of Boris Yeltsin (1991–99), the Russian state actively contributed to the creation of large private monopolies which gave birth to future transnational corporations (TNCs). However, at that time the Russian state did not have a policy supporting and promoting OFDI. The situation changed radically under the presidency of Vladimir Putin (1999–2008). The participation of the Russian state in the ownership of some TNCs and the government role in their internationalization (especially in the cases of Gazprom and Rosneft) became crucial. Thus, the internationalization strategies of the state-owned and state-controlled Russian TNCs became influenced by the goals of Russian foreign policy and the geopolitical interests of the Russian state. Of course, the fact that in most cases the MNEs from Russia and Kazakhstan are based on natural endowments has also predetermined their international development. Thus capital accumulation by these MNEs was enormous in the period of just ten years or so. It should be also stressed here that the model according to which MNEs from Russia and Kazakhstan develop is different from the Chinese model or the model of the Latin American countries, where an increasingly greater role is played by companies from the modern technology sectors, which efficiently compete with companies from developed economies. Moreover, it seems that having natural endowments is the main reason which led to the creation of MNEs in these two countries. As Goldstein (2009:150–1) writes, for an emerging MNE aspiring to become a profitable international player and recognized brand, the edge of low labour costs, which is an advantage of emerging economies in competing with Western rivals, is becoming less and less important. Consequently, competing with low labour costs on a global scale becomes less applicable in the internationalization of firms in emerging economies.

Companies from the new EU member states find themselves in a different situation from their Russian and Kazakhstani counterparts. Accessing the EU and adopting rules applicable to the common market have created obstacles for actively supporting companies in their growth and international development. Additionally, these countries do not have natural resources which would enable the creation of MNEs. According to Rugman and Doh's definition (2008), quoted at the beginning of this chapter, companies can generate less than 50 per cent of their sales in the home region and over 20 per cent in the other regions of the triad only in a knowledge-based economy. In fact, without additional competitive advantages, it is now difficult for CEE firms to compete at a global level. Therefore, a question is raised as to whether an economy based on knowledge can stimulate companies or create an appropriate environment – country specific advantages – to strengthen the international competitive position of firms.

To assess the relation between the level of internationalization of companies and the level of knowledge-based economy, I use two indices. The first one is OFDI stock to GDP and the second is the Knowledge Economy Index (KEI). KEI has been developed by the World Bank using Knowledge Assessment Methodology. KEI is an aggregate index that represents the overall level of development of a country or region in the Knowledge Economy. It summarizes performance over the four knowledge economy pillars, which include: economic incentive and institutional regime, innovation, education and information, and communication technologies (see Table 3.6). It is constructed as the simple average of the normalized values of the 12 knowledge indicators of the basic scorecard (see Chen and Dahlman, 2005).

Figure 3.1, as well as Table 3.7, presents the dependency between KEI and OFDI stock to GDP ratio for the transition economies analysed in this chapter. These countries have been divided into three clusters, depending on the KEI index adopted:

- First, where the value of the KEI index ≥ 8.0;
- Second, where 7.0 < KEI < 8.0;
- Third, where KEI ≤ 7.0.

As Figure 3.1 shows, the states with a higher KEI index are characterized by a higher share of OFDI stock in relation to GDP. For example, in Estonia this index amounts to 37 per cent, in Slovenia 17 per cent and in Hungary 11 per cent. However, in the case of Russia, this index equals 16 per cent with a KEI of as little as 5.03. This finding suggests that in the sector of modern technologies, MNEs from Russia will probably not be formed within the existing institutional conditions. In the group of countries where KEI > 8, an exception is the Czech Republic, in which the OFDI stock to GDP ratio equals 5 per cent only. With the exception of Russia, transition economies with a value of the OFDI stock to GDP index exceeding 10 per cent are relatively small open economies with a small domestic market, which clearly was one of the factors leading to an early internationalization of companies from these countries. One has to remember that with a small internal market, as is the case of Estonia and Slovenia, which are smaller than an average-sized European city, the companies had to start activities outside their country-of-origin in order to achieve any economies of scale. Moreover, in Estonia the early liberalization of the economy before the EU accession had a major role in the internationalization of the economy.

The second group of countries, where the value of KEI is between 7 and 8, includes Lithuania, Latvia, Slovakia, Croatia and Poland. Apart from Slovakia, in all these countries the value of OFDI to GDP ratio ranges from 4 to 6 per cent. In this group, all the countries are characterized by a small internal market, except for Poland. In the third group, the only EU members

Table 3.6 Knowledge Economy Index of transition economies

	KEI		Economic Incentive and Institutional Regime		Innovation		Education		ICT	
Country	*2010*	*1995*	*2010*	*1995*	*2010*	*1995*	*2010*	*1995*	*2010*	*1995*
Estonia	9.19	8.73	9.38	9.34	8.78	7.46	8.60	8.45	10.00	9.69
Slovenia	8.73	8.76	8.52	7.63	9.86	9.53	8.27	7.89	8.26	10.00
Czech Republic	8.36	8.32	8.52	9.54	9.07	8.12	7.98	7.09	7.88	8.52
Hungary	8.07	7.77	8.89	7.47	9.51	8.84	6.15	6.42	7.75	8.33
Lithuania	7.97	6.39	8.52	7.39	6.63	4.72	8.63	6.89	8.11	6.54
Latvia	7.82	6.18	8.52	6.39	6.52	3.51	8.62	7.28	7.64	7.53
Slovak Republic	7.55	7.59	8.15	7.77	7.40	8.40	6.24	6.23	8.39	7.96
Poland	7.15	6.94	7.65	6.56	7.44	6.37	7.13	7.97	6.37	6.85
Croatia	7.03	6.85	7.78	5.67	8.72	8.57	4.13	4.89	7.49	8.27
Bulgaria	6.42	6.71	7.16	6.70	5.94	7.22	5.87	5.15	6.72	7.78
Ukraine	5.45	5.68	3.46	3.43	4.99	5.37	8.02	8.62	5.35	5.31
Romania	5.39	4.68	6.91	6.79	4.85	4.20	3.91	2.66	5.89	5.06
Russia	5.03	5.65	1.48	2.80	6.87	5.53	5.91	8.10	5.87	6.17
Serbia	4.44	4.97	3.21	1.48	5.19	8.33	2.59	2.78	6.76	7.28
Belarus	4.38	5.65	0.86	2.49	5.05	4.64	7.75	8.99	3.84	6.48
Kazakhstan	3.77	4.29	4.32	3.33	1.92	2.22	5.86	6.60	2.96	5.00
Georgia	3.76	4.70	4.57	3.81	4.20	4.07	3.87	6.10	2.38	4.81
Bosnia & Herzegovina	3.05	3.06	3.46	4.81	1.85	1.48	2.51	1.67	4.37	4.26
Albania	2.19	2.53	3.21	5.04	1.32	1.67	1.74	0.38	2.50	3.02

Source: http://data.worldbank.org/indicator

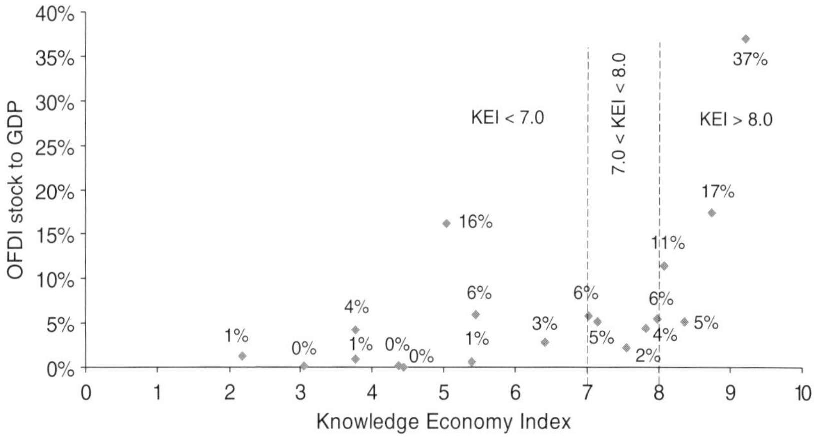

Figure 3.1 Knowledge Economy Index and OFDI stock to GDP for CEE and CIS in 2008
Source: UNCTAD (2009) for OFDI stock/GDP; http://data.worldbank.org/indicator for KEI.

Table 3.7 Knowledge Economy Index and OFDI stock to GDP for CEE and CIS in 2008

Country	KEI	OFDI stock to GDP (in percent)
Estonia	9.19	37.0
Slovenia	8.73	17.0
Czech Republic	8.36	5.0
Hungary	8.07	11.0
Lithuania	7.97	6.0
Latvia	7.82	4.0
Slovak Republic	7.55	2.0
Poland	7.15	5.0
Croatia	7.03	6.0
Bulgaria	6.42	3.0
Ukraine	5.45	6.0
Romania	5.39	1.0
Russia	5.03	16.0
Serbia	4.44	0.0
Belarus	4.38	0.0
Kazakhstan	3.77	4.0
Georgia	3.76	1.0
Bosnia & Herzegovina.	3.05	0.0
Albania	2.19	1.0

Source: UNCTAD (2009) for OFDI stock/GDP; http://data.worldbank.org/indicator for KEI.

are Bulgaria and Romania, the other countries are either aspiring to EU membership or CIS countries.

Similar to the values of the OFDI stock to GDP, where the highest values were reached by Estonia (37 per cent), Slovenia (17.5 per cent) and Hungary (11.4 per cent), the value of the OFDI stock per capita in these countries was also highest. The highest one was for Estonia, amounting to US$5,004, followed by Slovenia with US$4,291 and Hungary with US$1,414 (see Figure 3.2).

The Russian economy is once again an exception with US$1,434. In the case of transition economies, there is a regularity compliant with Dunning's IDP model where the higher the value of GDP per capita, the higher the value of OFDI stock per capita. Of course, one has to remember that the analysed countries differ in their economic structure. As Rugraff (2010) notes, there is quite a large difference amongst countries which are the largest investors in the region when it comes to the model of companies investing abroad. In the case of Hungarian and Czech investments, the group of largest investors is dominated by companies owned by foreign MNEs, which made investments in these countries. It results from a significant inflow of foreign investments by foreign corporations to these two countries in the last 15 years and, in a sense, using the knowledge of the Central European market possessed by their Hungarian and Czech subsidiaries. When it comes to Slovenian companies investing abroad, these are mainly Slovene-capital companies, whose investments result from the low penetration of this economy by foreign capital, as well as from the support given by governmental institutions to companies investing abroad. In the case of Polish foreign investments, a large share is held by companies where the decisive votes are

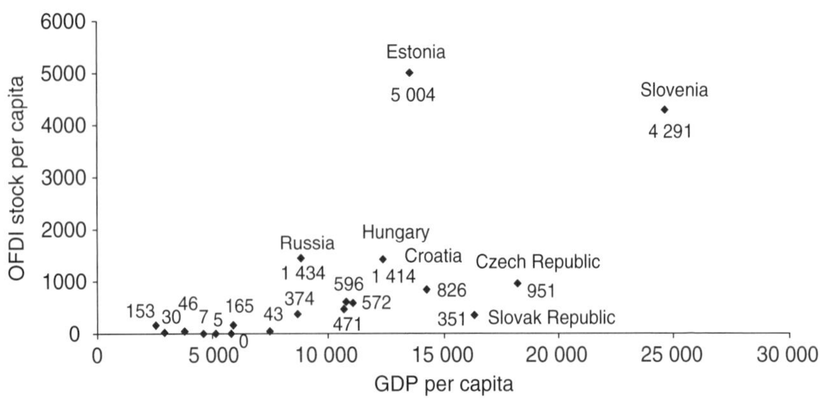

Figure 3.2 Outward FDI stock to GDP per capita in CEE in 2008

Source: UNCTAD (2009).

held by the government. These are often stock-listed companies in which some part of the stock is still held by the State Treasury.

Figure 3.3 shows the dynamics of increment of the annual average value of OFDI flows in the periods 1992–97 and 2007–08. It is obvious that there is a significant difference of the rate of FDI outflow between the two periods. Clearly one can posit that there has been a sudden increase of the average value of OFDI in the second period. With that in mind, one has to remember that the 1990s were the beginning of the systemic transformation in these countries, which resulted in such a large growth dynamics of investments, though still at a significantly lower level than in the triad region countries.

Figure 3.4 shows the share of OFDI stock in relation to IFDI stock in 2008. In the case of nine countries, the value of 10 per cent was exceeded, and only in Russia did the investments of Russian companies exceed the value of investment of foreign companies into the country. The countries with the largest value of this index are those in which the value of OFDI per capita is the highest one in the region.

The main source of data relating to the geographical structure of OFDI from transition economies is the Data Base on Foreign Direct Investment in Central, East and Southeast Europe 2010, developed by the Vienna Institute for International Economic Studies, based on statistical reports of

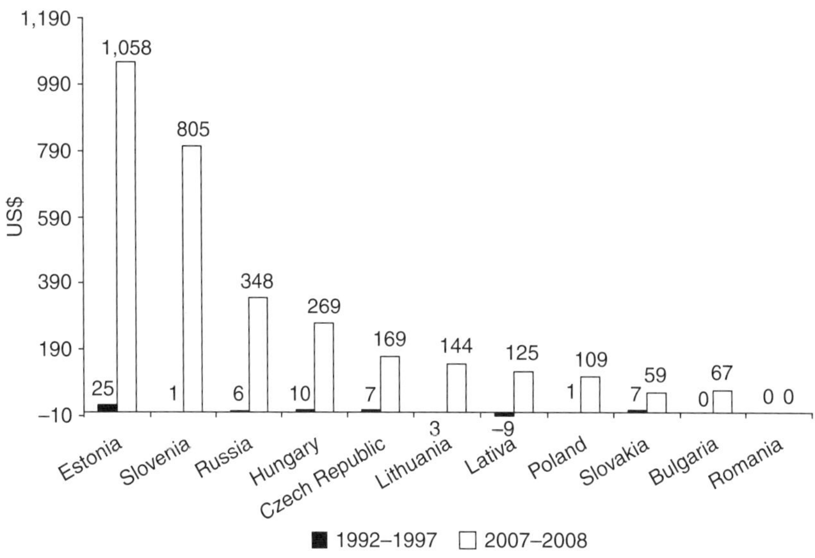

Figure 3.3 Average outward FDI flow per capita in the periods 1992–1997 and 2007–08

Source: Own calculations, data for outward and inward FDI from UNCTAD (1998, 2009).

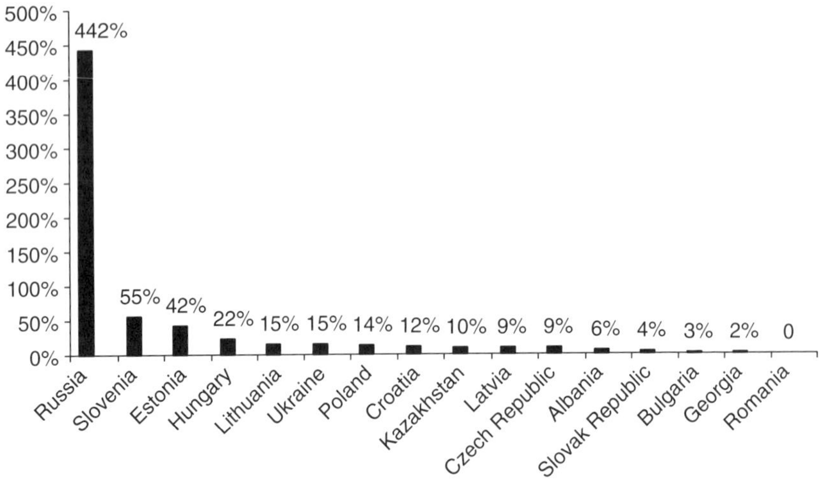

Figure 3.4 Outward FDI stock as a percentage of inward FDI stock in transition economies in 2007–08

Source: UNCTAD (2009).

the central banks in these countries. The data on geographical distribution of OFDI stock show that most investments are located in the countries of the region – in principle, the countries neighbouring the investor's country-of-origin. Using Rugman and Doh's (2008) perspective one might suggest that most companies from transition economies in CEE are home region firms, which is due to the fact that no investments are located outside Europe. Lack of investments outside Europe indicates also a relatively weak internationalization of companies from this region.

In the geographical structure of investments from CEE transition economies, it is important to note that as much as 58 per cent of OFDI has been targeted at countries not situated in the direct vicinity of the investor's country, such as Cyprus, the Netherlands, Switzerland and Luxembourg (see Table 3.8). The investments into these countries are not necessarily associated with their investment attractiveness, which is usually aligned with the size of the local market or with access to highly developed technologies. These are countries where taxation is favourable or it is easy for companies to engage in further reinvestments from that country. It seems that the percentage of investments coming into these countries is highest from transition economies with a higher, rather than a lower, degree of internationalization. For example, the largest investments into Cyprus, the Netherlands and Switzerland come from the Ukraine (93 per cent) and Russia (66 per cent). In their case, the important factor for investment location in the above mentioned states is an unstable home market and

Table 3.8 Geographical distribution of outward FDI from transition economies by selected host countries in 2008

Investing Country \ Host Country	Cyprus	Gibraltar	Liberia	Luxembourg	Marshall Islands	Netherlands	Switzerland	Virgin Islands	Percent of total outward FDI stock	Outward FDI stock	Outward FDI stock invested outside the CEE & CIS region
	(percent)									(million US$)	
Ukraine	93.0							0.3	93.0	7005	6529
Russia	30.0			1.0		28.0	5.0	3.0	66.0	202837	134075
Czech Republic	11.0	1.0		2.0		44.0			58.0	9913	5700
Croatia			7.0		5.0	41.0		0.2	54.0	3635	1952
Poland				21.0		9.0	22.0		51.0	21814	11169
Lithuania	6.0					21.0			27.0	1990	533
Latvia	6.0			2.0			16.0		23.0	1066	245
Hungary	4.0			4.0		2.0	7.0		17.0	14179	2340
Bulgaria	3.0			1.0	5.0		4.0		13.0	1248	162
Estonia	12.0			0.1		1.0			13.0	6686	889
Romania	12.0						1.0	1.0	13.0	912	120
Slovakia	1			11.0					12	1901	234
Slovenia	3	1	3			2	1		9	8650	787
Total									58	281836	164736

Sources: Own calculation based on Hunya and Schwarzhappel (2010), WIIW Database on Foreign Direct Investment in Central, East and Southeast Europe (2010).

political system, which makes companies want to seek safer investment contexts.

The division of OFDI from the point of view of economic activities in transition economies is not uniform; however, four sectors prevail. They comprise of manufacturing, wholesale, retail trade, repair of vehicles, financial intermediation, and property, renting and business activities (Table 3.9).

Sectors with very small importance are agriculture; forestry and fishing; construction; and hotels and restaurants. The sectoral structure of investments clearly indicates the small share of vertical investments and the predominance of horizontal investments, which may be caused by the dominant position occupied by services companies (and especially the foreign-owned banks) in the outward investments (Rugraff, 2010). Russian

Table 3.9 Outward FDI from transition economies by economic activities 2005–08 (in percent)

Economic activities \ Countries	Croatia	Czech Republic	Estonia	Hungary	Latvia	Lithuania	Poland	Russia*	Romania	Slovakia	Slovenia	Ukraine
Agriculture, forestry & fishing	1	0	0	0	0	0	0	0	0	0	0	0
Mining and quarrying	6	1	0	7	0	0	0	39	65	1	0	0
Manufacturing	22	11	3	38	6	13	9	37	3	18	33	2
Electricity, gas and water supply	0	12	0	0	1	0	2	0	0	-7	1	0
Construction	8	3	2	0	2	1	1	2	0	1	1	0
Wholesale, retail trade, repair of vehicles	39	6	6	7	32	17	7	3	7	19	21	2
Hotels and restaurants	0	0	0	1	1	1	0	0	0	0	1	0
Transport, storage and communication	12	0	14	1	3	9	2	6	9	1	10	1
Financial intermediation	7	7	34	23	30	14	5	13	15	22	18	3
Real estate, renting & business activities	–1	57	38	21	20	41	7	0	1	41	15	86
Public administration, defence	0	0	0	0	0	0	1	0	0	0	0	0
Other community & social services	6	2	2	0	0	0	0	0	0	0	1	
Other not elsewhere classified activities	0	2	1	0	5	0	66	1	0	4	0	
Private purchase & sales of real estate	0			2		4	2	0	0	0	0	7

Sources: Hunya and Schwarzhappel (2010), WIIW Database on Foreign Direct Investment in Central, East and Southeast Europe (2010), UNCTAD, cross-border M&A database.ww

investments are dominated by two sectors: mining and quarrying, and manufacturing, which together make up 76 per cent of Russian OFDI. The Russian Federation is an interesting case as it experiences the combined effects of 'system-escape' pressures (capital flight) and global corporate strategic aspirations supported by government initiatives. This has resulted in a major orientation towards OFDI, without having the levels of GDP per capita usually assumed as a precondition for such high levels of OFDI. The main reasons, enabling this dynamic development of Russian MNCs, are the largest natural gas and oil fields in the world and the lack of possibilities for effectively reinvesting the profits in Russia.

Russian enterprises are investing abroad for various corporate strategic reasons rather than just for export-supporting activities, as witnessed in the early 1990s. Their motivations have expanded to cover strengthening market positions, expanding markets overseas, internalizing control over value chains and accessing natural resources, including acquisition of strategic assets to improve competitiveness. The desire to diversify their activities out of the domestic business environment has also encouraged OFDI by Russian enterprises. These reasons have driven Russian companies to invest both in neighbouring countries and as far afield as Africa, Australia and the United States (Vahtra and Liuhto, 2005). Surely, a serious supporting factor for the dynamic expansion of Russian MNCs in the CEE and the EU is the dependence of the region on the supply of Russian fossil fuels. The degree of dependence on Russian energy supplies together with its potential role in political relations has become a genuine threat. The examples of temporary restrictions in the supply of natural gas to Belarus in 2004 and Ukraine in 2006 have shaken not only the energy security of those countries but also restricted the supply of those resources to end users.

Conclusions and further research

Based on the analysis above, the following conclusions could be drawn. Firstly, despite a significant increase in the value of OFDI stock from transition economies, its value amounted to only 2 per cent of the total world investments in 2008. Therefore, it is of low importance to the global economy. Secondly, the level of internationalization of transition economies is relatively low and the OFDI stock to GDP index is almost two and a half times lower than its value in developed economies. Thirdly, the geographical structure of the investments of MNEs from transition economies indicates a negligible share of global companies and a dominance of companies with European reach only. Fourthly, as opposed to FDI from developed countries, a very large part of investments from former communist countries, mainly from the Ukraine and Russia, is the so-called 'round-trip' FDI, which is OFDI by MNEs seeking to reinvest the same funds into the home country in the form of IFDI.

From among former communist countries, the largest capital was invested abroad by MNEs from Russia. The leaders among Central European and South European countries with respect to OFDI stock value are companies originating from the new EU member states, while, with respect to OFDI per capita, small countries lead the rankings. Due to the smallness of their domestic markets, they started the process of internationalization of companies fairly early. The analysis of the KEI indicates that knowledge oriented economies are characterized by a higher level of internationalization of companies. With respect to the sectoral structure of investments, those from CIS are based mostly on natural resources and power sector, which is not the case of investment structure of companies from the new EU member states. It could be suggested that, due to the operation in a common European market, companies from the new EU member states are in a different environment compared to companies from Russia, Kazakhstan or Ukraine. The latter may count on active governmental support in the process of OFDI expansion into foreign markets.

From the point of view of the competitiveness and internationalization of transition economies, it is important to define the factors and mechanisms that might lead to the creation of global companies, as the international companies from CEE are mainly with a local reach. One could also suggest that the importance of born-global companies from CEE could be studied in relation to their future engagement in international business activities. As compared to the traditional incremental approach to internationalization of companies, the concept of born global assumes the possibility of fast track internationalization of activities, which perhaps is at present the best way forward to speeding up the internationalization of companies from transition economies.

References

de Beule, F. and van Den Bulcke, D. (2009). Retrospective and prospective views about the future of the multinational enterprise. *International Business Review*, 18, 215–23.

Chetty, S. and Campbell-Hunt, C. (2004). A strategic approach to internationalization: a traditional versus a 'born-global' approach. *Journal of International Marketing*, 12(1), 57–81.

Dunning, J.H. (1980). Toward an eclectic theory of international production: some empirical tests. *Journal of International Business Studies* 11(1): 9–31.

Dunning, J.H. (1981). *International Production and Multinational Enterprise*. London: Macmillan.

Dunning, J. (1996). The economic theory of the firm as a basis of a 'core' theory of international production, in I. Islam and W. Shepherd (eds.) *Current Issues in International Business*, Aldershot, UK and Brookfield, US: Edward Elgar, 63–72.

Dunning, J.H. (2000). *Regions, Globalization, and the Knowledge Based Economy*. Oxford: Oxford University Press.

Dunning, J.H. and Narula, R. (1996). *Foreign Direct Investment and Governments*. London and New York: Routledge.
Gabrielsson, M., Kirpalani, M., Dimitratos, P., Solberg, C. and Zucchella, A. (2008). Born globals: propositions to help advance the theory. *International Business Review*, 17, 385–401.
Johanson, J. and Vahlne, J.-E. (1977). The internationalization process of the firm. *Journal of International Business Studies*, 8 (Spring–Summer), 23–32.
Kojima, K. And Ozawa, T. (1984). Micro- and macro-economic models of direct investment: Towards a synthesis, *Hitotsubashi Journal of Economics*, 25(1): 1–20.
Narula, R. (2010). Much ado about nothing or sirens if a brave new world? MNE activity from developing countries and its significance for development. OECD Development Centre.
Neuhaus, M. (2006). *The Impact of FDI on Economic Growth: An Analysis for the Transition Countries of Central and Eastern Europe*. Heidelberg: Physica – Verlag.
Ozawa, T. (1992). Foreign direct investment and economic development, *Transnational Corporations*, 1(1): 27–54.
Svetličič , M. and Rojec, M. (eds) (2003). *Facilitating Transition by Internationalization: Outward Direct Investment from Central European Economies in Transition*. Aldershot: Ashgate.
UNCTAD (1998). *World Investment Report: Trends and Determinants*, New York and Geneva.
UNCTAD (2009). *Trade and Development Report*, New York and Geneva.
UNCTAD (2010). *World Investment Report 2009: Transnational Corporations, Agricultural Production and Development*. New York and Geneva: UNCTAD.
Väätänen, J., Podmetina, D. and Pillania, R. (2009). Internationalization and company performance: a study of emerging Russian multinationals. *Multinational Business Review*, 17(2), 157–77.
Welch, L. And Luostarinen, R. (1988). Internationalization: Evolution of a concept, *Journal of General Management*, 14(2): 36–64.

Websites

www.worldbank.org
http://data.worldbank.org/indicator
www.imf.org/external/datamapper/index.php
'Data Base on Foreign Direct Investment in Central, East and Southeast Europe 2010' is a document that is on the following website http://lambda.qsensei.com/content/1n697b.
'Data Base on Foreign Direct Investment in Central, East and Southeast Europe 2010' is a document that is on the following website http://lambda.qsensei.com/content/1n697b.
Documents containing data on 'UNCTAD, cross-border M&A' can be found on the following webpage – http://www.unctad.org/templates/.

4

Foreign Direct Investment in New EU Member States from Central and Eastern Europe: An Investment Development Path Perspective

Marian Gorynia, Jan Nowak, Piotr Tarka and Radosław Wolniak

Introduction

The interface and interplay between inward and outward foreign direct investment (IFDI and OFDI), coupled with economic development, constitutes the essence of the Investment Development Path (IDP) paradigm, the central theoretical model in this study. In the context of this model, a comparative analysis is conducted of the IDPs of ten Central and Eastern European (CEE) countries, all members of the European Union (EU). They include Bulgaria, the Czech Republic, Estonia, Hungary, Latvia, Lithuania, Poland, Romania, Slovakia and Slovenia. This group of countries shows relative homogeneity in terms of sharing the same communist heritage, common experience in establishing and developing a market economy, and in acceding to the EU: with eight countries joining the EU in 2004 and two (Bulgaria and Romania) in 2007. All of these countries show relative homogeneity in terms of many socio-economic variables (Niroomand and Nissan, 2007) and have exhibited a tendency to economic convergence over the last two decades (Amplatz, 2003; Matkowski and Próchniak, 2007). At the same time though, there are considerable differences between them in their level of development and in completion of the transition process to the market-led system. In fact, one can distinguish more homogenous subregions in the CEE-10 group (see e.g. Caporale et al., 2009), namely the Central European countries (the CEE-5: the Czech Republic, Hungary, Poland, Slovakia and Slovenia), the Baltic countries (the B-3: Estonia, Latvia and Lithuania), and the two Balkan countries located in south-eastern Europe (the SEE-2: Bulgaria and Romania). Particularly the latter states are handicapped with a considerable development gap separating them from the transition leaders of the CEE-5. Thus in this study we undertake to determine how these factors of homogeneity in some areas and heterogeneity in other areas influence the individual countries' IDP trajectories.

The main purpose of this chapter is to determine the timing and explore the factors that have influenced the movement of these ten CEE countries through their IDP stages. Thereafter, conclusions and policy recommendations are presented, which are not only applicable to the analysed countries, but which might serve as guidelines or simply be of interest to other CEE states, particularly those that may be or want to be considered as prospective members of the EU.

The datasets used in this study have been derived from the *Handbook of Statistics* (UNCTAD, 2009) and the *Statistical Yearbook of the Republic of Poland* (GUS, 2000–09). The data collected cover the entire period of the ten countries' transition process up to 2008, the last year for which relevant data for all countries were available.

We set out by presenting the IDP model (paradigm) and briefly describing its five stages. We then review the relevant literature, focusing on those studies that applied the IDP model to CEE economies. In the subsequent section, we try to determine the current positioning of the ten countries on the IDP, using a graph depicting the relationship between net outward investment position (NOIP) per capita and GDP per capita, and tables presenting detailed data on IFDI and OFDI stocks and NOIP's absolute values. In doing so, we also highlight the EU accession effects on the countries' move through stages 2 and 3, and the effects of the recent economic and financial crisis on their NOIP dynamics. In a second analytical section, a regression analysis is conducted to verify findings from the previous section. Thereafter, we focus on the CEE-10 countries' OFDI and apply the OFDI performance index in our analysis of that outward investment. The index is used to supplement and enrich the analysis of the countries' IDP positioning conducted in the previous sections. In the concluding section, we summarize our findings and reveal a need to add new theoretical considerations to the IDP original model. We also outline future research avenues in the area of the IDP of CEE countries.

The IDP concept and its application in the studies of CEE countries

The concept of the IDP, which relates to FDI, was first proposed by Dunning in the early 1980s (Dunning, 1981). This was further refined by Dunning (1986, 1997), Dunning and Narula (1994, 1996, 2002) and Narula and Dunning (2000). Several other authors have made significant contributions to the development of the concept, including Lall (1996) and Durán and Úbeda (2001, 2005). According to the basic IDP proposition, the inward and outward foreign investment position of a country is tied with its economic development. Changes in the volume and structure of FDI lead to different

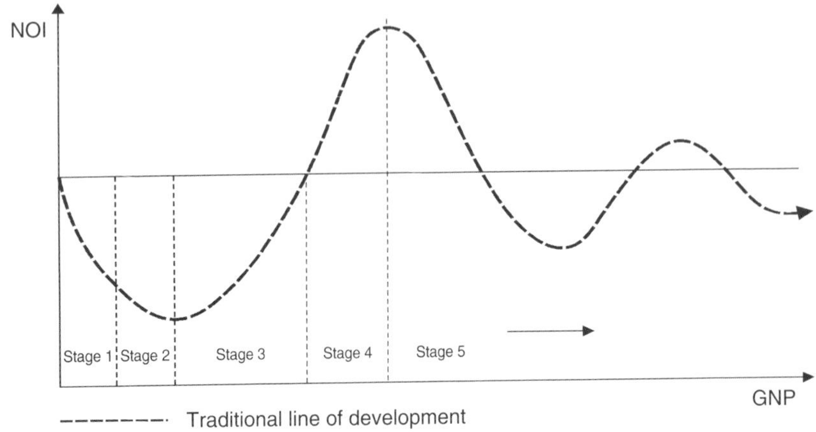

Figure 4.1 The pattern of the Investment Development Path

Note: Not drawn to scale. The IDP curve shown is called by Dunning and Narula (2002) a traditional one. On this traditional curve, they superimposed a curve, parallel to the traditional one but flatter (ibid.:139), that, according to these authors, reflects technological and organizational changes in FDI emerging in the 1990s.

Source: Dunning and Narula (2002:139).

values in the country's net outward investment (NOI) position, defined as the difference between gross outward direct investment stock and gross inward direct investment stock. The changing NOI position passes through five stages intrinsically related to the country's economic development (Dunning and Narula, 2002).[1] A diagrammatic representation of the IDP model is depicted in Figure 4.1

In Stage 1 of the IDP, the NOI position is initially close to zero and subsequently assumes negative, but rather small, values. IFDI is negligible and flowing mostly to take advantage of the country's natural assets. OFDI is also negligible or non-existent, as foreign firms prefer to export and import as well as to enter into non-equity relationships with local firms (Dunning and Narula, 2002:140). As a country develops and improves its L-specific advantages,[2] it experiences an increased inflow of FDI and enters Stage 2 of the IDP. With OFDI remaining still low but larger than in the previous stage, the NOI position continues to decrease, although towards the latter part of Stage 2 the rate of decrease slows down as the growth of OFDI converges with that of IFDI. Stage 3 is reached by a country when it experiences an improving NOI position, although it remains negative, due to an increased rate of growth of OFDI and a gradual slowdown in IFDI, geared in this case more towards efficiency-seeking motives and away from import-substituting production. OFDI is stimulated by domestic firms acquiring new O-specific advantages,[3] which are increasingly based on intangible assets and which reflect these firms' ability to manage and coordinate assets and activities across national borders (Dunning and Narula, 2002:142). In Stage 4, OFDI stock continues to rise faster than the inward one, and the country's NOI position crosses the zero level and becomes positive. Country L-specific advantages are now mostly derived from created assets and its firms' O-specific advantages develop and lead to their increased international competitiveness, as the indigenous firms seek to maintain their competitiveness by moving their operations to foreign countries. In Stage 5, the NOI position first falls and thereafter demonstrates a tendency to fluctuate around zero but usually with both IFDI and OFDI increasing. This stage is characterized by two main phenomena: (i) the growing propensity of MNEs to internalize their cross-border transactions (as opposed to relying on the market) and to engage in an increasingly complex web of cooperative agreements among themselves; (ii) a convergence of Stage 5 countries' economic structures and their international direct investment positions. Stages 4 and 5 are typical of the most developed countries (ibid.: 143–4).

A conceptual evaluation of the IDP model, as evidenced in developed as well as in developing and newly industrialized countries, is undertaken by Lall (1996). Lall maintains that structural changes in ownership and location factors influence trends in international capital flows, corporate behaviour and government policy. According to one of his suggestions the IDP could be better measured by the international transfer of intangible assets instead of relying only on FDI. His main observation is that countries exhibit long-term deviations from the IDP model, caused mainly by the nature and efficacy of government policy. This might necessitate extending and modifying the model itself to encompass all the identified subpatterns.

A more recent comprehensive evaluation of the IDP concept, its shortcomings and suggestions for its modification are found in the studies of Durán and Úbeda (2001, 2005). In calling for a new approach to the IDP, they draw attention to such methodological problems as the incompleteness of the concept of NOI position as an indicator for analysing the effects of structural changes on IFDI and OFDI, and then the insufficiency of GDP per capita as the indicator of a country's level of economic development. The first dilemma appears in countries where hardly any IFDI and OFDI is made and which are classified as being in Stage 1 of the IDP. Their NOI position will be close to zero, similar to developed countries in Stage 5 of their IDP. To solve this paradox, Durán and Úbeda propose looking at IFDI and OFDI in absolute and relative terms. Suggestions for dealing with the second issue revolve around the inclusion of structural variables, which would reflect not only the degree of economic development but also each country's peculiarities and the nature of its international trade.

Another significant contribution to the debate around the IDP concept made by Durán and Úbeda concerns their redefinition of Stage 4. In the amended version it is proposed to include developed countries which have: (a) a structural gap due to fewer endowments of created assets; (b) the same levels of IFDI as those in Stage 5 but smaller OFDI compared to those in Stage 5; and (c) a positive or negative NOI position, but in all cases lower than that of countries in Stage 5. All the proposed modifications depend on the availability of additional or more detailed data and offer much wider analytical possibilities.

The IDP model has been used as a framework in numerous empirical studies, which by and large have attempted to validate it by either employing cross-sectional or longitudinal datasets.[4] However, a relatively small number of studies could be identified that directly or indirectly deal with IDPs of CEE countries, of which only four represent a cross-nation comparative analysis.[5]

Boudier-Bensebaa (2008) undertakes a comparative analysis of the IDP in the whole region of CEE (including the former Soviet Republics) and the EU of 15 member states. The 'Eastern' countries concerned are classified into four distinct groups according to their per capita level of GDP and NOI. Their NOI places them in Stages 1 or 2 of the IDP, while that of the EU countries points to Stages 4 or 5. The first most advanced group of the Eastern countries consists of the Czech Republic, Estonia, Slovenia, Hungary, Slovakia, Poland, Latvia, Lithuania and Croatia. The said group is identified as moving towards the end of Stage 2 of their IDPs or even towards the beginning of Stage 3. The NOI of the Eastern countries' groups and subgroups reveals a tendency to converge. But as far as income levels are concerned, no convergence is found either inside the countries or between them and the EU. Finally the author draws attention to the fact that data on FDI stocks and GDP do not cover all the factors affecting FDI and development. In the FDI sphere, left out are the non-equity forms of investment. As for the effect on FDI, besides GDP, elements such as EU accession, globalization and the transformation process per se should be also taken into account. Boudier-Bensebaa focuses on cross-sectional analysis across countries and does not attempt to assess and explain the individual countries' IDP trajectories. This missing element is taken up by us in this study. We argue that individual countries' IDP idiosyncrasies can provide a deeper understanding and a more insightful explanation of the varying IDPs and their convergence or divergence within groups of countries.

In the second cross-nation study focused on CEE, Kottardi et al. (2004) attempt to integrate Dunning's IDP model with Vernon's Product Life Cycle and Hirsch's International Trade and Investment Theory of the Firm. These authors analyse the location determinants of IFDI and the interrelationship between IFDI and imports during the years 1992–2000 in eight new EU member states from CEE and two candidate countries – Bulgaria and Romania. They find evidence of the ten CEE countries going through the second stage of the IDP and gradually moving towards the third stage, which corroborates the findings of Boudier-Bensebaa (2008) with respect to the most advanced CEE economies, labelled CEECs1.

Studies by Kalotay (2004) and Svietličič and Jaklič (2003) focus on OFDI from CEE. While the former study uses the IDP framework, the latter does not. Kalotay (2004) examines OFDI from most of the 2004 accession CEE countries plus Croatia, placing these countries in Stage 2 of their IDPs. This author predicts that accession of the eight CEE countries to the EU in 2004 should give a major push to both their OFDI and IFDI, with an uncertain net impact of such a development on the IDP. However, based on the experience of Portugal (Buckley and Castro, 1998) and Austria (Bellak, 2001), Kalotay hypothesizes that CEE countries being at the time of accession to the EU on the verge of moving from Stage 2 to 3 will be held back in their transition.

Svietličič and Jaklič (2003), while not using the IDP paradigm as a framework, conduct a comparative analysis of several CEE countries' OFDI (the Czech Republic, Estonia, Hungary, Poland and Slovenia). Their analysis clearly demonstrates that major increases of FDI outflows started in the latter part of the 1990s. This is yet another indication of the CEE countries entering Stage 2 of the IDP during that period. At the same time Svietličič and Jaklič find positive correlation between a country's level of development and its rate of investment abroad, and observe that OFDI of the five countries under study tends to be geographically concentrated in countries with close historical or cultural ties.

Econometric analysis in IDP studies

Many of the IDP studies apply econometric modelling in testing the paradigm. Dunning himself (1981, 1986) and Dunning and Narula (2002) postulated and used a quadratic specification to describe the IDP curve (the formula for this specification is presented later in this chapter). A quadratic function allows for the non-linearity in the relationship. The same function has been used by several other authors analysing IDPs of individual countries or groups of countries (see e.g. Tolentino, 1987; Narula, 1996; Barry et al., 2002; Boudier-Bensebaa, 2008). Other authors (see e.g. Buckley and Castro, 1998; Bellak, 2001) found a cubic specification that fitted their empirical data better.[6]

Some other approaches to econometric analysis of IDP are also noteworthy. Durán and Úbeda (2001, 2005) for example applied factor and cluster analyses to identify the countries reaching specific stages of the IDP. These authors also applied panel data analysis for a number of Stage 4 countries. Similarly Boudier-Bensebaa (2008) applied a quadratic equation to a panel of 27 CEE countries and ran the regression not only for the entire sample but also for two clusters in that group.

Current positioning on the IDP

The last two years under consideration have brought significant changes in the positioning of the ten investigated economies on their respective IDP trajectories. As visualized in Figure 4.2, and further recorded in Table 4.1, five countries in descending order (Hungary, Estonia, Lithuania, Poland and the Czech Republic) were clearly in their IDP Stage 3. Their NOIPs[7] per capita increased in 2008 relative to the previous year (i.e. decreased in absolute values). The smallest increase was curiously recorded for the Czech Republic – the country exhibiting the highest GDP per capita of the above-listed group (US$20,815). Hungary had the highest increase but at a lower GDP per capita of US$15,408. The lowest GDP per capita was that of Poland in the Stage 3 group of countries (US$13,861). Those leaders were with respect to their level of development in the upper middle segment of all the analysed countries. At the least developed end, there was Bulgaria with decreasing (i.e. rising negative) NOIP and GDP per capita of only US$6,573 in 2008.

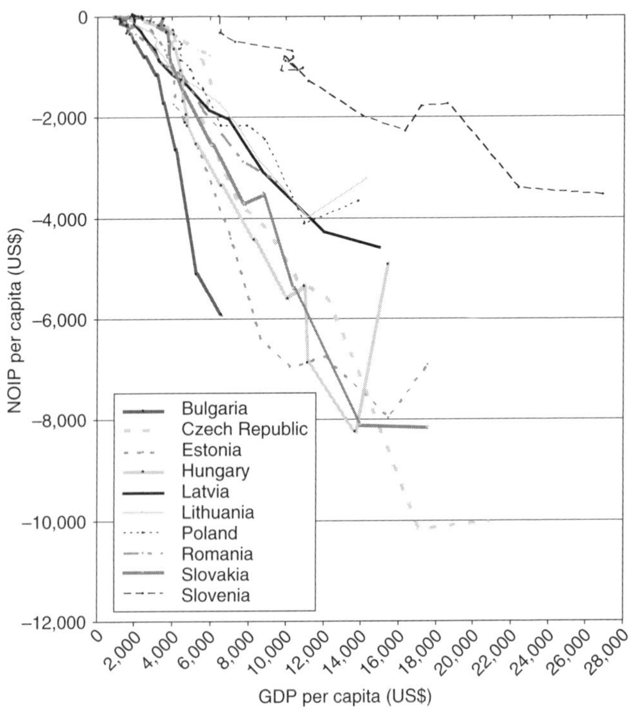

Figure 4.2 NOIP per capita and GDP per capita in US$, 1990–2008, CEE-10 countries

Source: Authors' calculations based on UNCTAD (2009) and (GUS, 2000–09).

At the other end was Slovenia with the top GDP per capita of US$26,905, though its NOIP in 2008 was still slightly decreasing, indicating the forthcoming advent into IDP Stage 3 as well. Bulgaria and Romania were still in the second half of their IDP Stage 2, as well as Latvia, which was closer to the beginning of its IDP Stage 3. Slovakia's NOIP per capita in 2008 was only very slightly higher than in 2007, indicating that the country was at the turning point from Stage 2 to Stage 3 of its IDP.

According to the original model of Dunning, the shift to IDP Stage 3 takes place when the NOIP, and in our case NOIP per capita, starts to rise. In the latest two years for which data are available such shifts in the whole group of countries under investigation has been described above. But it must be stressed that in four countries such shifts were already observed a few years earlier. In the case of Hungary, Slovenia and Slovakia such a shift was visible four years earlier, i.e. in 2004. In that year, all of them became full members of the EU and this accession effect could be held responsible for the said shift in their NOIPs. Also a reinforcing factor was that those three economies were considered to be the most developed in the group of CEE states and the most advanced in the transition process to the market-led economic system. In the case of Estonia, a relatively small Baltic economy, a similar shift occurred in 2005, indicating a somewhat delayed EU accession effect. Thus the closeness to the latest shifts observed in 2008 indicates that final conclusions as to the permanency of passing to IDP Stage 3 require more time for verification.

The underlying causes for the NOIP per capita movements in countries which as of 2008 have been positioned to be in Stage 3 of their IDP require more scrutiny of changes in their stocks of OFDI and IFDI. These changes are recorded in Table 4.2. In two cases, that of Poland and Estonia, the net outcome of a decrease in their NOIPs per capita was due to their OFDI stock increasing for at least two years before and the IFDI stock decreasing from 2007 inclusive. This indicated that as for OFDI expansion and thus competitiveness of their firms these two economies had shown a relatively positive performance in the face of the severe economic downturn which started to afflict the global economy towards the end of 2007. But simultaneously this same business cycle factor may have been responsible for the fall in IFDI stocks. Also it cannot be easily determined whether the continuing outward expansion via FDI from those two countries was due to competitive advantages of domestic firms (the desired expected outcome) or simply indirect FDI, signifying expansion of subsidiaries of foreign MNEs from those countries, thus reflecting their much stronger and sustainable competitive advantage versus their domestic rivals. The retreat of foreign investors in those two cases also demonstrates that the risk associated with recession is not dependent on the size of the internal markets of these two countries, since Poland had the largest market measured by population, whereas Estonia had a much smaller one. Hungary, on the other hand,

Table 4.1 NOIP per capita, GDP per capita in US$ and OFDI Performance Index (OFDIPI) for ten CEE countries, 1990–2008

	1990	1991	1992	1993	1994	1995	1996	1997
Bulgaria								
NOIP per capita	0.001	–0.006	–0.011	–0.016	–0.029	–0.041	–0.058	–0.120
GDP per capita	2,350	873	995	1,267	1,149	1,568	1,197	1,265
OFDIPI	–0.014	–0.093	–0.045	–0.029	0.000	–0.050	–0.223	–0.012
Czech Republic								
NOIP per capita				–0.314	–0.412	–0.679	–0.784	–0.845
GDP per capita				3,603	4,230	5,360	6,022	5,559
OFDIPI				0.257	0.269	0.055	0.188	0.027
Estonia								
NOIP per capita				–0.130	–0.278	–0.422	–0.506	–0.666
GDP per capita			2,859	2,813	2,874	3,114	3,365	3,622
OFDIPI				0.102	0.112	–0.170	0.203	0.275
Hungary								
NOIP per capita	–0.036	–0.182	–0.310	–0.518	–0.657	–1.067	–1.262	–1.683
GDP per capita	3,546	3,319	3,702	3,836	4,125	4,443	4,499	4,564
OFDIPI	0.042	0.093	0.000	0.029	0.110	0.105	–0.007	0.613
Latvia								
NOIP per capita				0.054	–0.055	–0.155	–0.296	–0.431
GDP per capita			2,095	1,854	1,938	1,991	2,310	2,568
OFDIPI				0.102	0.112	–0.170	0.203	0.275
Lithuania								
NOIP per capita				–0.037	–0.088	–0.097	–0.193	–0.284
GDP per capita			2,168	1,867	1,730	1,788	2,271	2,795
OFDIPI				0.102	0.112	–0.170	0.203	0.275
Poland								
NOIP per capita	0.008	–0.001	–0.025	–0.057	–0.086	–0.189	–0.278	–0.361
GDP per capita	1,694	2,189	2,406	2,446	2,813	3,603	4,059	4,073
OFDIPI	0.007	–0.010	0.018	0.020	0.026	0.025	0.026	0.018
Romania								
NOIP per capita	0.003	0.002	–0.002	–0.005	–0.013	–0.031	–0.043	–0.102
GDP per capita	1,659	1,254	854	1,157	1,327	1,575	1,576	1,583
OFDIPI	0.045	0.012	0.026	0.028	0.000	0.005	0.000	–0.016
Slovakia								
NOIP per capita				–0.093	–0.137	–0.216	–0.347	–0.347
GDP per capita				2,550	2,939	3,676	3,977	4,007
OFDIPI				0.102	0.112	–0.170	0.203	0.275
Slovenia								
NOIP per capita				–0.345	–0.511	–0.693	–0.799	–0.886
GDP per capita			6,445	6,496	7,347	10,329	10,393	9,992
OFDIPI				0.102	0.112	–0.170	0.203	0.275

Note: OFDIPI–OFDI performance index reflects the ratio of the share of a country's OFDI from the world's total in a given year to the share of the country's GDP from the world total GDP in a given year.

Source: UNCTAD (2009) and GUS (2000–09).

1998	1999	2000	2001	2002	2003	2004	2005	2006	2007	2008
−0.187	−0.297	−0.327	−0.362	−0.506	−0.799	−1.162	−1.728	−2.647	−5.100	−5.914
1,567	1,607	1,574	1,711	1,965	2,546	3,148	3,496	4,160	5,259	6,573
0.000	0.037	0.006	0.025	0.114	0.089	−0.419	0.6100	0.195	0.172	0.481
−1.323	−1.646	−2.046	−2.542	−3.646	−4.217	−5.248	−5.598	−7.106	−10.195	−10.036
6,030	5,880	5,549	6,058	7,379	8,959	10,615	12,165	13,863	17,004	20,815
0.088	0.042	0.019	0.113	0.167	0.149	0.444	−0.008	0.440	0.236	0.287
−1.169	−1.585	−1.742	−1.994	−2.616	−4.419	−6.413	−6.957	−6.754	−7.971	−6.922
4,102	4,152	4,108	4,544	5,385	7,093	8,638	10,230	12,038	15,471	17,538
0.281	−0.504	0.036	0.121	0.027	0.495	−0.024	0.178	0.267	2.126	1.517
−1.943	−2.181	−2.114	−2.537	−3.351	−4.422	−5.593	−5.343	−6.867	−8.249	−4.933
4,708	4,820	4,695	5,233	6,563	8,326	10,101	10,942	11,134	13,660	15,408
0.247	0.142	0.332	0.293	0.254	1.287	0.520	1.131	1.076	0.690	0.351
−0.529	−0.647	−0.866	−0.970	−1.148	−1.358	−1.850	−2.046	−3.095	−4.285	−4.581
2,788	3,041	3,293	3,520	3,972	4,802	5,944	6,969	8,781	12,013	14,956
0.281	−0.504	0.036	0.121	0.027	0.495	−0.024	0.178	0.267	0.310	0.224
−0.453	−0.578	−0.658	−0.752	−1.131	−1.401	−1.734	−2.187	−2.863	−3.980	−3.233
3,147	3,096	3,260	3,487	4,076	5,373	6,543	7,494	8,592	11,133	14,244
0.281	−0.504	0.036	0.121	0.027	0.495	−0.024	0.178	0.267	0.407	0.246
−0.553	−0.651	−0.864	−1.044	−1.222	−1.455	−2.174	−2.180	−2.436	−4.109	−3.662
4,487	4,364	4,458	4,959	5,165	5,655	6,592	7,951	8,916	10,978	13,861
0.078	0.005	0.002	−0.020	0.071	0.093	0.149	0.536	0.508	0.287	0.222
−0.197	−0.248	−0.308	−0.374	−0.349	−0.549	−0.932	−1.187	−1.891	−2.879	−3.299
1,885	1,600	1,673	1,824	2,090	2,726	3,475	4,557	5,684	7,726	9,518
−0.009	0.013	−0.009	−0.017	0.023	0.043	0.044	−0.016	0.012	0.042	−0.044
−0.466	−0.528	−0.811	−0.953	−1.493	−2.553	−3.727	−3.540	−5.391	−8.115	−8.153
4,164	3,825	3,795	3,917	4,552	6,122	7,800	8,804	10,402	13,958	17,566
0.281	−0.504	0.036	0.121	0.027	0.495	−0.024	0.178	0.267	0.129	0.089
−1.083	−1.038	−1.071	−0.808	−1.309	−1.985	−2.286	−1.782	−1.754	−3.422	−3.559
10,640	10,887	9,737	9,950	11,197	14,075	16,323	17,182	18,596	22,379	26,905
0.281	−0.504	0.036	0.121	0.027	0.495	−0.024	0.178	0.267	1.019	0.867

Table 4.2 Outward FDI stock, inward FDI stock and NOIP for CEE-10 countries, 1990–2008 (US$ millions)

	1990	1991	1992	1993	1994	1995	1996	1997	1998
Bulgaria									
OFDI Outward	124	118	116	112	113	105	76	74	75
IFDI Inward	112	168	210	250	355	446	555	1059	1597
NOIP	12	–50	–94	–138	–242	–341	–479	–985	–1522
Czech Republic									
OFDI Outward		70	91	181	300	345	498	548	804
IFDI Inward	1363	1886	2889	3423	4547	7350	8572	9234	14375
NOIP		–1816	–2798	–3242	–4247	–7005	–8074	–8686	–13571
Estonia									
OFDI Outward			57	63	65	68	108	215	198
IFDI Inward			96	258	473	675	825	1148	1822
NOIP			–39	–195	–408	–607	–717	–933	–1624
Hungary									
OFDI Outward	197	224	224	226	291	278	265	647	784
IFDI Inward	569	2107	3424	5576	7087	11304	13282	17968	20733
NOIP	–372	–1883	–3200	–5350	–6796	–11026	–13017	–17321	–19949
Latvia									
OFDI Outward			365	361	296	231	209	222	281
IFDI Inward			176	221	436	616	936	1272	1558
NOIP			189	140	–140	–385	–727	–1050	–1277
Lithuania									
OFDI Outward			0	0	0	1	3	26	17
IFDI Inward			107	137	321	352	700	1041	1625
NOIP			–107	–137	–321	–351	–697	–1015	–1608
Poland									
OFDI Outward	408	401	414	432	461	539	735	678	1165
IFDI Inward	109	425	1370	2621	3789	7843	11463	14587	22461
NOIP	299	–24	–956	–2189	–3328	–7304	–10728	–13909	–21296
Romania									
OFDI Outward	66	87	79	103	107	121	120	126	135
IFDI Inward	0	44	122	215	402	821	1097	2417	4527
NOIP	66	43	–43	–112	–295	–700	–977	–2291	–4392
Slovakia									
OFDI Outward		127	136	149	166	139	183	236	408
IFDI Inward	282	363	463	642	897	1297	2046	2103	2920
NOIP		–236	–327	–493	–731	–1158	–1863	–1867	–2512
Slovenia									
OFDI Outward			279	281	365	524	470	459	636
IFDI Inward			841	954	1365	1886	2043	2207	2777
NOIP			–562	–673	–1000	–1362	–1573	–1748	–2141

* According to UNCTAD data OFDI stock for Bulgaria in 2004 was negative, but no exact value is available. Therefore it was assumed that in this case outward FDI stock = 0.

Source: UNCTAD (2009) and GUS (2000–09).

1999	2000	2001	2002	2003	2004	2005	2006	2007	2008
11	85	68	81	103	*	181	343	528	1248
2403	2704	2945	4074	6371	9058	13565	20707	39484	46011
–2392	–2619	–2877	–3993	–6268	–9058	–13384	–20364	–38956	–44763
698	738	1136	1473	2284	3760	3610	5058	8557	9913
17552	21644	27092	38669	45287	57259	60662	77460	112408	114369
–16854	–20906	–25956	–37196	–43003	–53499	–57052	–72402	–103851	–104456
281	259	442	676	1028	1419	1940	3613	6174	6686
2467	2645	3160	4226	7002	10064	11290	12664	16815	15962
–2186	–2386	–2718	–3550	–5974	–8645	–9350	–9051	–10641	–9276
924	1280	1556	2166	3509	6018	7993	12693	17596	14179
23260	22870	27407	36224	48340	62585	61886	81760	100335	63671
–22336	–21590	–25851	–34058	–44831	–56567	–53893	–69067	–82739	–49492
244	24	39	59	114	235	284	447	880	1066
1795	2084	2328	2751	3277	4517	4993	7532	10637	11447
–1551	–2060	–2289	–2692	–3163	–4282	–4709	–7085	–9757	–10381
26	29	48	60	120	423	721	1183	1570	1990
2063	2334	2666	3981	4960	6389	8211	10939	15062	12847
–2037	–2305	–2618	–3921	–4840	–5966	–7490	–9756	–13492	–10857
1024	1018	1156	1457	2146	3223	6439	10705	19369	21814
26075	34227	41247	48320	57877	86366	89694	103616	175851	161406
–25051	–33209	–40091	–46863	–55731	–83143	–83255	–92911	–156482	–139592
144	136	117	144	208	273	214	278	1240	912
5671	6951	8350	7799	12188	20523	25894	41001	62961	71864
–5527	–6815	–8233	–7655	–11980	–20250	–25680	–40723	–61721	–70952
346	374	449	485	823	835	705	1282	1509	1901
3188	4746	5582	8530	14576	20910	19775	30327	45251	45933
–2842	–4372	–5133	–8045	–13753	–20075	–19070	–29045	–43742	–44032
626	768	988	1505	2350	3025	3515	3942	7197	8650
2682	2893	2594	4112	6308	7590	7077	7452	14048	15872
–2056	–2125	–1606	–2607	–3958	–4565	–3562	–3510	–6851	–7222

was the only country in the whole group which recorded falls both in IFDI and OFDI stocks, which contributed to the decrease in its NOIP per capita. This of course meant that the OFDI retreat was relatively smaller than the inward one. Thus the country leading in the movement into Stage 3 of its IDP was also the most sensitive to changes in the downturn of the business cycle. The effects of the recession in 2008 were also visible in Lithuania's IFDI stock rising in 2007 and then falling in the following year. At the same time its OFDI continued its unabated rise that had begun in 1998. The Czech Republic, as observed earlier, entered Stage 3 of its IDP, registering the smallest increase in NOIP per capita in the whole group. This was due to its OFDI stock rising slightly faster than its IFDI stock, which was also larger. The remaining countries in the group, i.e. Slovakia, Slovenia, Latvia, Romania and Bulgaria, all displayed slower rising OFDI stocks compared with faster rising IFDI stocks. This trend embraced relatively high GDP per capita countries (the first three) as well as the two least developed ones in the group.

Regression analysis

The above observations and findings based on descriptive analytical tools were subjected to verification using regression analysis. This was applied to the two principal variables of the IDP model: NOI per capita, as the dependent variable, and GDP per capita, as the independent variable. Two non-linear function specifications, quadratic and cubic, were applied.

In the analysis an attempt was made firstly to eliminate 'outliers' – extreme cases – and then to fit the appropriate curve to empirical data. Figure 4.3 shows the plot with country curves according to modelled data. The curves are different because of different data configuration. These regression curves were drawn through points on the scatter plot to summarize the relationship between the variables under investigation. All the curves slope down (from top left to bottom right), indicating an inverse relationship between the variables. Each regression curve represents the regression equation on a scatter plot. The regression equation shows the nature of the relationship between the two variables.

Data description

At first, a regression analysis based on a quadratic equation (in SPSS software) was conducted, related to the said variables. Non-linear regression was appropriate because the relationship between the dependent and independent variables was not intrinsically linear. It has been implemented according to Dunning's (1981) solution, with the idea of regressing NOI on GDP, and thus utilizing a quadratic specification (and further cubic one) in order to allow for the non-linearity in the relationship. As a result, a non-linear relationship was obtained between GDP per capita and NOI per capita.

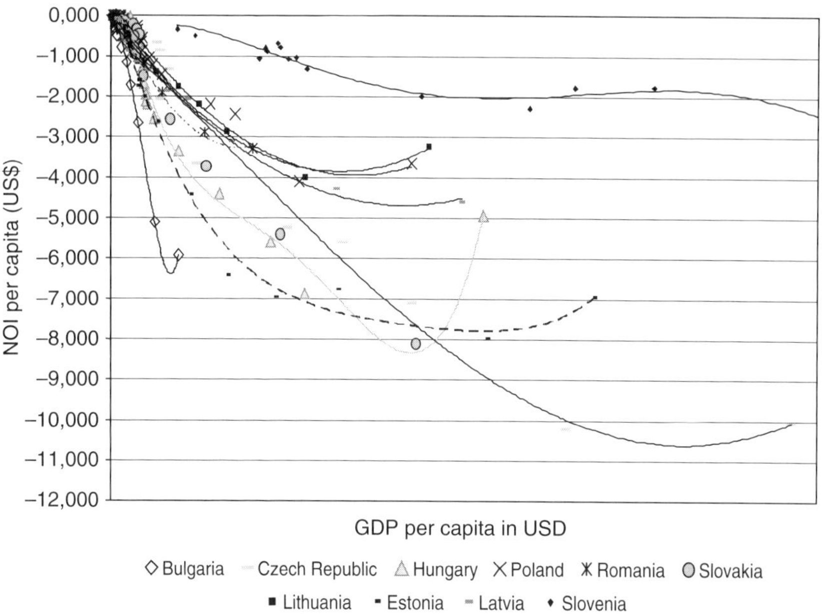

Figure 4.3 Non-linear relationship between NOI and GDP

Source: Authors' calculations.

A regression equation was primarily written as:

$$NOI = \alpha + \beta_1 GDPpc + \beta_2 GDPpc^2 + \mu \quad (1)$$

The equation specified the average magnitude of the expected change in *Y* given a change in *X*. In the course of examination according to available time series data the analysis embraced the period from 1990 to 2008 (for the countries Bulgaria, Hungary, Poland and Romania). A shorter period starting from 1993 to 2008 was used for the Czech Republic, Slovakia, Estonia, Latvia, Lithuania and Slovenia, because of the lack of data prior to 1993.

The analysis continued by experimenting with the regression function by allowing in a formula with a cubic equation, which was written in the following way:

$$NOI = \alpha + \beta_1 GDPpc + \beta_2 GDPpc^2 + \beta_3 GDPpc^3 + \mu \quad (2)$$

Where:

NOI – outward investment position of a country in a given year or at a given value of GDP per capita (NOI can be positive or negative) measured in US$ or EURO

GDPpc – gross domestic product per capita of a country in a given year measured in US$ or EURO

α, β, β and μ – coefficients depending on conditions in the countries for which NOI is calculated

Obviously the starting point of regression analysis was at first to fit a line to a number of points (crossing NOIP and GDP) in order to see at least the shape of the data on the plot. This is presented in Figure 4.3.

In proceeding further with the analysis based on quadratic and cubic formulas it was detected that regression coefficient values and fit of the models for quadratic assumptions were slightly lower than in the cubic ones. In some cases cubic formulas showed a much better fit of the variability being estimated. The relationship between the model and the dependent variable was quite strong. One can consider for example the R score as a multiple correlation coefficient.

The obtained R^2 values[8] were ranked in descending order (according to the non-linear regression quadratic function) of variability within the observed values. As a result, the variability of models could be explained for the investigated countries in the following descending order: (1) Latvia, (2) Romania, (3) Slovakia, (4) Czech Republic, (5) Bulgaria, (6) Poland, (7) Slovenia, (8) Lithuania, (9) Estonia and (10) Hungary. And as far as R^2 values were concerned, based on cubic calculations, the following descending order of countries was obtained: (1) Latvia, (2) Romania, (3) Slovakia, (4) Czech Republic, (5) Bulgaria, (6) Lithuania, (7) Poland, (8) Slovenia, (9) Estonia and (10) Hungary (see Table 4.3).

Having thus compared both types of analysis, one may infer that different characteristics in formulas result in only minor alterations (changes) in each country model's variability explanation. In some countries the R^2 values remain actually on the same level – no matter whether the quadratic or cubic equation is selected. This specific situation refers to countries such as Slovakia, Romania, Poland and Latvia. The biggest change appears in Bulgaria, Hungary and Lithuania.

The independent variable denotes NOI per capita and the dependent variable GDP per capita. The non-linear model provided very strong results for all parameters, which are highly significant in the overall model (F statistic at 5 per cent level).

Interpretation of findings

Based on the results of the regression analysis as shown in Figure 4.3, certain amendments to the findings based on the more descriptive analysis presented on pp. 000–000 need to be considered in this section. Firstly, Slovakia appears as the leader in the whole group, being the most

Table 4.3 Non-linear regression statistics for quadratic and cubic equations

	Bulgaria	**Czech Republic**	**Hungary**	**Poland**	**Romania**	**Slovakia**	**Estonia**	**Latvia**	**Lithuania**	**Slovenia**
Quadratic models $GDPpc^2$										
R – [Multiple R]	0.973	0.979	0.912	0.963	0.994	0.983	0.939	0.994	0.956	0.958
R^2 – [R – square]	0.946	0.959	0.831	0.927	0.987	0.967	0.881	0.988	0.913	0.917
Cubic models $GDPpc^3$										
R – [Multiple R]	0.979	0.981	0.928	0.964	0.994	0.983	0.941	0.994	0.964	0.960
R^2 – [R – square]	0.958	0.963	0.862	0.929	0.988	0.967	0.885	0.989	0.930	0.921

Source: Authors' calculations based on SPSS software.

advanced in Stage 3 of its IDP. In the descriptive approach it was positioned at the turning point from Stage 2 to Stage 3. Hungary, Lithuania and Estonia generally exhibit the same level of advancement to Stage 3 of their IDPs, whereas in the previous approach they were visibly differentiated, although they were also well into that stage. Poland, Latvia and the Czech Republic all are positioned at the beginning of Stage 3 of their respective IDPs, whereas earlier Latvia was described as being still positioned in Stage 2 of its IDP. In the regression analysis, Poland as the largest economy enters Stage 3 at a smaller GDP per capita than Latvia, and Latvia enters the same stage at a GDP per capita level still smaller than that of the Czech Republic.

Then there is the curious case of Slovenia. This country's positioning seems to show a fluctuation pattern around the turning point from Stage 2 to Stage 3 of its IDP. In the descriptive approach it was edging towards the end of Stage 2, with the highest GDP per capita of all the countries of the group positioned still in Stage 2 of their IDPs.

Romania and Bulgaria in the descriptive analysis were said to be somewhere in the second half of Stage 2 of their IDPs. But according to the regression analysis, Romania seems to be at the turning point from Stage 2 to Stage 3 of its IDP. However, the largest discrepancy concerns the positioning of Bulgaria. At first glance, Figure 3.3 suggests that Bulgaria is already in Stage 3 of its IDP, whereas descriptive analysis positioned its economy in the last place among the group of ten countries analysed, both with respect to the GDP per capita and the movement along its IDP. However, one cannot help noticing an atypical regression curve in the case of Bulgaria, which does not have the same shape as the curves of the Stage 3 countries. Bulgaria's curve first slopes to the left, which is an indication of a country going through the first part of Stage 2, and then it suddenly turns up at the end of the analysed period. Therefore it could be interpreted as a 'more dramatic' passage to the second part of Stage 2 rather than to Stage 3. Indeed, a closer look at the OFDI and IFDI stock statistics for Bulgaria (Table 4.2) confirms this assertion, i.e. that the country's OFDI remained negligible until 2006, when it started to grow rapidly and continued to do so over the next two years. However, even in 2008, when OFDI stock doubled compared to the previous year, it was still seven times lower than that of Slovenia, which incidentally recorded only a third of Bulgaria's IFDI stock in the same year. All of this seems to confirm Bulgaria's progress through Stage 2 but not yet passing to Stage 3.

Nevertheless both analytical approaches (the descriptive as well as the regressive) yield results confirming the undisputed leading role in the advancement of the IDP and a firm positioning in Stage 3 of Hungary, a medium sized advanced CEE economy. Lithuania and Estonia, the two Baltic states, and Poland, the largest country in the group, can also be classified in this leading category.

The outward FDI performance index

The analysis of the OFDI performance index (OFDIPI) provides an indication as to magnitude of OFDI which a country generates relative to the size of its economic potential, thus indirectly pointing out which country has the capacity to move to Stage 3 of its IDP or, being in that stage, to continue moving towards Stage 4. The values of the index that are less than 1 signify that OFDI is less than proportional to the size of the home country's economy as measured by its participation in the global economy as such. If, on the other hand, the values of the index are higher than 1 then the OFDI generated is more than proportional relative to the aforementioned size of the home economy. From the point of view of positioning on the IDP, the closer the index is to 1 or higher than 1 the more predisposed a given country is to advance on its IDP trajectory or in this case reach Stage 3 of its IDP, or to continue moving within Stage 3 faster than others.

In this context the values of the index as applied to the ten countries in this study are presented in Table 4.1. Among those countries Hungary was the unquestioned leader, recording the highest OPI values in 1991, 1995, 1997 and from 1999 onwards, surpassing in 2003, 2005 and 2006 the threshold value of 1, reflecting the highest relative effectiveness in OFDI expansion, which in turn was perceived to be the key factor in upgrading the country's international competitiveness. Until the end of 2006 no other country in the group recorded OFDIPI values higher than 1. At that moment Hungary showed the greatest propensity to be capable of being the first to move into its IDP Stage 3.

In the two ensuing years of 2007 and 2008, however, a radical change occurred in the OFDIPI values of certain countries. Estonia's value jumped from 0.267 in 2006 to the highest recorded value in the whole group so far of 2.126, thus succeeding Hungary as the new leader. The reason for that outstanding turnaround of Estonia was due to a sudden surge in OFDI, even in the face of rising IFDI stock. On the other hand Hungary's index fell to 0.69 indicating a substantial worsening of its international competitive position. Then in 2008, when the recession became prevalent, Estonia's index somewhat deteriorated, though still maintaining an impressive level of 1.51, showing sustained outward competitiveness in a difficult external environment. Hungary suffered more with its index going down to a mere 0.351.

A trend similar to that of Estonia was seen in the case of Slovenia's OFDIPI. In 2007, its value rose from 0.267 to a high of 1.019 in 2007, only to fall back to 0.867 in 2008. This also can be considered as evidence of a relatively small but well developed economy demonstrating a sustained capacity to maintain its competitiveness on foreign markets.

Then there is the case of the five countries of Latvia, Lithuania, Poland, Romania and Slovakia exhibiting a decline in their OFDIPI in 2007 and 2008. The first three registered in 2008 a similar level ranging from 0.222

for Poland to 0.246 for Lithuania, thus revealing that these economies (one with a large market and two with small internal markets) were underperforming in their OFDI relative to their economic potential, mainly as a result of recession. Thereafter is Slovakia, another small country, with its OFDIPI plunging down to 0.089 in 2008. And the lowest level of this index (–0.044) was recorded by Romania, confirming that also in this dimension the performance of this Balkan economy was in line with the second lowest GDP per capita level for the whole group, which in essence attested to its companies' paucity of significant competitive advantages that could be successfully exploited via FDI in foreign markets in addition to the negatively reinforcing effect of economic slowdown.

Bulgaria and the Czech Republic differentiated themselves from the rest by recording increased values of OFDIPI in 2007 and 2008, although both had higher values in 2006. Also worth noting is the fact that Bulgaria, the least developed in the group of all the ten countries, had a much higher OFDIPI of 0.481 in 2008 than the Czech Republic, the second most developed in the whole group with an OFDIPI of 0.287. This can be interpreted as evidence of rising international competitiveness of Bulgarian firms, stemming from an economy in the second half of Stage 2 of its IDP or, according to the regression analysis, even in Stage 3, especially when compared with their Czech competitors in foreign markets having behind them and being supported by a much more developed economic potential of an economy positioned at the beginning of its IDP Stage 3. Only these two countries, although being at opposing ends of the economic development scale, were able to withstand the onslaught of recession and improve in these challenging years their OFDIPI values.

Conclusions

The negative thrust of the last global recession exerted a surprising and paradoxical effect of pushing seven of the investigated CEE-10 economies well into Stage 3 of their IDPs. This provided a new theoretical consideration which could be added to the general IDP model in that exogenous macroeconomic factors, such as in this case a downturn in the business cycle which was not directly connected to and/or affecting changes in the NOIP construct, as envisaged originally by Dunning, could expedite the movement of an economy from one stage to another (in this case from Stage 2 to Stage 3). Moreover, in the case of two Balkan economies with a considerable development gap towards the rest (Romania and Bulgaria), this same factor accelerated movement along their IDP Stage 2 trajectory. This so far short-term effect, observed in a time frame of two years, has still to be proven to be sustainable since evidence from the past shows that in some cases such movement into Stage 3 can be reversible. This reversibility was observed previously as a consequence of accession to the EU: for Hungary in 2004, for

Slovenia and Slovakia one year later, and for Estonia two years later. Thus external factors or influences may exert a considerable impact on the IDPs of the former transition economies.

Evidence provided by the analysis of the OFDIPI also confirmed that the investigated countries weathered with different strengths and success the negative consequences for their international competitiveness and the sustainability of their competitive advantages in foreign markets brought about by the last global recession. Only a minority of the CEE-10 countries was able to improve its OFDIPI values. This of course brings into focus the necessity of all the remaining countries in the group to institute economic policy measures addressed to remedy and eliminate the existing unfavourable situation. From the point of view of the IDP paradigm, the key thrust lies in sustaining and promoting OFDI, especially by domestic MNCs and/or national firms, since subsidiaries of foreign based MNCs usually wield so much economic power that they are fully capable of re-exporting capital without additional host country assistance, encouragement or support. Of course the economic recovery underway in Western EU countries should lead to a resurgence of increased FDI flows to the CEE economies, and it remains to be seen how these increases will compare with increases anticipated in OFDI from the CEE region.

The analysis of the IDPs of the group of ten CEE countries leads to a general conclusion that, in their economic development viewed from a time perspective of 19 years from the start of the transition process, they have all followed the basic premises and trajectories as set forth in the original IDP model. The regression analysis showed that all of the investigated CEE economies, except those of Bulgaria, Slovenia and Romania, were well into Stage 3 of their IDPs. This observation can be construed as an indirect confirmation of the success of the transition process to a market led system, which those countries had implemented almost two decades ago, and of the role which FDI has been playing in this process and generally in the economic development of these economies. The Stage 2 economies were also in a specific positioning regarding IDP. Slovenia, much more developed than Bulgaria and Romania, showed a tendency to fluctuate around the border of IDP Stage 3, whereas Romania, according to the regression analysis, was about to enter its IDP Stage 3.

All the above country specificities can be attributed to external factors such as the effect of a downturn in the business cycle and to the idiosyncratic nature of development per se. The first effect is relatively short term, whereas the second effect is more long term; but both are prone to possible reversals. Thus all of those conclusions must undergo a further extensive verification process in the coming years since definite/sustainable patterns and trends are clearly visible only in a long-term approach. Also a comparative dimension is advisable with the remaining members of the EU and/or selected CEE countries, which are currently outside the EU.

Notes

An earlier version of this chapter was presented at the 36th Annual Conference of the European International Business Academy in Porto, Portugal, 9–11 December 2010.

1. In its original version (Dunning, 1981), the path had four stages. The fifth stage was added later (Dunning and Narula, 1996).
2. L-specific advantages denote a country's advantages as a locus for investment vis-à-vis other countries. Such advantages may include large markets, low input costs, tax and financial incentives or strategic geographic location.
3. O-specific advantages denote ownership advantages of firms, such as brand name, ownership of proprietary technology or lower costs due to economies of scale.
4. A succinct review of the two types of IDP empirical studies, cross-sectional and longitudinal, can be found in Gorynia et al. (2006).
5. Several studies focus on individual CEE countries' IDP. They either explicitly use the IDP framework or focus on some of its elements, typically on OFDI. A review of these studies is presented in Gorynia et al. (2008).
6. A cubic specification is as follows: $NOI = \alpha + \beta_1\ GDPpc^3 + \beta_2\ GDPpc^5 + \mu$.
7. The abbreviations NOI and NOIP are used interchangeably in this chapter but in both cases denote net outward investment position.
8. In linear regression models the quality of fit of a model is expressed in terms of the coefficient of determination, also known as theR^2. In non-linear regression, such a measure is, unfortunately, not readily defined. One of the problems with the R^2 definition is that it requires the presence of an intercept, which most non-linear models do not have. A measure relatively closely corresponding to R^2 in the non-linear case is $R^2 = 1 - SS(Residual)/SS(Total_{Corrected})$. The degree to which the predictor (independent variable) is related to the dependent variable is expressed in the R^2, which can assume values between 0 and 1.

References

Amplatz, C. (2003). The economic convergence performance of Central and Eastern European countries. *Economics of Planning*, 36, 273–95.

Barry, F., Gorg, H. And McDowell, A. (2002). Outward FDI and the investment development path of a late industrialising economy: Evidence from Ireland, University College Dublin, Belfield, The Economic Department.

Bellak, C. (2001). The Austrian Investment Development Path. *Transnational Corporations*, 10(2), 68–107.

Boudier-Bensebaa, F. (2008). FDI-assisted development in the light of the Investment Development Path paradigm: Evidence from Central and Eastern European countries. *Transnational Corporations*, 17(1), 37–63.

Buckley, P.J. and Castro, F.B. (1998). The Investment Development Path: the case of Portugal. *Transnational Corporations*, 7(1), 1–15.

Caporale, G.M., Rault C., Sova R. and Sova A. (2009). Financial development and economic growth: evidence from ten new EU members. Economics and Finance Working Paper Series No. 09–37, London: Brunel University.

Dunning, J.H. (1981). Explaining the international direct investment position of countries: towards a dynamic or developmental approach. *Weltwirtschaftliches Archiv*, 117, 30–64.

Dunning, J.H. (1986). The investment development cycle revisited. *Weltwirtschaftliches Archiv*, 122, 667–77.

Dunning, J.H. (1997). *Alliance Capitalism and Global Business*. London and New York: Routledge.

Dunning, J.H. and Narula, R. (1994). Transpacific direct investment and the Investment Development Path: the record assessed. *Essays in International Business*, 10, 1–69.

Dunning, J.H. and Narula, R. (1996). The Investment Development Path revisited: some emerging issues, in J.H. Dunning and R. Narula (eds), *Foreign Direct Investment and Governments: Catalysts for Economic Restructuring*. London: Routledge, pp. 1–41.

Dunning, J.H. and Narula R. (2002). The Investment Development Path revisited, in J.H. Dunning (ed.), *Theories and Paradigms of International Business Activity. The Selected Essays of John H. Dunning*, vol. 1. Cheltenham: Edward Elgar, pp. 138–72.

Durán, J.J. and Úbeda, F. (2001). The Investment Development Path: a new empirical approach. *Transnational Corporations*, 10 (2), 1–34.

Durán, J.J. and Úbeda, F. (2005). The Investment Development Path of newly developed countries. *International Journal of the Economics of Business*, 12(1), 123–37.

Gorynia, M., Nowak, J. and Wolniak, R. (2006). The Investment Development Path of Poland re-visited: a geographic analysis. Paper presented at the 32nd Annual EIBA Conference, Fribourg, 7–9 December.

Gorynia, M., Nowak, J. and Wolniak, R. (2008). Poland's Investment Development Path and industry structure of FDI inflows and outflows. *Journal of East–West Business*, 14(2), 189–212.

Gorynia, M., Nowak, J., Wolniak R. (forthcoming). Investment Development Paths of Central European Countries: a comparative analysis. *Argumenta Oeconomica*.

GUS (Central Statistical Office of Poland) (2000–09). *Statistical Yearbook of the Republic of Poland*. Warsaw: Central Statistical Office.

Kalotay, K. (2004). Outward FDI from Central European Countries. *Economics of Planning*, 37, 141–72.

Kottardi, C., Filippaios, F. and Papanastassiou, M. (2004). The Investment Development Path and the Product Cycle – an integrated approach: empirical evidence from the new EU member states of CEE. Economics and Management Discussion Papers 003, University of Reading.

Lall, S. (1996). The Investment Development Path: some conclusions, in J.H. Dunning and R. Narula (eds), *Foreign Direct Investment and Governments: Catalysts for Economic Restructuring*. London: Routledge, pp. 78–100.

Matkowski, Z. and Próchniak, M. (2007). Economic convergence in the EU accession countries. *Eastern European Economics*, 45(1), 59–76.

Narula, R. (1996). *Multinational Investment and Economic Structure: Globalisation and Competitiveness*, London: Routledge.

Narula, R. and Dunning, J.H. (2000). Industrial development, globalization and multinational enterprises: new realities for developing countries. *Oxford Development Studies*, 28(2), 141–67.

Niroomand, F. and Nissan, E. (2007). Socio-economic gaps within the EU: a comparison. *International Advances in Economic Research*, 13, 365–78.

Svietličič, M. and Jaklič, A. (2003). Outward FDI by transition economies: basic features, trends and development implications, in M. Svetličič and M. Rojec (eds), *Facilitating Transition by Internationalization: Outward Direct Investment from Central European Economies in Transition*. Aldershot: Ashgate, pp. 49–76.

Tolentino, P.E.E. (1987). *The Global Shift in International production: The Growth of Multinationals from Developing Countries – The Philippines,* PhD Thesis, University of Reading.

UNCTAD (United Nations Conference on Trade and Development) (2009). *Handbook of Statistics and the Statistical Yearbook of the Republic of Poland.* New York and Geneva: UNCTAD.

UNCTAD (2009). *Trade and Development Report,* New York and Geneva.

5

Sustainable Foreign Direct Investments: Regional Development and Transition Economies

Marjan Svetličič

Introduction

We believe we know much about the role of foreign direct investment (FDI) in development, but the present economic and financial crisis has called for a renewed attention towards the role of FDI in the economic development of nations and regions. The instability in the world economy and the pressing need for investment in the developed world have given birth to a much greater economic nationalism that has induced more restrictive approaches to outward foreign direct investment (OFDI) based on the argument that firms should give priority to investing in their domestic market. Many investors have frozen their plans for overseas investments; and some have even disinvested or shifted operations from foreign markets back to their home country or another cheaper location. The number of investors who are actively engaged in reinvesting their profits in host economies has substantially decreased. Profits earned overseas have started to flow back to home countries, which has had a negative effect on the balance of payments of host countries. The trade-off between high growth and vulnerability has shifted towards a much greater economic security and less vulnerability.

Such developments have influenced the approaches and strategies adopted by home country governments and firms towards the FDI process. Government policies have shifted from a focus on the contribution of FDI to national growth and competitiveness to achieving greater sustainability of FDI over the long run. More and more emphasis is devoted to balanced regional development and the role FDI can play in achieving this goal. The issue of how host countries can attract more sustainable FDI[1] to stimulate their own sustainable development has moved to centre stage. Sustainability of FDI implies economic, social and environmental impacts of FDI that are reflected in their contribution to a country's long-term sustainable development by enhancing local production capacity for environmentally friendly production, using resources efficiently in the long run and adhering to low carbon emission standards. Social sustainability or socially responsible FDI assumes that FDI should be contributing to local capacity buildings, long-term employment and more equal distribution of income/wealth, strengthening social resilience and solidarity. Investors are expected to behave responsibly also in terms of labour and environmental standards, conditions within global supply chains and minimizing the potential negative economic effects of FDI such as crowding out of local investors, substitution of local with foreign suppliers, a race to the bottom by incentives, corruption (leading to inefficiencies), and degrading the environment and working conditions.

I start with a conceptual framework for sustainable FDI and then look into empirical evidence on the role of FDI in the sustainable development in the evaluated regions. Subsequently, I present the results of a survey with special emphasis on transition economies, before concentrating on the policy measures for promoting sustainable regional development by promoting FDI inflows. Conclusions and some general policy recommendations are given at the end of the chapter.

FDI and the development of regions: theoretical framework and results of empirical studies

There is an extensive literature on FDI. It is clear that the benefits and costs of it do not happen automatically and evenly, rather they depend much on the environment in which it takes place. There is not a universally accepted agreement about the effects of FDI on the development of host and, even less so, home economies. Nevertheless, extant research claims that FDI can have a positive impact on the development and competitiveness of host economies. For example, Ghosh and Wang (2009:12) state that 'one percent increase in the growth of the inward stock of FDI resulted in 0.01 percent growth of GDP in OECD countries in the period 1980–2004. The coefficient for outward growth is also positive and statistically significant and its estimated value is around 0.01'. The OECD (2006:7) acknowledges the ability of FDI, as well as that of domestic investment, to 'expand an economy's productive capacity, drive job creation and income growth, and in the case of international investment, is a conduit for the local diffusion of technological and enterprise expertise and spurs domestic investment, including through the creation of local supplier linkages. Such benefits can act as a powerful force for development and poverty eradication'. The potential positive effects mentioned in these studies are not God given but depend to a large extent on the policies of host governments and local communities. FDI effects are therefore policy specific and not policy neutral. Impacts are contingent not only on policy content and clarity per se, but even more significantly on the implementation of existing policies.

There is less agreement on the spillover effects of FDI which are considered as most important. Largely because FDI effects depend on the absorptive capacity of local firms (see Damijan et al., 2003), those with high absorptive capacity are likely to benefit. Such capacity depends also on the technology gap between home and host economies (investor and local partner/suppliers). A widely cited study of Blomström and Kokko (1998) points out that the positive effects of FDI tend to increase with the level of local capability and competition. However, even when there is a wide technology gap, a host economy may gain from demonstration effects in countries which have lower levels of GDP per capita. The potential for enhancing productivity is hence positively correlated with the technology gap between foreign and domestic firms in a specific industry (see for example Meyer and Sinani, 2009:1076, 1077). However, such a hypothesis is valid only under very restrictive conditions (standardized and non-proprietary technology, and possibilities for reverse engineering). Since we are looking at EU regions, such effects are not central to our study as most EU members are expected to be developed, despite some differences in their development level. Therefore, absorptive capacity, although highly relevant in general, is less important in the case of similarly developed regions (see Table 5.3).[2] This means that the effects of FDI are contingent on the development level of the host countries and the technological/development gap between home and host countries and firms. The effects of FDI depend also on the motives of foreign investors and types of FDI. From resource-seeking investments one cannot expect substantial spillover effects, which are of course more important in efficiency-seeking or strategic FDI. Similarly, market-seeking FDIs imply better consumer satisfaction, but one cannot expect firms to export such products from the host country, for instance. Instead, levels of export engagement may fall.

There are plenty of studies on regional effects of FDI, but certainly few on their development in general. Thus we do not have unanimous agreement on these issues in the scholarly community. A usual assumption in evaluating the role of FDI in regional development is that FDI would contribute to the erosion of regional inequalities by government policies designed to direct FDI to less developed regions, consisting mostly or exclusively of emerging economies, bringing about convergence of incomes. Nevertheless, FDIs as private agents, driven by private profit-making motives, have in the past contributed to widening regional inequalities both in emerging and developed economies (see for instance Wei et al., 2009 for China; and Bode and Nunnemkamp, 2007 for the USA). Foreign investors find well-developed regions within countries as more attractive locations for FDI compared to less-developed regions. Therefore policies should address the question of how to reconcile the positive effects of FDI on economic growth with their negative effects on regional inequalities. Moreover, policy-makers should consider ways in which FDI could foster convergence among regions. There are almost no studies looking at the impact of FDI on sustainable regional development because it is only recently that the economic crisis has had a much greater impact on less developed regions, thus calling for special attention to regional distribution of FDI gains.

Among studies evaluating the relationship between FDI and regional development, the most comprehensive and representative one for the purpose of our research is the EC 2006 study evaluating EU25 regions plus Bulgaria and Romania.[3] The analyses show that the location of foreign firms in Europe is guided mostly by firm-specific characteristics and only a minor part of the location pattern can be explained by observable regional/national factors.[4] This is no surprise. The study identifies some very systematic and fundamental economic characteristics of the countries and regions in which foreign investors are interested in. These include the following:

- Access to a large national market (national market-size effect);
- Borders with the home country and/or language proximity with home country (proximity and culture effect);
- A high level of business English proficiency (internationalization effect);
- Low corporate taxation (fiscal incentive effect);
- Many advanced consumers with high purchasing power (national GDP per capita effect);
- Low unemployment level (proxy for little rigidity in the labour market).

Given the choice of country, the study shows that FDI is attracted to regions with:

- A large share of other foreign investors (signal effect);
- Good infrastructure and accessibility, especially to home region (access effect);
- A highly educated regional workforce (skill effect);
- A high level of spending on R&D (innovation effect);
- Penetration of information and communication technologies (ICT effect);
- A large local presence of competitors, clients and suppliers within the firm's industry (agglomeration and clustering effect).

While regional characteristics have proved to be important for the location pattern of FDI across Europe, it has been observed that the best fitting explanatory model includes national characteristics (such as the size of the national market, language and the national level of purchasing power). National GDP comes out as a significant explanatory variable in all estimations explaining the observed distribution of foreign ownership across Europe. The result holds regardless of industry and geographical subregion. The lesson is that it is important for foreign firms to be present in each national European market. At the same time, there are many, and an ever increasing number of, examples of outsourcing to low cost regions within Europe and signs of escalating agglomeration in fewer European locations for certain industries. However, the general pattern of investments in our study is not associated with a large scale agglomeration in fewer locations with the purpose of serving the entire European market from them. The study has found a more diversified picture with many regional subcentres across Europe. It also reveals that, regardless of the type of FDI and regardless of the region groups, the long-term effect from FDI induced productivity gains on labour demand are positive. FDI increases the international competitiveness of regions and total regional output. Derived demand is generally strong enough to counter-balance the lay-offs engendered by the foreign owners or induced by the competitive restructuring resulting from the presence of foreign firms. It shows also that foreign takeovers of local firms through mergers and acquisitions generally lead to restructuring and company downsizing in which local staff are made redundant, although the net result on labour demand cannot be judged a priori, and the sign of the net effect depends on a number of conditions in the local labour market, as well as employment protection policies. This study allows us to conclude that the net effect from FDI on labour demand is generally positive in Eastern Europe (Group 1) and in the regions facing weaknesses in competitiveness and employment (Group 3). The study derives very robust results showing that the net labour market effect in the cohesion regions (Group 2) is negative. In those regions, the lay-offs after foreign takeovers and the within-industry competitive effect are stronger than the effect from induced demand from other sectors.

Regarding the geographic dimension of FDI, proximity in terms of distance to the home region is an important factor in explaining the pattern of FDI across regions. Therefore regions close to large sources of FDI tend to receive more inflow than distant and remote regions. Furthermore, border regions (especially border regions with developed economies) receive more FDI, all other things being equal, than inland regions of a country. This effect is further enhanced if the two regions share a common language (as for example with Germany and Austria; the UK and Ireland; Sweden and Finland, as Swedish is the second official language in Finland).

The major conclusion of the study is that FDI plays an important role in raising a region's technological level, its productive efficiency and its ability to compete internationally. Therefore the presence of foreign firms can improve regions' competitiveness, but fears can also be raised that foreign competitors crowd out and threaten the survival and growth of local firms, thus reducing the local capital base. The net positive effect of FDI on regional economic development cannot be taken for granted.

The study finds strong empirical support for the economic benefits of FDI across all types of regions and industries in the following directions:

- Host region productivity spillovers from FDI are generally positive and significant. A productivity gain of up to 40 per cent for local firms can be measured as a maximum increase. Significant positive spillovers in 24 of 36 best-fit estimations, and significantly negative spillovers in only two of the 36 estimations, were found.
- Labour demand is not always negatively affected by FDI. Over time, FDI leads to more demand for labour, not less. Even though the results are slightly less robust than the productivity effects above, the study finds no systematic evidence of long-term negative labour market effects from FDI. However, the level of development and the economic structure and vitality of host countries may have an effect on different levels of labour demand.
- FDI is attracted by regional policy factors. Most regions can improve their attractiveness to FDI. Analysing the location patterns of FDI across European regions, the study finds a number of factors that are significant in identifying regional attractiveness to FDI. They include good infrastructure and accessibility, a highly educated regional workforce and a high level of spending on R&D. Good penetration of information and communication technologies and a large pool of competitors, clients and suppliers within the firm's industry are also shown to attract FDI. However, other factors that cannot be influenced at the regional level, such as firm specific conditions, national macro-conditions, market size, geography and language, are equally or even more important.
- The current pattern of FDI coupled with the current levels of host region productivity spillovers can enhance growth and convergence at large. The two large groups of regions with below average regional income per capita, namely the cohesion regions and the regions in Eastern Europe, have benefited from FDI through productivity spillovers, and this in itself had led to greater convergence. There are exceptions to this general pattern as is the case of the remote regions in the Nordic countries, the British Isles and Mediterranean regions. Regions in the EU15, in terms of the lack of competitiveness, do not have sufficient absorptive capacity to benefit from FDI. Thus, FDI has generally increased regional growth, and many European regions have seen benefits from attracting foreign investment.

My research finds strong empirical support for the pivotal role of FDI in regional growth and development in Europe's lagging regions, but the details of the policies to attract foreign investors also matter. Well-designed regional FDI policies have positive implications on the European economy, both in terms of the overall growth possibilities and in terms of promoting regional convergence, as well as in the catching up by the least developed regions in Europe. Poorly designed policies, however, can work in the opposite direction.

Results of the survey among FDI promotion agencies in selected European regions

My survey is based on a questionnaire[5] with 16 questions sent to 620 addresses in 34 countries (all EU member countries plus the Western Balkans and Turkey). Almost two-thirds of the sample is regional and national government (ministry, FDI agency) organizations, while a quarter are economic intelligence or research organizations. Therefore we can assume that the survey reflects a much more regional than national dimension. From some countries, we have received responses from more than one institution.[6] While most responses received are from EU members states (14), there was no response from 12 countries.[7] Nine out of 44 valid responses were from organizations based in countries which are not EU members, namely Croatia, Serbia, Switzerland and Turkey. In three-quarters of the cases, organizations pursue public interests. Not all respondents have answered all questions; therefore representativeness is lower in some cases. I also recognize that the results show the perceptions of the respondents, rather than hard statistical data.

My survey demonstrates clearly that FDI plays an important role in the development of host economies and regions and their competitiveness. Around 68 per cent of respondents claim that FDI plays a very important role in enhancing competitiveness, 16 per cent believe that FDI has an important role to play. While more than 50 per cent of respondents are convinced that the level of FDI in their region is below the generally desirable level, 13 per cent think that it is even substantially below. They expect an increasing role of FDI as the economic crisis, that has affected most developed economies heavily, begins to wither. Of these, the transition economies are much more optimistic in this regard.

The share of those convinced that FDI plays an important role and that this role will be further enhanced after the crisis has increased from 84 to 95 per cent. No respondent thinks that FDI will not play an important role in the future. This is in line with the expectations that in the future, multinational corporations (MNCs) will increase the value of their FDI (Tuerk, 2010).

Despite the prevailing opinion that the major benefit of FDI is the inflow of capital[8] it brings to the local economy, my survey clearly indicates that major benefits are also associated with the potential for new employment. Capital inflow is important, particularly at the time of a severe credit crunch, while, under normal economic conditions, we would assume that access to a regional or country market and access to technology would be positioned higher as they are perceived FDI benefits (Table 5.1).

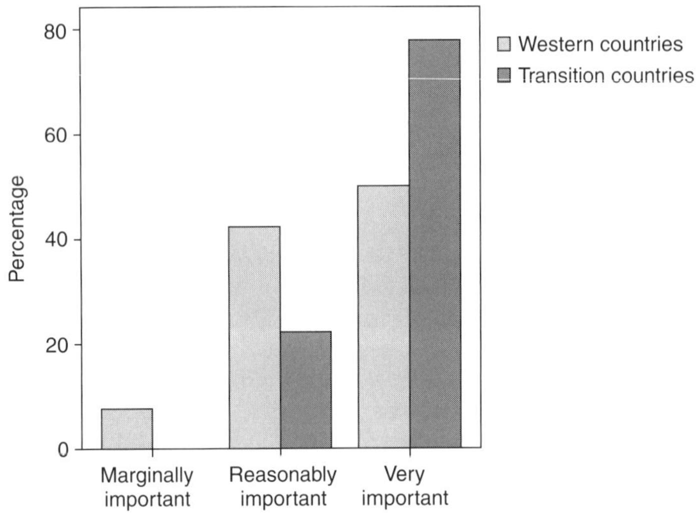

Figure 5.1 Importance of FDI for a country/region's competitiveness in the future

Table 5.1 Main benefits from FDI for a country/region (survey results, percentage)

	Total	Transition countries	Western countries
New employment opportunities	77	89	69
Inflow of capital	61	78	50
Transfer of state-of-the-art technology	45	22	62
Access to new markets	20	44	42
Improved competition in domestic market	32	39	27
Improvement of management performance	18	22	15
Other	7	0	12

Note: Percentages add up to more than 100 per cent because up to three responses were possible. Twenty-six of the responses are from Western and 18 from transition countries.

The three major differences between the Western and transition economies in their evaluation of benefits from FDI can be summed up as technology, capital and employment (in order of relative importance). Surprisingly, developed countries consider the transfer of modern technology to be almost three times more important than transition economies. It seems that the more developed an economy is, the more modern technology it wishes to attract as it may have an important dynamic effect on integration.

Respondents from transition economies still place significantly higher importance on the capital contribution of FDI, which may be partly due to the lower capital stock in transition countries compared to that in the more developed European economies. It can be argued that in transition countries the economic crisis has contributed significantly to the stronger relative importance assigned to FDI as a source of capital inflow. In spite of the fact that unemployment is a common phenomenon in the developed and transition economies, the latter place much more weight on new employment opportunities arising from FDI. This is understandable in view of the usually higher unemployment rates in transition economies, which was not a problem during their socialist past.

Interestingly the role of local competition, not so frequently documented as an important consideration, is somehow underestimated. Enhancing competition is particularly relevant to transition economies. This verity is reflected in the greater weight these economies put on the role of competition than Western economies. The precondition for a positive FDI effect is therefore the undisrupted competition and increased firm competitiveness in the local market.

Improving management performance was also not identified among the major benefits from FDI. However, indirectly, 'high dependence on foreign decisions' as a major disadvantage of FDI (as shown in Table 5.2) may be

Table 5.2 Major disadvantages and negative effects of FDI experienced by firms (survey results, percentage)

	Total	Transition countries	Western countries
Excessive dependence on foreign investor's decisions	76	61	52
Demands on government subsidies	62	39	52
Increased dependence on foreign instead of local suppliers	41	39	24
Reduced competition on the domestic market	34	33	19
Increased unemployment	28	22	19
Crowding out of local investors/firms	28	28	14
Reduced R&D activities	21	17	14
Increased dependence on selected export markets	21	22	10
Other	10	6	10

Note: Percentages add up to more than 100 per cent because up to three responses were possible. Percentages are calculated on 39 valid responses, of which 21 are from Western and 18 from transition countries.

an indicator that the lack of appreciation for (independent) local managerial expertise is a significant problem associated with IFDI. The problem is even worse for transition economies, which are lagging much behind in their management expertise and performance. The economic crisis and its effects on transition economies can only support this, as in many countries managers responded too slowly or inappropriately to the crisis and, hence, foreign-owned firms performed a lot better than those in which local decision-making prevailed.

Compared to the advantages from FDI, there are even fewer differences when the respondents address the disadvantages of FDI (Table 5.2). The top two differences with 15 and 14 percentage points, respectively, are in the areas of dependence on foreign instead of local suppliers and reduced competition in the domestic market. Transition countries register stronger criticism of increased dependence on foreign suppliers. This can be explained either by the fact that FDI is focused on industries or type of products where there is no adequate local supply of intermediate products, or by the wrong perception that foreigners tend to source abroad even if there is a local supplier. Interviews with local managers do not confirm that foreigners prefer overseas to local sourcing. On the contrary, FDI is attracted to locations where a strong local suppliers' network exists, and where other FDIs with local sourcing are present.[9] Considering the second difference, transition economies consider reduced competition to be a much more negative factor than Western respondents. The frequent substitution of domestic with foreign monopolies may be one explanation. In the absence of adequate domestic competition policy, this has frequently happened in the first wave of privatization through foreign takeovers of domestic monopolies. Interestingly enough, the only category where respondents from the transition countries are less worried compared to their Western counterparts is regarding the demands on government subsidies. This can be explained by the fact that the respondents from the developed European countries favour fiscal measures for attracting and sustaining FDI (Kunčič and Svetličič, 2011) and so do not see it as a serious negative effect. Prediction that incentives work better in the case of countries at a similar level of development obviously holds true.

The usual public accusations that FDI increases unemployment and crowds out local businesses or even reduces R&D activities have, overall, not received strong support. The major reason for the unfavourable impact of FDI is considered to be excessive dependence on foreign investors' decisions and (high) demands for subsidies. A relatively high score for dependence on foreign suppliers seems to confirm the usual public opinion attitude that foreign investors tend to substitute local with foreign suppliers. Cases have not confirmed such perceptions because foreign investors are actually attracted by local suppliers, provided that they are of quality. In the absence of local suppliers,[10] investors would source abroad rather than trying to develop a local supply network, provided that this is not a government requirement. There are some differences by groups of countries (Table 5.2). Transition economies see FDI more as a negative factor or as a disadvantage in relation to the crowding out of local investors,[11] increased dependence on selected export markets is somewhat reduced because of the decreased competition in certain local markets.

Frequently firms are taken over when they are in difficulties (the 'fire sale' FDI which is so frequent during a crisis). In such cases FDI actually contributes positively to employment by keeping jobs. In addition, it usually abolishes low paid jobs and creates better paid ones, contributing to more value added activities; thus the assumption is that positive effects out pace negative ones.

For designing the right policy/institutional framework, it is important to see what the reasons for negative effects are. Respondents were not satisfied with regulatory frameworks and more particularly with the consistency and enforcement of regulations in transition economies. It is surprising that respondents from Western economies are more afraid of speculative foreign investors. In contrast to the evaluations of the positive effects of FDI where robust economic factors prevail, more psychological/political factors have been indicated as major reasons for the unfavourable effects of FDI (see Table 5.3).

Table 5.3 Reasons for unfavourable impact of FDI (survey results, percentages)

	Total	Transition countries	Western countries
Our regulatory framework and implementation policies did not provide for effective protection of the interests of our economy	38	44	32
Inadequate local competition policy	27	33	21
Due to our poor negotiating skills, unfavourable conditions were accepted, and foreign owners don't care when hurting our economic interests	30	33	26
Lack of consistent legal and policy environment brings to us only investors with speculative, 'quick-buck' motivation	35	33	37
Unfavourable general economic fundamentals	30	28	32
Lack of local suppliers	16	22	11
Excessive technology gap prevents more absorption of foreign knowledge	11	22	0

Note: Percentages add up to more than 100 because up to three responses were possible. Percentages are calculated on 37 valid responses, of which 19 are from Western and 18 from transition countries.

Somehow surprising is the low importance attributed to low absorption capacity, which is indicated in the literature as among the major barriers to positive effects of FDI. However, it is certainly a much bigger problem in transition economies. Lack of soft negotiating skills is still frequently considered responsible for many unfavourable effects of FDI. Respondents from transition economies frequently think that better negotiating skills may have a more positive effect on FDI.[12] The importance of supplier networks is somehow lower than usually assumed in the FDI literature.

My survey confirms the findings of previous research claiming that good infrastructure (Table 5.4)[13] and general economic fundamentals are more important than specific policies for attracting FDI. Nevertheless, it places a much stronger emphasis on the role of qualified personnel, good infrastructure and general economic conditions. All countries consider regulations and prioritizing selected regions as the most important instruments for influencing foreign investors.

Surprisingly, there are not many differences by group of countries. The only really noticeable difference is that Western respondents put relatively more weight on local development objectives/plans in comparison with the transition countries and slightly less on keeping some sectors unavailable to foreigners. The correlation coefficient between good economic fundamentals and financial subsidies and fiscal incentives was negative (see Svetličič and Kunčič, 2010:20). It seems that countries try to compensate for bad economic fundamentals with fiscal incentives which have proved inefficient. Although most of the countries rely heavily on financial subsidies and fiscal incentives, my respondents claim that provision of information is more important. However, while some respondents are still convinced that

Table 5.4 Key reasons for FDI presence in a country/region (as a result of 'your country's policy instruments/measures') (percentage)

Key reasons	Strongly agree	Agree	Neither agree nor disagree	Disagree	Strongly disagree
Qualified personnel	45	43	9	0	2
Good infrastructure, legal and logistical support	27	52	5	5	11
Good general economic fundamentals	0	77	16	2	5
Information services	20	52	20	5	2
Financial subsidies to greenfield FDI	9	43	14	34	9
Fiscal incentives (such as tax holidays)	11	20	23	20	11

incentives work, others are strongly against them. Therefore it is surprising that most of the investment promotion agencies (IPAs) still rely strongly on incentives.

Three explanations for this are possible. One reason is that they are too low to be effective or that they are not implemented effectively. Another reason may be a 'race to the top' argument, i.e. if others do it, we have to follow. A third reason is that it is possible that financial subsidies and fiscal incentives are not deemed important from the perspective of IPAs since they may not be under the direct control of IPAs but under the control of government directly or some other government body such as the ministries of economy. More respondents agree than disagree that fiscal subsidies for greenfield FDI are key for attracting FDI, and more agree than disagree with the statement that more sustainable FDI inflows can be achieved by providing special fiscal and other incentives.

Regional agencies believe more in the importance of good infrastructure than national agencies. This may well be a result of a specific policy to increase regional attractiveness for FDI with a greater emphasis on geographic advantages. Equally, one may argue that regional agencies may have fewer instruments for the promotion of FDIs compared to national agencies. Representatives of regional agencies claim that foreign investors simply want some additional 'cherries on the cake' in the form of incentives.

Regulations in general,[14] and particularly government strategic thinking identifying priority sectors for FDI in accordance with development priorities, are considered crucial for attracting sustainable FDI. It seems that priority areas for FDI are considered more important than general development objectives/plans.

In spite of experiencing a 'race to the bottom' in investment incentives by many investment promotion agencies (see Figure 5.2), respondents said that these agencies should put more emphasis on economic fundamentals and implementation of policies. Survey results confirm that the implementation of policies is frequently more important than the very existence of institutions. It is therefore not surprising that a high percentage of respondents claim that they have a systematic FDI policy and effective institutions working in the field, but are not all satisfied with the implementation and consistency of such policies. Nearly half of the respondents from countries with IPAs claim that the implementation of their policies is not satisfactory and that, although policies exist, they are not really consistent. The only noticeable difference between transition and Western economies regarding FDI policies is in the consistency and level of implementation of policies, being considered a lot more important in transition economies (see Svetličič and Kunčič, 2011).

The majority of respondents believe that institutions can influence FDI flows, particularly if they have an adequate systemic framework, channelling FDI in development priority areas more than general regional development

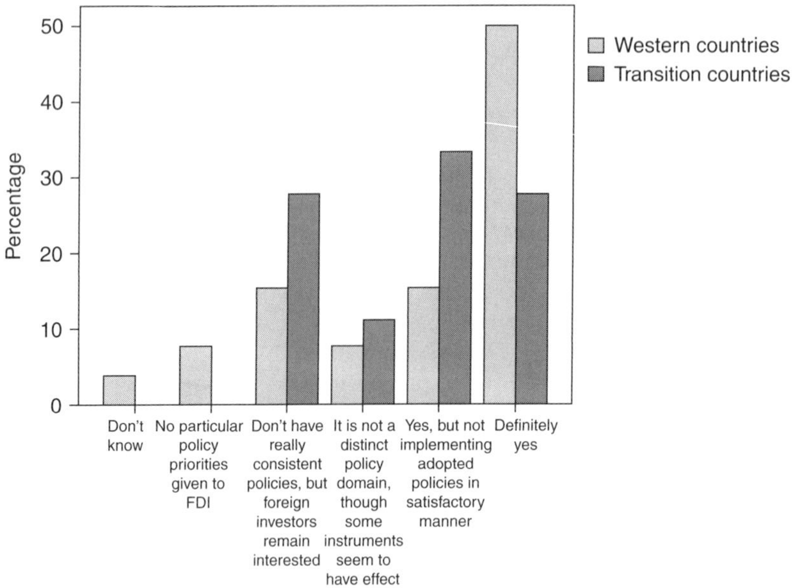

Figure 5.2 Existence of FDI policy as part of the country's development strategy

Table 5.5 Impact of authorities on foreign investors to act sustainably and respect a country/region's interests (percentage)

Impact of authorities	Strongly agree	Agree	Neither agree nor disagree	Disagree	Strongly disagree
Through the regulatory framework	21	45	29	0	5
By directing foreign investors to regions/ countries' priorities	13	53	11	13	11
By well developed local development objectives/plans	11	37	26	16	11
By keeping some sectors inaccessible to FDI	0	8	26	42	24

objectives (Table 5.5). Keeping sectors out of reach of foreign investors has not proved to be an option for most respondents.

My study demonstrates that IPAs are doing their best in terms of acting as a one-stop service shop, providing information, legal and other support to investors by their qualified personnel. Listing personnel as less important among excelling factors means that there is still room for improving the qualifications and efficiency of the cadre in IPAs. Contrary to prevailing policies relying much on incentives, respondents think that providing information in an effective way to promote FDI is more important than providing fiscal incentives (Table 5.6). This has been very important in transition economies (71 per cent compared to 48 per cent in Western economies). Transition economies place greater emphasis on providing legal and other advice (64 per cent compared to 29 per cent for Western economies). However, Western economies place much more weight on the role of fiscal incentives. This difference can be explained by the relatively higher importance of other factors like economic fundamentals in transition economies (Svetličič and Kunčič, 2011:16).

The first task of any organization is to improve its present activities before embarking on some major strategy changes (Table 5.7). A smaller number of respondents (34 out of 43) indicate that others are rather satisfied with a

Table 5.6 Excelling factors of IPAs

Excelling factors of IPAs	Frequency	Percentage
Providing one-stop services	20	66
Information services	18	57
Legal and other advice/consultancy, and logistical support	13	43
Providing qualified personnel	11	33
Financial subsidies for greenfield FDI	5	19
Fiscal/tax incentives	5	33
Other	0	0

Note: Percentages add up to more than 100 because up to three responses were possible.

Table 5.7 Weaknesses of the national Foreign Investment Promotion Agency (survey results, percentage)

	Total	Transition countries	Western countries
Inadequate financial and human resources	56	71	44
Inadequate instruments of operation	50	71	33
Organizational problems, including weak management	38	71	11
Don't have one stop agency for FDI promotion; services are divided among several agencies	44	14	67
Low general standing and too limited statutory responsibilities	19	14	44
Other	6	14	0

Note: Percentages add up to more than 100 because up to three responses were possible. Percentages are calculated on 16 valid responses, of which nine are from Western and seven from transition countries.

respective IPA, after we asked them to respond only if an IPA is not performing satisfactorily. Those who responded indicated that financial and human resources and inadequate instruments are major weaknesses. Traditional instruments are obviously not performing well and new initiatives are scarce.

The first lesson is that underfinanced and understaffed agencies cannot produce good results. They need to achieve a certain threshold in order to perform well. Secondly, the existing instruments used are not performing satisfactorily and novelties are needed together with improvements in the management and organization of such agencies. Although general standing and too limited statutory responsibilities have been indicated as marginal problems for IPAs, there is room for improvement in this regard.

Answers differ a lot in all categories regarding the origin of respondents. This implies that transition economy IPAs are facing completely different problems compared to their Western counterparts. Main difficulties for transition economies are poor management and organizational problems, which is considered the top problem in Eastern countries, along with difficulties with instruments of operation and understaffing, coupled with financial difficulties. Simply put, transition countries have a long way to go to develop effective and successful IPAs. On the other hand, organizational, staffing and financial problems do not bother Western IPAs, but they do see the absence of a one-stop agency as a major weakness. Western investment promotion agencies might be more decentralized, with dedicated regional IPAs. This would then explain the difference in responses regarding the one-stop agency. Additionally, statutory limitations seem to be more of a problem in the west than the east, which might be explained with the fact that transition countries have traditionally had strong governments with lots of interference in the economy; and it would seem that some of those levers have survived.

How to promote sustainable FDI and regional development

Although there is not a consensus about the impact of FDI on development, positive effects are still perceived to prevail. The question is therefore how to promote FDI and what the role of incentives is compared to other factors. Are incentives instrumental at all? Is public money invested in them well consumed? How can we promote sustainable FDI in the long run?

Drivers of FDI

Any FDI promotion policy should carefully consider FDI motives. The key driving force of FDI location is firm specific characteristics. Nevertheless, policy-makers commit mistakes by putting too much weight on macro, national or regional factors and thus underestimate the firm specific determinants on the part of investors and on the side of the host country partners. Very little in the location patterns can be explained by national/regional specific factors. Among them general economic fundamentals, level of development stability and transparency of the system play major roles. However, their roles can change in time and in different configurations of location specific factors and levels of development.

When it comes to specific location decisions, structural and market factors – such as market size, availability of resources and suppliers, possibilities for improving efficiency or some other strategic opportunities in addition to the investment climate, including entrepreneurship – are of main importance. They all represent the general framework of location-specific determinants that play a role.

Why FDI incentives?

Theoretically, FDI incentives are justified by two general principles. Firstly, incentives are needed to correct for market failures specific to the production of MNEs and 'capture wider benefits from externalities of production' (UNCTAD, 2003:124; Koko and Gustavsson, 2004). In this regard, foreign entry may increase the efficiency of indigenous firms. Such efficiency gains could result, for instance, from intensified competition and knowledge spillovers. But as MNEs will not include these externalities in their private assessment of the costs and benefits of investing abroad, they may invest less than what would be socially optimal. The motive for public subsidies to foreign investors is therefore to bridge the gap between the private and social returns, thus promoting larger inflows of FDI. Correcting for the market failures may require policies that can increase the amount of FDI over the volumes driven on the basis of private supply. This requires the provision of public goods (e.g. a stable business environment) and/or the correction of imperfect information on locations[15] (location incentives). But the question is whether or not it is better to correct for market failures directly rather than compensating such failures by incentives.

Secondly, in conditions of limited supply of private resources – which are needed for the operation of certain public services and/or for dealing with imperfect information about location possibilities (Loewendahl, 2009:5) – public intervention is necessary. As private investors are driven by their private profit interests, it is necessary to bridge the gap between private and public yields because MNEs do not take external economies of scale in their calculations of investment yields. Incentives are now more justified since competition for FDI has become tougher as foreign investors have become more 'choosy about location factors' (Bellak, 2007:4).

Do incentives work?

There is no agreement on whether incentives really stimulate FDI. Until the early 1990s, there was a strong consensus in the literature that FDI is mainly attracted by strong economic fundamentals, like market size, income, skills, infrastructure and political and macroeconomic stability. In 2006, market size and a skilled workforce still dominated the list of attraction factors.[16] A case study of Switzerland (see Ernst & Young, 2006:5) put more weight to quality of life. About 72 per cent of the executives who participated in the survey rated quality of life as very important. The second factor mentioned was flexible labour law and low tax rates or tax incentives. Other important factors were long-term stability, liberal legislation and protection of free competition, and government cooperation. The relative weight of factors is obviously quite different when it comes to highly developed countries and regions compared to less developed ones.

Global and regional trade and investment liberalization have made incentives a more significant determinant of international investment decisions. Incentives are important in conditions of more liberalized international business and greater competition for limited resources (see Clark, 2000; Taylor, 2000; Kokko and Gustavsson, 2004:125). The executives of MNEs who used to downplay the role of incentives some years ago, now readily admit their increasing importance for investment decisions (Easson, 2001). The effectiveness of incentives has been the subject of intense debate, and little consensus has emerged. Some experts have argued that there is little evidence that such incentives are effective (James, 2009). Others have argued that investment incentives have contributed to the rapid economic growth of countries such as the Republic of Korea, Mauritius and Singapore' (ibid.: iv). Incentive programmes are effective (see Kokko and Gustavsson, 2004), if correcting market failures and providing public goods (externalities) when there is a lack of supply of private ones (no private investors' interest). Otherwise, subsidies to attract foreign investors (such as tax holidays) tend to shift profits and welfare away from the host regions towards foreign firms and their home regions.

Regarding the justification of incentives Bellak (2007) clearly states that policies for attracting FDI are not productive if they do not result in sustainable FDI. FDI attraction without a strategy to make the attracted FDI sustainable is probably not worth the resources invested (ibid.: 6). Contrary to this, Wells and Wint (1990:57) are convinced that efficient investment promotion activities are highly cost effective. His analysis demonstrated that expenditure of US$570 incurred to attract one job can bring benefits with a present value of US$1,917 to the country. To conclude, incentives are under certain conditions efficient, but only in combination with other measures (see Rojec et al., 2007:104).

Nevertheless, many countries have found themselves in a prisoner dilemma. They have to match the incentives offered by other countries to be able to compete on the global market for FDI. In doing this they engage in a race to the bottom in terms of benefits of such schemes since they may consume too much public money, placing it in the hands of foreign investors, which could imply an inappropriate spending of public funds. They perform better if they are temporary and if there are provisions[17] 'stipulating the return of incentives if conditions are not met' (UNCTAD, 2003:126). It is also suggested that by enhancing the local supply of human capital and modern infrastructure, and by improving other fundamentals for economic growth, a country/region does not only become a more attractive host for foreign firms, but also increases the likelihood of benefits for the host economy through the spillover mechanisms. Enhancing R&D and soft skills, particularly negotiation and cross-cultural communication skills, can also improve the bargaining position of host countries/regions to a greater extent than financial/fiscal incentives. This can be done by introducing more soft skills training, both in regular education programmes and in special training for managers and public administrators, because experts possessing such skills can better negotiate with potential investors. Without appropriate multilingual and multicultural skills no FDI attraction programme can be effective.

Although investment promotion programmes are usually about attracting IFDI, gradually and in parallel with economic development more and more emphasis should be given to outward investments and establishing own MNEs. OFDI can enhance local development and restructuring. Inward internationalization is a step in the direction of later outward internationalization,[18] of the creation of own multinationals. Therefore countries, regions or firms have to develop a comprehensive approach to internationalization with an initial emphasis towards IFDI and, later, on stimulating OFDI. My assumption is that in many small countries, the ownership structure of the firms can be in the future something like 40/40/20. This means that 40 per cent of firms may be foreign owned, 40 per cent are own multinationals and the remaining 20 per cent are firms operating in local industries which are not global by definition. In the absence of domestic MNCs, foreign ownership would necessarily increase, but this may have negative consequences for the host economy in the long run with overdependence on foreign capital, low reinvestment of profits and a questionable innovation pattern. Therefore stimulating the development of domestic MNCs is of paramount importance.

Incentives and development level

The relative weight of factors influencing FDI incentives is different when it comes to highly developed countries/regions as compared to less developed ones. Evidence shows that incentives perform better in developed countries with more stable economic conditions and transparent systems, where the investment climate is enhanced by high levels of GDP per capita and a better system of institutions and governance, while financial and fiscal incentives applied in less developed countries have limited reach. This limitation is due to the real (private) driving forces behind FDI, which are inbuilt in the motivation of firms for location decisions. Incentives for FDI attraction to transition economies should carefully consider foreign investors' strategies. Incentives cannot compensate for an otherwise unfavourable investment climate, a bad infrastructure or a generally unattractive economic structure. Incentives are only the 'icing on the cake', which can influence decisions when very similar locations are competing against each other. However, they can be used to direct FDI to economic sectors of national and regional priority, aiming at achieving a more balanced regional development. Less developed regions and those more distant from agglomerations of economic development – as well as those which are not bordering countries providing substantial outflows of FDI – demand special incentives.

National/regional policies

The rationale for regional policies for attracting FDI stems from the conclusions of the empirical studies demonstrating that regions can improve their attraction for FDI particularly by improving on infrastructure and accessibility, education and R&D spending, penetration of information and communication technologies (ICT), and a large pool of competitors, clients and suppliers within the firm's industry (agglomeration effects). By enhancing the local supply of human capital and creating modern infrastructure, and by improving other fundamental conditions needed for economic growth, a region does not only become a more attractive host region for foreign firms, but it also increases the likelihood for benefits from foreign firms through spillover mechanisms. Case studies have also shown that subsidies or tax relief can hardly compete with regions investing in underlying long-term growth factors such as education, research, ICT infrastructure and regulations fostering entrepreneurship.

Development and regional strategy are still central for harnessing sustainable FDI. A major precondition for FDI is a coherence of it with national/regional development strategies. FDI policies should form an integral part of regional growth strategies/policies aiming to create new employment and to promote economic growth in the regions. If such plans do not promote a greener economy, FDI cannot do it either. Efficiency of FDI promotion programmes depends to a large extent on the development strategy of a country/region. The general precondition for sustainable FDI is directing development of regions/countries towards sustainable development and a greener economy.

The major objective of regional FDI incentive programmes is first to differentiate a specific region from the crowd by indicating what the region can offer vis-à-vis competitors and how the region supports steady economic growth and sustainable development. The evidence of the EU 2006 study suggests a move away from policies based on traditional regional FDI incentive packages towards policies recommending the integration of regional inward investment agencies into regional growth strategies that aim to inform and help foreign investors to see the potential of a region and help the region to overcome regulatory barriers.

Decentralized and coherent development strategy provides a much better framework for regions to attract FDI as centralized development strategy usually attracts FDI to central regions or capital cities. In this respect, country programmes giving priorities to selected regions are immensely important. The reach of regions for promoting FDI is limited, and is really only a supplement to national incentive schemes. However, I argue that investment promotion needs to be coordinated at the national and regional levels. Regional agencies within a country are often competing for the same investment projects (Oman, 2000), and it is essential that there is effective coordination of agencies to avoid wasteful competition and a duplication of effort and resources (see Loewendahl, 2001:9).

The EU's regional support programmes affect FDI flows, but it is not clear whether the impact is strong enough to narrow down the income gaps between central and remote regions. The reason is that FDI may still cluster to the central locations, where other fundamental determinants of investment location are stronger. Thus, the positive impact of investment subsidies may be too weak to compensate for the disadvantages of the regions qualifying for support (Koko and Gustavsson, 2004:126).

My general conclusion when it comes to promoting FDI at the regional level is that two strategies can be applied. There is a broadly-based strategy at the country level, which creates generally enabling 'infrastructural' conditions and a generally favourable climate for FDI, increasing the international visibility of less known countries/regions. Such a strategy has to be combined with a targeted strategy, which gives certain priorities to the development of selected regions within a country. However, such 'national' policy can be amended at the regional level by some specific measures, which regions can take to attract FDI. Regions can attract FDI also by special industrial zones or technology parks equipped with necessary infrastructure to facilitate investors' operations. Regarding the type of activities, more scope for regional actions is mainly in the domain of post-investment-service activities whereby regions can try to create their own image internationally.

Type of incentives

Contemporary FDI incentive programmes have four major trends:

- Less automatic and more selective/discriminatory measures;
- Less general incentives and more specific functions (application of modern technology, export and R&D promotion, employment of ecological projects);
- Less grants and more returnable incentives;
- Regular project evaluation of incentives and sanctions in the case of non-performance. (Kostevc et al., 2009:16).

Incentives have to be selective, targeted at development priorities and refundable. Authorities have to evaluate regularly their effectiveness and efficiency in order to build upon good incentives and eliminate less successful ones.

According to James, 'whatever incentives a government decides to offer and however it structures them, every effort should be made to ensure that incentives are:

- Affordable: forgone income should not severely undermine government revenue streams.
- Targeted: targets for incentives should be based on research to confirm that they will benefit the country in ways that would not have been possible if there were no incentives, thereby reducing revenue costs.
- Simple: incentive administration should permit easy accessibility and determination of eligibility.
- Reviewed periodically: investment incentives should be regularly reviewed to determine their relevance and economic benefit relative to their budgetary and other costs, including long-term impacts on resource allocation ... Incentives should be used minimally, i.e. mainly to address market failures and generate multiplier effects and to the extent possible, linked to investment growth (that is, based on performance), and tax holidays should be avoided.' (James, 2009:35, v).

Although these recommendations were made for countries they can be applied to regions as well.

Impacts of Sustainable FDI

FDIs can become more sustainable by providing improved infrastructure and human capital. This goes hand in hand with making FDI coherent with regional/country development priorities and economic fundamentals as well as with the creation of local supplier networks. FDI sustainability in the long run means that priority should be given to *foot-stick/hold* activities which cannot run away as soon as wage differentials start working against a certain locality or when incentives disappear. Finally, existing FDIs should be made more sustainable. High incentives may result in a shorter time horizon for investments, and perhaps also weaker links to local industry (see also Koko and Gustavsson, 2004:126). Foreign investment attracted mostly by incentives may well move on after the subsidization period has expired. There is a trade-off between incentives and footlessness or sustainability of FDI. Given that firms most likely respond to investment incentives are probably also the most footloose, implies that attracting such firms is not the best policy to make FDI instrumental for sustainable development.

The easiest short-term instrument for enhancing sustainability of FDI is to keep already active foreign investors and to stimulate them to upgrade their investments to higher value added activities. Generating more local supplies by enhancing their integration in the local economy and stimulating local purchasing of intermediate products can also increase FDI sustainability. Developing special skills suited to the needs of foreign investors (local universities or other schools/training) can also support existing foreign firms to stay longer and upgrade their activities. Upgrading existing investments along the value chain enhances sustainability of FDI because existing FDIs are 'a signal of good investment climate because happy and profitable investors are the best promoters' (Loewendahl, 2009:16). It implies that countries/regions should also improve investor post-investment services.[19] At the same time such a policy is also instrumental for attracting long-term inflow of desired FDI in R&D. Targeting existing investment means 'reducing risk of closure. This is becoming more important with ongoing rationalization and reorganization of TNC operations' (Loewendahl, 2001:26) as a reaction of MNCs to the economic crisis.

Emphasizing sustainable FDI implies less reliance on incentives since foreign investors are more inclined to move to other locations if their decisions are incentive-based. Establishing standards for sustainability of FDI, based on a combination of international and local standards in terms of local sustainable development priorities and sustainability indicators, can help governments and institutions to evaluate and preselect sustainable FDI inflows to a country/region.

Conclusions

In spite of the limited sample of our survey, we can still draw some tentative conclusions which mostly conform to previous empirical studies and prevailing theories on the role of incentives in promoting FDI. However, there are some differences in terms of emphasis and priorities due to changes in the global investment environment.

There is not a single one-size-fits-all strategy for promoting FDI to stimulate regional development. Promotion programmes are highly idiosyncratic, tailored to the specific conditions and needs of the regions, as well as to the desires of foreign investors.

Regional policy for attracting FDI can be productive but cannot compensate for poor general economic fundamentals or generally unattractive economic structure of a country since, on their own, incentives have limited promotional reach. This is particularly relevant for transition economies. Development/regional strategy is still central in harnessing sustainable FDI for the goals of a country.

The more the development strategy is decentralized and polycentric, the greater can be the role of FDI in narrowing regional development gaps.

A centralized development strategy in transition economies implies less convergence among the regions.

The regional promotion of FDI should concentrate on some priority areas, because resources are even scarcer at the regional than at the national level. Under the conditions of scarcity of resources and ongoing consolidation of TNC operations it is wise for countries/regions to focus on enhancing existing FDI projects. This can be achieved by upgrading the activities of existing foreign-owned firms to a higher value added and by stimulating local suppliers.

A major FDI priority is to attract R&D intensive activities[20] and those in green industries. It can be done by providing specific services to foreign investors in R&D before the actual investment (pre-investment services), during the investment process (implementation services) and after the investment takes place (post-investment servicing). Post-investment services are particularly important.

A three-edged FDI promotion policy has proved to be most productive. This should

- Focus on improving the investment climate, economic fundamentals, infrastructure and a coherent (regional) development strategy;
- Target specific value added activities (areas)[21] and task-oriented incentives;
- Be selectively directed to specific groups of investors (existing, investment brokers, strategic firms, diasporas and new actors).[22] With such a strategy regions can single themselves out from their competitors.

Enhancing human capital, R&D and soft skills, particularly languages, negotiation and cross-cultural communication skills, may improve the investment attractiveness of regions. They can also enhance the bargaining position of host countries/regions more than financial/fiscal incentives. Those implementing the policies should also be well trained in soft skills which should become major criteria for recruiting the staff working in IPAs. 'Private sector experiences and language proficiency' (Ortega and Griffin, 2009:12) are instrumental to such an end.

It is also necessary to eliminate frequent attitudinal barriers: the scepticism regarding IFDI and OFDI. Attitudes based on economic nationalism can be a major barrier against an inflow of FDI in spite of all attractive incentives. The target public for FDI promotion programmes should therefore not be foreign investors only but also the domestic public in order to eliminate such attitudinal barriers.

Notes

1. There is no clear definition of sustainable FDI. Bellak defines sustainable FDI 'as the opposite of footloose FDI. Hence sustainable FDI is investment that is kept

in one location but changes the value-added activities in reaction to changes of location factors like market instabilities or changes in trade costs. Footloose FDI changes the location but keeps the same value-added activities' (2007:3). We could also call them 'foot-hold' or 'foot-stick' FDI. This is a narrow definition of sustainable FDI, while a broader one should include more 'social equity, avoiding careless exploitation of natural resources and environmental damage that will harm later generations' (Stopford and Strange, 1991:13). Broadly defined sustainable FDIs are those which, paraphrasing Paul Kleindorfer's (2010) INSEAD definition of sustainability, will leave to our children and grandchildren the opportunity to have a quality of life roughly the same as that we have or perhaps even better at the local, regional and global level (see www.50globalviewpoints.com). Sustainable FDI should lead to 'equitable and sustainable well-being', preservation of the environment, more equitable development patterns, more equitable distribution of benefits among all stakeholders, and more equitable governance.

2. Ghosh and Wang also confirm that FDI exerts positive influence on both host and source countries' economic growth in the case of all OECD members for the period 1988–2004, irrespective of human capital or absorptive capacity threshold (Ghosh and Wang, 2009:12).
3. If not otherwise stated, I present here the most important results of this study based mainly on its summary (pp. 4–15). This was based on an econometric location choice model, supplemented by case studies. Country and regional levels were both evaluated, particularly as to whether foreign investors started by choosing firstly the country or directly the region. The study has estimated the location factors for approximately 100,000 foreign firms in Europe and the impact of these FDIs on local firms. There were around 2.2 million local firms in the sample representing all 268 EU27 regions. Data covers the period 1995–2004, but only the most recent data were entered into the estimations. The study includes foreign firms from other European countries and firms from outside the EU. The study is thus based on an unprecedentedly large, exhaustive and detailed amount of firm level data.
4. Regional and national characteristics variables used by the model were: market size, host country's development level, agglomeration (localization and urbanization), share of FDI, taxes, infrastructure, accessibility and proximity to the home region, capital dummy, skills, unemployment rate, language in common with host region, level of innovation, and ICT.
5. The survey was undertaken by the Slovenian Business and Research Association in Brussels. We received 44 responses in total, from 19 different countries. They were further grouped into transition countries, consisting of Croatia, the Czech Republic, Hungary, Romania, Serbia, Slovenia and Turkey on the one hand, and Western countries consisting of Austria, Belgium, Denmark, Finland, France, Italy, Luxembourg, the Netherlands, Spain, Sweden, Switzerland and United Kingdom on the other hand.
6. Austria, Belgium, Croatia, Finland, Italy, the Netherlands, Romania, Serbia, Slovenia, Spain, the UK and Turkey.
7. Bulgaria, Cyprus, Estonia, France, Germany, Greece, Ireland, Latvia, Lithuania, Malta, Poland, Portugal and Slovakia.
8. Every student of economics should know that credits are less expensive financially than FDI because a foreign investor expects financial remuneration for the risks he or she is taking. Therefore the financial costs of FDI are higher than those of credits. However, all the risks in the case of credits are taken by the credit takers, while in the case of FDI they are taken by a foreign investor. FDIs

are therefore reasonable only when local firms are not able to undertake certain projects due to lack of capabilities, while foreign investors do have such an ability. If local firms have the knowledge, they would simply go to a bank, get a loan and undertake a project.

9. Foreign automotive producers have been attracted to the Czech Republic and Slovakia after foreigners invested there and strong local supplier network was developed.
10. This is a frequent case because the foreign investors tend to bring into the host economy new, higher, valued-added production, which local suppliers are not able to serve or are too small to become suppliers to the whole network of large foreign multinationals.
11. My findings contradict the empirical findings that FDI doesn't crowd out local investors in less developed countries but can produce such effects in advanced countries (see Moran et al., 2005). The effects are however different in the case of greenfield FDIs and takeovers. Greenfield FDI creates in the long run more new jobs than takeovers of existing firms (see EC, 2006:4). However it is important to take into consideration the opportunity costs of such a takeover, i.e. what would have happened to the acquired firm without the takeover?
12. This supports the increasing role of soft competences in today's turbulent and unpredictable business and political environment, which was also confirmed by the evaluation of the Slovene presidency of the EU Council in 2008. It was not lack of knowledge about the EU but the lack of language, communication and negotiations skills that caused a problem. Respondents also wanted to get training in these fields for future activities.
13. There is almost no difference in terms of the influence of local policy on the sustainability of FDI. This is the reason why I do not differentiate between transition and other economies. This is elaborated in Svetličič and Kunčič (2011).
14. The relatively high share of 'undecided' responses indicates that there are some doubts regarding the role of regulations for attracting FDI; and similarly regarding well developed local development objectives/plans and keeping one sector inaccessible to FDI.
15. Companies will typically only consider countries for investment which (i) they have invested in before, (ii) their competitors have invested in, (iii) have major customers or suppliers, (iv) appear in location attractiveness rankings, (v) have positive reports in business press and media, (vi) they have visited, and (vii) they have family roots in (see Loewendahl, 2009:5).
16. In Western Europe, a skilled workforce was the most important factor, with market size ranked third, while investment agencies and government support ranked second. In Eastern Europe, market size was number one, low costs came second and the presence of suppliers ranked third (EC, 2006:28).
17. 'Claw back' provisions applied by the US government, for instance (UNCTAD, 2003:126).
18. Autio et al. (2000) found that 'earlier initiation of internationalization and higher knowledge intensity is associated with faster international growth' (cited by Schwens and Kabst, 2009:510).
19. PwC's study in 2009 put after-care services for target firms and links to target firms and networks as the top two factors of investment generation (scores 5 and 4.8 out of 5). According to a *Financial Times* study, after-care services for existing firms got the highest score of effectiveness among investors targeting techniques (score of 4.1) (Loewendahl, 2009:9, 10).

20. As these are driven, according to Birkinshaw, by three groups of factors – parent company strategies, subsidiary potential and host country characteristics – governments that aim at attracting R&D-intensive FDI may act upon each of those three groups of factors. (Guimón, 2008:2). Enhancing local R&D and research infrastructure is a crucial attraction, together with skilled personnel and fiscal and financial incentives to corporate R&D.
21. See for instance the programme of industry upgrading (1986) in Singapore, the related industry enhancing in Ireland (1998), local supplier developments in the Czech Republic (Loewendahl, 2009:36) and cluster development in Slovenia.
22. Local firms/diasporas can increase IFDI by 50 per cent. New actors (sovereign wealth funds, governments in the Middle East and Japan) are also important new targets for FDI (see Loewendahl, 2009).

References

Autio, E., Sapienza, H.J. and Almeida, J.G. (2000). Effects of age of entry, knowledge intensity, and international growth. *Academy of Management Journal*, 43(5), 909–24.

Bellak, C. (2007). How to attract sustainable foreign direct investment? *AIB Insights*, 7(1), 3–6.

Blomström, M. and Kokko, A.O. (1998). *Multinational Corporations and Spillovers*. London: Blackwell.

Bode, E. and Nunnenkamp, P. (2007). Does foreign direct investment promote regional development in developed countries? A Markov chain approach for US states. Kiel Working Paper 1374. Kiel: University of Kiel.

Clark, S.W. (2000). Tax incentives for foreign direct investment: empirical evidence on effects and alternative policy options. *Canadian Tax Journal*, 48(4), 1139– 80.

Damijan, J., Majcen, B., Knell, M. and Rojec, M. (2003). The role of FDI, R&D accumulation and trade in transferring technology to transition countries: evidence from firm panel data for eight transition countries. *Economic Systems*, 27, 189–204.

Ernst & Young (2006). *European Investment Monitor: 2006 Report*. www.eyeim.com/pdf/EIM%20Report%202006.pdf.

Easson, A. (2001). Tax incentives for foreign direct investment: recent trends and countertrends. *Bulletin for International Fiscal Documentation*, 55(7), 266–74.

Ghosh, M. and Wang, W. (2009). Does FDI accelerate economic growth? The OECD experience based on panel data estimates for the period 1980–2004. *Global Economy Journal*, 9(4), 1–21.

Guimón, J. (2008). Government strategies to attract R&D-intensive FDI. OECD Global Forum on International Investment, Paris. (www.oecd.org/investment/gfi-7).

James, S. (2009). *Incentives and Investments: Evidence and Policy Implications*. Washington DC: World Bank. (www.ifc.org/ifcext/fias.nsf/AttachmentsByTitle/PublicationMT_IncentivesandInvestments/$FILE/IncentivesandInvestments.pdf).

Kleindorfer, P. (2010) Business Week Special Advertising Sections. (www.50globalviewpoints.com/full_articles/GlobalViewpoints_November_2009.pdf). Kokko, A. and Gustavsson, P. (2004). Regional integration, foreign direct investment, and regional development. *EIB Papers*, 9(1), 111–35.

Kostevc, Č., Redek, T. and Rojec, M. (2011). Scope and effectiveness of FDI policies in transition countries, in: E. Rugraff, and M. W. Hansen (eds.), *Multinationals and Local Firms in Emerging Markets*, Amsterdam: Amsterdam University Press, 155–180.

Kunčič, A. and Svetličič, M. (2011). Who's who in FDI promotion: Keynesians versus Neoclassicals. *Eastern European Economics*, 49(3), 66–88.

Loewendahl, H. (2001). A framework for FDI promotion. *Transnational Corporations*, 10(1), 1–42.

Loewendahl, H. (2009). The role of investments in investment promotion. Paper presented at the WAIPA-JAPTI Focus Meeting on Investment Incentives in FDI Attraction, 23–24 November, Ljubljana, Slovenia.

Meyer, K. and Sinani, E. (2009). When and where does foreign direct investment generate positive spillovers? A meta-analysis. *Journal of International Business Studies*, 40, 1075–94.

Moran, T., Graham, T. and Blomström, M. (2005). *Does Foreign Direct Investment Promote Development*? Washington, DC: Institute of International Economics.

OECD (2006). *Policy Framework for Investment*. Paris. OECD.

Oman, C. (2000). *Policy Competition and Foreign Direct Investment: A Study of Competition Among Governments to Attract FDI*. Paris: OECD.

Ortega, C. and Griffin, C. (2009). Investment promotion essentials: what sets the world's best investment facilitators apart from the rest? Investment Climate in Practice, 6. Washington DC: The World Bank. (www.fias.net/ifcext/fias.nsf/Content/Pubs_InvestmentPolicyandPromotion). Rojec, M., Redek, T. and Kostevc, Č. (2007). Omejitve in možni elementi slovenske politike spodbujanja neposrednih tujih investicij. *Revija IB*, 41(3/4), 102–15.

Schwens, C. and Kabst, R. (2009). How early opposed to late internationalizers learn: experience of others and paradigms of interpretation. *International Business Review*, 18, 509–22.

Stopford, J. and Strange, S. (1991). *Rival States, Rival Firms: Competition for World Market Shares*. Cambridge: Cambridge University Press.

Svetličič, M. and Kunčič, A. (2010). The regional FDI strategy and politics for sustainable knowledge based competitiveness. EREF-2010 Graz Preparatory Workshop, 23 April.

Svetličič, M. and Kunčič, A. (2011). FDI, the Crises and Competitiveness of Transition Economies. Mimeo. Ljubljana: Centre of International Relations.

Taylor, C.T. (2000). The impact of host country government policy on US multinational investment decisions. *World Economy*, 23(5), 635–48.

Tuerk, E. (2010). The role of FDI in developing knowledge-based competitiveness in European Regions. Paper presented at the European Regional Economic Forum, Geneva.

UNCTAD (2003). *World Investment Report 2003*. New York and Geneva: United Nations.

Wei, K. and Yao, S. and Liu, A. (2009). Foreign direct investment and regional inequality in China. *Review of Development Economics*, 13(4), 778–91.

Wells, L. and Wint, A. (1990). Marketing a country: promotion as a tool for attracting foreign investment. Occasional Paper. Foreign Investment Advisory Service, Washington, DC.

6

Born-Global Firms from China and Norway: A Comparison

Siv Marina Flø Karlsen, Youzhen Zhao and Randi Lunnan

Introduction

The first study of fast internationalizing small to medium-sized enterprises (SMEs) was conducted by Rennie (1993). He identified a 'new breed' of Australian firms which were 'born-global'. According to this study, born-global firms tended to be small with, for example, average sales of less than US$16 million and to be relatively young in age (for instance with an average age of 14 years). They should have begun exporting, on average, two years after their establishment and have generated three-quarters of their total sales via exporting. Such companies were found in all industries, but they all applied new technologies to developing unique products or a new way of doing business and, according to Junkkari (2000), as a result were strikingly competitive against established large players. Born-global firms or international new ventures (INVs) are firms that are international and entrepreneurial in their business dealings. Wright and Ricks (1994) highlighted international entrepreneurship (IE) as a newly emerging research arena and they defined internationalization speed as: time between discovery of an opportunity and first foreign entry, speed with which country scope is increased (market selection and spreading), and speed of international commitment (mode of entry versus export share). Oviatt and McDougall (1994) found that many of the firms they studied were not truly global and thus decided to call INVs these new fast internationalizing SMEs instead of born globals or global start-ups. There is a problem with the different definitions (of born-global firms) for comparing research results. This issue was pointed out by Gabrielsson and Kirpalani (2004). In this chapter the following definition will be used: 'Fast internationalizing SMEs are defined as business organizations that from inception [seek] to derive significant competitive advantage from the use of resources and the sale of outputs in multiple countries' (Oviatt and McDougall, 2005a:538).

Existing literature on the internationalization of emerging economy SMEs is scarce. China opened its doors to the world in 1978 (Deng, 2004) and has since then had great success in attracting foreign direct investment (FDI). In 2002 China surpassed the US as the largest recipient of FDI in the world. The Chinese government launched the 'go global' strategy in 1999, urging Chinese enterprises to invest more overseas in order to sharpen their competitive edge and materialize their international business presence (ibid.: 14). 'A number of leading Chinese firms have begun to internationalize with a view to becoming global players in international markets' (Child and Rodrigues, 2005:337). In 2004 China was the fifth largest foreign investor (Yiu et al., 2007). The Chinese government has played a crucial role in shaping the structure of China's outward foreign direct investment (OFDI) since the country is still very much a state-owned, state-directed and state-controlled economy. Only one out of the twelve largest Chinese multinationals is privately owned. Chinese multinationals' investment strategies thus largely reflect government directives and priorities. Most of the works on the national and international expansion of Chinese companies are based on large companies, but, according to the Ministry of Commerce of the People's Republic of China, the Chinese authorities are actively pursuing the development as well as the national and international expansion of domestic SMEs (Cardoza and Fornes, 2009). Since the adoption of the policy of economic reform and opening to the outside world in late 1978, China's economy has experienced very rapid changes, and its impact on the world economy has progressively increased (Fishman, 2006). Related to this, the issue of internationalization of Chinese firms has attracted much attention. There has recently been a large media focus on high-profile international acquisitions and takeover bids by Chinese companies (Liu et al., 2008). In reality, these high-profile Chinese companies belong to a very small group of the so called 'national teams or champions' (Zeng and Williamson, 2003). We need to understand how ordinary Chinese firms go international. We know that born-global firms are different in a number of aspects from traditionally internationalizing firms. They are small, young and niche-oriented. It is also known that Chinese firms have other problems apart from competing with firms from developed economies. Consequently it is interesting to compare a group of Chinese born-global firms with a group of born-global firms from a Western economy, and to compare the expansion processes of the Chinese born-global companies with the existing theory on born-global firms. Thus the aim is to identify the differences that Chinese companies possess in terms of their internationalization process. This chapter explores what these differences are and how they come into existence using the new stream of theory on international entrepreneurship with a special focus on the role of social networks. Network relationships have long been recognized to be indispensable for SME development in order to achieve international growth (Johanson and Mattsson, 1988; Reuber and Fischer, 1997). However, a particular focus on social networks has been limited to date (Harris and Wheeler, 2005). Empirical findings show that social networks are vital to the identification of new opportunities. Zhou et al. (2007) found that newly internationalizing Chinese SMEs can leverage home-based social networks to enhance firm performance.

A dynamic theory of the process of firm internationalization relevant to the economic conditions of the 1990s is lacking (Dunning, 1995). Thus, our ability to explain accelerated internationalization is limited, especially for business activities originating from emerging economies. Internationalization is defined as a process in which a firm develops increasing involvement in operations outside of its home country (Welch and Luostarinen, 1988:2). The most widely recognized theory concerning the dynamics of internationalization and the one that has been relevant for young and small firms in the past, according to Oviatt and McDougall (1999), is the Uppsala stage model (Johanson and Vahlne, 1977, 1990). The Uppsala model reads very much as a theory of constraints. It drew heavily on the behavioural theory of the firm (Cyert and March, 1964) and on the theory of the growth of the firm (Penrose, 1959). The model is believed to have assumed away individual strategic choice (Autio, 2005:12). The key contribution by Oviatt and McDougall (1994) is seen as a direct challenge to the risk-averse firms, a constrained posture described by the Uppsala model. It is claimed that international new ventures are possible, because entrepreneurs are able and willing to make strategic choices, as well as to accept risks associated with an aggressive international expansion (Autio, 2005).

This chapter proceeds with a theoretical overview of the new stream literature on IE. The methods used for data collection will be described before we compare the 12 cases from China and Norway. This is followed by a discussion concerning the differences and similarities of the two categories of born-global firms, before we move on to suggest reasons and plausible explanations.

International entrepreneurship

Competitive advantage has in recent years shifted away from firms of large size and long experience towards firms with unique knowledge and swift response capabilities (Oviatt and McDougall, 1995). Technological and competitive forces have made the slowly staged efforts of firms to be risky undertakings for an increasing number of them (for example, operating in global industries). Traditionally international business researchers have focused on large multinational enterprises (MNEs) (Kirpalani et al., 2008) and, following from this, much of the focus has been on how and when to carry out FDI. Entrepreneurship researchers have focused primarily on venture creation and the management of SMEs within a domestic context. In recent years, the demarcation segregating international business and entrepreneurship has begun to erode (Gabrielsson et al., 2004). The literature on such topics has currently reached the point of specifying that 'international entrepreneurship is a combination of innovative, proactive, and risk-seeking behaviour that crosses national boundaries and is intended to create value in organizations' (McDougall and Oviatt, 2000:903).

Morrow (1988) introduced IE. In this publication he highlights technological advances and cultural awareness that appeared to open previously untapped foreign markets to new ventures (Oviatt and McDougall, 2005b). A series of globalization drivers (for instance growing interdependence of national economies, improved international communications and transportation, as well as homogenization of markets) has contributed to an overall trend towards integration of markets and globalizing of completion. This trend is believed to simplify and shorten the process of firm internationalization, which means that firms may skip stages of their international development. Thus what has been observed in the past presently may not occur in stages at all. The recent emergence of IE as a distinct field of research is an important milestone. Oviatt and McDougall's (1994) award winning article questions whether research in international business alone is sufficient to understand the internationalization process of entrepreneurial firms. This article is seen as providing a theoretical base for studying international new ventures. The authors examine how and why entrepreneurial processes of opportunity discovery, evaluation and exploitation vary across nations. They challenged the extant internationalization process theories and established a new exciting research area of internationalization, that of IE. The greatest value of their contribution lies within the creative tension that they generated in the field of international business studies by mounting a direct challenge to the established Process Theory of Internationalization (Johanson and Vahlne, 1977) and by highlighting the increasing prevalence of international new ventures. The contrast between emphasizing firm-level versus individual-level knowledge naturally reflects the different empirical scopes of the two perspectives. They open a way towards building a more comprehensive theory of new firm internationalization.

From an entrepreneurial learning perspective, Zhou (2007) argues that the tension with regard to the role of foreign market knowledge between the process models of internationalization and the early internationalization of born-global firms can be resolved by understanding the sources of knowledge. Cardoza and Fornes (2009) study internationalization of SMEs in one of the least developed regions of China, identifying several internal and external barriers to internationalization. Their findings showed that the barriers are related mainly to weak management skills and knowledge. Finance does not seem to be a barrier for the internationalization of Chinese SMEs as is the case for most Western SMEs. This may be explained by the active role played by the supportive and resourceful Chinese government in funding the development of local SMEs. Theories explaining born-global internationalization have stressed foreign market knowledge as a key factor for the understanding and explanation of the rapid internationalization of firms

(Oviatt and McDougall, 1994; Knight and Cavusgil, 2005). Interestingly, the knowledge factor has also been emphasized in the traditional models of internationalization (Eriksson et al., 2000; Johanson and Vahlne, 2003). Zhou (2007) expected that firms with international entrepreneurial proclivity have the dynamic capability to develop foreign market knowledge rapidly and internationalize early. Thus, the international entrepreneurial proclivity is what distinguishes the born-global approach from the traditional ones. The young internationalizing firms must develop other mechanisms to acquire the requisite knowledge and resources in comparison, for instance, to the traditional way of experience-based accumulation of knowledge. Entrepreneurial proclivity is defined as the firm's predisposition to engage in entrepreneurial processes, practices and decision-making, characterized by its organizational culture for innovativeness, risk taking and proactiveness (Matsuno et al., 2002). In the context of internationalization, the term 'IE orientation' is adopted by extending the conceptual domain to the processes and activities across national borders (Knight and Cavusgil, 2005). Zhou (2007) argues that the innovative dimension of entrepreneurial proclivity promotes acquisition of knowledge through market scanning and information utilization, whereas the risk-taking dimension provides a base for knowledge gained from 'trial and error' activities. Proactiveness, referred to as a forward-looking perspective, the tendency of taking initiative to anticipate rising opportunities in the marketplace (Lumpkin and Dess, 1996), results in an increased level of market knowledge by pursuing new market opportunities (Matsuno et al., 2002). According to Matsuno et al. (2002) entrepreneurial learning of market knowledge is not confined to organizational routines and administrative structures, but rather is characterized by an exploration and out-of-the-box thinking approach to the pursuit of entrepreneurial opportunities.

It is clear that entrepreneurship and internationalization are complementary fields with complementary theoretical interests and empirical developments (Jones and Coviello, 2005). Coviello (2006:2) focuses on the impact of networks on international new venture: 'network theory and analysis are fundamental to international entrepreneurship research'. Hite and Hesterly (2001) argue that in the emergent stage of firm existence, networks are cohesive and composed primarily of socially embedded ties. As the firm moves into the growth stage, the networks change to encompass a balance of embedded and arm's-length economic ties that are more intentionally managed to exploit growth. The networks will gradually shift over time from being 'identity based' (path-dependent) to being more calculative (intentionally managed). Social ties are thus seen as particularly important in the initial stages of firm evolution and with diminishing influence over time. Once engaged in international activities, new start-up ventures have their establishing process complete and organizational needs are believed to become more complex, necessitating non-social relationships (Coviello, 2006).

An important difference between theoretical approaches concerning multinational enterprise and theoretical approaches relating to international ventures seems to be the unit of analysis. IE theories argue that some firms start out internationally because of certain entrepreneur-specific capabilities (rather than firm-specific ones) (Knight and Cavusgil, 1996; McDougall and Oviatt, 1996). When the entrepreneur creates a new enterprise, there are no routines in place, but the entrepreneur has a vision and a network of contacts that he or she is going to build up further. Thus, the study of international ventures has to be concerned with the individual learning by the entrepreneur as well as with the organizational learning of the emerging entrepreneurial firm. From Fletcher's (2004) study of two case firms' international development, it is possible to argue that the language of strategy and structure, which is often prescribed by many models of international business to enable firms to survive in competitive global markets (Levitt, 1983; Bartlett and Ghoshal, 1989; Ohmae, 1989), is somewhat limited for explaining small business internationalization. Close consideration of small business practice highlights the importance of multifaceted frameworks of analysis, which go beyond the structural, strategic and behavioural aspects, and which take account of the often chaotic, opportunistic and incremental process through which entrepreneurs build international relationships and realize cross-border transactions (Buckley, 1991; Andersen, 1993; Calof and Beamish, 1995; Bell and Young, 1996; Jones, 1999). This 'means that when evaluating the international activity of small firms, there is a closer relationship to entrepreneurship than there is to international strategy and structure that has tended to dominate small business research' (Fletcher, 2004:294). For fast internationalizing SMEs the realization of entrepreneurial activities cannot be separated from the international business context and the market in which they are being created. IE is a tightly integrated process whereby entrepreneurs envision and realize the emergence of their business as an international entity. For such firms, internationalization is not an extension of what has already occurred or 'has been' in the home market. For small firms that internationalize some years after start-up, on the other hand, the international arena is seen as another 'site' in which entrepreneurial activities are tried out or practised. Internationalization is seen as an extension of what has already occurred in the home market. As a result of Fletcher's (2004) analysis, it is argued that, in staged or gradual internationalization, IE is characterized by the extension and broadening of entrepreneurial capabilities that have already been developed at home.

In the study by Liu et al. (2008) where 16 cases were investigated, entrepreneurship was regarded as the most important factor influencing the internationalization process. It is not novel to apply entrepreneurship to firm internationalization, but it is clear that 'normal' entrepreneurship embedded in and prevailing in a developed market economy might not be able to provide a satisfactory explanation of the Chinese IE experience. Liu et al.

(2008) argue that the so-called 'bounded entrepreneurship' argument may be better applied to Chinese firms. This argument proposes that the founders of such a group of firms are entrepreneurial by nature, but that their cognition and ability are bounded by their limited education and international experience and by China's unique institutional barriers.

Determinants of the pace of internationalization

Individual resources: experience and networks

The experience and background of firm founders and their relationships are important resources for the new entity and are important drivers or facilitators of the internationalization process. International experience is defined as the understanding and realistic perceptions of foreign operations, risks and returns in foreign markets (Aulakh and Kotabe, 1997). The reasoning here, which is based on the organizational capability of the firm, is that firms are initially risk-averse when entering new markets, and therefore not willing to invest substantial resources in unfamiliar contexts. As a firm's management gets a better feel of foreign markets, it gains better understanding of the existing risks and opportunities and becomes more confident and aggressive, but also more realistic. This may be manifested by the willingness to commit more resources to overseas operations and it may also enable management to make better investment decisions. For firms, international experience has traditionally been measured by making an assessment of the geographic scope and depth of the firm's experience. This is done by registering the number of different countries in which a firm is active and the length of experience in each of those countries (Erramilli, 1991).

In this study, the variables were analysed at the individual level. Information about the founder(s)' and/or other key employees' international experience were collected. Several studies (Oviatt and McDougall, 1994; Reuber and Fischer, 1997; Ellis, 2000) show that key employees in born-global firms very often have extensive international experience from previous employment. Furthermore, Reuber and Fischer (1997) argue that decision-makers with more international experience are more likely to have a foreign business network in place and are more likely to have developed the skills needed to identify and negotiate with firms in a different culture. Oviatt and McDougall (1994) argue that partnerships provide concrete critical resources: specific skills and finances, as well as more abstract resources, such as legitimacy and market power. These resources are seen as being particularly important when a new firm, with relatively limited resources, attempts to increase foreign sales. The founders' or other key employees' relationships from previous employments may enable such firms to enter new markets at a faster rate than otherwise (for example, by providing the firm with complimentary resources and by opening up markets). This view is supported by Ellis's (2000) findings, which sustain the notion that awareness of foreign market opportunities, which has been identified as being a critical antecedent of foreign market entry, is commonly acquired via existing social ties. Zhou et al. (2007) in their study of 163 Chinese SMEs found that home-based social networks play an important role in the relationship between firm internationalization and performance and recommend that international business managers should consider such networks as an efficient means of helping internationally oriented SMEs to internationalize quickly and more profitably. McGaughey et al. (1997) emphasize the important role of personal networks in triggering initial export inquiries or orders. They found that the key individuals of a network affected significantly the international activities of the studied firms. These people were critical of both the content and direction of the company's internationalization: 'much of the ability of the company to initiate and carry through international operations resided in the decision-makers' personal networks' (ibid.: 179).

Global reach and product characteristics

One reason for the differences observed in the speed by which traditional multinationals and fast globalizing firms become international/global may be due to different environmental conditions. Thus 'the slowness of the whole process is a consequence of incremental adaptations to changing firm and environmental conditions rather than the result of a deliberate strategy' (Knight and Cavusgil, 1996:13). In other words, when the environmental conditions change rapidly, as they do when globalization intensifies, the process of firm internationalization is likely to speed up as well. In a closed domestic industry, a company accustomed to weak competitors and undemanding customers has little to fear, for there are no new competitors that might grow strong in more demanding competitive arenas. In an open global industry, new and existing strong competitors abound (Yip, 1992). As a consequence, it is important to understand just how the industry globalization drivers affect the competitive environment of SMEs. When moving to industry and company level, it has been argued (Lindqvist, 1991) that increasing speed in the development of new technologies leads to shorter product life cycles (PLCs) and higher innovation intensity, which in turn leads to intensified global competition. Shorter PLCs have led to more emphasis on R&D and on recognizing new opportunities and exploiting them as rapidly as possible with successful timing (for example in the cases of personal computers and mobile phones). In short, product characteristics are an important issue requiring considerable attention. For firms with small home markets it may be difficult to achieve competitive advantage in terms of economies of scale from pure domestic operations. In the case of certain products, significant economies can be achieved only by operating in multiple countries. The shorter the PLC is then the shorter is the time period for return on investments made in product development. Consequently, companies with small domestic markets need large volume realization, so that the costs for product development can be apportioned.

Conceptual framework

Based on the above discussion, a conceptual framework is proposed where four main factors are posited as having an impact upon a firm's pace of internationalization. These factors are: (1) the experience and background of the firm's founders and/or other key employees; (2) the personal network of the founder and/or key employees; (3) the globalization of the industry in which a firm does its business; and (4) the product characteristics (see Figure 6.1).

Boundaries between domestic and international markets are becoming less relevant as businesses increase their activities abroad. In order to find an explanation as to why some SMEs still follow a more step-by-step approach, while others choose a faster and more erratic approach that leapfrogs over stages, Madsen et al. (2000) argue that globalization may enable firms to choose more freely their own model for becoming international. International sales become simultaneously easier and more difficult, in the sense that international markets have become more accessible for most firms, but the level of competition and the demand for international competence have been augmented. There is both a 'positive' pressure, from the increased level of globalization, in the form of an increase in the accessibility to markets, and a 'negative' pressure from tougher competition and

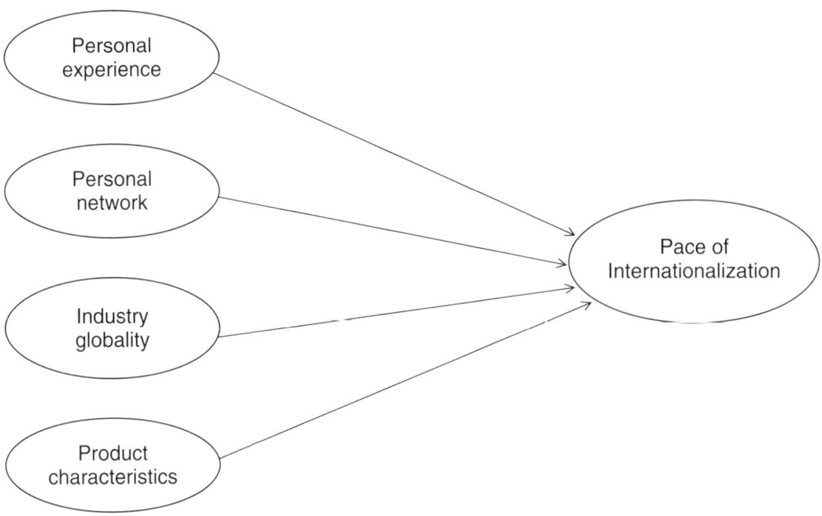

Figure 6.1 Conceptual framework

more sophisticated markets, since it has become a necessity for a host of new companies to be present in many markets. Both of these pressures work to increase the pace of internationalization. The positive pressure lures the company to explore opportunities in new territories, while the negative pressure forces the company to find new markets.

These pressures may work differently depending on the size of the home market. According to Bloodgood et al. (1996), new European firms are more likely to consider internationalizing some of their activities than new US firms. Like the USA, China also has a large home market. A new Chinese firm, operating in a 500-mile radius around its base, may do so without crossing national borders; a European firm, with the same operating radius around its base, may have to deal with the contexts of five or six other countries. Luostarinen and Gabrielsson (2002) state that global firms from large countries globalize because of the demand-based pull forces in global markets, but global firms from small open economies globalize because they are pushed to do so. Small domestic markets and the fear of expected future competition from global firms in large countries puts a lot of pressure on new internationalizing firms, pushing them to find new markets overseas. According to Hamel and Prahalad (1985:146), companies that safely nestle in their home beds will increasingly experience a resource disadvantage: 'they will be unable to marshal [the] forces required for a defense of the home market'.

Research method

This study compares and contrasts the internationalization processes of six Norwegian firms with six Chinese cases of born-global firms. The purpose is to discover the major differences and similarities of Chinese and Norwegian born globals and to establish whether the existing theory is applicable for describing the internationalization process of these firms. The method adopted entails a qualitative, primarily explanatory research perspective on the internationalization processes of Chinese and Norwegian SMEs. Multicase study research strategy has been applied, allowing data manipulation using three modes of analysis, including: pattern matching, explanation building and time series (Yin, 2003).

Multiple case design follows a 'replication' logic and is different from a 'sampling' logic (Yin, 2003:46–7). Consistent with Eisenhardt (1989), multiple cases have been chosen within each category in terms of degree of internationalization (for example the number of foreign countries/continents in which international business operations are performed and the export share in total revenue) to allow findings to be replicated within categories. Thus, if common patterns of internationalization emerge from different types of firms within the Chinese and the Norwegian economy, this will increase the generalizability of the findings.

Most of the interviewees have been firm founders. The data were collected mainly by the use of in-depth interviews supplemented with archives to 'provide stronger substantiation of constructs and hypotheses' (Eisenhardt, 1989). Archival data were obtained from company reports, newspaper clippings as well as company websites. The time length for an interview was between 1.5 and 3 hours. Interviews were tape-recorded unless the interviewees objected. All interviews were conducted in 2002 except for the Shanghai case which was conducted in 2008. Some follow-ups by email and/or telephone conversations were conducted in 2003 and 2006. While the interviews were carried out in line with a predesigned interview guide based largely on existing theories, open questions were also often asked to allow for possible theoretical deviations.

Analysis of findings

According to Cardoza and Fornes (2009) there is a problem with the definition of SMEs. Firms with employability within the scope of up to 200 employees in wholesaling to 3,000 employees in the construction and transportation industry are considered SMEs (National Bureau of Statistics of China, 2007). Zhou (2007) defines SMEs as firms with less than 500 employees, and Freeman and Cavusgil (2007) as firms with less than 200 employees. Knight et al. (2004) found out that most of the rapidly internationalizing firms have less than 100 employees. These differences in defining SMEs make the task difficult. Thus for instance what is considered a small firm in China is regarded as a large firm in Norway. This might be explained by the environment in which these firms are established. In China the domestic market is huge, whereas the Norwegian market is small on a comparative basis. Moreover, while Chinese firms have a strong cost advantage concerning labour and material cost, Norwegian firms have no such advantage and have to rely on other advantages to compete successfully in the international marketplace, for instance by offering unique and specialized products. In the Norwegian cases SMEs were firms with less than 100 employees and in the Chinese cases firms with less than 2,000 employees. The basic characteristics of the 12 case firms are presented in Table 6.1.

Apart from the clear difference in the size of Chinese and Norwegian SMEs the type of products also differs significantly. Two countries of the Norwegian firms offer products for the industrial market while most of the Chinese firms operate as original equipment manufacture (OEM). Zhou's (2007) findings show that the majority of the firms in the sample of 775 SMEs were producing textiles, garments, shoes and accessories. Many of the Chinese cases have a very high export share. This might be due to what Cardoza and Fornes (2009) label as the 'unusually fragmented' Chinese market. It has been reported that 'access to foreign markets is easier and cheaper than access to most of the country's domestic markets' (Boisot and Meyer, 2008:354, 356).

Table 6.1 Summary of the key features of the studied SMEs

	No of employees	Founded (export)	International sales (after3 years)	Products	Type of FOM most used	No of market areas in 2001
Chinese firms						
Aroma	600	1995	100%	Candles	Direct exporting	2–3
Eral	99	1997	70%	Textiles	OEM	3–4
Lisi	2000	1993	100%	Plastics	OEM (FDI sales)	worldwide
Shanghai	87	2005	94%	Refrigerator parts	OEM	1–2
Smal	1100	1995	100%	Electric appliances	OEM	worldwide
YDH	500	1989	70–80%	Car components	OEM	3–4
Norwegian firms						
Dolphin	10	1991(92)	90% (90%)	Hardware	Agents	3–4
Fras	4	1996(98)	80% (20%)	Fluid sampling	Follow cust.out	worldwide
ICAS	61	1989(93)	50% (10%)	Smoke detectors	Agents	2–3
Incatel	65	1993/4(97)	80% (50%)	Software	Direct exp.	2–3
Opera	110	1995(95)	99% (99%)	Software	Direct exp.	worldwide
Optoflow/ BioDetect	10	1993(97)	90% (85%)	Cytometer	sAgents	4–5

Note: All the numbers from the Norwegian interviewees were verified with transcripts from the Brønnøysund Register Centre (a government body under the Norwegian Ministry of Trade and Industry, consisting of several different national computerized registers).

In addition to being larger, the Chinese SMEs also take longer steps in terms of overcoming psychological distance than the Norwegian firms do when venturing abroad. One explanation for this might be that Chinese firms need to take larger steps in order to catch up for their late internationalization. In addition, since Chinese firms often establish themselves in countries where they can reap the benefits of existing networks (Child and Rodrigues, 2005; Zhou et al., 2007), they may find it viable to go to far away countries such as the USA, since there exists in that country a large Chinese population.

What is similar for all cases regardless of country of origin is the prevalence for using low commitment modes of entry such as OEM, direct exporting and use of intermediaries. This is not surprising as, for most SMEs, FDI is not an option as many of them do not have financial and other resources as well as the will for undertaking FDI. They might prefer to use lower-commitment modes for coordinating their activities abroad (Pedersen and Petersen, 1998; Madsen et al., 2000). Table 6.2 provides a summary of the case firms using five different dimensions.

As presented in Table 6.2, in order to distinguish the similarities and differences between case firms, the data material, consisting of detailed answers from each interviewee, has been reduced, and each variable has been given relative values on a continuum basis. The *experience* continuum has values that vary from having some experience at the low end, to experienced in the middle and very experienced at the high end. The network variable has been termed *relational*. The term indicates whether the founder or another key employee has a network of importance or not, and reflects his or her relational approach. This variable is a continuum from not relational at the low end, through varying, when the firm occasionally uses a relational approach, suggesting placement in the middle of this continuum, to very relational at the high end. The *globality* characteristics of an industry are found to vary from low, to medium, to high and to very high, based on the founder's perceptions of the industry in which he or she does business. When characterizing the *product*, S means that the product is specialized, U means that the product is unique, and the PLC is described as being long, medium or short. The dependent variable, the *pace of internationalization*, varies on a continuum from slow, to medium, to fast and to very fast. The relative values assigned are based upon the number of countries entered and the export rate measured three years after founding. If the firms with most significant global operations on both dimensions are examined, namely Opera and Lisi, it is seen that they have very experienced founders in terms of international exposure. This has made them less sceptical to venture abroad. As one founder put it: 'it is not worse out there than here'. This is in line with Johanson and Vahlne's (1977) argument that practised founders experience less psychological distance and are thus not as risk averse when it comes to choosing which and how many new markets to enter. Lisi and Opera also have products with short PLCs

Table 6.2 Key findings of the six case study firms

	Norwegian firms					
	Optoflow	**Dolphin**	**Fras**	**ICAS**	**Incatel**	**Opera**
Experience	Experienced	Some	Experienced	Some	Very	Very
Relational	Varying	Varying	Very	Varying	Very	Very
Globality	High	Very high	Very high	Low	Medium	Very high
Product	S, U, long PLC	S, U, med PLC	S, U, long PLC	Long PLC	S, U, long PLC	S, U, short PLC
Pace of Int.	Very fast	Fast	Fast	Slow	Medium	Very fast
	Chinese firms					
	Aroma	**Eral**	**Lisi**	**Shanghai**	**Smal**	**YDH**
Experience	Some	Very	Very	Very	Little	Experienced
Relational	Very	Very	Varying	Very	Varying	Varying
Globality	Medium	High	High	High	Very high	High
Product	Med	Short	Short	Long	Short	Long
Pace of Int.	Medium	Fast	Very fast	Medium	Very fast	Fast

Note: S = specialized; U = unique.

and this, at least for firms with small home markets, is believed to contribute to an increase in the firm's pace of internationalization. The shorter the PLC, the shorter the time in which a return on the investment in product development can be earned. Thus, companies with small domestic markets need global volumes to reduce the cost per unit (Alahuhta, 1990). Opera's product is unique and highly specialized, which is more or less the case for all Norwegian cases except ICAS. This firm turned out not to be a born global; rather it can be classified as a traditionally internationalizing SME. This result is in line with Knight and Cavusgil's (2004) findings, that the most important strategies employed by born-global firms (at least in the Western economies) underscore global technological competence, unique product development, quality focus and leveraging foreign distributor competence. In addition, Bloodgood et al. (1996) found out that ventures were significantly more internationalized if they were seeking competitive advantage through product differentiation. This belief corresponds well with what several of the Norwegian founders answered when asked about competition. The founder of Opera and Optoflow pointed out in 2002 that 'the strongest competitor for our product is the application of old methods'. This informant also stated that 'what we do is very much research based and working towards markets we believe will be realized in the next few years'. This is a vision very typical of entrepreneurial minds as they see opportunities before others with the proactiveness dimension of entrepreneurial proclivity (Matsuno et al., 2002), referred to as a forward-looking perspective. This is summarized by the tendency of taking the initiative in anticipating rising opportunities in the marketplace (Lumpkin and Dess, 1996). Opera and Optoflow belong to an industry which can be considered to have a high degree of globalization. This finding is consistent with the assumption that firms internationalizing in industries characterized by a high degree of globalization are either forced to go global fast, due to tough competition even in the home market, or are lured out of the home market because of the increased accessibility to foreign markets (Masden and Servais, 1997; Madsen et al., 2000).

With regard to the relationship variable, the findings were inconsistent. The relationship approach was supported for the Norwegian cases. Several of the founders (of Fras, Opera, Incatel and Optoflow) stated that they aimed at securing particular customers. They were not concerned about the markets in various countries. These firms pursued relationships with suitable customers, wherever they were found to be, and they did not pay much attention to international borders. The fact that it was more varying for the Chinese cases might not be so surprising as firms ultimately aiming at consumer markets are, by contrast, more likely to focus upon market potential at a country level (Andersen and Buvik, 2002).

The firms studied were chosen with the expectation that differences would be found in the pace of internationalization. Finding differences would enable the placing of these firms in different global categories. According to several studies (Knight and Cavusgil, 1996; Masden and Servais, 1997; Harveston, 2000; Madsen et al., 2000; Junkkari, 2000), born-global firms are defined as SMEs with an export rate of more than 25 per cent within three years of their establishment. Such a criterion is rather unspecific, particularly in the Norwegian case. It can be expected, for instance, that a Norwegian SME will export at least 30 per cent of its products in value terms to Sweden and Denmark within three years of its establishment. Thus such a firm cannot be categorized as a born global. In other words, one needs to incorporate the type and the number of the overseas markets an SME is present in before deciding whether it is a born-global firm or not. Moreover, most of the global SMEs usually have a far higher percentage of foreign sales than 25 per cent (Luostarinen and Gabrielsson, 2002). For the purposes of this study, a born-global firm is defined as an SME that exports at least 50 per cent of its products within three years of its establishment. However, to be defined as a 'true born global' (TBG), the SME has to be present in more than one continent simultaneously. To exemplify, a Norwegian SME that exports 80 per cent of its products to European countries would not be classified as a TBG as would be the case for a Chinese SME that exports 80 per cent of its produce to Japan. The TBG is found in the upper right corner of Figure 6.2, and the firms that gradually become international are found in the lower left corner. The upper left corner categorizes born-global firms when considering the market dimension: that is the born-global market (BGM) dimension. The lower right corner categorizes born-global firms when considering the export dimension: that is the born-global export (BGE) dimension.

The world markets of the studied firms were divided into several parts related to the increasing psychological distance from the home markets of China or Norway. This division is in accordance with Junkkari (2000:160), who classifies areas as hot (business transactions are close-by, in terms of distance) or cold (far away destinations in which business transactions are considered distant).

Based on the degree of internationalization as presented in Table 6.2, it was found that one firm, ICAS, qualifies to be classified as gradually internationalizing. One firm, Fras, qualifies to be classified as born global on the market dimension. Six firms (Aroma, Dolphin, Eral, Incatel, Shanghai and YDH) qualify to be classified as born global on the export dimension and four firms to be classified as true born-global firms (Lisi, Opera, Optoflow and Smal).

Discussion

Chinese firms are likely to use the relational systems such as Guanxi at their start-up phase. This is less the case for firms from developed economies such as Norway. But theories relating to born-global firms state that

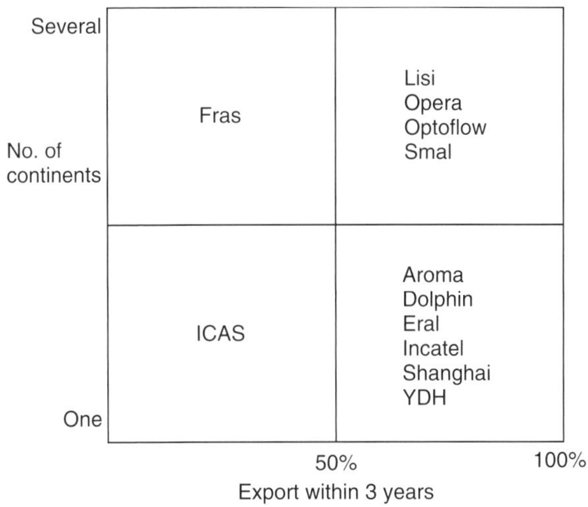

Figure 6.2 Different categories of born-global firms

they make greater use of networks than traditional SMEs. Such a practice is even seen as a precondition for the creation of born-global SMEs (see for instance, Knight and Cavusgil, 1996; Reuber and Fischer, 1997; Burgel and Murray, 2000; Chetty and Campbell-Hunt, 2004). This fact suggests that Western born-global SMEs might be more similar to Chinese born-global SMEs than traditional Western SMEs. This is especially the case in terms of making use of networks in their international growth of born-global firms. The use of networks and the central element of trust are seen as relatively new notions in the Western world. Traditionally, Western theories have focused on the importance of internalizing activities to protect oneself against opportunism. In the Eastern world the traditional way of doing business is to make extensive use of networks. Trust creation, as well as trust building, between business partners are also seen as vital to the establishment of business relationships, before any business transactions have taken place. Having relational orientation of Chinese businesses in mind one can deduce that theories which focus on opportunism and firm protection against it might not be valid in the Chinese context. Otherwise, theories that focus on networks and experiential learning can be more appropriate for explaining the internationalization process of Chinese SMEs. Norwegian born-global SMEs belong to dynamic industries characterized by a high degree of globalization. The internationalizing Chinese SMEs also belong to global industries. They are disadvantaged as they lag behind in their international development due to many years of entrepreneurial discouragement and isolation. The Chinese born-global firms have different characteristics than the Norwegian born-global SMEs, the latter being significantly smaller, high-tech and niche-oriented. Meanwhile their

Chinese counterparts are large, use high-tech in the production process rather than have it as a feature of the product, and are prone to penetrate and serve large markets with big potential. Another difference is that Norwegian born-global SMEs have a non-existent or tiny home market due to their focus on small market niches. This is not the approach to globalization of Chinese SMEs. They have in general an enormous home market. As their products are not niche focused, they target the mass market. Despite these differences, the founders of the case firms seem to have a similar approach to globalizing their businesses quickly, namely to take advantage of market opportunities. This is in accordance with the entrepreneurial proclivity argument that entrepreneurial behaviour provides international firms with dynamic capabilities to engage in cross-border activities and trade (Toyne and Walters, 1993). Such behaviour is viewed as a way of promoting a greater level of information-scanning activities and it fosters an increased knowledge base and responsiveness related to the external market environment (Matsuno et al., 2002). The relationship aspect which is seen as crucial for rapid and profitable internationalization (Zhou et al., 2007) is not seen as vital for the analysed cases. The main explanatory factors may thus be that the founder is proactive, innovative and risk-taking and also that the firms in question are entering a market characterized by a high degree of globalization, where the founders need to act fast before the window of opportunity closes.

It can be assumed, due to the radical change of economic regime in China – when it opened its doors to the world in 1978 (Deng, 2004) and when it launched the 'go global' strategy in 1999 – that the changes that are important drivers of the born-global phenomenon are compressed into a very short time frame. Thus the strong globalization pressures are more evident in China than in economies in which the advancement of globalization has been gradual. As a consequence of the competition that surfaced with China's trade liberalization, it can be assumed that many Chinese firms considered exporting to be an easier option to conduct business than continuing to serve the increasingly more competitive home market. This situation is similar to what was observed in New Zealand after 1984 when their economy was deregulated (Chetty, 1999). After the liberalization of an economy local firms are forced to accelerate their internationalization process in order to survive in an environment that is dramatically more competitive because of its exposure to global rivalry (Chetty and Campbell-Hunt, 2004).

Conclusion and suggestions for future research

The process of swiftly internationalizing Chinese and Norwegian SMEs has been studied at the individual level. Initially the pre-start-up processes have been analysed in line with Autio's (2005:11) argument: 'given the emphasis on the enabling effect of individual-level (pre-firm) internationalization experience for early and rapid internationalization, a more detailed examination of this issue appears necessary'. Globalizing SMEs that have evolved through to the later stages – using multiple case studies in different contexts of Western Europe with six Norwegian cases and South East Asia represented by six Chinese cases – have been investigated. The similarities between the cases were the way born-global SMEs consider the speed of their globalization. They all became global rather fast after their start-ups, considering the two dimensions of BGM and BGE. However, the firms varied in size and velocity of growth. The Chinese firms were bigger and grew faster in comparison to the Norwegian firms. For example, the Chinese firm Eral had a value for its exports of US$60 million three years after start-up, while the average export value for a born-global SME according to a study by Rennie (1993) should be about US$16 million. One reason for the fast growth of the Chinese firms, and their having a much larger export share than expected for a born-global SME, may be the active role played by the supportive and resourceful Chinese government in funding the development and internationalization of Chinese SMEs (Cardoza and Fornes, 2009).

This study sets the question – do we need a new theory to explain the globalization of Chinese SMEs? It seems that the existing theories on born-global firms may be sufficient. However, the role of the government needs to be taken more into consideration and studied in depth. The 'relational framework' thus needs to incorporate networking among firms, including the central and provincial governments and relevant institutions, in future studies of globalizing Chinese firms.

Appendix: milestones of the case firms

Dolphin AS – Hardware

1991/92	Dolphin AS was established by 20 previous employees of Norsk Data
1992	Direct export started to the US market
1994	Ownership of Dolphin AS moved abroad to the US, i.e. parent company located in the US, but the owners are the same as at the outset
1996	Buy-up in the US
1997	Dolphin AS established an agent in France
2000	Dolphin AS established an agent in England
2002	Dolphin established an agent in Germany. Their focus for the future is on the US and the Chinese market.

Fras AS – Fluid sampler

1975	Mr Fjerdingstad (founder of Fras) established a subsidiary of Parker Haneyfin in Norway

1986	Fjerdingstad established a subsidiary of Hägglunds Drive in Norway
1990	The first step for the product was to follow a customer out – namely they followed Norske Skog to France
1991	Fjerdingstad was employed at Veritas as a strategy to prepare a platform for the product
1996	Fras AS was established by Fjerdingstad
1998	Fras AS established contact with Lloyds of London
1999	Fras AS sold licences to Germany
2000	Fras AS followed Statoil to China
2003	Fras AS is currently looking for new investors. They do not focus on country markets but on product markets: offshore, ships, process industry and energy production.

ICAS AS – Smoke detectors

1989	ICAS AS was established by Mr Olving
1990/91	Legislation required that all homes in Norway have smoke detectors. ICAS AS started production in Norway.
1991	All production moved to the Czech Republic (55 employees) – only marketing and sales in Norway (five employees)
1993	Established agent in Finland
1997	Started selling to Sweden – considered as the most important market for ICAS AS
2000	Some sporadic sales to Australia
2001	Some sporadic sales to South Africa
2003	Established subsidiary with one employee in England. The markets they focus on in the future are Germany and England. The entry mode most used is agents or importers.

Incatel AS – Software

1959	The founder of Incatel AS, Mr Vedeld, wrote his first computer program
1961	Vedeld started to work for IBM
Early 1980s	There was a pilot (INKA) in what was then called Televerket – the idea was based on the fact that if you could keep track of accounts by using computers it should be possible to keep track of a telephone network as well
1987	A firm called SysScan won a bid from Televerket to deliver a computer solution that should manage the telephone network – the solution was not complete
1989	A new company with former employees from SysSan was established, it was called Amis. It was to complete the

product development. IBM had entered the scene and was to supply Amis with the Unix platform on which Televerket had demanded INKA to be developed – IBM Europe agreed to fund the product development in exchange for the marketing rights all over the world.

1991 Amis demanded more funding which IBM refused – and it thus went bankrupt. The owners of Amis had put money into the project with intellectual property rights as security without IBM's knowledge – they moved these rights into an American company called Cimage Corp.

1992 IBM Europe established a new firm called Corena which was to continue the development that Vedeld was employed in at Televerket

1993/94 Cimage Corp came up with the best solution – Corena was dissolved. Televerket made an agreement to buy the solution of Cimage Corp with IBM Norge as integrator. Cimage Corp was closed down in Norway, and Incatel AS was established – it is owned by Telenor Venture (40%), IBM Europe (40%), Norpet/Vedeld (10%) and employees (10%).

1997 Incatel AS sold their software to Tele Danmark

1999 Incatel AS sold their software to Czech Telekom (KPN)

2001 Incatel AS sold their software to Belgia Telekom

2002 Incatel AS sold their software to the Swedish telecom, Telia. They are currently working on getting a contract with the French and British telecompanies.

Opera Software AS – Software

1991 One of the founders, Mr Tezchner started to work for Telenor Research

1994 The Opera browser started out as a Telenor project

1995 Telenor did not wish to pursue this product and Tezchner and Ivarsøy founded Opera Software AS – they got permission to keep the research

1996 The first Opera browser was released on the internet

1998 Embraced emerging market of internet devices

2000 Opera Software AS teamed up with key players in the internet device market: Ericsson, Nokia, Sony, IBM and Psion. Opera Software AS acquires Hern Lab (Sweden).

2001 Opera Software AS became part of Symbian (a strategic alliance of leading handset and mobile computing manufacturers: Ericsson, Motorola, Nokia, Panasonic and Psion). They aim for the mobile phone and the digital-TV market.

Optoflow AS – Cytometer

1993	Gjelsnes established Optoflow AS
1994	Gjelsnes was awarded a Reodor Prize for his invention
1995	The product is ready for sale – first sale to Norway
1996/97	A prototype was sold to England – it was an OEM contract

The firm was sold and changed its name to BioDetect in 2000. BioDetect got a distributor in Japan (and has remained in that market. Optoflow has sold to 12 countries: Sweden, Denmark, Germany (distributor), England (distributor), Belgium, the Netherlands, France (agent), Italy (agent), Jordan, USA (two agents), Japan (distributor) and Singapore. The founder prefers agents – he is disappointed with the performance of the distributors.

References

Alahuhta, M. (1990). *Global Growth Strategies for High Technology Challengers*, PhD Thesis, Helsinki: Helsinki University of Technology.

Andersen, O. (1993). On the internationalisation process of firms: a critical analysis. *Journal of International Business Studies*, 24(2), 209–31.

Andersen, O. and Buvik. A. (2002). Firms' internationalization and alternative approaches to the international customer/market selection. *International Business Review*, 11(3), 347–63.

Aulakh, P.S. and Kotabe, M. (1997). Antecedents and performance implications of channel integration in foreign markets, *Journal of International Business Studies*, 28(1), 145–175.

Autio, E. (2005). Creative tension: the significance of Ben Oviatt's and Patricia McDougall's article 'Toward a theory of international new ventures'. *Journal of International Business Studies*, 36, 9–19.

Bartlett, C.A. and Ghoshal, S. (1989). *Managing across Borders: The Transnational Solution*. Boston, MA: Harvard Business School Press.

Bell, J. and Young, S. (1996). Towards an integrative framework of the internationalisation of the firm. Proceedings of the Academy of International Business Conference, 24–25 March.

Bloodgood, J.M., Sapienza, H.J. and Almeida, J.G. (1996). The internationalization of new high-potential U.S. ventures: antecedents and outcomes. *Entrepreneurship Theory and Practice*, 20, 61–76.

Boisot, M. and Meyer, M. (2008). Which way through the open door? Reflections on the internationalization of Chinese firms. *Management and Organization Review*, 4(3), 349–65.

Buckley, P.J. (1991). The analysis of international corporate strategy: an integrated framework and research agenda, in H. Vestergaard (ed.) *An Enlarged Europe in the Global Economy*, Proceedings of the 17th Annual European International Business Academy Conference, Copenhagen: Copenhagen Business School Press, Volume 1, 541–575.

Burgel, O. and Murray, GC. (2000). An integrated market entry choice of start-up companies in high technology industries, *Journal of International Marketing*, 8(2), 33–62.

Calof, J.L. and Beamish, P.W. (1995). Adapting to foreign markets: explaining internationalization. *International Business Review*, 4(2), 115–31.

Cardoza, G. and Fornes, G. (2009). The internationalisation of SMEs from China: the case of Ningxia Hui autonomous region. *Asia Pacific Journal of Management*, 1–23 October.;http://www.springerlink.com/content/ah2h53630660372g/fulltext.pdf.

Casson, M. (1987). *The Firm and the Market*. Cambridge, MA: Massachusetts Institute of Technology Press.

Chetty, S. (1999) Dimensions of internationalisation of firms in the apparel industry. *European Journal of Marketing*, 33(1&2), 121–142.

Chetty, S. and Campbell-Hunt, C. (2004). Internationalisation strategy and its impact on learning during the process,. *Journal of Asia Pacific Marketing*, 3(2), 37–51.

Child, J. and Rodrigues, S.B. (2005). The internationalization of Chinese firms: a case for theoretical extension? *Management and Organization Review*, 1(3), 381–410.

Coviello, N.E. (2006). The network dynamics of international new ventures. *Journal of International Business Studies*, 37, 713–31.

Cyert, R. and March, J.G. (1964). *A Behavioral Theory of the Firm*. London: Blackwell.

Deng, P. (2004). Outward investment by Chinese MNCs: motivations and implications. *Business Horizons*, 47, 3, 8–16.

Dunning, J.H. (1995). Reappraising the eclectic paradigm in an age of alliance capitalism. *Journal of International Business Studies*, 26(3), 461–91.

Eisenhardt, K.M. (1989). Building theories from case study research, *The Academy of Management Review*, 14(4), 532–550.

Ellis, P. (2000). Social ties and foreign market entry. *Journal of International Business Studies*, 31(3) 443–69.

Eriksson, K., Johanson, J., Majkgård, A. and Sharma, D. D. (2000). Effects of knowledge accumulation in the internationalization process, *International Studies of Management and Organization*, 30(1), 26–40.

Errammili, M.K. (1991). The experience factor in foreign market entry behavior of service firms, *Journal of International Business Studies*, 21(3), 479–501.

Fishman, T. (2006). *China Inc.: The Relentless Rise of the Next Great Power*. London: Simon & Schuster.

Fletcher, D. (2004). International entrepreneurship and the small business. *Entrepreneurship and Regional Development*, 16, 289–305.

Freeman, S. and Cavusgil S.T. (2007). Toward a typology of commitment states among managers of born-global firms: a study of accelerated internationalization. *Journal of International Marketing*, 15(4), 1–40.

Gabrielsson. M and Kirpalani, V.H.M. (2004). Born-globals: how to reach new business space rapidly. *International Business Review*, 13 (5), 555–71.

Gabrielsson, M., Sasi, V. and Darling, J. (2004). Finance strategies of rapidly-growing Finnish SMEs: born internationals and born-globals. *European Business Review*, 16(6), 590–604.

Hamel, G. and Prahalad, C.K. (1985). Do you really have a global strategy? *Harvard Business Review*, July–August, 139–48.

Harris, S. and Wheeler, C. (2005). Export market development activities: entrepreneur relationships as exchange based activities, *International Business Review*, 14(2), 187–207.

Harveston, P. (2000) *Synoptic versus Incremental Internationalization: An Examination of "Born Global" and "Gradual Globalizing" Firms*, PhD Thesis, Memphis, University of Memphis.

Hite, J.M. and Hesterly, W.S. (2001). The evolution of firm networks: from emergence to early growth of the firm. *Strategic Management Journal*, 22(3), 274–86.

Johanson, J. and Mattsson, L.-G. (1988). Internationalisation in industrial systems: a network approach, in N. Hood and J.E. Vahlne (eds), *Strategies in Global Competition*. New York, NY: Croom Helm, pp. 283–305.

Johanson, J. and Vahlne, J.-E. (1977). The internationalisation process of the firm. *Journal of International Business Studies*, 8, 23–32

Johanson, J. and Vahlne, J.-E. (1990). The mechanisms of internationalisation. *International Marketing Review*, 7(4), 11–24.

Johanson, J. and Vahlne, J.-E. (2003). Business relationship commitment and learning in the internationalization process. *Journal of International Entrepreneurship*, 1, 83–101.

Jones, M.V. (1999). The internationalisation of small high technology firms. *Journal of International Marketing*, 7(4), 15–41.

Jones, M.V. and Coviello, N.E. (2005). Internationalisation: conceptualising an entrepreneurial process of behaviour in time. *Journal of International Business Studies*, 36, 284–303.

Junkkari, J.M. (2000). Born-global: The Globalization Strategies of Small and Medium-sized High Technology Manufacturers. Master's Thesis, Helsinki School of Economics.

Kirpalani, V.H.M., Gabrielsson, M., Dimitratos, P., Solberg, C.A. and Zucchella, A. (2008). Conceptualization to advance born-global definition: a research note. *Global Business Review*, 9(1), 45–50.

Knight, G. and Cavusgil, S.T. (1996). The born-global: a challenge to traditional internationalization theory. *Advances in International Marketing*, 8, 11–26.

Knight, G. and Cavusgil, S.T. (2004). Innovation, organizational capabilities, and the born-global firm. *Journal of International Business Studies*, 35(2), 124–41.

Knight, G. and Cavusgil, S.T. (2005). A Taxonomy of born-global firms. *Management International Review*, 45(3), 15–35.

Knight, G., Madsen, T.K. and Servais, P. (2004). An inquiry into European and American born-global firms. *International Marketing Review*, 21(6), 645–65.

Levitt, T.(1983). The globalization of markets. *Harvard Business Review*, May–June, 92–102.

Lindquist, M. (1991). *Infant Multinationals: The Internationalization of Young, Technology-based Swedish Firms*, PhD Thesis, Stockholm: Stockholm School of Economics.

Liu, X., Xiao, W. and Huang, X. (2008). Bounded entrepreneurship and internationalisation of indigenous Chinese private-owned firms. *International Business Review*, 17, 488–508.

Lumpkin, G.T. and Dess, G.G. (1996). Clarifying the entrepreneurial orientation construct and linking it to performance, *Academy of Management Review*, 21(1), 135–172.

Luostarinen, R. and Gabrielsson, M. (2002). Globalization and global marketing strategies of born-globals in SMOPECs. Paper presented at EIBA Conference in Athens, Greece, December.

Madsen, T.K. and Servais, P. (1997). The internationalization of born-globals: an evolutionary process. *International Business Review*, 6(6), 561–83.

Madsen, T.K., Rasmussen, E. and Servais, P. (2000). Differences and similarities between born-globals and other types of exporters. *Advances in International Marketing*, 10, 247–65.

Matsuno, K., Mentzer, J.T. and Özsomer, A. (2002). The effects of entrepreneurial proclivity and market orientation on business performance. *Journal of Marketing*, 66, 16–32.

McDougall, P. and Oviatt, B. (1996). New venture internationalization, strategic change, and performance: a follow-up study, *Journal of Business Venturing*, 11(1), 23–40.

McDougall, P.P. and Oviatt, B.M. (2000). International entrepreneurship: the intersection of two research paths. *Academy of Management Journal*, 43(5), 902–6.

McGaughey, S., Welch, D. and Welch, L. (1997). Managerial influences and SME internationalization, in I. Bjørkman and M. Forsgren (eds), *The Nature of the International Firm*. Copenhagen: Copenhagen Business School, pp. 165–88.

Morrow, J.F. (1988). International entrepreneurship: a new growth opportunity. *New Management*, 3, 59–61.

National Bureau of Statistics (2007). *National Economy Kept Steady and Fast Growth*, Beijing, National Bureau of Statistics.

Ohmae, K. (1989). Managing in a borderless world. *Harvard Business Review*, 67, 152–61.

Oviatt, B.M. and McDougall. P.P. (1994). Toward a theory of international new ventures. *Journal of International Business Studies*, 25(1), 45–64.

Oviatt, B.M. and McDougall. P.P. (1995). Global start-ups: entrepreneurs on a worldwide stage. *Academy of Management Executive*, 19(2), 30–43.

Oviatt, B.M. and McDougall. P.P. (1999). A framework for understanding accelerated international entrepreneurship, in A. Rugman and R. Wright (eds), *Global Strategic Management: International Entrepreneurship*. Stamford, CT: JAI Press, pp. 23–40.

Oviatt, B.M. and McDougall. P.P. (2005a). Defining international entrepreneurship and modelling the speed of internationalization. *Entrepreneurship Theory and Practice*, 25, 537–53.

Oviatt, B.M. and McDougall. P.P. (2005b). The internationalization of entrepreneurship. *Journal of International Business Studies*, 36, 2–8.

Pedersen, T. and Petersen, B. (1998). Explaining gradually increasing resource commitment to a foreign market. *International Business Review*, 7(5), 483–501.

Penrose, E. (1959). *The Theory of the Growth of the Firm*. London: Basil Blackwell.

Rennie, M.W. (1993). Global competitiveness. *The McKinsey Quarterly*, 4, 45–52.

Toyne, B. and Walters, P.G.P. (1993). *Global Marketing Management: A Strategic Perspective*, 2nd edn. Boston, MA: Allyn and Bacon.

Reuber, A.R. and Fischer, E. (1997). The influence of the management team's international experience on the internationalization behavior of SMEs, *Journal of International Business Studies*, 28(4), 807–825.

Welch, L.S. and Luostarinen, R. (1988). Internationalisation: evolution of a concept. *Journal of General Management*, 14 (2), 34–64.

Wright, R.W. and Ricks, D.A. (1994). Trends in international business research: twenty-five years later. *Journal of International Business Studies*, 687–701.

Yin, R. K. (2003). *Case Study Research, Design and Methods*, Third Edition, Newbury Park: Sage Publications.

Yip, G.S. (1992). *Total Global Strategy: Managing for Worldwide Competitive Advantage*. London: Prentice-Hall.

Yiu, D.W., Lau, C.M. and Bruton, G.D. (2007). International venturing by emerging economy firms: the effects of firm capabilities, home country networks, and corporate entrepreneurship. *Journal of International Business Studies*, 38, 519–40.

Zeng, M. and Williamson, P.J. (2003). The hidden dragons. *Harvard Business Review*, 81(10), 92-99, 137.

Zhou, L. (2007). The effects of entrepreneurial proclivity and foreign market knowledge on early internationalisation. *Journal of World Business*, 42, 281–93.

Zhou, L, Wu, W.P. and Luo, X. (2007). Internationalisation and the performance of born-global SMEs: the mediating role of social networks. *Journal of International Business Studies*, 38, 673–90.

7

Becoming a True Born Global without Any Experiential Market Knowledge: Three Chinese Cases

Tiia Vissak and Xiaotian Zhang

Introduction

Internationalization processes have been very actively researched for about the last five decades. During this period, many views about companies' foreign involvement have emerged. Some of them, including the Uppsala (U) model, the innovation-related internationalization (I) models and the Finnish (Helsinki) model, emphasize the importance of experiential knowledge for internationalization. They state that the lack of knowledge forces firms to internationalize slowly by entering culturally and geographically closest countries and by using initially simpler foreign operation modes such as direct and indirect exporting. Only after acquiring the necessary experiential knowledge are they able to enter other countries and use more complicated entry/operation modes. Some other research streams, including the literature on international new ventures, born globals and other fast internationalizers and the network approach to internationalization, have shown that internationalization does not have to be that slow, as knowledge can be also acquired by other means rather than through experience. Consequently, some enterprises may start their internationalization from farther markets, even from other continents, without having any activities on its home continent. They may also use more advanced entry modes and skip the earlier stages of internationalization.

Unfortunately, the current literature does not pay enough attention to how these companies manage to obtain such mostly non-experiential knowledge and how acquiring it impacts on their internationalization. Thus, during the current decade, several authors have emphasized the need to examine the acquisition and use of knowledge and its impact on internationalization (see, for example, Mitra and Golder, 2002; Morgan et al. 2003; Saarenketo et al. 2004; Pedersen and Petersen, 2004; Bengtsson, 2004; Lingyee, 2004; Weerawardena et al., 2007; Brennan and Garvey, 2009; Casillas et al., 2009; Freeman et al., 2010). It is especially interesting to study this subject in the context of China, as, after the period of reforms and opening up, many firms were established there without any experiential knowledge and several of them became successful born globals.

In this chapter we will study how three Chinese firms have become true born globals without having any experiential market knowledge. We define 'true born globals' as firms that have entered at least two other continents, apart from operating on the home continent, within three years since their foundation, and have achieved at least a 25 per cent export share from outside their home continent during this period, and at least a 75 per cent export share by the ninth year since their establishment. The chapter starts with a literature review of all the main approaches to explaining the importance of experiential market knowledge for fast internationalization and continues with an overview of studies on acquiring foreign market knowledge. Then, after a methodology section, we present three Chinese case studies. We then discuss the results and some managerial and research implications.

Literature review

The importance of experiential market knowledge for fast internationalization

This section starts with an overview of the literature on slow (sometimes also called 'gradual') internationalization. It shows that several authors have argued that internationalization depends on the acquisition of experiential foreign market knowledge. The section continues with an overview of the literature on international new ventures, born globals and other fast internationalizers and explains why some firms, who may lack such knowledge, can manage to internationalize much faster than the literature on slow internationalization would have expected.

A large amount of research has been based on the Uppsala (also called the U or the internationalization process) model. Its authors (including Johanson and Wiedersheim-Paul, 1975; Johanson and Vahlne, 1977, 1990; Vahlne and Johanson, 2002) have made the following three assumptions:

- Experiential market knowledge, for example knowledge about doing business in a specific foreign country, is the driving force of the internationalization process as it generates business opportunities, but also reduces market risk and uncertainty.
- Lack of knowledge about foreign markets is a very important obstacle to the development of a firm's international operations. The necessary knowledge can be acquired mainly through the firm's own experience, in other words through its operations abroad. The acquisition, integration and use of such knowledge are quite often gradual and relatively slow. Thus, the internationalization process is usually long, slow and incremental.

- Because of a lack of knowledge about foreign countries and a propensity to avoid uncertainty, firms usually start their international activities from exporting to neighbouring countries or some others that are comparatively well known and culturally similar. In a specific country, they make stronger commitments incrementally as they gain experience from their activities there. This means that they pass through steps from (1) having no regular export activities to (2) exports via independent representatives or agents, and (3), later, after acquiring more experiential knowledge, establish overseas sales and (4) production (manufacturing) units.

The authors of the U-model have brought out three main exceptions to their model (Johanson and Vahlne, 1990). Firstly, to some extent, also explaining why some firms may internationalize faster than this model expects, large or resourceful enterprises can internationalize more easily than smaller companies. Secondly, in stable market conditions, relevant market knowledge can be also obtained in other ways, not only through experience. Thirdly, if a company has gained considerable experience from similar markets, it may also use it for entering some other countries. Vahlne and Johanson (2002) have also stated that IT companies tend to internationalize faster by entering far away countries and establishing subsidiaries or by acquiring other firms there very rapidly.

Innovation-related internationalization (or I-models) focus on the learning sequence connected with the adoption of an innovation. They are derived from the five stages of the individual innovation adoption process, namely awareness, interest, evaluation, trial and adoption of an innovation (Rogers, 1962). These models agree with the above-discussed Uppsala model that a firm's foreign market expansion is incremental and thus depends on the firm's experiential learning and the uncertainty regarding its decision to internationalize (Fina and Rugman, 1996; Morgan and Katsikeas, 1997).

In these models, the number of 'stages' varies. For instance, Leonidou and Katsikeas (1996) discuss three broad phases, i.e. the pre-engagement phase, the initial phase and the advanced phase (the first two include different types of firms), while Reid (1983) identified eight. Some authors suggest some other foreign entry and operation modes apart from exporting and establishing foreign sales and production subsidiaries. For instance, Cavusgil (1980) and Reid (1983) include licensing. Still, the authors of these models have agreed that internationalization is a gradual process and that it can be subdivided further (Czinkota, 1982). Unlike the U-model, the innovation-related internationalization models have demonstrated that knowledge is not always the only factor influencing the speed of internationalization. For instance, according to some authors, foreign-owned firms may internationalize faster as the initial exporting decision could be made in the parent company's headquarters, whereas sales may be organized through its global marketing network (Wiedersheim-Paul et al., 1978).

The Finnish model (sometimes also called the Helsinki model or the target country internationalization process model) agrees with the two previously discussed approaches in the sense that, firstly, firms tend to start their activities from their home market and, after that, they penetrate physically, politically, economically and culturally the closest countries, as in the case of farther markets uncertainty is perceived to be high. It acknowledges the importance of experiential knowledge, but states that some knowledge can be also acquired from other sources. In this model, cultural distance between the home and foreign countries is defined as the 'sum of factors creating, on the one hand, a need for knowledge, and on the other hand, barriers to the knowledge flow and hence also for other flows between the home and target countries' (Luostarinen, 1989:131–2).

This model supposes that as firms gain confidence from the home market and some closest countries, they may start seeking more distant markets, but it does not exclude fast internationalization. For example, in his work, Luostarinen (1989:81) identifies some 'immediate international business involvers', i.e. firms that start internationalizing in the year of their establishment (they formed 9.4 per cent of his total sample of 941 Finnish companies). The model also acknowledges that as enterprises internationalize, they may change the method(s) of operation from more simple to more complicated ones (Welch and Luostarinen, 1988; Luostarinen, 1989; Luostarinen and Welch, 1997). In addition to the two dimensions of markets and market operation modes already discussed in the previous two models, the authors of this model add four more: sales objects, firm characteristics, decision-maker characteristics and firm competencies, including market knowledge (Welch and Luostarinen, 1988; Chetty, 1999).

While other internationalization process studies usually include export operations and foreign investments in the form of establishing foreign sales and production subsidiaries, the Finnish model examines in total 16 outward investment and non-investment marketing and production operations. It proposes that firms usually start internationalization from non-investment marketing operations and then continue with direct investment marketing operations, non-investment production operations and direct investment production operations (Luostarinen, 1989). The model suggests that several firms can speed up their internationalization by leapfrogging some stages (Chetty, 1999). It also claims that inward internationalization may precede and influence the development of a firm's outward activities and vice versa (Korhonen, 1999). For instance, many companies have their first international contacts as customers of foreign enterprises. Through these activities, they may acquire foreign market knowledge and reduce risk, uncertainty and the time required to establish new international operations (Karlsen et al., 2003). The Finnish model also shows that de-internationalization, i.e. decreasing a firm's foreign activities, completely or partially over a period, may occur at any stage, especially during the earlier steps of their export development (Welch and Luostarinen, 1988). It may be followed again by advancing steps that are called re-internationalization (Luostarinen, 1994). This, in turn, should be easier as such enterprises already have some experiential market knowledge.

The interest in born globals, international new ventures and fast internationalizers arose in the early 1990s. In the literature, such firms have been defined differently. For example, Madsen and Servais (1997:579) state that they should 'seek to derive significant advantages from the use of resources from the sale of outputs to multiple countries/continents right from their legal birth'. Kuivalainen et al. (2007) claim that true born globals should internationalize during the first three years after their establishment, enter culturally distant foreign countries and achieve at least a 25 per cent share of turnover from abroad during this period. Gabrielsson et al. (2004), in turn, note that such companies should generate at least a half of total sales from outside their own (home) continent after a maximum of 15 years from starting operations, while Hashai and Almor (2004) state that born globals should internationalize within nine years of establishment and reach at least a 75 per cent export share. In this study, true born globals are defined as firms that have entered at least two other continents besides their home continent within three years of foundation and have achieved at least a 25 per cent export share from outside their home continent during this period and at least a 75 per cent export share by the ninth year since their establishment. This relatively strict definition was selected as this guarantees that the firms that are true born globals according to the above-mentioned criteria are also classified as born globals by all the definitions introduced above.

Despite using relatively different definitions and classifications, the authors belonging to this research stream have shown that, although such companies are young and small, and their markets are very volatile (Oviatt and McDougall, 1994), they are also growth-oriented, flexible and ready to take risks (Spence and Crick, 2009). Thus, they internationalize very fast instead of moving through the numerous 'steps', 'phases' or 'stages' suggested by the U- and I-models and also, to some extent, by the Finnish (Helsinki) model. So, from the very beginning of the firm's existence, its marketplace comprises all firms (McDougall et al., 2003). Some of these firms may even start exporting before having any domestic sales (Bell, 1995). Still, this does not mean that such firms always follow a clear plan or vision: some foreign market entries may be completely unplanned (Crick and Spence, 2005). Moreover, some born globals may still internationalize gradually in terms of their market or foreign entry mode selection (Hashai and Almor, 2004).

It has been stated that these enterprises may be able to compensate for the lack of foreign market experience (Oviatt and McDougall, 1994) and their relatively modest resource base by using a narrow but very important set of skills (Wolff and Pett, 2000). They may also focus on one or a couple of relatively narrow market niches (Saarenketo et al., 2004). Such firms may use their founders' and/or owners' pre-existing knowledge (Weerawardena et al., 2007) and international business experience (McDougall et al., 2003; Zucchella et al., 2007), but also their business and personal relationships for fast internationalization. Such relationships may also help them create new relationships (Casillas et al., 2009; Freeman et al., 2010) and learn from others quickly (Saarenketo et al., 2004). In addition, such firms may manage to form strategic alliances to use foreign resources, such as manufacturing capacity or marketing, instead of establishing foreign sales or production subsidiaries (Oviatt and McDougall, 1994). Hiring internationally experienced managers and/or other staff may also allow them to become more competitive abroad (Wolff and Pett, 2000; McDougall et al., 2003; Spence and Crick, 2009). In some cases, these firms may also hire export consultants (Zucchella et al., 2007) or find internationally experienced distributors (Spence and Crick, 2009). Still, being a born global in itself will not automatically guarantee a company's long-term success or even survival (Pajunen and Maunula, 2008).

Ways of acquiring foreign market knowledge

According to Slater and Narver (1995), three main sources of information can be identified: (1) direct (own) experience, (2) organizational memory, and (3) the experience of others. Eriksson et al. (2000), in turn, identify three types of experiential knowledge: (1) business knowledge (about customers, competitors and foreign market conditions), (2) institutional knowledge (about the foreign country's government, institutional frameworks, norms, rules and values), and (3) internationalization knowledge (the firm's knowledge of its capabilities and resources necessary for internationalization). The following paragraphs introduce the ways in which necessary knowledge can be acquired.

The network approach to internationalization has partly grown from the U-model. From the point of view of the authors belonging to this research stream, an enterprise's internationalization means that it establishes and develops business relationships in networks located in other countries (Johanson and Mattsson, 1988). Thus, a firm's international progress and internationalization route depend on its total business network (Axelsson and Johanson, 1992): not only on its direct partners, but also on its partners' partners (Ford, 1998). The existing relationships can be, in turn, also used as bridges to other relationships and networks (Johanson and Vahlne, 1990).

According to this approach, relationships can tie together resources, including technology, materials and knowledge, that are required by the organization to succeed in its commercial activities (Håkansson and Snehota, 1992; McLoughlin and Horan, 2000). Through network relationships, a firm can gain access to other enterprises' knowledge without necessarily going through exactly the same experiences (Eriksson et al., 1998; Brennan and Garvey, 2009). In addition to learning about its partners' capabilities, needs and strategies, it can also obtain knowledge about their business conditions and market networks (Johanson and Johanson, 1999). Thus, by joining the nets, a typical internationalization sequence has changed from gradual international development to expansion in leaps (Hertz, 1996). For example, some firms may enter a market directly with their own manufacturing unit (Björkman and Eklund, 1996) and not start from exporting as the U- and I-, but also the Finnish (Helsinki), models suggest. On the other hand, even in networks, acquiring knowledge takes time. A better understanding of relationships and networks can only be gained later on by becoming active in the network (Blankenburg, 2001). In addition, network relationships do not only drive and facilitate internationalization, instead, in some cases, they can also inhibit it (Ford, 1998).

Substantial research has been done on the relationships between foreign direct investment (FDI) and host country exports. Several scholars have shown that foreign subsidiaries are usually more international (for example, they tend to export more) than locally owned firms. This is caused by two main reasons (Blomström, 1990; Dunning, 1994; Lauter and Rehman, 1999; Hadley and Wilson, 2003):

- Subsidiaries have better international business contacts, more advanced marketing and management skills, superior technology, greater know-how and they can use their parents' brand names;
- The owners can help them in setting up a distribution network, following industrial norms, safety standards and consumer tastes, and in dealing with product design, packaging, servicing, distribution and shaping a new product image.

There are also several other ways for acquiring foreign market knowledge besides forming network relationships with foreign owners and other long-time partners: for instance, conducting market research and making pre-entry visits (Pedersen and Petersen, 2004), but they may not provide knowledge about a particular customer's way of working, decision-making and needs for goods and services (Eriksson et al., 1997). Hiring other companies' former expatriates may be useful for obtaining such information, as they have customer contacts and first-hand knowledge of foreign markets and some foreign companies (Downes and Thomas, 1999). People employed in other firms having presence on a specific market may also have such information (Bengtsson, 2004; Brennan and Garvey, 2009). The experience and knowledge of immigrants could be used as they have often contacts and good knowledge of both their new and former home country (Pécoud, 2002). In addition, some near-market knowledge may be acquired from a company's subsidiaries located in economically and culturally similar countries

(Mitra and Golder, 2002) through acquisition of enterprises (Pajunen and Maunula, 2008) located in the target country or through cooperation with them (Bengtsson, 2004). In this area, the importance of social relationships should not be under-emphasized, but it must be kept in mind that such relationships may sometimes also inhibit a firm's internationalization (Ling-yee, 2004).

Some companies have also acquired knowledge and other assistance from trade missions, as they can combine several important export marketing facets: assessment of market opportunities, establishment of direct contacts and a high profile in a target market, assistance in seeking representation or finding prospective customers and exchanging experience with other participants (Seringhaus and Mayer, 1988). Industry associations and governmental organizations may be also very useful for knowledge acquisition (Hadley and Wilson, 2003). Sometimes firms may unintentionally come across interesting information about the internationalization strategies and practices of other enterprises and use it for quickening their own internationalization (Bengtsson, 2004).

Table 7.1 summarizes the main ways of foreign market knowledge acquisition and internationalization. Based on this table and the literature review, the following main conclusions about internationalization and the importance of knowledge acquisition can be made:

- If a firm lacks foreign market knowledge, it tends to start its internationalization from nearby countries and simpler market entry modes. Afterwards, when it has acquired the necessary (experiential) knowledge, it may progress to more distant markets and more demanding market entry/operation modes.
- Apart from direct market experience, several other ways for acquiring foreign market knowledge can be used, including conducting market research, hiring competent people, forming strategic alliances and participating in trade fairs.
- If a company has actively acquired foreign market knowledge (not necessarily through its own experience), it may considerably quicken its internationalization. Still, at times, some knowledge acquisition ways may fail and this may, instead of quickening, inhibit its internationalization process.

Methodology and case study evidence

Methodology

To examine the above described three main conclusions, case study methodology was chosen. This method has become an important form of research in the social sciences and management (Chetty, 1996). By combining

Table 7.1 The ways of foreign market knowledge acquisition and internationalization

Approach/research stream	**Foreign market knowledge acquisition is…**	**Internationalization is…**
The Uppsala model	…possible mainly through operations abroad. It is gradual and relatively slow (except in stable market conditions).	…usually long, slow and incremental, driven by experiential market knowledge acquisition.
Innovation-related internationalization models	…also possible through other sources, not just experience: for instance, foreign owners may also provide some.	…incremental and dependent on an enterprise's experiential learning (but also on other factors).
The Finnish model	…possible through experience, but also inward activities (for instance, imports and inward FDI) and other sources.	…quite slow, but some firms may do it faster (some may also pull back from abroad and return later). Knowledge is very important.
The literature on born globals/international new ventures/other fast internationalizers	…possible not only through experience but also, for example, through employing internationally experienced managers and involving foreign investors; some firms may also benefit from their entrepreneurs' earlier acquired knowledge and experience.	… very rapid (in terms of export share, but also market and entry mode selection), even if a firm lacks experience. Some companies internationalize without having any domestic sales. Still, not all firms succeed.
The network approach (to internationalization)	…possible through direct and indirect network relationships. Personal experience is not always necessary.	…dependent on network relationships. It may happen in leaps, instead of gradual expansion (but not always).
Research on the relationships between FDI and host country exports	…sometimes easy, if the firm has a foreign owner (its other subsidiaries and network relationships are also helpful).	…usually fast if a firm has a foreign owner. For locally owned enterprises it may be slower.
Other literature on internationalization and knowledge acquisition	…possible through many ways: network relationships (with the firm's owner and its owner's other subsidiaries), acquisition of foreign enterprises, conducting market research, making pre-entry visits, hiring immigrants and former expatriates of other companies, visiting trade missions, industry associations and governmental organizations and, in some cases, even by chance.	…fast if the necessary knowledge has been acquired and (personal) network relationships developed. Still, sometimes, (personal) network relationships may strongly inhibit a firm's internationalization, instead of quickening it.

previously developed theories and new empirically derived insights (Yin, 1994), it is especially appropriate in studying new research topics and areas. This method allows transcending the local boundaries of the investigated cases and capturing new layers of reality. Its use can result in developing novel, testable and empirically valid theoretical and practical insights (Eisenhardt, 1989; Tsoukas, 1989; Voss et al., 2002).

In this chapter, the multiple case study approach was used. This may reduce the depth of study (especially if an excessive number of cases have been chosen; see Piekkari et al., 2009) but it can augment the results' external validity and help to reduce observer bias (Voss et al., 2002). There is no ideal number of cases in the multiple case study approach. For example, Eisenhardt (1989) recommends choosing a number between four and ten, while Gummesson (2003) has stated that any number of cases – from one to even several hundreds – can be justified, but, naturally, this depends on the research purpose and questions. Still, it has to be acknowledged that once a pattern has emerged, each new case (field site) adds to the research data at a diminishing rate (Stuart et al., 2002). This chapter is based on three Chinese cases. These firms were selected carefully after searching several relevant websites and databases to represent the phenomenon under study: these three companies became successful true born globals although they were established without having any experiential knowledge. The cases were selected by replication logic rather than by sampling logic. In other words, these firms were chosen because the data from them could be used for replication in producing some contrasting results (Yin, 1994), rather than because they were representative of the total population (Chetty, 1996). Thus, they also represented different industries and had different owners and employees.

The information about Firm A (due to the request of the companies' owners to retain anonymity, all case firms' names and some financial data have not been disclosed) was collected in March–June 2010 through 12 interviews with the firm's general manager, deputy manager and a local city official who was asked about the economic background of the early 1990s. The total interview time was around 20 hours. The information about Firm B was collected in March–June 2010 through ten interviews with the firm's owner/manager; the total interview time was around 23 hours. The information from Firm C was collected in December 2010 through three interviews with the firm's founder, who is also the owner and general manager of the company; the total interview time was around four hours. All interviews had semi-structured open-ended questions that were sent to the interviewees before the interview. In all three case firms, the interviewees were asked additional questions about the establishment of their firm, its first export orders and other cross-border activities, the further development pattern of the company, its main reasons of success so far, the firm's future plans and strategies and other related topics. All these interviews were recorded digitally and transcribed verbatim. In addition, field notes were made. For data triangulation and ensuring that important information had not been ignored, secondary data sources such as the firms' websites, annual reports and other materials, and the business press, were also used. In addition, the interviewees also sent several documents to the authors. The full texts of the interviews and the resulting case stories were sent to all interviewees for possible corrections and clarifications. All these activities helped to establish a chain of evidence and guarantee construct validity (Lee, 1999). In the following section, the case descriptions are provided. The results are discussed in the final part of the chapter.

Case study evidence

Firm A

Firm A is located in Qinlan, Anhui Province, Eastern China. This town is well-known for its cluster of electronics firms. In the early 1990s, it started attracting foreign investors and global customers actively and its efforts were successful due to low manufacturing costs and convenient transportation links. According to the city official's words, 'there were too many orders, so, many firms could not handle all the projects'.

Firm A was established in May 1993 by two Chinese brothers that had no previous business experience. Before establishing the company, the older brother had been a construction worker, while the younger one had been a farmer. The older brother's friend was a deputy manager of an electronics company producing TV remote controls and other electronic components. The friend told him that this firm was supported by the local government and they got so many orders from abroad that they could not finish all of them on time. As that company obviously lacked production capacity, the older brother thought that it could be a perfect opportunity for him and his family to start a business. So, he and his younger brother borrowed the starting capital from their relatives, friends and also some from the construction firm. In the beginning, their production capacity was low due to lack of capital. They bought an outdated second-hand production line and employed 25 workers. Their first products were components of TV remote controls. Due to its relatively small size, the firm's structure was very simple (see Figure 7.1).

Despite outdated technology and lack of experience, the company became international from the beginning. Its first order came from a buyer in the USA. Firm A was recommended to them by another Chinese company that received 15 per cent of the firm's profits for helping them with the export process. This buyer from the USA is still Firm A's customer, but now they are communicating directly.

The company started growing fast (see Table 7.2). In 1994, its owners participated in a local annual trade fair and managed to find two German customers. In the second half of that year, their buyer from the USA

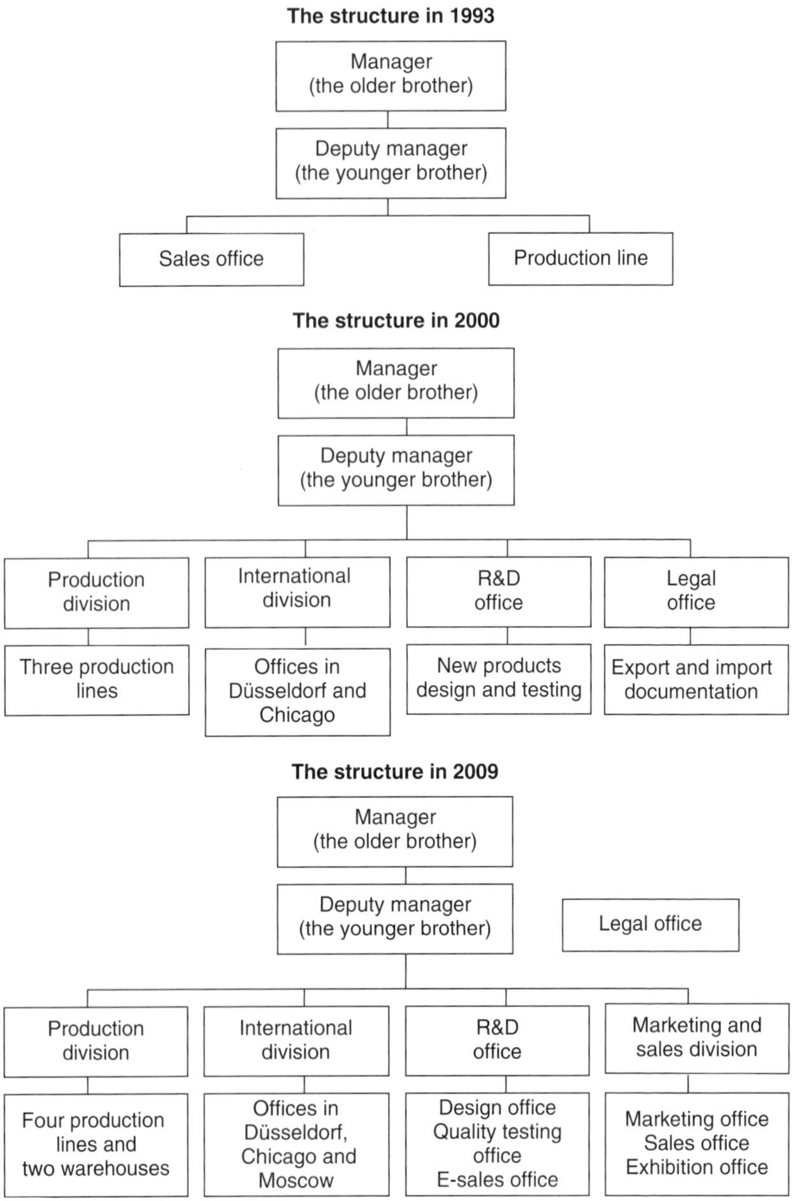

Figure 7.1 Structure of Firm A in 1993, 2000 and 2009

Table 7.2 Export performance of Firm A, 1993–2009 (US$ million)

	1993	1994	1995	1996	1997	1998	1999	2000	2001	2002	2003	2004	2005	2006	2007	2008	2009
USA	0.02	0.05	0.07	0.11	0.21	0.35	0.52	0.51	0.55	0.62	0.85	0.92	1.81	2.03	2.00	1.15	1.96
Germany		0.01	0.05	0.07	0.09	0.11	0.89	0.82	0.80	0.81	0.78	0.75	1.00	1.02	0.91	0.50	0.53
France				0.005	0.007	0.007	0.008	0.01	0.01	0.03	0.05	0.03	0.05	0.02	0.02	0.02	0.03
UK				0.003	0.004	0.003	0.005	0.007	0.011	0.015	0.012	0.02	0.02	0.02	0.011	0.01	0.02
Poland								0.01	0.02	0.04	0.05	0.03	0.12	0.33	0.29	0.28	0.41
Holland								0.03	0.05	0.05	0.07	0.12	0.23	0.55	0.62	0.51	0.58
Malaysia									0.11	0.15	0.39	0.45	0.50	0.79	0.65	0.69	0.92
Vietnam									0.08	0.09	0.16	0.19	0.30	0.62	0.52	0.52	0.62
Russia											0.10	0.22	0.50	0.61	0.49	0.47	0.61
Ukraine													0.05	0.09			0.10
Total exports	0.020	0.060	0.120	0.260	0.231	0.470	1.423	1.387	1.631	2.075	2.462	2.730	4.700	6.060	5.511	4.150	5.780

suggested Firm A to another customer from the same country. In 1995, they got a loan from the Industrial and Commercial Bank of China. After that, they became able to employ two technicians and an English translator and to build a new product line that enabled them to both produce and assemble TV remote controls. In addition, they also renewed some of their older equipment. In 1995–98, they exported to six customers from the USA, three from Germany, one from France and one from the UK.

In 1999, their growth speeded up even more: they started to use the Six Sigma Production and Management System and gained the ISO 9001 certificate. They also participated in some international electronics fairs in the USA and Germany. As a result, they also found new customers from the USA, the Netherlands and Poland. In 2000, the firm's structure was changed considerably. An R&D office was established and more staff with foreign language skills was employed. They also started exporting multi-functional remote controls and opened a new production chain of automatic dry type flame lighters.

In 2001, they also started exporting to South East Asia, including Malaysia and Vietnam. In 2003, they participated in an international trade fair in Moscow (Russia) and started exporting to Eastern Europe. Two years later, they established a sales office in Moscow with five employees who started searching for new customers in Russia, Belarus and the Ukraine. Until the end of 2007, the firm's export performance kept growing relatively fast, but, during the world financial crisis, the amount of orders declined. At the end of 2009, their sales started increasing again.

During the interviews, the managers were asked how the firm had become so successful. They answered that it had been lucky to start its activities at the beginning of the 1990s. It had always focused on exports. To internationalize fast, it has actively acquired knowledge from trade fairs and from international trade with their foreign partners. In addition, its long-term business partnerships (built on trust) have guaranteed the stability of their business.

Firm B

Firm B was established in September 1997 in Yangzhou, Jiangsu province: the large Chinese 'toy town' located along the east coast. This city's famous toy production cluster has specialized in manufacturing and exporting plush toys. This industry started developing in 1992 when some small firms started exporting hand-made toys. In 1995, the local government started offering special conditions for land use and taxation to encourage exports. Moreover, they started organizing investment seminars and trade fairs to attract foreign investors and buyers (translators were provided for local firms) and helped firms to participate in international exhibitions.

The founder of Firm B was a farmer who used to grow rice and vegetables. He had no business experience or education as he had only studied for two years in the elementary school in his village. He visited a local trade fair once and thought that he could also start a business producing some toy parts. So, he borrowed the starting capital from relatives and friends. He also took a loan from the Agricultural Bank of China by using his and his parents' houses as collateral. The first 20 workers were his relatives, friends and some other vegetable growers from his village. At first, half of them did not even know how to do needlework (they did not have any machinery in the beginning).

The founder rented a small warehouse and became the manager of his company. He participated in a trade fair in 1997, but did not get any orders as potential foreign buyers were not certain that this young firm could produce in the necessary quantities. In November 1997, he got the first order from another firm in Yangzhou to make 5,000 red hearts for plush bears. They finished the order on time and got the first payment. These hearts were exported to the USA by another company. In the first eight months, they kept getting orders from other Chinese firms to supply different toy parts.

In the second half of 1998, the manager decided that, in the long term, remaining a subcontractor for other enterprises from Yangzhou would not be a good strategy. So, the company started to search for direct export opportunities. The owner got more capital from his wife's relative in Nanjing and also an additional loan from the Agricultural Bank of China. By the end of 1998, the firm had managed to build up its own half-automatic production lines and it had also bought some new sewing machines. The manager also employed 12 additional workers to operate the machinery. In 1999, he again participated in a local trade fair and found three customers at once: two from the USA and one from the Netherlands (for export data, see Table 7.3). Firm B started to produce half-finished toys for them. Soon after, he found five more customers: three from the USA and two from Germany. In 1999, the company ended all domestic projects and concentrated on exports only.

As the exports were very successful, Firm B established its own sales department in 2000 and started participating in international fairs in Cologne and California. This has increased the number of orders from Germany and the USA. In 2003, a new production line of plush toys was

Table 7.3 Export performance of Firm B, 1999–2009 (RMB tens of millions)

	1999	2000	2001	2002	2003	2004	2005	2006	2007	2008	2009
USA	0.191	0.453	0.785	0.826	0.999	1.112	1.491	1.992	2.755	2.023	2.235
Netherlands	0.138	0.198	0.239	0.200	0.398	0.555	0.626	0.799	0.703	0.655	0.738
Germany	0.121	0.352	0.688	0.795	0.999	2.001	2.322	2.928	3.101	3.423	3.502
Finland					0.090	0.125	0.233	0.300	0.252	0.221	0.249
Russia									0.122	0.100	0.152
Romania									0.200	0.205	0.229
Total exports	0.450	1.003	1.712	1.821	2.486	3.793	4.672	6.019	7.133	6.627	7.105

opened. The firm received the quality licence for exporting toys from the China Import and Export Commodity Inspection Bureau and the licence for self-administrated imports and exports from the Chinese Ministry of Foreign Trade and Economic Cooperation. In 2004, Firm B obtained the ISO 9001 issued in 2000 certificate, and also the Wal-Mart and Target certificates. They hired three part-time toy designers from the USA and decided to open a refrigerator-magnet production line. Three representative offices (with seven employees in total) were opened in Hamburg, Los Angeles and Moscow (see Figure 7.2).

The company was not as successful in 2007–09 due to the financial crisis, but still they started exporting to new markets including Russia and Romania. Although the orders from the USA declined, they managed to keep most of their European customers. In the second half of 2009, the firm's export performance improved and they kept exporting to six countries and importing cotton and other materials from the Netherlands and Finland (see Table 7.4).

To the question of how Firm B had become successful, the manager explained that the main reason was that the government attracted foreign investors and customers to the city, so even people like him could find business opportunities and connections for the future. In addition, they focused on exports and participated successfully in international trade fairs and exhibitions. Thus, they have kept learning and improving during all these years. The last reason he mentioned was quality control, as good quality keeps customers. In 2011, the manager plans to start exporting to

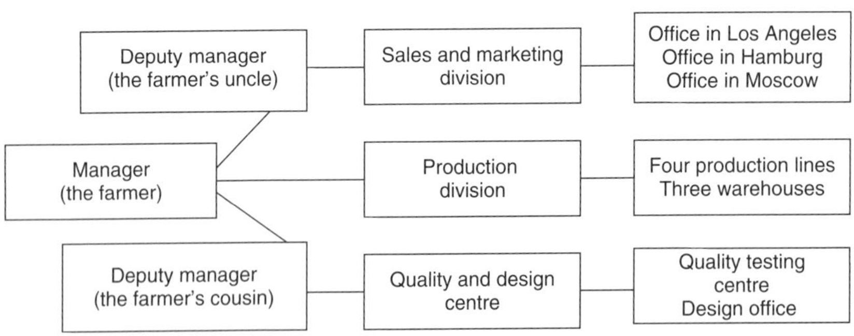

Figure 7.2 Structure of Firm B in 2010

Table 7.4 Import performance of Firm B, 2003–09 (RMB tens of millions)

	2003	2004	2005	2006	2007	2008	2009
Netherlands	1.12	2.23	2.25	2.98	3.03	3.12	3.23
Finland	1.01	2.52	2.99	3.08	4.55	3.39	4.00

South Asian countries and establish a representative office in Ho Chi Min, Vietnam. In 2015 he plans to open a new factory.

Firm C

Firm C was established at the end of 1998 in Tiangchang. This city was among the first in Anhui province (Eastern China) that was opened up to attract foreign customers and investors. In the mid-1990s, the city officials started developing foreign business contacts following the example of a neighbouring Jiangsu province. In 1996, they started offering special conditions for land use and developed more favourable taxation policies to encourage exporting. As Tiangchang had a strong light industry, especially clothing and footwear production, main attention was paid to developing these production areas. Learning from the experience of other cities, they started organizing investment seminars and trade fairs and also invited business people from other parts of China. As such an approach was very efficient, they also started inviting foreign investors and customers from 1997. Through these events, they identified those companies that could have a good exporting potential, while local enterprises got a good opportunity to find foreign partners.

The founder of Firm C participated in one of the export promotion events in 1998. He heard that foreign countries, especially the USA and Germany, had a large demand for footwear products and so he decided to start a business to meet the demand, although he had no background in this industry. (At that time, he was in his mid-thirties. He joined the military after graduating from high school. After finishing his service, he returned to Tiangchang and became a sales assistant in a shop. He also tried some other jobs but had not worked in the footwear business. He did not speak English and had never been abroad.)

The founder had a couple of former high school classmates who were employed by a local clothing producer (a Chinese–US joint venture). One of them was the head of its purchasing division. The founder contacted him and discussed his business ideas and decided to go forward with his business. At first, he employed 16 workers: local unemployed youths (for the structure of Firm C, see Figure 7.3). He got the starting capital from his parents (enough to acquire 12 second-hand half-automatic machines) and started production in his father's old warehouse. The firm's first customer was the Chinese–US joint venture where his former classmate worked: Firm C started producing some parts of footwear accessories and its customer exported the finished footwear to the USA.

The partnership was relatively successful for Firm C as the relationship with its only customer was stable. Still, the founder was not completely satisfied with his firm's business performance, so he started looking for other opportunities. He joined a local trade fair in spring 1999 and found a couple of customers from the USA who were interested in buying shoe accessories

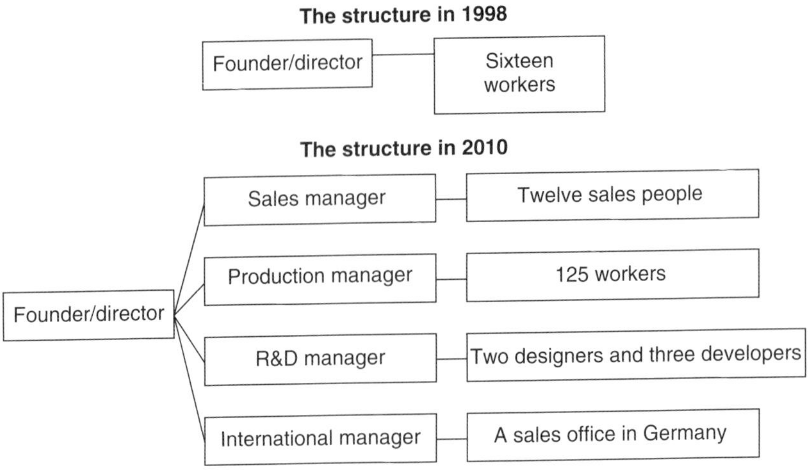

Figure 7.3 Structure of Firm C in 1998 and 2010

from Tiangchang and selling them in their home country. So, Firm C closed a deal with one of them and started exporting to the USA. At first, it involved a local trade agency that was familiar with the necessary export documentation and customs procedures.

The exports to the USA were successful and this helped Firm C to get other orders from some other firms located there, but also some from China. In the second part of 1999, the other American buyer whom the founder of Firm C had met at the trade fair also started ordering from them. By the end of 1999, the company had increased the number of employees to 48 and its export share had reached 27 per cent. The construction of a new factory building (adjacent to the old warehouse) began. Firm C employed an English teacher from a nearby high school as a part-time translator.

To cut exporting costs and become more flexible, Firm C decided to apply for the licence of self-administered imports and exports issued by the Chinese Ministry of Foreign Trade and Economic Cooperation. The licence was granted in 2000. In the same year, the founder visited the Guangzhou International Trade Fair and found two customers from Germany and one from the Netherlands. By the end of 2000, the firm's number of employees exceeded 100: 75 per cent of them were workers, 15 per cent technical staff, while the rest were managerial and sales staff. Its export share increased to 95 per cent of turnover as the firm decided to stop its cooperation with its first customer, i.e. the local Chinese–US joint venture.

In 2001, Firm C got a loan from the Industrial and Commercial Bank of China to update the machinery. The company bought a second-hand (but relatively up-to-date) computer-operated embroidery machine and a CAD computer design system for apparel. This increased the firm's production capacity and helped to get larger and more complicated orders. In 2001, the founder, his deputy manager and translator visited trade fairs in the USA and Germany. Although they did not rent a booth for their firm, they managed to find many useful contacts. One of them was a new customer from the UK. As the firm had enough export orders, it had no sales in China in 2001.

The firm's growth continued after 2001. In 2003, they started exporting to Japan and, in 2004, Russia followed. In that year, the firm also received the Quality Award of Anhui Province and the ISO 9001 certificate. In addition, it established a design division which also became responsible for R&D. The firm opened two new production lines and established a sales office (with two sales managers) in Hamburg, Germany. In 2007, the firm started exporting to the Ukraine.

The economic crisis was not favourable for Firm C as some customers from the USA decreased their orders, but it managed to get more orders from other countries. Its exports even increased (see Table 7.5).

The founder of the firm thought that the real reason behind its success was perfect timing. In the 1990s, it was possible to start a successful business without much knowledge: it was enough to work hard and have good personal connections, while nowadays it is much harder to start a business without experience and knowledge (for this reason, he sent his daughter to get her MBA in the USA). In the beginning, the local government's help was also important for the firm's successful development as they attracted investors and customers to the city and helped local people to develop new business connections. The founder added that now his firm's success is mainly based on constant innovation, high quality and active marketing.

In 2012, Firm C plans to start exporting to South Asia and in 2013 they wish to establish a sales office in Moscow. They also plan to build a new factory by 2015, invest more in R&D and develop their brand further.

Discussion, conclusions and implications

As was concluded from the literature review, internationalization may be slow and incremental, but it may also be very fast, as in the case of born globals, international new ventures and other fast internationalizers. If a firm manages to acquire necessary foreign market knowledge by other ways than through experience, it may internationalize faster: by using more advanced foreign market entry modes and by starting its internationalization from farther markets.

The case results are summarized in Table 7.6. They demonstrate that these companies managed to acquire foreign market knowledge through their cooperation partners, but also through trade fairs and exhibitions, and by hiring some skilled staff. As a result, their internationalization has been

Table 7.5 Export performance of Firm C, 1999–2010 (RMB millions)

	1999	2000	2001	2002	2003	2004	2005	2006	2007	2008	2009	2010 (estimated)
USA	0.6	1.1	2.6	3.3	5.3	7.9	11.8	11.5	9.5	9.3	10.8	11.9
Germany		0.9	1.5	3.2	6.5	7.1	8.9	10.5	10.2	9.1	9.9	10.5
Netherlands		0.2	0.9	1.1	1.5	3.0	3.0	3.0	2.5	2.9	3.3	4.5
Japan					0.3	1.0	3.0	5.5	6.3	7.5	7.8	7.7
Russia						0.3	1.5	2.3	2.3	3.5	3.0	4.7
Ukraine									0.1	0.3	0.5	0.5
Total exports	0.6	2.2	5.0	7.6	13.6	19.3	28.2	32.8	30.9	32.6	35.3	39.8

Table 7.6 An overview of the internationalization of the three case companies and their ways of foreign market knowledge acquisition

	Foreign market knowledge acquisition	Internationalization
Firm A (electronics; founded in May 1993)	Initially, the firm's owners/managers had no educational background or business experience. The first customer came through another firm. The firm actively participated in trade fairs: at first, only in China, but since 1999 also in the USA and Germany. In 1995, they hired two technicians They have also tried to learn from their long-term cooperation partners.	The first customer was found in 1993 from the USA; in 1994, the firm also started exporting to Germany. In 1996, France and the UK followed. Since 2000, it also exports to Poland and the Netherlands; from 2001, to Malaysia and Vietnam; from 2003, to Russia; and from 2005, to the Ukraine (but has not exported to the latter every year). It has sales offices in Düsseldorf (Germany, founded in 2000), Chicago (USA, 2000) and Moscow (Russia, 2005). It has never had any local sales.
Firm B (toys; founded in September 1997)	Initially, the firm's owner/manager had no suitable educational background or business experience. At first, he tried to learn from his Chinese cooperation partners. He participated actively in investment and trade fairs: at first, only in China (financed by the Chinese government), but since 2000 also in the USA and Germany. In 2004, he hired toy designers from the USA.	First indirect exports started in 1997 (to the USA), first direct exports in 1999 (to the USA, the Netherlands and Germany). From 1999, it had no local sales. Since 2003, it also exports to Finland and from 2007, to Russia and Romania. In 2004, it established sales offices in Hamburg (Germany), Los Angeles (USA) and Moscow (Russia). It imports from the Netherlands and Finland. In 2011, it plans to start exporting to South Asian countries and establish a representative office in Ho Chi Min, Vietnam.
Firm C (footwear; founded at the end of 1998)	Initially, the firm's owner/manager had no educational background or experience of the footwear industry. At first, he tried to learn from his former classmate, but also from the firm's initial partner: a local trade agency. He participated actively in investment and trade fairs: at first, only in China (financed by the Chinese government), but since 2001 also in the USA and Germany.	First indirect exports started in 1998 (to the USA) and first direct exports in 1999 (to the USA; in 2000, the Netherlands and Germany followed). Local sales finished at the end of 2000. Since 2003, it also exports to Japan; since 2004, to Russia; and since 2007, to the Ukraine. In 2004, it established a sales office in Hamburg (Germany). In 2012, it plans to start exporting to South Asia and in 2013 it wishes to establish a sales office in Moscow (Russia).

relatively successful. Firm A has never had any sales in China and its first customer, a firm from the USA, still orders from them. In addition, this company exports to Germany, France, the UK, Poland, the Netherlands, Malaysia, Vietnam, Russia and the Ukraine (but has not exported to the latter every year). It has sales offices in Düsseldorf (Germany), Chicago (USA) and Moscow (Russia). Firm B has also internationalized successfully. Its first products were later indirectly exported to the USA, and in less than two years since foundation it ceased all local sales. In addition to the USA, it started exporting to the Netherlands and Germany. Soon, Finland, Russia and Romania followed. In addition, the firm has sales offices in Hamburg (Germany), Los Angeles (USA) and Moscow (Russia). It imports from the Netherlands and Finland and soon plans to start exporting to South Asian countries and to establish a representative office in Vietnam. Firm C's internationalization can be also regarded as a success. Its first products were later indirectly exported to the USA, and in about two years since establishment it ceased all local sales.

Comparing the empirical results with the theoretical conclusions, it becomes evident that, in all three investigated cases, the internationalization process has been quite different from the one predicted by the Uppsala (Johanson and Wiedersheim-Paul, 1975; Johanson and Vahlne, 1977, 1990) and the innovation-related internationalization models (Cavusgil, 1980; Czinkota, 1982; Reid, 1983; Fina and Rugman, 1996) and, to some extent, also by the Finnish (or Helsinki) model (Welch and Luostarinen, 1988; Luostarinen, 1989; Luostarinen and Welch, 1997). They argue that firms without prior experiential knowledge internationalize slowly, selecting nearest markets first, using exporting as the only operation mode for a relatively long period. Even if we take into account these models' exceptions (Wiedersheim-Paul et al., 1978; Johanson and Vahlne, 1990; Vahlne and Johanson, 2002), we can still state that they were not shown in the case of the three investigated firms: their markets were not stable, these firms were not large, their owners/managers did not have any previous business experience, the companies were not foreign-owned and they were not active in the IT sector. Moreover, the three case firms did not experience inward internationalization before their outward internationalization that could have quickened the development of their outward activities (Korhonen, 1999).

All three case companies chose the USA and Germany as their first foreign markets (Firm C also entered the Netherlands in the year when it started exporting to Germany) although they did not have any previous experiential knowledge of these markets. Their founders (who were also owners and managers) had not studied or worked on these markets and they had also not been employed by any firms with activities in these countries. Firms A and B established sales offices in the USA, Germany and Russia while C still has only one, in Germany, but plans to establish one in Russia in 2013. Firm A has never had any domestic sales while Firm B ceased all less than two years since foundation and Firm C less than three years since establishment. Also, all three companies have mainly concentrated on exporting to other continents (Firm A also has some activities in Vietnam and Malaysia, but these markets were entered eight years after the first foreign market, the USA, was entered; Firm C entered its first Asian foreign market, Japan, five years after establishment; for both firms the share of these markets has never exceeded 25 per cent of total exports). Thus, all three case firms can be called true born globals. They are also born globals according to all the criteria suggested by Madsen and Servais (1997), Gabrielsson et al. (2004), Hashai and Almor (2004) and Kuivalainen et al. (2007).

Although the chapter is based only on three cases, some managerial implications can be drawn. It is evident that if a company wishes to internationalize quickly, it should try to obtain foreign market knowledge very actively through different channels. These three companies mainly concentrated on participating in trade fairs and exhibitions, but also on learning from their friends and cooperation partners. Although they have become successful, other companies should also concentrate on other ways of knowledge acquisition. Some of them, for instance involving foreign investors or creating strategic alliances or joint ventures, may also be beneficial for acquiring capital, ideas and raw materials, developing products and raising a company's efficiency. Some others, for example employing foreign immigrants, may not instantly bring such benefits, but, in the future, they may also prove very useful in other ways, in addition to knowledge acquisition.

It is also necessary to note that having or sharing foreign market knowledge in itself will not guarantee a company's automatic success on one, several or all foreign markets. This may depend on many factors both controllable (for instance, product quality and design) and uncontrollable (for example, the global economic crisis or the changes in some countries' economic policies) by the enterprise. Sometimes, despite having made large efforts, internationalization may fail in some sense: for example, a firm's activities on a specific market may be temporarily stopped. Thus, both foreign markets and sources of foreign market information should be selected with great care.

As this chapter is based only on three Chinese cases and the subject has still not been very widely researched, it is important to study the ways of foreign market knowledge acquisition and their impact on the internationalization processes further. Without a doubt, more cases should be examined. It would be interesting to compare different countries, firms and industries: for example, to find out whether enterprises from smaller countries tend to use different ways of knowledge acquisition; whether there is a difference between more advanced and less advanced countries; and between smaller and larger, or older (more experienced) and more recently established, firms. One could study the likelihood of more international firms and industries obtaining knowledge via different routes – for instance if they cooperate among each other more or less intensively or if they are more or less active in involving foreign investors or using the services of export agencies – and, if they do so, then how much this has impacted on their international success. Collecting some survey evidence may also be useful for making more general conclusions about these issues.

Further research may also focus on the type of necessary foreign market knowledge (about a specific customer, about the ways of acquiring state support, about tax deductions on a specific market, about internationalization as a process, in general, and so on) that determines the means of its acquisition. The costs and benefits of foreign market knowledge acquisition should also be studied more thoroughly. This would enable researchers to help firms to select the right knowledge acquisition methods for them and, as a result, to internationalize faster. It is very important to examine the problems and failures of knowledge acquisition and internationalization and to discuss how 'successful internationalization' should be defined, i.e. whether it is important to take into account (only) the number of foreign markets or foreign subsidiaries, export share or market share, net profit or other data. Only after examining these issues does it become possible to offer more specific managerial and export or foreign direct investment policy suggestions for achieving successful internationalization.

Note

The research was financed by the Estonian Science Foundation's Grant no. 7405 and the target financing of the Estonian Ministry of Education and Research no. 0180037s08.

References

Axelsson, B. and Johanson, J. (1992). Foreign market entry: the textbook versus the network view, in B. Axelsson and G. Easton (eds), *Industrial Networks: A New View of Reality*. London: Routledge, pp. 218–34.

Bell, J. (1995). The internationalization of small computer software firms: a further challenge to 'stage' theories. *European Journal of Marketing*, 29(8), 60–75.

Bengtsson, L. (2004). Explaining born globals: an organisational learning perspective on the internationalisation process. *International Journal of Globalisation and Small Business*, 1(1), 28–41.

Björkman, I. and Eklund, M. (1996). The sequence of operational modes used by Finnish investors in Germany. *Journal of International Marketing*, 4(1), 33–55.

Blankenburg, D. (2001). A network approach to foreign market entry, in K. Möller and D.T. Wilson (eds), *Business Marketing: An Interaction and Network Perspective*, 2nd edn. London: Kluwer Academic, pp. 375–405.

Blomström, M. (1990). *Transnational Corporations and Manufacturing Exports from Developing Countries*. New York: United Nations.

Brennan, L. and Garvey, D. (2009). The role of knowledge in internationalization, *Research in International Business and Finance*, 23(2), 120–33.

Casillas, J.C., Moreno, A.M., Acedo, F.J., Gallego, M.A. and Ramos, E. (2009). An integrative model of the role of knowledge in the internationalization process. *Journal of World Business*, 44(3), 311–22.

Cavusgil, S.T. (1980). On the internationalization process of firms. *European Research*, 8(6), 273–81.

Chetty, S. (1996). The case study method for research in small- and medium-sized firms. *International Small Business Journal*, 15(1), 73–85.

Chetty, S. (1999). Dimensions of internationalisation of manufacturing firms in the apparel industry. *European Journal of Marketing*, 33(1/2), 121–42.

Crick, D. and Spence, M. (2005). The internationalisation of 'high performing' UK high-tech SMEs: a study of planned and unplanned strategies. *International Business Review*, 14(2), 167–85.

Czinkota, M.R. (1982). *Export Development Strategies: US Promotion Policies*. London: Praeger.

Downes, M. and Thomas, A.S. (1999). Managing overseas assignments to build organizational knowledge. *Human Resource Planning Journal*, 22(4), 33–48.

Dunning, J.H. (1994). Re-evaluating the benefits of foreign direct investment. *Transnational Corporations*, 3(1), 23–51.

Eisenhardt, K.M. (1989). Building theories from case study research. *Academy of Management Review*, 14(4), 532–50.

Eriksson, K., Johanson, J., Majkgård, A. and Sharma, D.D. (1997). Experiential knowledge and cost in the internationalization process. *Journal of International Business Studies*, 28(2), 337–60.

Eriksson, K., Johanson, J., Majkgård, A. and Sharma, D.D. (1998). Time and experience in the internationalization process, in A. Majkgård (ed.), *Experiential Knowledge in the Internationalization Process of Service Firms*. Uppsala: Department of Business Studies, pp. 185–217.

Eriksson, K., Majkgård, A. and Sharma, D.D. (2000). Path dependence and knowledge development in the internationalization process. *Management International Review*, 40(4), 307–28.

Fina, E. and Rugman, A.M. (1996). A test of internalization theory and internationalization theory: the Upjohn company. *Management International Review*, 36(3), 199–213.

Ford, D. (1998). Two decades of interaction, relationships and networks, in P. Naudé and P. Turnbull (eds), *Network Dynamics in International Marketing*. Oxford: Elsevier, pp. 3–15.

Freeman, S., Hutchings, K., Lazaris, M. and Zyngier, S. (2010). A model of rapid knowledge development: the smaller born-global firm. *International Business Review*, 19(1), 70–84.

Gabrielsson, M., Sasi, V. and Darling, J. (2004). Finance strategies of rapidly-growing Finnish SMEs: born internationals and born globals. *European Business Review*, 16(6), 590–604.

Gummesson, E. (2003). All research is interpretive. *Journal of Business & Industrial Marketing*, 18(6–7), 482–92.

Hadley, R.D. and Wilson, H.I.M. (2003). The network model of internationalisation and experiential knowledge. *International Business Review*, 12(6), 697–717.

Håkansson, H. and Snehota, I. (1992). Analysing business relationships, in H. Håkansson and I. Snehota (eds), *Developing Relationships in Business Networks*. London: Routledge, pp. 24–49.

Hashai, N. and Almor, T. (2004). Gradually internationalizing 'born global' firms: an oxymoron? *International Business Review*, 13(4), 465–83.

Hertz, S. (1996). The dynamics of international strategic alliances. *International Studies of Management and Organization*, 26(2), 104–30.
Johanson, J. and Johanson, M. (1999). Developing business in Eastern European networks, in J.-Å. Törnroos and J. Nieminen (eds), *Business Entry in Eastern Europe: A Network and Learning Approach with Case Studies*. Helsinki: Kikimora Publications, pp. 46–71.
Johanson, J. and Mattsson, L.-G. (1988). Internationalization in industrial systems: a network approach, in N. Hood and J.-E. Vahlne (eds), *Strategies in Global Competition*. London: Croom Helm, pp. 287–314.
Johanson, J. and Vahlne, J.-E. (1977). The internationalization process of the firm: a model of knowledge development and increasing foreign market commitments. *Journal of International Business Studies*, 8(1), 23–32.
Johanson, J. and Vahlne, J.-E. (1990). The mechanism of internationalization. *International Marketing Review*, 7(4), 11–24.
Johanson, J. and Wiedersheim-Paul, F. (1975). The internationalization of the firm: four Swedish Cases. *Journal of Management Studies*, 12(3), 305–22.
Karlsen, T., Silseth, P.R., Benito, G.R.G. and Welch, L.S. (2003). Knowledge, internationalization of the firm, and inward–outward connections. *Industrial Marketing Management*, 32(5), 385–96.
Korhonen, H. (1999). Inward–outward internationalization of small and medium enterprises. PhD thesis, Helsinki School of Economics and Business Administration, Finland.
Kuivalainen, O., Sundqvist, S. and Servais, P. (2007). Firms' degree of born-globalness, international entrepreneurial orientation and export performance. *Journal of World Business*, 42(3), 253–67.
Lauter, G.P. and Rehman, S.S. (1999). Central and East European trade orientation and FDI flows: preparation for EU membership. *International Trade Journal*, 13(1), 35–52.
Lee, T.W. (1999). *Using Qualitative Methods in Organizational Research*. Thousand Oaks, CA: Sage.
Leonidou, L.C. and Katsikeas, C.S. (1996). The export development process: an integrative review of empirical models. *Journal of International Business Studies*, 27(3), 517–51.
Ling-yee, L. (2004). An examination of the foreign market knowledge of exporting firms based in the People's Republic of China: its determinants and effect on export intensity. *Industrial Marketing Management*, 33(7), 561–72.
Luostarinen, R. (1989). *Internationalization of the Firm: An Empirical Study of the Internationalization of Firms with Small and Open Domestic Markets, with Special Emphasis on Lateral Rigidity as a Behavioral Characteristic in Strategic Decision-Making*. Helsinki: Kyriiri OY.
Luostarinen, R. (1994). *Research for Action: Internationalization of Finnish Firms and their Response to Global Challenges*. Finland: UNU Wider.
Luostarinen, R. and Welch, L. (1997). *International Business Operations*. Helsinki: Kyriiri OY.
Madsen, T.K. and Servais, P. (1997). The internationalisation of born globals: an evolutionary process? *International Business Review*, 6(6), 561–83.
McDougall, P.P., Oviatt, B.M. and Shrader, R.C. (2003). A comparison of international and domestic new ventures. *Journal of International Entrepreneurship*, 1(1), 59–82.
McLoughlin, D. and Horan, C. (2000). Business marketing: perspectives from the markets-as-networks approach. *Industrial Marketing Management*, 29(4), 285–92.

Mitra, D. and Golder, P.N. (2002). Whose culture matters? Near-market knowledge and its impact on foreign market entry timing. *Journal of Marketing Research*, 39(3), 350–65.

Morgan, R.E. and Katsikeas, C.S. (1997). Theories of international trade, foreign direct investment and firm internationalization: a critique. *Management Decision*, 35(1/2), 68–78.

Morgan, N.A., Zou, S., Vorhies, D.W. and Katsikeas, C.S. (2003). Experiential and informational knowledge, architectural marketing capabilities, and the adaptive performance of export ventures: a cross-national study. *Decision Sciences*, 34(2), 287–321.

Oviatt, B.M. and McDougall, P.P. (1994). Toward a theory of international new ventures. *Journal of International Business Studies*, 25(1), 45–64.

Pajunen, K. and Maunula, M. (2008). Internationalisation: a co-evolutionary perspective. *Scandinavian Journal of Management*, 24(3), 247–58.

Pécoud, A. (2002). Weltoffenheit schafft jobs: Turkish entrepreneurship and multiculturalism in Berlin. *International Journal of Urban and Regional Research*, 26(3), 494–507.

Pedersen, T. and Petersen, B. (2004). Learning about foreign markets: are entrant firms exposed to a 'shock effect'? *Journal of International Marketing*, 12(1), 103–23.

Piekkari, R., Welch, C. and Paavilainen, E. (2009). The case study as disciplinary convention: evidence from international business journals. *Organizational Research Methods*, 12(3), 567–89.

Reid, S.D. (1983). Firm internationalization, transaction costs, and strategic behaviour. *International Marketing Review*, 1(2), 45–56.

Rogers, E.M. (1962). *Diffusion of Innovations*. New York, NY: Free Press.

Saarenketo, S., Puumalainen, K., Kuivalainen, O. and Kyläheiko, K. (2004). Dynamic knowledge-related learning processes in internationalizing high-tech SMEs. *International Journal of Production Economics*, 89 (3), 363–78.

Seringhaus, F.H.R. and Mayer, C.S. (1988). Different approaches to foreign market entry between users and non-users of trade missions. *European Journal of Marketing*, 22(10), 7–18.

Slater, S.F. and Narver, J.C. (1995). Market orientation and the learning organization. *Journal of Marketing*, 59(3), 63–74.

Spence, M. and Crick, D. (2009). An exploratory study of Canadian international new venture firms' development in overseas markets. *Qualitative Market Research: An International Journal*, 12(2), 208–33.

Stuart, I., McCutcheon, D., Handfield, R., McLachlin, R. and Samson, D. (2002). Effective case research in operations management: a process perspective. *Journal of Operations Management*, 20(5), 419–33.

Tsoukas, H. (1989). The validity of idiographic research explanations. *Academy of Management Review*, 14(4), 551–61.

Vahlne, J.-E. and Johanson, J. (2002). New technology, new companies, new business environments and new internationalisation processes? in V. Havila, M. Forsgren and H. Håkansson (eds), *Critical Perspectives of Internationalisation*. Amsterdam: Pergamon, pp. 209–27.

Voss, C., Tsikriktsis, N. and Frohlich, M. (2002). Case research in operations management. *International Journal of Operations and Production Management*, 22(2), 195–219.

Weerawardena, J., Sullivan Mort, G., Liesch, P.W. and Knight, G. (2007). Conceptualizing accelerated internationalization in the born global firm: a dynamic capabilities perspective. *Journal of World Business*, 42(3), 294–306.

Welch, L.S. and Luostarinen, R. (1988). Internationalization: evolution of a concept. *Journal of General Management*, 14(2), 34–57.

Wiedersheim-Paul, F., Olson, H.C. and Welch, L.S. (1978). Pre-export activity: the first step in internationalization. *Journal of International Business Studies*, 9(1), 47–58.

Wolff, J.A. and Pett, T.L. (2000). Internationalization of small firms: an examination of export competitive patterns, firm size, and export performance. *Journal of Small Business Management*, 38(2), 34–47.

Yin, R.K. (1994). *Case Study Research Design and Methods*. London: Sage.

Zucchella, S., Palamara, G. and Denicolai, S. (2007). The drivers of the early internationalization of the firm. *Journal of World Business*, 42(3), 268–80.

8

From National Leaders to Global Players: Evidence from Russian MNEs in the High Technology Sector

Andrei Panibratov

Introduction

In this chapter the process of internationalization of Russian hi-tech multinational enterprises (MNEs) is analysed with a focus on telecommunications and IT companies that are expanding abroad. Of particular interest are the choices that Russian MNEs make when facing entry challenges, environmental constraints and investment alternatives.

While the theory of firm internationalization has been built to explain the motives and strategies of firms from developed countries (mostly European and North American) that are expanding to developing markets, there have been several attempts to test the applicability of the established concepts to explain internationalization of companies from emerging economies. MNEs and foreign direct investment (FDI) from developing economies were investigated in the early pioneering studies of Heenan and Keegan (1979), Lall (1983), Lecraw (1983) and Wells (1983), and in more recent works of Globerman and Shapiro (2006), Benito and Narula (2007), Goldstein and Shaw (2007), Luo and Tung (2007) and Sethi (2009).

Despite the interest and novelty of the topic of emerging multinationals, the focus of most studies has been on Chinese, Indian and Brazilian MNEs, overlooking their Russian counterparts. While a range of studies on Russian MNEs was developed after the second part of the 1990s (Bulatov, 1998, 2001; Heinrich, 2003, 2006; Kets de Vries et al., 2004; Crane et al., 2005; Filatotchev et al., 2007; Liuhto and Vahtra, 2007; Kalotay, 2008;) the research in this field remains scarce.

Previous research showed that FDI legislation varies across industries even in the same host country (Beamish, 1993; Zaheer and Zaheer, 1997). Gaining a firm legal station is considered as particularly important for MNEs in the context of developing economies due to frequent government interference and strong environmental volatility (Hoskisson et al., 2000; Zhou and Li, 2008). In industries encouraged by the home governments, such as infrastructure and telecommunications, foreign firms face relatively favourable or stable policies (Luo, 2005) in sectors where the government has a strong tendency to protect local companies, though MNEs face an unfavourable regulatory environment.

According to Child and Rodrigues (2005) as well as Luo and Tung (2007), emerging MNEs use international expansion as a springboard to compensate for their competitive disadvantages, to counter-attack global rivals in their home country market, to alleviate constraints and explore preferential treatment from the home market, and to exploit their competitive advantages in other developing markets. The application of these motives towards Russian MNEs in the hi-tech industry may be promising in terms of understanding their results and prospects.

The structure of this chapter has the following objectives. Firstly, the literature of emerging multinationals in general and Russian MNEs, in particular concerning their outward FDI (OFDI), is analysed. Next, the case-study-based methodology is introduced and explained. The main part consists of the case studies of four MNEs in the Russian hi-tech sector. The chapter ends with a discussion on how the adopted theoretical approach and supportive findings can advance new research on Russian MNEs and their OFDI.

Conceptual framework

Earlier studies on emerging multinationals and Russian MNEs

While MNEs from developed economies concentrate on advanced technology and marketing skills to differentiate their products (Wells, 1983), and see their competitive advantage in having a large variety of assets, as well as in integrating operations across national boundaries (Bartlett and Ghoshal, 1989), MNEs from emerging economies have been considered to rely mostly on maturing technologies, originally developed in the Western countries. The prototypes of Russian MNEs already existed in the time of the former USSR. In Russia as well as in China, most of the leading MNEs had roots going back to the days of strict central planning, long before they were partially or wholly privatized (Ramamurti, 2008). In his study of foreign operations of Soviet firms (which were all state-owned), Hamilton (1986) refers to these companies as 'red multinationals'. His observations show that in most cases these firms carried out only marketing and sales operations. Few of these red multinationals showed signs of developing as Western multinationals had done (McMillan, 1987).

The former USSR exercised strict control upon these companies, and they were usually majority-owned by their Soviet parents (Vahtra, 2006). Most of these firms were involved in supporting Russian exports abroad. They conducted their activities very intensively, selling more than half of all Soviet exports.

After the collapse of the Soviet Union at the end of 1980s, Russian companies were mostly involved in restructuring and consolidating assets inside the country. After having gained enough power, they started to look for foreign markets. Several studies have documented the process of transformation of these former state-owned enterprises (see for example King et al., 1995).

A wave of FDI from Russia started to grow much faster at the end of the 1990s, the main share of which took the form of cross-border mergers and acquisitions as well as greenfield investments. Russian investors preferred to apply mergers and acquisitions to their international expansion in order to go for quick returns on their investments and to compensate for the lack of internationalization experience.

The outward investment policy of Russian firms changed overtime. Kuznetsov (2010) points out a special type of Russian MNEs. These are companies with foreign capital participation. Thanks to these inward investments, Russian companies can reinforce significantly their own investment activities.

Although the majority of Russian MNEs are believed to be exclusively engaged in natural endowment based industries, the pioneering study of Elenkov (1995) helps us to understand the roots of the technology-based internationalization of Russian companies. He has highlighted and investigated the importance of the military sector in the context of the coopetition (cooperation and competition) of Russian and Western technologically developed firms in the aerospace industry. While the non-military sector was technologically obsolete, due to the lack of strong technical staff, close linkages with technologically advanced institutes using modern equipment, the strong Russian military industry was nurtured at the expense of the largely neglected civilian sector (ibid.). While promising, the Russian military sector, more than any other hi-tech industry, has suffered from serious expansion-related restrictions based on the sensitive nature of knowledge and technology transfer relating to this sector. The Russian aerospace MNEs have also introduced a new dimension of competition, which has been characterized by aggressive development and effective implementation of new technology to produce advanced aircraft and related products via consistently keeping the total cost down (ibid.).

An international springboard perspective, provided by Luo and Tung (2007), generalizes several strategies undertaken by emerging MNEs. They are: cumulative benefits from inward investment before undertaking OFDI; a leapfrog trajectory; and coopetition with global players.

The most common destinations for Russian OFDI are the countries from the Commonwealth of Independent States (CIS) and Eastern Europe. In these contexts Russian MNEs have the advantage of originating from an emerging economy operating in a familiar environment, and which is hostile to that of the MNEs in developed countries (Cuervo-Cazurra and Genc, 2008).

The strategies and characteristics of MNEs originating from emerging markets, for example those of Chinese firms, are analysed and discussed by Child and Rodrigues (2005). According to them MNEs from emerging markets have stronger catch-up capabilities than expected. The characteristics of Chinese firms, such as government involvement in the internationalization of large companies and the necessity to overcome their latecomer disadvantages, can be recognized in the Russian context as well.

Western MNEs, which have invested in Russia over the last two decades, have demonstrated an orientation to high quality products and services, effective marketing policy and the formation of partnerships with local firms (Panibratov, 2009). Hence, partnership benefits have not only been financial but have involved experience and knowledge acquisition for both foreign firms and their Russian counterparts.

Previous research on OFDI from Russia: motives and destination perspectives

OFDI from Russia has been examined by Kalotay (2001, 2005), Liutho (2001, 2005), Liutho and Jumpponen (2003), Sauvant (2005), Liutho and Vahtra (2007), Filatotchev et al. (2007) and Kuznetsov (2010), among others. The research focus has been the interest of Russian firms to diversify their holdings via international investment. The studied firms have been in a limited number of industries, mostly oil and gas, mining, metallurgy and telecommunications.

The mainstream research of the internationalization of MNEs from emerging economies has focused on the amount of OFDI such firms have invested overseas. FDI outflows from emerging economies have been often taken as a proxy for the activities of emerging multinationals (Filippov, 2008). Such an approach should be challenged since the particular business motives and corporate strategies are neglected if studying Russian MNEs is conducted primarily or exclusively from the perspective of their OFDI. Business motives of Russian MNEs have been indeed investigated in several works. An increase of market-driven OFDI has been expected, as well as an increase of the share in the total amount of outward investment by non-resource-based firms (Vahtra and Liuhto, 2005).

The internationalization motives of emerging market MNEs are considered to be the same as those of companies from developed economies with market, material and human resources, and technology seeking motives that prevail over the rest (Rasiah et al., 2010). In the case of Russian MNEs resource-seeking and market-seeking motives are most often the initial ones, regardless of industry specifics.

OFDI from Russia is often seen as similar to system escape as firms driving OFDI invest abroad due to the negative characteristics of the Russian business environment. This phenomenon has been largely discussed in the case of MNEs from developed economies, where institutional barriers in the home country set constraints encouraging firms to escape through international investment (Boddewyn and Brewer, 1994; Witt and Lewin, 2007). This situation has also been the case for Russian firms with capital flight for investing abroad to provide a higher rate of return on their investments overseas (Kalotay, 2001).

The Russian OFDI flows amounted to US$46.1 billion in 2009 (Bank of Russia, 2010). At the same time, over a half of the OFDI by non-banking firms went to offshore destinations (Cyprus, the Netherlands, Gibraltar, Luxembourg, Switzerland and the British Virgin Islands), which fact asks a question as to whether this investment is real or pseudo-FDI. This situation might account for a reverse in capital flight due to system-escape motives. Such capital flight investments decreased sharply after 1999 but started to bounce back in 2008. The paradox is that it is the hostility of the home country business environment (rapidly changing legislation, weak law enforcement, corruption, political pressure), on the one hand, and the home government incentives expected, on the other hand, that stimulates Russian capital to go abroad (Panibratov and Kalotay, 2009).

The internationalization motives of Russian MNEs vary significantly. It is not surprising that the most typical motives of Russian MNEs are market-seeking and resource-seeking. Besides, some investments are motivated by strategic asset-seeking, and are rarely efficiency-seeking. Sometimes, OFDI from Russia is driven as well by image-building motives or considerations designed to prevent domestic political risks (IMEMO-VCC, 2009).

The effects of the historical and cultural ties as well as physical proximity are evident in the geographical distribution of Russian OFDI. The fluctuation of its geographical priorities is very interesting (see Table 8.1). According to Kuznetsov (2010), international Russian firms evolve from intra-regional multinationals (which operate only within the CIS) or bi-regional multinationals (operating in the CIS and Europe) to global multinationals (operating in three or more regions).

Table 8.1 Regional distribution of Russian OFDI

Destination	2007 (US$ million)	2007 (percent from total)	2008 (US$ million)	2008 (per cent from total)	2009 (US$ million)	2009 (per cent from total)
All the world	45,211	100.00	54,202	100.00	44,868	100.00
Non-CIS countries	41,967	92.82	51,789	95.55	41,760	93.07
CIS countries	3,244	7.18	2,413	4.45	3,109	6.93

Source: Bank of Russia (2010).

Research methodology

The internationalization of Russian MNEs is difficult to evaluate quantitatively, unless studied in the context of a systematic questionnaire survey of top managers. Even then respondents may be reluctant for a variety of reasons to disclose information. This is why this study has aimed at analysing managerial perceptions in the process of their internationalization attempts, with a prime objective to determine the actual sources of competitive advantage of Russian firms. Possible political influences in the process have been sought as well as the impact of competitors on the issues studied. Case study methodology has been applied in the investigation.

A key reason for adopting a case study approach is that the internationalization of firms from emerging economies requires conceptualization and theory building. As Eisenhardt argues (1989), the case study approach is especially appropriate in the investigation of new topic areas. Given the main characteristics of Russian MNEs in forming partnerships and alliances abroad, reference is made to the discussions by Halinen and Törnroos (2005) concerning the applicability of qualitative approaches in examining strategies of international partnership formation.

Russian MNEs are studied from the perspective of obtaining market leadership via investment abroad. The research focused on the process of foreign market entry selection. The firms selected are key players, which have obtained distinctive domestic competitiveness in a major Russian industry over all local firms and other foreign players operating in Russia, prior to their internationalization attempts. Since case study research faces the issue of generalization, the research design attempted to ensure a relatively broad geographic focus within a specific industry. Four case studies with a similar time span have been analysed. The case studies – MTS, VimpelCom, Kaspersky and Sitronics – all fit initial sample specifications, coming from two major hi-tech industries in Russia (telecommunication services and IT solutions), and all four firms are said to have obtained significant success in entering foreign markets of developed and developing countries.

The study combines multiple collection methods. The role of domestic strategy was initially studied. Key data sources are published materials, supplemented by face-to-face interviews with experts in related Russian industries. Top managers of companies (foreign and Russian) that were associated with the major players of the Russian hi-tech industry sector were also interviewed. Obtained information was cross-checked and data from different sources used to increase reliability and accuracy.

Case studies

Telecommunications services providers

The Russian telecommunications sector has recently recorded extremely buoyant growth, which has been fuelled by initially low entry level barriers, combined with strong economic growth, boosting significantly real disposable incomes. Few industries have reflected the consumer boom and growing middle class in Russia prior to 2008 to such a significant extent as telecommunications. Total telecommunications sector revenue amounted to US$42.6 billion in 2008, up from just over US$27 billion in 2006. The mobile phone market accounted for 57 per cent of the whole market, or US$24.2 billion, and the fixed-line market accounted for the remaining 43 per cent, or US$18.4 billion. The share of the fixed-line segment in the total telecommunications market has fallen in recent years, owing to relatively slower growth than in mobile telephony. Mobile telephony experienced explosive growth in Russia in the 2000s, and the market was the fourth largest in the world in the period 2008–09, only after those of China, India and the USA. This sector is fast growing and one of the most attractive for Russian and foreign investors.

Case study 1: MTS

MTS is the largest mobile communications services company in Russia. The company began its foreign expansion in 2002, establishing a subsidiary in Belarus. By the end of 2009 it had subsidiaries in five CIS countries: Belarus, the Ukraine (from 2003), Uzbekistan (from 2004), Turkmenistan (from 2005) and Armenia (from 2007). In 2007, it started its mobile telephone business in India, where it took over the communications firm Shyam Telelink.

MTS initiated its internationalization in several neighbouring CIS countries. The main reasons for choosing these country markets were related to historical and cultural traditions summarized by psychological proximity, common infrastructural networks inherited from the Soviet era, and relatively similar business practices. In addition to that one should take into consideration the geographical proximity, which clearly favoured international expansion, though several potential country markets (such as Uzbekistan) are located relatively far from the main Russian economic centres.

Despite all tensions and difficulties, political and economic relations of CIS countries tend to develop positively. Integration within the CIS region seems to be a political goal of the Russian government. Considering the significant role of the state in the mobile communications sector, this political issue favouring cooperation, helps Russian companies enter CIS markets.

Internationalization via expansion to CIS countries fits the strategy of the company of following your customers. Many Russian firms, being MTS corporate clients, had previously entered markets of CIS countries and actively developed economic cooperation. Human migration within the CIS is also an important reason, as it formed an initial basis as well as incentive for internationalization by enhancing cooperation between mobile operators from Russia and other CIS countries supplying international roaming services. Table 8.2 presents information concerning the internationalization of MTS.

Table 8.2 Internationalization of MTS

Key characteristics	Internationalization results
Internationalization start	2002: established joint-venture subsidiary in Belarus.
Foreign destinations	CIS countries and India.
Main assets abroad	Subsidiaries in Belarus (2002), Ukraine (2003), Uzbekistan (2004), Turkmenistan (2005) and Armenia (2007).
Market entry modes	Acquisitions of country market leaders. The only exception is a joint-venture formation in Belarus.
Recent major deals	In 2007, started mobile telephone business in India via the acquisition of Shyam Telelink.
Expansion approach	Application of 'follow your consumer' strategy. Russian firms that were MTS corporate clients had previously entered CIS markets – MTS followed them there.
Role of the state	The political factor favoured internationalization and cooperation within the CIS region.

Case study 2: VimpelCom

VimpelCom is the leading Russian firm in the field of mobile communications, with over 25 per cent of the domestic market. VimpelCom Group provides voice and data services across a wide range of mobile, fixed and broadband technologies under the Beeline brand.

International expansion of the company began with the acquisition of large shares of Norwegian Telenor (in 1998) and the Russian Alfa-Group in 2001. Currently, VimpelCom has 30 and 44 per cent of the shares of the above operators respectively. Companies of the VimpelCom Group operate in Kazakhstan (from 2004, with 43 per cent of the Kazakhstani market), the Ukraine and Tajikistan (from 2005), Uzbekistan, Georgia and Armenia (from 2006), and Vietnam and Cambodia (from 2008). In the internationalization process, acquisitions always played the most important role. First the company acquired the Kazakhstan mobile operator Kar-Tel in 2004. At the end of the 2000s it turned to South East Asia where it strived to build mobile networks: in 2008 it established a joint venture in Vietnam named GTEL-Mobile in which it had a 40 per cent share, and it acquired 90 per cent of the firm Sotelco in Cambodia. Cambodia and Vietnam with a total population of 100 million people represent a huge market with enormous potential. Moreover, VimpelCom focused on expansion in the CIS region where the mobile coverage is still at a relatively low level and developing the CIS market represents another huge potential for future expansion.

The series of acquisitions let VimpelCom not only enter many markets with high growth potential but also strengthen its home market position. At the end of 2010, it had more than 64 million subscribers, about

Table 8.3 Internationalization of VimpelCom

Key characteristics	Internationalization activities
Internationalization started	In 1998 acquisition of 30 per cent of Norwegian Telenor.
Internationalization destinations and main assets abroad	Operates in Kazakhstan (from 2004, with present share of 43 per cent of the host market), Ukraine and Tajikistan (from 2005), Uzbekistan, Georgia and Armenia (from 2006), and Vietnam and Cambodia (from 2008).
Entry modes	Mainly acquisitions, but also international joint venture formation and licensing.
Major deals and projects	Focus on South East Asia with the aim to build mobile networks: in 2008 it established a joint venture GTEL-Mobile in Vietnam with a 40 per cent ownership stake; in 2009 it acquired 90 per cent of Sotelco, Cambodia; in 2009 it invested in Laos.
Expansion approach	Intends to go global with major destinations in the CIS region, South East Asia and Europe.
Role of the state	Despite a high level of regulation of the telecommunication industry by the Russian government, VimpelCom has insignificant governmental support in its internationalization.

51 million in Russia, among them 11 million in Moscow. The largest foreign markets of the firm are Kazakhstan with more than 6 million subscribers and Uzbekistan with 3.6 million. Its market share in Russia at the end of 2009 was estimated at 24 per cent and at the end of 2010 at 24.4 per cent (A&M Consulting, 2010). The key aspects of the internationalization of VimpelCom are presented in Table 8.3.

Case companies' results: entry through M&A

The mergers and acquisitions (M&As) activity of Russian telecom players has been significant in their expansion in the CIS region since the early 2000s. Being aggressively active in M&As in the first half of the 2000s, Russian telecom companies reduced their investment activities at the end of the decade, with no major deals recorded in the period 2007–09 (see Table 8.4). Nevertheless, OFDI activity is predicted to reactivate in the near future.

From the CIS region, Kazakhstan, Ukraine and Uzbekistan have been the most attractive countries for investment by Russian telecom operators. They have substantial growth potential because of the large combined population and a comparatively low penetration rate of telecommunications services. Russian operators have also been active in Belarus, but the fixed-line and the broadband Belorussian markets were previously conquered and

Table 8.4 Major acquisitions in the CIS region by Russian telecom operators, 2001–09

Year	Operator	Country and acquisition target	Stake (%)	Amount invested ($ millions)
2001	Megafon	Tajikistan: TT-Mobile	75	Co-founder
2002	MTS	Belarus: MTS Belarus	49	Co-founder
2003	MTS	Ukraine: UMC	100	373
2004	VimpelCom	Kazakhstan: Kar-Tel	100	350
2004	MTS	Uzbekistan: Uzdunrobita	74	121
2005	MTS	Turkmenistan: BCTI	100	47
2005	MTS	Kyrgyzstan: Bitel	51	150
2005	VimpleCom	Ukraine: URS	100	231
2005	VimpleCom	Tajikistan: Takom	60	12
2006	VimpleCom	Georgia: Mobitel	51	13
2006	VimpleCom	Uzbekistan: Buztel	100	60
2006	VimpleCom	Uzbekistan: Unitel	100	200
2006	VimpleCom	Armenia: ArmenTel	100	475
2006	Altimo	Kyrgyzstan: Sky Mobile	100	n/a
2006	Comstar UTS	Armenia: Callnet	75	n/a
2006	Comstar UTS	Ukraine: DG Tel, Technology Systems	100	5
2007	MTS	Armenia: K-Telecom	80	425
2009	MegaFon	Abkhazia: Aquafon; South Ossetia: Ostelecom	51	28.5

Source: UNCTAD (2010)

monopolized by Beltelecom, a firm owned by the Belorussian government. Two of the three local GSM mobile operators had previously been sold to Western investors. Thus the telecommunications market structure and supply in Belarus were settled before the attempted entry by Russian firms.

Once most of the mobile communications markets of the CIS had been penetrated by Russian operators they started expanding into the host fixed-line and broadband markets. These areas of expansion are going to become the busiest in the M&As arena in the CIS region in the next decade. This will be more significant for the countries in the region with high population densities (such as Ukraine), whereas in countries with low population densities (such as Kazakhstan) operators will prefer to develop the next generation of mobile services, which will allow them to offer high-speed mobile broadband.

In should be noted that both case companies, MTS and VimpelCom, explored M&As with regard to gaining access to, for example, knowledge, skills, and access to suppliers and customers. In the case of VimpelCom the acquisition of an important subscriber base and the possibility of applying new technologies to broaden its networks has been most beneficial. The main reasons for internationalization success have been the significantly expanded network and substantial increase in the number of users. The fact that VimpelCom penetrated the developing CIS markets allowed the firm to use existing technology to develop the infrastructure of host countries, which act played a positive and highly important role in improving relationships with local national governments. Some of the acquisitions helped the company to overcome competitors by striking contracts with local companies to develop the 'Beeline network' for roaming.

An issue of key importance has been the establishment of relationships with the host governments of the countries VimpelCom entered. The main component of the company's entry strategy in a new market was establishing partnerships with the local mobile operators. Such partnerships were crucial for obtaining specific knowledge of the market. When entering the Uzbekistani market in 2006, VimpelCom first bought Unitel for US$207.7 million and then Buztel for US$62.4 million. The two VimpelCom subsidiaries merged in 2007. The prices for the two acquisitions were very high. Still, such a strategy was fully justifiable as obtaining communications licences in Uzbekistan by foreign operators was excessively expensive as the Uzbek government wanted to be sure that a foreign player would be loyal and committed.

IT companies

In 2008 the Russian IT market generated total revenues of US$4,500 million. The Russian digital economy indicators concerning personal computers, the internet and broadband penetration rates have been growing positively in the last decade. The major factor that affected the Russian IT industry negatively was the global financial crisis that started in 2008. The crisis led to significant problems in the industry, primarily linked with decreasing demand. In 2008 export of software and software development services decreased drastically. The export target of US$3,000 million set by the Russian IT union Russoft for 2009 was not attained. Instead export volume in value terms only reached US$2,650 million. The most lucrative business for the Russian software market in 2008 was home use application software sales, generating total revenues of US$1,100 million, equivalent to 23.6 per cent of the market's overall value. The software market is expected to drive the market to the value of US$12,300 million at the end of 2013.

Case study 3: Kaspersky

Kaspersky Lab or Kaspersky is a Russian IT company, founded in 1997 in Moscow. Due to its high level of professionalism and dedication, Kaspersky Lab has become one of the market leaders in the development of antivirus protection. By the mid-2000s the company had grown into an international company, employing over 1,500 computer specialists. The company sells its products all around the globe in more than 100 countries. It is headquartered in Moscow with several regional offices in Europe (the Netherlands,

Germany, France, the UK, Poland, Romania and Sweden), Asia (Japan, China and South Korea) and in North America (the USA).

While the majority of businesses in the IT industry grow via mergers and acquisitions, Kaspersky follows a path of organic expansion. The company aims to achieve global growth, and its expansion strategy is that of enterprise-oriented solutions, regional growth and an increased number of partnership formations. In order to serve its customers better, Kaspersky has established relationships with distributors in various countries, starting its international expansion via exporting. One key step in the company's internationalization was engaging in partnerships in order to penetrate and conquer the North American market. In 2001, it announced a partnership with Itamigo, a developer of internet security services. This partnership formation enabled the company to launch the first Kaspersky anti-virus products on the US market.

The European market was entered via the launch of European retail sales in 2001. The company made use of local retail and distribution networks. These developments were followed by opening regional sales offices in a number of countries.

In 2003 a regional office in Beijing was opened, which was the beginning of Kaspersky's penetration into large emerging economies. Presently the company is establishing its presence in the African market. Results of its internationalization are presented in Table 8.5.

Table 8.5 The internationalization of Kaspersky

Key characteristics	Internationalization results
Internationalization started	2001
Foreign destinations/main assets abroad	Regional sales offices in Europe (the Netherlands, Germany, France, the UK, Poland, Romania, Sweden), Asia (Japan, China, South Korea) and North America (the USA).
Entry modes	Starting with an export via establishing relationships with distributors in foreign countries. Establishing multiple strategic partnerships with leading IT firms.
Major deals and projects	In 2001, launching of European retail sales and partnership with Itamigo (US developer of internet security services). In 2003, opening of a regional office in Beijing, China. Strategic partnerships established with Microsoft, Intel, IBM, Novell, Check Point and Linux Solutions.
Expansion approach	Opening regional offices in various European countries.
Role of the state	Insignificant.

Internationalization through partnerships with industry leaders

Kaspersky Lab has established multiple strategic partnerships with leading firms in the software industry. With partners all over the world, the company has been able to expand its presence in the global market. Among its key strategic partners were Microsoft, Intel, IBM, Novell, Check Point and Linux Solutions. In partnership with Microsoft, Kapersky Lab has worked on several joint projects and has optimized its systems for Intel products. The two firms are also founding partners of the National Coalition Against Spam. Via partnership formation Kaspersky Lab has shown great potential for further grow and international expansion. The firm has focused on global expansion and continuous penetration of new markets via successful partnerships and the launch of an online shop.

Case study 4: Sitronics

Sitronics is one of the largest national players in the hi-tech industry. Established in 2002, the company was set up as a scientific centre, focusing on microelectronics and telecommunications equipment and software development. In 2004, the company established a business line related to IT-services. The company gained stakes in several companies, including the largest IT company in Ukraine (Kvazar-Mirco). Presently, as a result of its internationalization, Sitronics is the largest hi-tech company in Eastern Europe operating in the field of IT, telecommunications solutions, system integration and consulting, and the development and manufacturing of microelectronics products.

The company is a key partner with government institutions for infrastructural transformations in Russia and the CIS region. In its international expansion, it implements the strategy of public–private partnership formation, taking part in scientific research funded by the Russian government. The company has subsidiaries in more than 30 countries and employs over 10,000 people. It is one of the top three Russian IT companies. Its major international competitors are Microsoft, IBM and SAP AG.

Having more than 3,500 clients worldwide the company exports to over 60 countries in Western and Eastern Europe, the Middle East, North America, North Africa, and Central and South East Asia. Manufacturing is internationalized and done in Russia, Greece, the Czech Republic, Romania and China. The key production sites are in Prague and Athens for telecommunications solutions, in Kiev for IT and in Zelenograd and Moscow for microelectronics solutions.

Sitronics's key markets are Russia, the CIS region, Greece, Eastern Europe, the Middle East and South East Asia. All these markets have high growth potential. The company participates in joint projects in the telecommunications area with Ericsson (for 3G network designs) and Cisco Systems (for network solutions for fixed and mobile communications). The most important international results of Sitronics are presented in Table 8.6.

Table 8.6 The internationalization of Sitronics

Key characteristics	Internationalization results
Internationalization started	In the mid-2000s.
Foreign destinations	The CIS region, Greece, Eastern Europe, the Middle East and South East Asia. The major enterprises are located in Prague, Athens, Kiev, Zelenograd and Moscow.
Main assets abroad	Subsidiaries in over 30 countries.
Entry modes	Strategic partnerships and joint ventures.
Major deals and projects	Strategic partnership with Nokia Siemens Networks. Joint projects in the telecommunications area with Ericsson (3G network designs) and Cisco Systems (network solutions for fixed and mobile communications). Strategic alliances with Cisco Systems, STMicroelectronics, Infineon and Giesecke and Devrient in relation to the most important products and services. Vendor relationships with Siemens, Ericsson, Motorola, Oracle, Intel, Sun Microsystems and Microsoft.
Expansion approach	Exporting to over 60 countries in Western and Eastern Europe, the Middle East, North America, North Africa and Central and South East Asia. Key customers abroad are OTE, Cosmote, Vodafone, Ericsson, Arcelor Mittal and TCL. Manufacturing in Russia, Greece, the Czech Republic, Romania and China.
Role of the state	High because of business–government partnership.

Internationalization through partnerships with industry leaders

The expansion strategy of Sitronics is based on strong partnerships with key global and regional players. The company has developed strategic alliances with Cisco Systems, STMicroelectronics, Infineon and Giesecke and Devrient in relation to the most important products and services. The firm has vendor relationships with Siemens, Ericsson, Motorola, Oracle, Intel, Sun Microsystems and Microsoft. Key customers are both local companies (MTS, Comstar-UTS and MTT) and international firms (OTE, Cosmote, Vodafone, Ericsson, Arcelor Mittal and TCL).

Sitronics uses strategic partnerships and joint venture modes of market entry and market serving in order to get knowledge and experience from new markets and to benefit from established networks. One recent strategic partnership was established with Nokia Siemens Networks, a global enabler of communications services. Within the framework of this partnership an agreement was signed according to which Sitronics Microelectronics (a subsidiary of Sitronics) became the official global supplier of analogue power management electronic components for Nokia Siemens Networks products.

Sitronics launched its operations in the fastest growing ICT market in the world, India, using the name Sitronics India and with a head office in New Delhi. The group started operating in the Indian market in May 2008, and has had a permanent presence there since November 2008. The formal registration of the new subsidiary was in April 2009. In India the telecommunications sector, transport industry, educational system, state organizations and educational systems are major targets. The primary objective of the new subsidiary has been to introduce the complete range of Sitronics's products and solutions to the Indian market.[1] Expansion and development of services in India provided the firm with numerous opportunities for growth even in such a difficult market and period of stagnation. At the end of 2009, the company announced that it had launched a billing platform for pan-Indian telecommunications operator Sistema Shyam TeleServices, which traded under the MTS-India brand. The new platform, after being implemented in Mumbai (India's financial capital) and the state of Maharashtra, was intended to be introduced in other regions of the country.

An important deal for the company was the joint venture established in the city of Hangzhou in East China. Sitronics held a 51 per cent stake in this venture, with ZTE Corporation owning the remaining 49 per cent. The aim of the new enterprise was to enable the company to relocate its mass manufacturing and production sites from Europe to South East Asia, thereby improving efficiency and reducing costs.[2]

Sitronics was engaged in aggressive international regional expansion via various strategies. It used strategic partnerships and international joint venture formation in order to penetrate new attractive markets and to benefit from established networks and cheaper resources.

Findings and discussion

This study advances the notion that in strategic sectors of the Russian economy motives of internationalization of national firms may be explained with the fast growth of the local market, low cost opportunities and home government incentives. In the sector of telecommunications:

- In the period 2008–09 the Russian market was the fourth largest in the world;
- This sector is one of the most attractive for Russian and foreign investors;
- The development of the local market is stimulated by OFDI.

In the sector of IT:

- Russian companies exploit their advantage of highly educated employees with relatively low pay;
- There are incentives for local IT enterprises to improve the quality of their operations to become service providers for foreign firms operating in Russia.

The findings of this study have implications for the entry strategy of firms in their internationalization. The relatively fast development of the hi-tech sector in Russia has led to the rise of advanced technologies and a highly skilled, relatively cheap labour force. Hence, obtaining technology and upgrading technological capabilities through collaborations with foreign companies are the primary objectives of domestic companies and the governments in emerging economies (Beamish, 1993; Meyer, 2004). Hi-tech Russian companies are more focused on acquisition of customers than of advanced technologies when expanding abroad.

Concerning the geographical distribution of international activities of the studied firms it is obvious that Russian hi-tech firms have predominately targeted emerging economy markets and firms, mainly in the CIS region, Eastern Europe and Asia. A preferred starting destination has been the area of the former USSR, namely the economies and firms from the CIS region. Acquisition as a way of international expansion among other positive outcomes has been preferred because of the usually higher cost of greenfield investment (Muller, 2007). Hence, partnerships via international joint venture formation and strategic alliances can be considered as appropriate modes of entry as they allow Russian hi-tech firms quick access to host country infrastructure before the application of an acquisition strategy. This is particularly important for telecommunications firms that are internationalizing, which tend to be protected by host governments.

Taking into account technological differences when applying greenfield strategy, such an internationalization strategy can be advantageous only if a significant technological gap exists between the major competitors in the industry. As the technological advancement of Russian and leading foreign hi-tech firms is more or less the same, the partnership strategy of internationalization followed by acquisition strategy are the most appropriate ways for the international expansion of Russian hi-tech firms. When expanding overseas, Russian telecommunications MNEs often acquire an equity stake in existing host firms. Such stakes range from minority to 50/50 ownership structures. Meanwhile, hi-tech industries in a number of countries are under high government protection and surveillance, and a rise of shares in the ownership structure aiming at creation of wholly owned subsidiaries have in certain cases proven difficult or even impossible.

OFDI from Russia is considered 'exodus' and 'expansion' in terms of the role of the home-country factors that encourage firms to invest abroad and the attractiveness of foreign locations (Vahtra and Liuhto, 2006). The exodus factors causing escape of firms from a hostile host environment was very strong in the early 1990s, followed by less intensive escape in the mid-1990s. The crisis of 1998 prompted a significant rise in capital escape, followed by a legal approach to foreign investment initiated with the start of Vladimir Putin's presidency. The crisis of 2008 prompted a move towards exodus once again. Nevertheless the government role and institutional support limit the impact of this. Thus, in analysing the internationalization of hi-tech Russian MNEs, it seems that exodus plays a much smaller role than expansion orientation. Industry characteristics also contribute to such internationalization specificity.

The findings from this study have important implications for the internationalization strategies of Russian MNEs as they depend on Russian and host governments. The Russian state facilitates internationalization of domestic firms via imposing ownership restrictions on foreign firms in hi-tech industries. This policy protects local companies, helping them to establish leading

Table 8.7 International results of Russian hi-tech MNEs

Sector	Foreign destinations	Entry modes	Expansion approach	Role of state
Telecommunications	CIS region; Eastern Europe; Asia (focus on India)	Strategic partnerships. Rarely, international joint ventures and licensing. Acquisitions of leading host firms.	'Follow the customer' strategy. Expansion in various forms with regional and global attempts.	The sector is surveyed and controlled by the government with varying forms and extent of interference. Government support particularly helpful in the cases of expansion into the CIS region.
IT	CIS region; Europe; Asia; The Middle East; Southeast Africa.	Exporting. Strategic partnerships and international joint venture formation are core modes of international expansion.	Manufacturing in countries with cheap high quality labour force. Opening regional offices in Europe and the CIS region to serve the markets better.	Russian government support available. The sector seems less dependent on state regulation and help than the telecommunications sector.

positions in their home market. Thus Russian MNEs generate profits sufficient to self-finance their acquisitions abroad. Host country governments, mostly in emerging economies, are often interested in attracting Russian investments and ease the implementation of Russian government policy for international expansion. This is mostly true for countries in the CIS region. A summary of the international results of case companies are presented in Table 8.7.

Research validity and limitations

Data were compiled from published sources, the interviews with managers, and the information provided by experts from the selected industries related to the hi-tech sector. To minimize the effects of subjective biases during the face-to-face interviews the most important issues were discussed considering a variety of aspects. Trends and conclusions were based on the general common views resulting from the whole investigation process.

The validity of the results of this study is limited by the choice of cases. The case companies are leading Russian hi-tech firms which are the most significant investors abroad. The target sector has been hi-tech, but the telecommunications industry has a stronger emphasis as two of the four studied companies are telecommunications services providers and one is partly involved in the telecommunications business.

Conclusions

Due to the fast development of the Russian hi-tech sector, there has been a significant rise of advanced technologies in the sector employing a highly skilled labour force. Thus in the process of their internationalization Russian MNEs have been more focused on the acquisition of assets and customers than advanced technologies.

Increasing OFDI diversification provides Russian MNEs with capabilities to match the moves of their global counterparts. Domestic sustainable economic growth, low cost opportunities for international extension, Russian government support and a large high quality cheap workforce are likely to continue to drive the expansion of Russian firms abroad. For this Russian firms rely on strategic partnerships and acquisitions. As the development of Russian hi-tech firms is mainly driven by economic factors, they seem to be not so much 'escaping' the host environment as 'investing' overseas, which is probably less the case with their natural endowment dependent counterparts.

Finally, while the global crisis impacted on the internationalization of Russian MNEs its role was not critical in negative terms. Nevertheless there is a need for upgrading the global competitiveness of Russian firms to enable them to be more successful, in spite of the severe rivalry worldwide. This will require more efforts beyond strategic partnership formation, aggressive acquisitions and government support.

Notes

1. Sitronics Establishes Subsidiary in India [electronic resource] – Wireless News. - http://bmi.com/
2. Sitronics Establishes Joint Venture with ZTE Corp. [electronic resource] – Wireless News. - http://bmi.com/

References

A&M Consulting (2010). Market information, www.acm-consulting.com/news-and-data.

Bank of Russia (2010). Russian Federation: Outward Foreign Direct Investments of Nonbanking Corporations by Country. (www.cbr.ru/eng/statistics/print.aspx?file=credit_statistics/inv_out-country_e.htm). Bartlett, C. and Ghoshal, S. (1989). *Managing Across Borders*. Boston, MA: Harvard Business School Press.

Beamish, P.W. (1993). The characteristics of joint ventures in the People's Republic of China. *Journal of International Marketing*, 1(2): 29–48.

Benito, G. and Narula, R. (eds) (2007). *Multinationals on the Periphery*. London: Macmillan.

Boddewyn, J.J. and Brewer, T.L. (1994). International business political behavior: new theoretical directions. *Academy of Management Review*, 19 (1): 119–43.

Bulatov, A. (1998). Russian direct investment abroad: main motives in the post-Soviet period. *Transnational Corporations*, 7(1): 69–82.

Bulatov, A. (2001). Russian direct investment abroad: history, motives, finance, control and planning. *Economics of Planning*, 34(3): 179–94.

Child, J. and Rodrigues, S. (2005). The internationalization of Chinese firms: a case for theoretical extension? *Management and Organization Review*, 1(3): 381–410.

Crane, K., Peterson, D.J. and Oliker, O. (2005). Russian investment in the Commonwealth of Independent States. *Eurasian Geography and Economics*, 46(6): 405–44.

Cuervo-Cazurra, A. and Genc, M. (2008). Transforming disadvantages into advantages: developing-country MNEs in the least developed countries. *Journal of International Business Studies*, 39(6): 957–79.

Economist Intelligence Unit (2010). *Russia, Country Report*. London: Economist Intelligence Unit.

Eisenhardt, K.M. (1989). Building theories from case study research. *Academy of Management Review*, 14(4): 532–50.

Elenkov, D.S. (1995). Russian aerospace MNCs in global competition: their origin, competitive strengths and forms of multinational expansion. *The Columbia Journal of World Business*, Summer: 66–78.

Filatotchev, I., Buck, T. and Wright, M. (2007). Soviet all-union enterprises as new multinationals of the CIS. *The International Executive*, 35(6): 525–38.

Filatotchev, I., Strange, R, Piesse, J. and Lien, Y.-C. (2007). FDI by firms from newly industrialised economies in emerging markets: corporate governance, entry mode and location. *Journal of International Business Studies*, 38 (4): 556–73.

Filippov, S. (2008). Russian emerging multinationals: trends and issues. Working Paper Series, Paper 062, the United Nations University and Maastricht University.

Globerman, S. and Shapiro, D. (2006). Outward FDI and the economic performance of emerging markets. Paper presented at The International Conference on the Rise of Transnational Corporations from Emerging Markets: Threat or Opportunity? Columbia University.

Goldstein, A. and Shaw, T.M. (2007). *Multinational Companies from Emerging Economies: Composition, Conceptualisation and Direction in the Global Economy*. London: Macmillan.

Halinen, A., and Törnroos, J.-A. (2005). Using case methods in the study of contemporary business networks. *Journal of Business Research*, 58(9): 1285–97.

Hamilton, G. (ed.) (1986). *Red Multinationals or Red Herrings? The activities of Enterprises from Socialist Countries in the West*. New York, NY: St Martin's Press.

Heenan, D.A. and Keegan, W.J. (1979). The rise of third world multinationals. *Harvard Business Review*, 57(1): 101–9.

Heinrich, A. (2003). Internationalisation of Russia's Gazprom. *Journal of East European Management Studies*, 8(1): 46–66.

Heinrich, A. (2006). Russian companies in old EU member states: the case of Germany. *Journal of East–West Business*, 11(3/4): 41–59.

Hoskisson, R., Eden, L., Lau, C.M. and Wright, M. (2000). Strategy in emerging economies. *Academy of Management Journal*, 43(3): 249–67.

IMEMO-VCC Survey (2009). *Russian Multinationals Continue their Outward Expansion in Spite of the Global Crisis*. Moscow and New York: IMEMO-VCC.

Kalotay, K. (2001). The contribution of foreign direct investment to transition revisited. *Journal of World Investment*, 2(2): 259–76.

Kalotay, K. (2004). Will foreign direct investment take off in the Russian Federation? *Journal of World Investment and Trade*, 5(1): 119–38.

Kalotay, K. (2005). Outward foreign direct investment from Russia in a global context. *Journal of East–West Business*, 11 (3/4): 9–22.

Kalotay, K. (2008). Russian transnationals and international investment paradigms. *Research in International Business and Finance*, 22: 85–107.

Kets de Vries, M., Shekshina, S., Korotov, K. and Florent-Treacy, E. (2004). The new global Russian business leaders: lessons from a decade of transition. *European Management Journal*, 22(6): 637–48.

King, R., Hill, M., and Cornforth, J. (1995). From 'red multinationals' to capitalist entrepreneurs? *European Journal of Marketing*, 29(13): 6–22.

Kuznetsov, A. (2010). Industrial and geographical diversification of Russian foreign direct investments. *Electronic Publications of Pan-European Institute*, 7. (www.mgimo.ru/files2/p86/173286/675b1e735662f553f371b04b7cd8166c.pdf). Liuhto, K. (2001). Russian gas and oil giant conquer markets in the West: evidence on the internationalization of Gazprom and LUKoil. *Journal of East–West Business*, 7 (3): 31–72.

Lall, S. (1983). *The New Multinationals*, New York: Wiley.

Lecraw, D.J. (1983). Performance of transnational corporations in less developed countries, *Journal of International Business Studies*, 14(1), 15–33.

Liuhto, K. (ed.) (2005). *Expansion or Exodus: Why Do Russian Corporations Invest Abroad?* Binghamton, NY: Haworth Press.

Liuhto, K. and Jumpponen, J. (2003). The Russian eagle has landed abroad: evidence concerning the foreign operations of the Russian Federation's 100 biggest exporters and banks. Research Report 141, Finland: Lappeenranta University of Technology.

Liuhto, K., and Vahtra, P. (2007). Foreign operations of Russia's largest industrial corporations: building a typology. *Transnational Corporations*, 16 (1): 28–36.

Luo, Y. (2005). Transactional characteristics, institutional environment and joint venture contracts. *Journal of International Business Studies*, 36: 209–30.

Luo, Y., and Tung, R. (2007). International expansion of emerging market enterprises. *Journal of International Business Studies*, 38: 481–98.

McMillan, C. (1987). *Multinationals from the Second World: Growth of Foreign Investment by Soviet and East European Enterprises*. New York: St Martin's Press.

Meyer, K.E. (2004). Perspectives on multinational enterprises in emerging economies. *Journal of International Business Studies*, 35: 259–76.

Müller, T. (2007). Analyzing modes of foreign entry: greenfield investment versus acquisition. *Review of International Economics*, 15(1): 93–111.

Panibratov, A. (2009). Internationalization process of Russian construction industry: inward investments perspective. *Journal for East European Management Studies*, 14(2): 210–28.

Panibratov, A. and Kalotay, K. (2009). Russian outward FDI and its policy context, in *Columbia FDI Profiles, Vale Columbia Center on Sustainable International Investment*. Columbia University. (www.vcc.columbia.edu/files/vale/documents/FDI_Profile-_Russia.pdf).

Rasiah, R., Gammeltoft, P. and Jiang, Y. (2010). Home government policies for outward FDI from emerging economies: lessons from Asia. *International Journal of Emerging Markets*, 5(3/4): 333–57.

Sauvant, K. (2005). New sources of FDI: the BRICs. Outward FDI from Brazil, Russia, India and China. *Journal of World Investment and Trade*, 6(5): 639–709.

Sethi, D. (2009). Are multinational enterprises from the emerging economies global or regional? *European Management Journal*, 27: 356–65.

Sutyrin, S. (2009). Internationalization of Russian economy: threats and opportunities in time of crises. *Electronic Publications of Pan-European Institute*, 4. (www.tse.fi/FI/yksikot/erillislaitokset/pei/Documents/Julkaisut/Sutyrin%200409%20web.pdf).

Economist Intelligence Unit *The Russians are Coming: Understanding Emerging Multinationals* (2006). London: Economics Intelligence Unit. (www.rusal.ru/UploadedFiles/RussiansAreComing_eng.pdf).

UNCTAD (2010) *World Investment Report: Investing in a Low Carbon Economy*, New York and Geneva: United Nations.

Vahtra, P. (2006). Expansion or exodus? The new leaders among the Russian TNCs. *Electronic Publications of Pan-European Institute*, No. 13. (www.tse.fi/FI/yksikot/erillislaitokset/pei/Documents/Julkaisut/Vahtra_Russian_TNCs_global_economic_crisis_2009_web.pdf).

Vahtra, P. and Liuhto, K. (2005). Russian corporations abroad: seeking profits, leverage or refuge? in K. Liuhto and Z. Vincze (eds), *Wider Europe*. Turku, Finland: Turku School of Economics and Business Administration, pp. 225–54.

Vahtra, P. and Liuhto, K. (2006). An overview of Russia's largest corporations abroad, in K. Liuhto (ed.), *Expansion or Exodus: Why do Russian Corporations Invest Abroad?* New York, NY: International Business Press.

Wells, L. (1983). *Third World Multinationals: The Rise of Foreign Direct Investment from Developing Countries*. Cambridge, MA: MIT Press.

Witt M.A. and Lewin A.Y. (2007). Outward foreign direct investment as escape response to home country institutional constraints. *Journal of International Business Studies*, 38: 579–94.

Zaheer, S. and Zaheer, A. (1997). Country effects on information seeking in global electronics networks. *Journal of International Business Studies*, 28(1): 77–100.

Zhou, C. and Li, J. (2008). Product innovation in emerging market-based international joint ventures: an organizational ecology perspective. *Journal of International Business Studies*, 39(7): 1114–32.

Websites of Russian multinational firms

www.kaspersky.com
www.kaspersky.co.uk/homeuser
www.vimpelcom.com
www.vimpelcom.com/index.wbp
www.sitronics.com
www.sitronics.ru
www.comverse.com/press_releases.aspx?newsId=1094
www.mtsgsm.com

9

Analysing Culture in a Cross-Border Acquisition: An Indian–Finnish Deal in Focus

Niina Nummela and Mélanie Raukko

Introduction

Worldwide, cross-border investments increased up until 2007. Since then, cross-border acquisitions have led the recovery of foreign direct investment (FDI) (*World Investment Report*, 2010). Accordingly, cross-border mergers and acquisitions (M&As[1]) increase their importance in international business transactions. Due to their international nature, cross-border acquisitions involve unique challenges, because of the various economic, institutional or regulatory, and cultural diversity structures (Hoecklin, 1995; Child et al., 2001; Very and Schweiger, 2001).

The cross-border context brings additional challenges to post-acquisition integration, as representative parties are from different nationalities and, thus, lack a common cultural frame of reference. Often firms underestimate the complexity of cross-border acquisitions (Nadolska and Barkema, 2007). The institutional contexts may differ between the countries involved and associated obstacles may increase the perceived cultural differences between parties (Olie, 1994b). The relationship concerning culture and the outcome of acquisitions is very complex, hence research findings remain contradictory (e.g. Teerikangas and Very, 2006; Stahl and Voigt, 2008). From managerial perspectives the primary objective after acquisitions is to integrate the companies into a well-functioning, but not necessarily an integrated, unit sharing a common organizational culture. The need for integration varies considerably, ranging from relatively loose integration consisting of a few changes in top management and strategy to more comprehensive integration with selective merging of some functions (Janson, 1994; Lees, 2003).

Cultural integration usually refers to acquisition-related changes in the culture of the target company. These changes may manifest themselves, for example, in the values of self-image, work-related norms, organizational practices (management and control, treatment of employees, artefacts) and the power structure in the firm (cf. Cartwright and Cooper, 1992; Lees, 2003). The process of cultural integration may vary both in depth (see e.g. Cartwright and Cooper, 1993) and in length, because change processes in organizational culture are complex, slow and bound to encounter resistance (Schein, 1989).

Cultural integration is challenging and does not always result in desired outcomes. The lack of cultural compatibility is, not surprisingly, frequently mentioned as a potential factor leading to acquisition failures (see e.g. Cartwright and Cooper, 1993; Weber, 1996; Teerikangas and Very, 2006). The relationship between cultural integration and acquisition performance is far from straightforward. A recent meta-analysis of 46 studies clearly indicates that cultural differences not only affect significantly acquisition performance, but they also represent a 'double-edged sword' contributing both benefits and risks as an acquisition outcome (Stahl and Voigt, 2008). Consequently, more research is needed to analyse the role of culture in acquisitions (cf. Teerikangas and Very, 2006; Stahl and Voigt, 2008) and whether key decision-makers are likely and able to prioritize cultural differences (Janson, 1994). Prior meta-analyses (King et al., 2004) call for greater recognition of the process and organizational dimensions of acquisitions (cf. Cartwright and Schoenberg, 2006). Understanding the role of culture in cross-border acquisitions remains limited (cf. Björkman et al., 2007) and to some extent inconsistent because of the ambiguous and overlapping use of key concepts.

The aim of this chapter is to clarify the conceptual foundation of culture in cross-border acquisitions and suggest ways for analysing its role in the future. It addresses and clarifies the link between the key culture-related constructs, such as cultural awareness, fit, distance and acculturation, and the acquisition process. Based on a comprehensive literature review, a framework is proposed and applied to a longitudinal real-time case study of an Indian–Finnish acquisition in the IT field. The case itself provides an interesting view of the phenomenon as research on acquisitions in emerging markets is limited.

We address theoretical and methodological issues. First, we add to the theory by combining analysis of cultural differences and change to highlight the dynamics of culture (as called for in Janson, 1994; Zander and Lerpold, 2002). Second, the longitudinal, mixed-method research strategy used in the study is a novel approach compared with earlier research (cf. Meglio and Risberg, 2010). The chapter is divided into five sections. The first one defines the key concepts and links them together. The second section describes the case company and the method used in the empirical study. The third section presents the key findings, and the fourth discusses the results within the context of existing literature. The chapter ends with conclusions and suggestions for future research.

Key culture concepts in cross-border acquisitions

Cultural distance: evaluating cultural differences of national cultures

Organizations are embedded in national cultures reflecting shared historical experience and institutional structures. Members of one nation are expected to share a common set of values that shape their preferences for many issues (Hofstede, 1980). The culture interfaces in cross-border acquisitions extend beyond a single culture hence the parties involved are bound to encounter differences (Lees, 2003) originating from culture heterogeneity. Moreover, organizations possessing distinct national cultures are likely to favour diverse means in order to implement the desired changes (Laurent, 1989).

When evaluating cultural similarities or differences among various national cultures, two related and partly overlapping concepts are often addressed: cultural distance and psychic distance. Beckerman (1956) considers psychic distance as short when a country is 'nearer' to another country in psychic evaluation. The Uppsala school defines psychic distance in the context of firm internationalization as 'the sum of factors preventing or disturbing the flows of information between firms and markets' (Johanson and Wiedersheim-Paul, 1975:308).

In the international business literature, psychic distance is an important predictor of international market selection (Brewer, 2007) and more critical than the geographical distance (cf. Hofstede, 1980; Fang et al., 2004; Vaara et al., 2006). Traditionally, both geographical and psychic distances are perceived to be negative factors in cross-border acquisitions (Johnson et al., 2006). While psychic distance is often evaluated at an individual level (i.e. based on respondents' subjective perceptions), cultural distance is an organizational-level construct that refers to the differences concerning cultural values among countries (Sousa and Bradley, 2006). Thus, cultural distance is 'the sum of factors creating, on the one hand, a need for knowledge, and on the other hand, barriers to the knowledge flow and hence also for other flows between the home and the target countries' (Luostarinen, 1979:131–2). Sousa and Bradley (2006) argue that cultural distance together with other factors determine psychological distance. Consequently, cultural distance is a viewable component of psychic distance (Dow and Karunaratna, 2006).

In the context of cross-border acquisitions, cultural distance necessitates the acquirer to apply its strategic advantages to a different location (Shimizu et al., 2004). A lower cultural distance is likely to ease integration of companies. The national cultural distance, therefore, appears to have a substantial effect on cross-border acquisition performance as managers access diverse routines and repertoires that are beneficial to their performance (Morosini et al., 1998). Instead of 'distance', both parties' familiarity with the business environment or socialization may be decisive factors (Weber et al., 1996; Larsson and Lubatkin, 2001).

The conflicting notions and findings are probably, at least partly, due to conceptual ambiguity. Many studies use the terms 'cultural distance' and 'psychic distance' interchangeably (Sousa and Bradley, 2006). Despite differences in meaning, cultural distance and psychic distance are measured with the same indicators, mostly based on Hofstede's (1980) cultural dimensions and/or Kogut and Singh's (1988) index modified from Hofstede's (1980) four dimensions of culture. Another explanation may be the paradox of perceived closeness. Perceived similarity can prevent executives from learning about critical differences that leads to failure as the executives do not prepare for differences (O'Grady and Lane, 1996). Consequently, when a cross-border acquisition takes place in countries with seemingly similar cultures, the acquiring company may consider the markets to be similar to its own and not consider seemingly small but crucial differences (e.g. Angwin and Savill, 1997; Fang et al., 2004). Hence, national cultural distance is an important factor to consider when planning and implementing a cross-border acquisition (Morosini et al., 1998). However, cultural clashes may result not only from cultural distance highlighting the differences between national cultures, but also from a lack of cultural fit between organizations.

Cultural fit: analysing cultural differences at an organizational level

In the literature, diverse schools of thought view compatibility concerning mergers and acquisitions differently. The strategic school focuses on issues related to the strategic fit and synergy realization, while organizational behaviour scholars are more concerned about issues related to the impact of acquisition on individuals and the organizational culture as a whole, as well as issues concerning the 'cultural fit' (Datta, 1991; Haspeslagh and Jemison, 1991; Birkinshaw et al., 2000). The degree of compatibility, or cultural fit, between two merging organizations is one of the reasons why many acquisitions fail to meet expectations (Buono and Bowditch 1989; Cartwright and Cooper, 1993; Olie, 1994b).

'Cultural fit' is within the labels of cultural differences and cultural clashes (Datta, 1991; Cartwright and Cooper, 1993; Weber, 1996). The greater the dissimilarity between organizational culture types, the more problematic and longer the integration phase (Cartwright and Cooper, 1993). Interpretation of this relationship is not straightforward. Some studies suggest that the cultures of merging organizations are not necessarily bound to clash simply because they are different (cf. Very et al., 1997; Larsson and Lubatkin, 2001). Cultural similarity is not a prerequisite for successful integration; on the contrary, in some cases, it may even be an impediment to successful integration. In other words, successful cultural integration depends on multiple factors. Although cultural clashes are more likely to occur in acquisitions where the need for integration is important (Nahavandi and Malekzadeh, 1988; Weber et al., 1996), even an undemanding need for integration is not a sufficient prerequisite for a smooth cultural integration. Successful cultural integration also depends on the willingness of the two organizations to fit and to integrate (e.g. Cartwright and Cooper, 1993; Olie, 1994b).

Furthermore, both the target and the acquiring company should agree on the aspects of each other's culture they think are worth preserving; that is, whether the integration aims at a single culture, multiple cultures or a mixed culture (cf. Pribilla, 2002). Surprisingly, employees prefer a situation where the dominant acquirer imposes its own practices and culture on the target organization to one in which the issue remains undecided for a long period of time (Buono et al., 1985; Cartwright and Cooper, 1993). Thus, management of ambiguities (cf. Risberg, 2001) may turn out to be crucial for improving the cultural fit.

Although (lack of) cultural fit or compatibility is frequently mentioned as a potential factor leading to failures, the construct has not been well-defined (e.g. Cartwright and Cooper, 1993; Teerikangas and Very, 2006; Weber, 1996) nor well-researched empirically (Datta and Puia, 1995; Veiga et al., 2000; Björkman et al., 2007). Attempts to assess corporate culture primarily examine dimensions of a single culture but not the dynamics of compatibility between two merging cultures.

Due to the lack of measures of cultural compatibility, understanding of the relationship between cultural fit and acquisition outcomes remains limited, and the studies with meaningful cross-cultural comparison across organizations and nations are scarce (Weber et al., 1996; Veiga et al., 2000). Whether analysing cultural differences on a national or organizational level, cultural compatibility does not have value per se. Cultural compatibility only becomes valuable through understanding and if the knowledge of cultural differences is taken into consideration when preparing for the post-acquisition integration. Therefore, researchers and executives can manage cultural fit only through another concept: cultural awareness (Risberg, 2001).

Cultural awareness: the prerequisite for cultural integration

Cultural awareness refers to situations where researchers and executives perceive cultural dimensions as being different. Consequently, the individual knows that his or her culture is different from another's but also knows what to expect from the culture of other individuals.[2] Thus, managers with cultural awareness have skills greater than others to exploit culture-general and culture-specific knowledge (Hofstede, 1980). When identifying differences, managers know how to select appropriate tools (Fraser and Zarkada-Fraser, 2002) as well as the appropriate integration strategy (cf. Janson, 1994; Zander and Lerpold, 2002) to deal with differences successfully. A company may have limited awareness of its own culture before encountering another culture or may ignore the cultural differences of a seemingly similar culture

(Fang et al., 2004). On the other hand, even high cultural distance in combination with low cultural awareness does not necessarily result in major failures if the cultural differences are in areas of less significant importance (cf. Janson, 1994). Not all conflicts in the target organization are related to cultural differences, the acquisition itself or poor management of the process may raise employees' resistance to integration (Janson, 1994).

Previous research implies that in cross-border acquisitions cultural differences are expected and acquirers tend to have high cultural awareness. The managers of the acquired company are less likely to resist changes because of those differences (Risberg, 2001). Employees' resistance is often due to the misinterpretations in interaction with people from different cultural backgrounds, diverse management styles or emotional reactions due to historical or other reasons (Risberg 2001; Fang et al., 2004; Kusstatcher and Cooper, 2005; Sinkovics et al., 2010). Here, cultural differences at the national and organizational levels are tightly intertwined, so therefore, in cross-border acquisitions, cultural awareness should be broadly understood as awareness of cultural ambiguities.

Conducting an in-depth culture audit in order to identify similarities and differences between core values, beliefs, attitudes and managerial style of the target company and the potential acquirer is one way to improve cultural awareness in relation to the particular acquisition (e.g. Cartwright and Cooper, 1993; Pribilla, 2002). A successful acquisition requires careful planning to reach congruence between two companies concerning the implementation of integration (cf. Nahavandi and Malekzadeh, 1988). Cultural audits include various methods such as using observations, interviews or questionnaires (Cartwright and Cooper, 1993). Researchers refer to this audit as 'cultural due diligence', and it includes evaluation of hierarchies and symbols, management style, openness of interaction, decision-making, error tolerance and other indicators for corporate culture (Pribilla, 2002).

During due diligence, the culture, the vision, the strategy and the goals of both companies are evaluated to determine whether the two companies can be productive together (Chaudhuri and Tabrizi, 1999). Unfortunately, this kind of auditing is quite rare in practice (e.g., Lodorfos and Boateng, 2006), perhaps because of the confidential nature of negotiations and limited access to data prior to any agreement to purchase (Cartwright and McCarthy, 2005). However, acquirers with the same cultural distance and seemingly similar cultural fit may still succeed differently in their activities. For example, Reus and Lamont (2009) suggest that increased diversity can lead to more unique and innovative exploration and exploitation of opportunities. This study particularly draws attention to the cultural differences in the process of cross-border acquisition, something that has already been called for (e.g. Janson, 1994), recognizing that the three concepts of cultural distance, fit and awareness are bound in time and therefore change during the acquisition process.

Culture in post-acquisition integration

All firms have unique organizational cultures shaped by its members' shared history and experiences (Schein, 1989). The shared experiences help organizational members develop a repertoire of symbols and shared meanings that enhance organizational identification and the formation of a new organizational culture (cf. Buono et al., 1985). From this point of view, acquisition is not an end but the beginning of a complex social identity-building process at both the organizational and the individual level (Vaara et al., 2003). In this lengthy process, a new social identity is created based on joint experiences, beliefs, values and assumptions (Olie, 1994a, 1994b; Larsson and Lubatkin, 2001). The aim is a jointly shared, constructive culture (Larsson et al., 2004).

In acquisitions, two simultaneous processes take place: reconstructing one's own identity in relation to the other party (images of 'us' and 'them') and constructing a common identity in the new organization (images of a 'common future') (Vaara et al., 2003). Additionally, as mentioned earlier, in a cross-border acquisition acculturation is double-layered, requiring adjustment both to a foreign national and to a foreign organizational culture (Barkema et al., 1996). The co-existence of two layers of culture with which the companies must contend creates potential for additional conflict (Hitt and Pisano, 2004). This process of contact, conflict and adaptation is referred to as 'acculturation' (Cartwright and Cooper, 1993).

In order to succeed in acculturation, employees of formerly independent organizations must learn to understand each other's cultural assumptions and find ways to bridge the gaps between them. Moreover, they need to learn to avoid cultural clashes that would lead to disintegration (Bijlsma-Frankema, 2001). Several practices can facilitate the acculturation process. For example, involving employees in introduction programmes, training, cross-visits, celebrations and other such socialization rituals would enhance the creation of a joint organizational culture as long as these employees are allowed autonomy. Joint informal interactions appear to be especially effective in supporting acculturation (cf. Larsson and Lubatkin, 2001).

Despite all good intentions and measures, the members of the acquired company are likely to experience some kind of acculturative stress when they are expected to adapt to another culture, and the level of this stress depends on the perceived cultural differences between the acquirer and the acquired (Very et al., 1996). The progress of acculturation (or the lack thereof) can be followed through employee resistance, that is, employees' reaction to the acculturation process (cf. Janson, 1994; Hartog, 2004). The sources of employee resistance may be individual or collective; and they may originate from cultural differences, communication problems and negative effects of acquisition at the individual level (Larsson et al., 2004). Resistance is highest in situations that involve high levels of both organizational and personal uncertainty (Hartog, 2004).

To conclude, research shows that: no universal way exists for acculturation to occur, numerous paths lead to the same end result, and the degree of acculturation may vary. A dynamic model of acculturation suggests that over time the acquiring and acquired company move from one mode of acculturation to other modes, and thus the degree of congruence between each party's preferences may change (Nahavandi and Malekzadeh, 1988). Acculturation takes time, which presents a challenge for research to draw any definite conclusions on the phenomenon. Additionally, organizational culture is a dynamic phenomenon constantly undergoing change (Schein, 1989). Therefore, acquisition should not be viewed as the end of one culture but as a critical turning point in the development path towards a new joint organizational culture between the integrating organizations.

Linking the key concepts

The role of culture in cross-border acquisitions

An acquisition that brings together two organizations inherently includes a confrontation of cultural differences that needs to be managed (Schweiger and Goulet, 2005). The concept of culture in cross-border acquisitions is complex and multi-layered. Although culture is defined in numerous ways, in the context of cross-border acquisitions, most authors focus on one level of culture – most often corporate or national culture – even though, in this context, cultural differences should be interpreted broadly, taking both corporate level and national level culture into account (Weber et al., 1996).

In this chapter culture is a very dynamic element in the process of cross-border acquisition. Figure 9.1 links the culture-related concepts to the

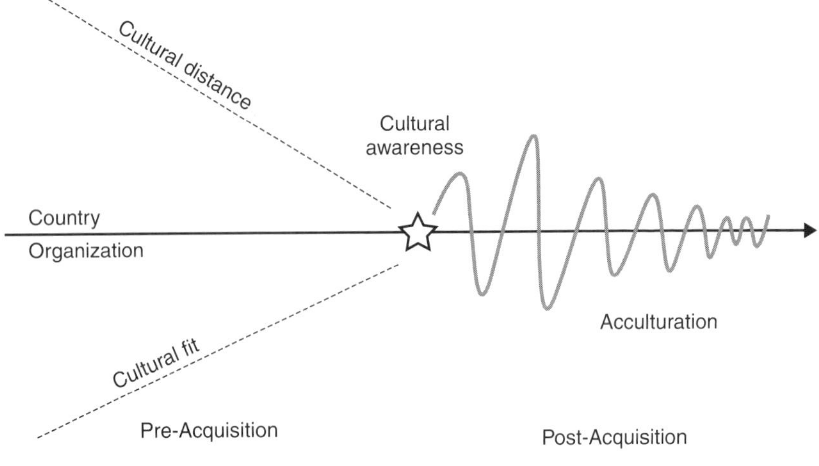

Figure 9.1 Culture in the process of cross-border acquisition

acquisition process. The timeline is divided into two phases, pre-acquisition and post-acquisition, because until the time of the deal two separate cultures are clearly distinguished. Prior to the acquisition, cultural differences can be evaluated with the concepts of cultural distance (referring to the differences between national cultures) and cultural fit (referring to differences originating from organizational cultures). Cultural awareness includes alertness to both national and organizational cultural differences. The importance of cultural awareness increases significantly at the time of the deal when differences need to be identified, evaluated in terms of their importance and taken into account when making the integration plan. Cultural awareness as a concept combines both the organizational and national levels of investigation, but particularly highlights the role of the individual.

In the post-acquisition phase, the acculturation process that takes place, particularly in the target company but also in the acquiring company, should be the focus of studying culture. In the acculturation process, the organizational and national cultures are closely intertwined making separation of the organizational and national dimensions in analysis difficult. Over time, the cultures of the acquirer and acquired come closer, and the acculturation process gradually slows down. However, employees may need years to develop a 'we' feeling (e.g. Kusstatcher and Cooper, 2005), making the acculturation process lengthy and lasting for years.

Teerikangas and Very (2006) report that the research setting often leads to oversimplification of the problem, and both the complexity of the cultural setting involved and the dynamic nature of the acquisition process need to be taken into account (for instance, instead of asking whether cultural differences impact on performance ('yes/no'), researchers should ask 'how' they impact on the acquisition performance). As a response to Teerikangas and Very (2006), this study takes into account the dynamics inherent in cross-border acquisitions and links the key concepts with the acquisition process.

Now, a real-life case – a cross-border acquisition between a Finnish and an Indian partner – is described with the help of the proposed framework.

Research design

A longitudinal case study approach

In order to obtain a better understanding on the dynamics of cultural integration, the study uses a longitudinal case study approach (cf. Leonard-Barton, 1990; Pettigrew, 1990). A case study method retains the holistic and meaningful characteristics of real time events, and provides a good research strategy for longitudinal field research using both quantitative and qualitative research methods (e.g. Pettigrew, 1990; Yin, 2003). It also allows the researchers to make their interpretations specific to situations, as recommended by Weick (1979) and Dubois and Gadde (2002), and to minimize retrospective bias. Retrospective data often contain retrospective errors, especially data based on recollections (Golden, 1992; Taris, 2000). In addition, prior knowledge of the outcome of an acquisition may bias any findings (e.g. a successful acquisition may accentuate positive attitudes and vice versa) (cf. van de Ven, 1992). Longitudinal studies on acquisitions are still relatively rare, mainly because maintaining a representative sample size over time is difficult (cf. Meglio and Risberg, 2010). In this study, data were collected in real time for a period of two years. The time frame was selected according to case-specific reasons, the most important of which was the length of the key persons' retention contracts. The research was limited to when the key informants were available.

This research is a single case study in which the case needed to fulfil several requirements. The most important selection criterion was that the acquisition had to be a cross-border deal. In addition, as this research required much time and commitment from the organization, access to key informants guided the selection process. This study uses a mixed-method strategy (it combines quantitative data collection and analysis with qualitative data collection and analysis) (cf. Hurmerinta-Peltomäki and Nummela, 2006). By combining qualitative and quantitative methods this study makes a strong empirical contribution towards understanding culture in cross-border acquisitions. The case selected for this research, an Indian–Finnish acquisition that took place in 2006, fulfils all the above-mentioned criteria.

In order to protect the anonymity of the companies, the names of the two organizations are not revealed. One was a small-to-medium-sized Finnish hi-tech company (Alpha Group) operating as a subcontractor in the field of telecommunications, employing around 250 workers. Alpha Group was acquired in 2006 by an Indian company referred to as Gamma. Gamma was bigger than the target company as it had around 3,000 employees and could be considered a medium-sized firm in its domestic industry and market. The nature of the deal can be defined as friendly because both companies were looking for a partner in order to grow and become more international.

Many other companies in the hi-tech sector in Europe had already transferred all or parts of their production and R&D to low-cost countries in Asia. The Indian company was looking for new customers, new know-how and a foothold in Europe. The acquisition type could be defined as a concentric acquisition as both companies operated in the same field (cf. Cartwright and Cooper, 1992) although in different areas: Gamma from India operated in the field of software engineering, while Alpha Group from Finland operated in the field of both software and hardware engineering.

Data collection

This study uses a mixed-method approach that allowed us to study culture both at the level of the organization (quantitative data) and at the level of the individual (qualitative data). Figure 9.2 illustrates the data collection

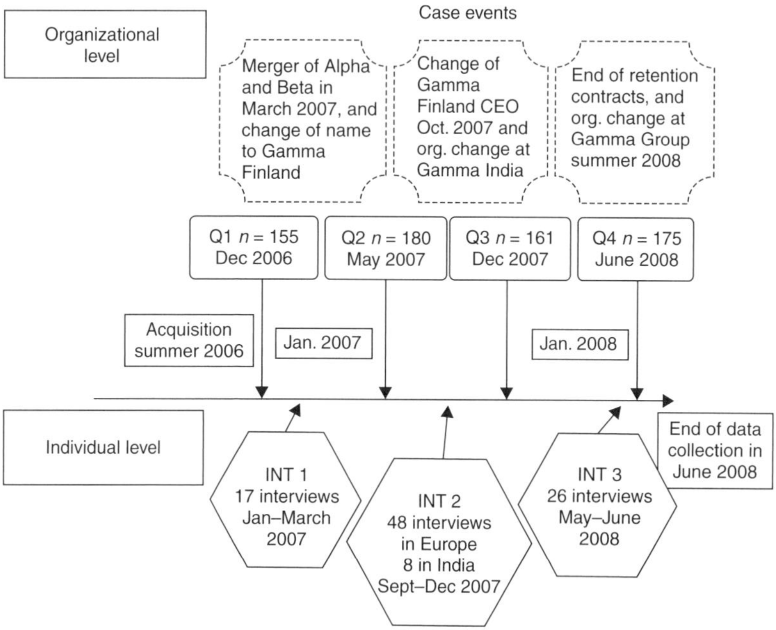

Figure 9.2 Data collection process

process. Besides the regular data collection process, critical events in the case company were followed in real time by observations and informal conversations. The data collection was mostly real time to emphasize the post-acquisition phase of the process with retrospective data playing a minor role.

The main purpose of the quantitative data collection was to analyse various employee attitudes and the integration experience. Data were collected from the employees of the acquired company, as they were the ones expected to experience acculturative stress (cf. Very et al., 1996). The quantitative data were collected through four questionnaires every six months during the first two years following the acquisition. The scales were borrowed from well-known and established scales in academic literature. The questionnaire includes the acculturative stress scale (based on Very et al., 1996) that includes five dimensions: participation and cooperation; personal and societal responsibilities; assertiveness and achievement; autonomy and innovativeness; and performance and reward objectives (see Table 9.1).

Since the scale was originally in English, it was translated. The questionnaire was administered electronically using software called Webropol and was sent individually via email to the entire work force of the acquired target company. The response rate was about 50 per cent (see Table 9.2). The

Table 9.1 Scales and reliabilities of the full questionnaire

Variable	Scale	Scale borrowed from	No items	Round 1 Dec 2006	Round 2 May 2007	Round 3 Dec 2007	Round 4 June 2008
Organizational commitment	OCQ (Organizational Commitment Questionnaire)	Porter et al. (1974)/ Mowday et al. (1979)	15	N = 112 α = 0.90	N = 133 α = 0.93	N = 122 α = 0.915	N = 140 α = 0.919
(i) towards acquired/target organization							
(ii) towards acquiring organization	(Items 10 and 15 were removed in the scale, since employees had not chosen this organization)			N = 72 α = 0.91	N = 116 α = 0.92		N = 127 α = 0.925
Organizational identification		Mael and Ashforth (1992)	6	N = 131 α = 0.81	N = 169 α = 0.89	N = 143 α = 0.806	N = 164 α = 0.858
(i) towards acquired/target organization							
(ii) towards acquiring organization				N = 89 α = 0.88	N = 172 α = 0.88		N = 156 α = 0.909
Career commitment		Blau (1985)	8	N = 112 α = 0.82	N = 149 α = 0.81	N = 134 α = 0.851	N = 151 α = 0.852
Work/task commitment	Job involvement	Kanungo (1982)	10	N = 120 α = 0.84	N = 175 α = 0.86	N = 155 α = 0.850	N = 169 α = 0.831
Job satisfaction		Warr et al. (1979)	10		N = 162 α = 0.85	N = 146 α = 0.837	N = 154 α = 0.839

Turnover intentions		Meyer et al. (1993); Kim et al. (1996)	6		N = 170 α = 0.89	N = 147 α = 0.868	N = 159 α = 0.909
Alternative job opportunities		Arnold and Feldman (1982); Price (2000); Kim et al. (1996)	3	N = 146 α = 0.66		N = 149 α = 0.644	N = 158 α = 0.661
Name	Raukko		8		N = 138 α = 0.86		
Integration	Level of integration	Cording (2004)	12	N = 72 α = 0.99	N = 48 α = 0.90		
	Speed of integration*		2	N = 57 α = 0.41**			
Culture	National*		7	N = 60 α = 0.81			
	Organizational*		10	N = 58 α = 0.46**			
Role ambiguity		Rizzo et al. 1970	10			N = 141 α = 0.83	N = 154 α = 0.828
Interactional justice		Moorman (1991)	6			N = 127 α = 0.914	N = 140 α = 0.920
Acculturative stress		Very et al. (1996)	23			N = 44 α = 0.926	N = 73 α = 0.932

* Designed by the researcher.

** Acceptable level $\alpha > 0.60$.

Table 9.2 Response rate and final sample by survey round

Questionnaires	Time	Total personnel	Final sample	Response rate (%)
Q1	December 2006	279	155	55
Q2	May 2007	308	180	58
Q3	December 2007	338	161	48
Q4	June 2008	355	175	49

distribution of the respondents represented the overall organization well, both hierarchically and geographically. The age and sex distribution corresponded to the company average: around 90 per cent of the personnel are men, and the average age in the organization is thirty.

The reliability of the scales used in the questionnaire was assessed using several means. First, the items and the construct of the scales were assessed through factor analysis (using varimax rotation). Both the factor analysis and Cronbach alpha values indicated that there was no reason to eliminate a single item. In general, the Cronbach alphas were very strong, well above $\alpha > 0.70$, which is considered to be the acceptable level (see Table 9.1; cf. Hair et al., 2006).

In order to obtain a deeper understanding of the cultural integration following a cross-border acquisition, interview data were also collected. Altogether 94 semi-structured interviews were conducted in the acquired company during 2007 and 2008 in three rounds (later termed spring 2007, autumn 2007 and summer 2008). In addition ten interviews were conducted in India at the parent company. Due to the demanding longitudinal real-time case study design, this research used a semi-structured approach (cf. King, 1994; Ghauri and Grønhaug, 2002).

The panel data were formed of identified key people mainly because they were involved in the acquisition process and also because their departure could be harmful for acquisition success (e.g. Ranft and Lord, 2000). However, interviews were also conducted within each of the employee groups (tester, support, engineer, lead/senior engineer, project/engineering manager, directors). The snowball technique was also used to select relevant interviews.

All the sites of the target company were visited as well as the headquarters of Gamma in India. The majority of the interviews were conducted in the mother tongue of both the interviewer and the interviewees (supported by Welch et al., 2002) and were tape-recorded with the consent of each interviewee. Most of the interviews were conducted face-to-face either in a conference room or at the office of the interviewee. The duration of the interviews varied from a mere 30 minutes to 1 hour and 20 minutes. In addition to interview data, photos of the various offices and locations, observations and annual reports were collected. A case diary was kept containing observations during the interviews at different locations (cf. Kvale, 1996).

Data analysis

The quantitative data were transferred from Webropol via Excel to SPSS for further analysis. Once the researcher had assessed the reliability of the items and scales through factor analysis and scale reliability (i.e. Cronbach alpha), the reverse coded items were recoded and then recomputed into sum variables.

The main tools of analysis compared means with the 'Means' function, tested statistical significance with ANOVA and measures of associations (ETA), T-tests and Mann-Whitney U-tests. The researcher mostly used non-parametric tests as the majority of the variables were not normally distributed and the measurement scale used was a Likert-type scale which is considered to be an ordinal one (cf. Hair et al., 2006). The quantitative analysis remained explorative and no causalities were analysed, mainly due to limitations concerning the data.

The interviews were analysed qualitatively. Due to their large number, the interviews were transcribed verbatim by an agency. The transcription of all 104 interviews (including interviews from the parent company in India) resulted in 1,362 pages of text. To facilitate the analysis of this extensive interview dataset, the researcher used software called Nvivo7. The coding was based initially on theory and the research problems. Nevertheless, codes were also emerging from the data. In addition, the 'find' function was used to identify all texts related to, for example, 'culture'.

The analysis began after arranging, coding and reducing the data. In order to capture the changes over time, the data were organized using the 'matrix coding query' function in Nvivo that allows the data to be organized in matrices based on the codes and the three data collection times (i.e. three interview rounds). The results were verified at the end of the research process by delivering the report to the CEO of Gamma Finland and by a meeting in which the results were debriefed and discussed (cf. Kvale, 1996).

Culture issues

Cultural distance between the acquirer and the acquired

Cultural distance was analysed here as perceived cultural differences. When measured with cultural distance, Indian and Finnish cultures seem to be fairly different from each other. According to Hofstede's (1997) dimensions, the greatest differences between the two national cultures would be in power distance and in long term orientation, although the countries differ significantly also in the masculinity/femininity dimension.[3] Power distance in Finland is noticeably lower than in India, whereas long-term orientation is considerably higher in Finnish culture than in Indian culture. Especially when compared with each other, Indian culture can be described as masculine and Finnish as quite feminine, although India does not have the top scores on masculinity. Both individualism and uncertainty avoidance are slightly higher in Finland than India, but also in the Finnish culture the scores are about average.

In summary, the cultural differences at the national level were apparent, and a visit to all sites helped to obtain a deeper understanding of the fundamental differences related to everyday life at the different locations of Gamma India and Gamma Finland. Interestingly, both parties claimed the other had a bureaucratic culture – but for each of them bureaucracy clearly meant something different. From the Indian perspective, Gamma Finland was bureaucratic despite its small size because it was slow. For Finns, bureaucracy referred to the increasing reporting and control and the need for 'red tape' that was evident after the acquisition.

The masculinity/femininity dimension could be seen in employees' different attitudes towards work: Indian's were perceived to be more career-oriented than Finns, who seemed to be more family-oriented. The cultural distance was evident also in terms of attitudes towards rules and regulations: the Finns were obviously more tolerant and used to follow strict laws and instructions because of the higher uncertainty avoidance embedded in their culture. For Indians, the differences in legislation came sometimes as a surprise, and the top managers at Gamma Finland spent a great deal of time explaining why the Indian way is not possible in Europe. On the other hand, different environmental factors, such as religion, had a different role in the two societies.

> Indian society still lags behind Finnish society in many ways, e.g. regarding social security, legislation, taxation, contractual issues, business practices, etc.... We have seven of these issues relating to work – there are seven agreements that are binding on both employers and employees, and we have to follow these rules. Indians find it difficult to understand that we are serious about these issues, for example, that we have to have development discussions with our employees – what on earth are they all about? (A director at Gamma Finland, autumn 2007)

> India and Finland differ quite a lot as regards work culture... and they have a different cultural background, too – religion, all that kind of thing... That's probably the biggest challenge, to make both parties understand, so that we understand how the Indians operate and the Indians understand how we operate. (A project manager at Gamma Finland, autumn 2007)

However, in this case the high awareness of the cultural distance was noticeable. From the very beginning, Gamma India respected the culture of Gamma Finland and chose a very loose integration strategy, not least because they were unfamiliar with the culture of the acquired organization. Another reason for the lower degree of integration was the fact that the acquired firm had been successful so far – they did not want to break the positive development in the company; on the contrary, they were allowed to do business as usual:

> Many companies try to impose their own culture on the acquired entity post-acquisition. Gamma India has never tried to do that. It has always respected the local sentiments. I don't recall any single incident where Gamma India had to impose its own value on Gamma Finland. In some sense I would say that expect for the name change to Gamma Finland, I don't think that the life of average employee has changed. He or she continued to work in the same way he or she has been working earlier. (An Indian manager)

In summary, cultural distance can be obvious in cross-border acquisition, but anticipating the problems is difficult. Often a slower integration approach allowing both organizations to get to know each other is recommended in such acquisitions. In this case Gamma India avoided imposing its own culture on Gamma Finland, but some clashes related to the differences in Finnish and Indian cultures occurred, nevertheless. Cultural distance may be diminished with cultural awareness.

Cultural fit and awareness

The acquiring company and the target company had a similar company history and shared the same values, to a large extent. Concrete challenges regarding the post-acquisition integration included the fact that the Finnish company was geographically spread over six cities. In addition, the Finnish company had grown through smaller acquisitions and, as a consequence, the company had two main sites: Alpha and Beta. Headquarters were in City A where Alpha was located. Furthermore, the target company had smaller sites in other cities, usually close to or even within the premises of key customers when the employees worked at their customers' projects. Both Alpha and Beta had strong, distinct identities and, based on the interviews, the cultural differences between the two sites were substantial. Six months after the acquisition by Gamma, Alpha and Beta still required further integration. At that point in time, Alpha Group was renamed Gamma Finland. The key actors are summarized in Figure 9.3.

The data indicate that the employees at Gamma Finland are relatively culturally aware. For example, some key people mentioned their past work experience in Asian countries. Quite a few also mentioned that the cultural training offered soon after the acquisition gave good insights into Indian

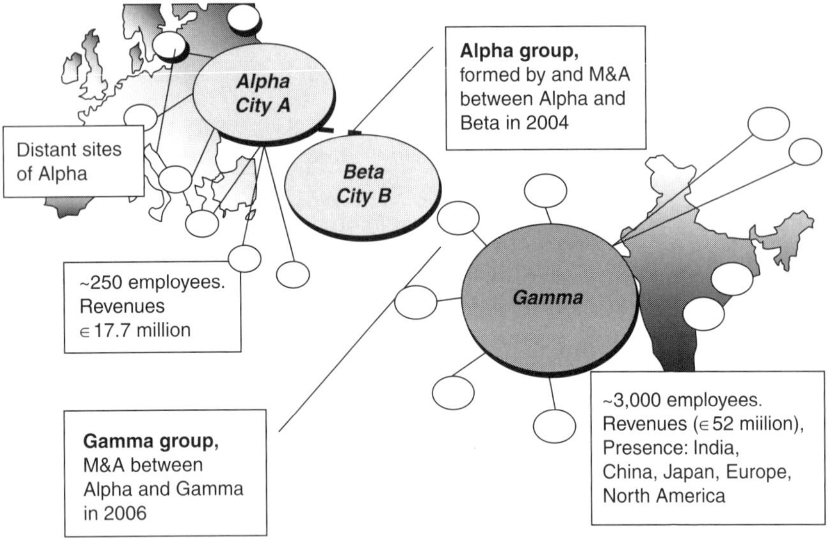

Figure 9.3 The organizational division of Alpha Group, Beta Group and Gamma Group

culture. In contrast, employees of the parent company, Gamma India, did not know much about the national cultural origins of Gamma Finland. Due to historical reasons Indians are very familiar with the UK culture but the cultural differences within Europe were surprising to some:

> Finland is different from the rest of Europe in terms of culture and from an Indian point of view because we have been used to the British because of historical reasons and business links with them, but Finland is very different from the UK, irrespective of the face that it comes from the same continent. So managing the cultural issues, and breaking the language barrier, was a big learning experience for me. (An Indian manager)

The interviews revealed that the due diligence was conducted by a Finnish bank, but the management of Gamma India did not visit any of the facilities before the deal was done. Nevertheless, both parties were aware of the cultural distance, as the statement of an Indian manager indicates:

> When you acquire within your own country or within your own culture, it's easy to forget that there are cultural differences ... While, when we acquired Alpha Group, it was clear to everybody that it was a different culture. So I think everybody was sort of on guard anyway. (An Indian manager)

Cultural differences in the analysed case

In practice, and in spite of the sensitivity to cultural differences, the lack of cultural fit was evident in this study. The main cultural differences between the acquiring and acquired company were related to work culture, communication and the conceptualization of time. The employee–manager relationship was said to be different, and Finnish subordinates felt their Indian managers were not as systematic as the superiors they were used to in their Finnish or Western culture. For example, development discussions were not common in the Indian organization's culture, and managers did not seem to set personal goals together with their employees. Indian workers took less initiative and required more monitoring, while in Finland employees were expected to be more conscientious about their work.

According to the interviewees several differences regarding the working day were found: Indians spent long days at the office, but their effectiveness was different as the days involved socializing in addition to work. In Finland, the work was effectively done between 8 a.m. and 4 p.m. The Indian work culture was also found to be more competitive than in Europe. In addition, the job descriptions were broader in Gamma Finland so that the work of an assistant there was more varied and involved more responsibilities than at Gamma India.

> Well there are quite a lot of differences in attitudes towards work...we Europeans are hard workers and serious about our work. When you tell us to do something, we do it, and some report on the results of the work immediately it's done, while some don't report and you have to ask them. On the other hand, Indians, when you give them a task, they start off with great enthusiasm and they tell you how they are going to do it, but whether they ever get it done – that's another story...Another thing is that we like to work on our own. When we are given a task, we'll do it and if there are problems we may ask or we may not, but we do it. Indians are different, they are used to their superior watching over their shoulder to see how the work is going – this makes them feel that their superior is interested in what they are doing and in that way present. (An engineering manager from Gamma Finland, autumn 2007)

Communication with the Indians was the biggest issue raised. Challenges related to the use of language and the understanding of meanings also posed problems. According to the Finns, Indian colleagues did not say 'no' easily or emphatically. Based on the interviews, a certain language barrier hindered communication and Finnish employees felt uncomfortable using their English. For example, meetings became much quieter than normal when conducted in English because the employees said only what they really had to say. Additionally, technical problems or issues (e.g. bad connections or talking over one another in conference calls) added to the communication challenges. Nevertheless, as interaction increased employees became more adept at using English.

In the interviews some Gamma Finland employees said that they could not trust what their Indian colleagues or managers said because it could change the next day. While a few informants did not report problems related to communication, others raised a number of issues such as slow response, escalation, communication tools and language. Some expressed frustration that they did not receive replies to their enquiries as fast as they needed or received answers to only some of their questions. Although escalation often speeded up the process, it was also viewed as a waste of superiors' time. Moreover, the overall communication culture was not perceived to be as open in India as it was in Finland. For example, subordinates felt they could not criticize or disagree with their superior. Sometimes a lack of communication caused problems (e.g. information about changes in contact people in India in the case of employee turnover was not passed on to Finland).

Finns and Indians clearly differ in their preferred mode of communication. Indians prefer using the telephone while Finns prefer sending emails. Although many questions could have been quickly answered with one phone call, Finns felt more comfortable formulating the questions or the issue in writing, and emails were often perceived to be a more efficient way to communicate based on that view. The quotation below illustrates the challenges relating to communication.

> Differences in ways of communicating – we use e-mail more, while they tend to use the phone more. Another difference is that we can maybe discuss things more openly, while they tend to rely more on interpersonal communication. We can be much more direct in public situations, for example, when someone puts an idea forward, we might criticise it, which happens quite often, whereas they might first say in public, 'Yes, very good', but then in a one-on-one private discussion it may turn out that they disagree completely. (An account manager from Gamma Finland, spring 2007)

Additionally differences in the concept of time were often mentioned. Some employees felt frustrated about the lack of punctuality, while others never had problems with punctuality (e.g. being punctual for meetings or conference calls). Meeting deadlines was another concern or challenge related to the conceptualization of time. Other issues that were mentioned as cultural differences were, for example, that in Finland employees are more autonomous. Although the culture training and Indian participants emphasized that the caste system no longer prevails, some interviewees felt it was still strongly present. For example, it was suggested that some top managers in

Gamma India were in their position more due to their social background than their managerial competence.

Figure 9.4 illustrates the main cultural differences at different stages of the integration process. In the figure the bolded differences, namely communication, concept of time and work culture represent differences that were mentioned at two or more interview rounds.

Figure 9.4 shows how, over time, the perceived cultural differences increase from the more obvious national cultural differences to the organizational cultural differences. This can be explained by the increased interaction between Gamma Indian and Gamma Finland as the integration proceeds. In the early post-acquisition phase, only key people had contact with the Indian Gammians, and the cultural differences were more related to differences of national background (i.e. Finnish or Indian national differences). As the integration progressed and contacts with the parent company increased, cultural differences began to show up in the differences in organizational culture, such as decision-making methods and manager and employee relations (that also reflect national differences). This progression is natural as the contacts between the parent company and the subsidiary increase and become deeper. As daily work-related contacts increased, more differences related to organizational culture emerged.

Acculturation and cultural clashes in the case

Cultural clashes in the analysed case

In order to analyse the level of acculturation and cultural clashes in the case, acculturative stress was measured cross-sectionally in December 2007 and June 2008, that is, one and a half and two years after the acquisition.[4] In general, acculturative stress slightly increased in June 2008 compared to December 2007, except with regard to the variable that 'measures individual performance in a clear, understandable manner', which increased just

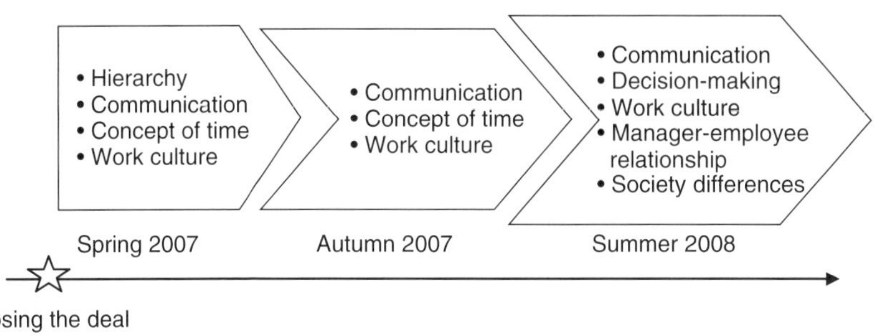

Figure 9.4 Main cultural differences at different stages of the integration process

Figure 9.5 Acculturative stress at Gamma Finland

slightly (see Figure 9.5). This increase might reflect the increased level of organizational integration and increased amount of bureaucracy. The findings indicate that the employees of Gamma Finland felt that the parent company Gamma India would not necessarily provide lifetime job security and that it did not delegate decision-making to the lowest possible levels.

Finnish employees felt only moderately that Gamma India is an organization people can identify with. However, contact with the parent company was at that time still relatively limited, and thus respondents might not have known enough about the company to identify with it. On the other hand, the results show that the employees of Gamma Finland felt that the parent company challenged them to give their best effort and to act in a responsible manner towards the environment, discrimination, etc.

The level of acculturative stress is very moderate (4.05 in December 2007, and 3.70 in June 2008), suggesting that the level of clashes is rather moderate. Nevertheless, based on the results, as the integration proceeds and the contacts between the two companies increase, acculturative stress slightly increases. This can be expected as acculturation in general requires interaction and cultural clashes are more evident when employees and managers interact than when they do not. Consequently, the results suggest that the less contact the respondents have with Indian colleagues or managers, the lower their actual level of acculturation stress ($p < 0.01$, December 2007).

Nevertheless, the results suggest that acculturative stress is higher among those respondents who experienced the acquisition negatively. Accordingly, the results imply that the acquisition experience is strongly related to the acculturative stress ($p < 0.01$ in December 2007 and $p < 0.000$ in June 2008). In line with this reasoning, those who perceived the integration process to be successful felt less acculturative stress than those who did not ($p < 0.01$ in June 2008). Interestingly key people felt more acculturative stress than other employees. They were mainly top and middle managers and prior owners or minority shareholders who had the most contact with the Indian parent organization. Some of them visited India once, twice or even more.

Work-related contacts ranged from email enquiries to offers of joint projects, which remained relatively limited. In general, only top managers had Indian superiors, while a few project and engineering managers had Indian subordinates. To the majority of the employees of Gamma Finland, the contacts with the parent company were limited to the visits of the top managers at the quarterly meetings or to the Indians that came through the engineer exchange programme. Some interviewees felt that meeting their Indian colleagues or superiors face-to-face either in India or in Finland enhanced personal contacts, and some interviewees were positive about seeing top managers from India in the quarterly meetings.

However, even those employees who did not have direct work-related contacts could have had a glimpse of their Indian colleagues in local corridors. The perceptions about the parent company were analysed in order to understand more deeply the attitudes towards the parent organization and the cultural differences those attitudes involved. Even though the majority of the interviewees had never heard about Gamma before the acquisition, the first information meetings were informative and many interviewees recognized the similar background and history the companies shared so that the employees of both Alpha and Beta could identify with Gamma India. The perceptions of the parent company were very positive six months after the acquisition. As the parent company become more visible and the contacts between the companies increased, the perceptions of the parent company became more concrete.

Some Finns were surprised at the high level of knowledge and know-how their Indian colleagues possessed. Others were surprised with the decision-making in the parent organization which they perceived to be ad hoc and noted that some decisions could be reversed the next day. The decision-making process was also considered to be very hierarchical and slow. Some thought that Gamma was much bigger than it was. With time, some informants said that the parent company did not feel that big any more and it had turned out to be medium-sized in the global market, just as Alpha was, in its market, before the acquisition.

Gamma was thus considered smaller than the big players in the market. Additionally, some felt that Gamma was still very India-oriented and not as global as they first thought. Two years after the deal, negative attitudes and disappointment had grown. The interviews indicated that the main reasons for disappointment were that expectations regarding both the parent company and the integration process had failed to materialize. Some thought that a bigger company acquiring Alpha would help them to grow and internationalize, that is, move to the next level. However, they did not realize that the parent company Gamma was in transition as well and did not have the solutions that the target company would have required.

Additionally, the employees at Gamma Finland's distant sites were the most 'distant' from the parent company. They had the least contact with their Indian colleagues, and as they were most often working at the customer's premises, they had the least interface with the parent organization – reflecting an underlying cultural clash. As contact and cooperation with the parent company increased, the organizational culture became more visible. The positive perceptions were related to the similar background of the companies and their level of knowledge and know-how, while negative perceptions were related to the slow decision-making process, the hierarchical and bureaucratic organization of the parent company, and the India-centred view of the parent company.

In the summer of 2008, joint procedures and communication remained the major challenges of collaboration between the acquirer and the acquired. Differences in processes and methods of executing them were seen as a challenge that also affected the launching of multisite projects. In addition, the time and schedules of the projects were seen as a challenge, although interviewees were aware of the cultural differences related to the concept of time. Naturally, cultural differences also created difficulties for cooperation and collaboration between Finns and Indians.

Discussion and conclusions

Cultural integration is a very complex phenomenon in the context of cross-border acquisitions. In this study several constructs are presented to analyse cultural integration in a cross-border acquisition. The constructs are strongly intertwined and their relationships require clarification. The key findings of the study are threefold. First, successful cultural integration requires not only cultural fit and awareness, but also understanding of which cultural differences require action and which do not. Second, the results imply that in a cross-border acquisition the perceived cultural differences vary during the process: in the beginning the differences due to cultural distance between the countries are highlighted, whereas later in the integration process the fit of organizational cultures becomes more important. In the process, cultural learning occurs and enhances cultural integration, and in order to increase cultural awareness of both parties, cultural due diligence should continue throughout the integration process. Third, findings also suggest that acculturation may also lead to negative outcomes if expectations concerning the integration process are not met. The case study illustrates very well how cultural integration is a very complex phenomenon. In this Indian–Finnish case, the cultural differences were obvious so that cultural awareness was relatively high. Both companies were aware of the obvious cultural distance although the level of awareness varied: the target company was more aware of Indian culture and history than the acquirer was of the target company's culture and history.

Nevertheless, high cultural awareness did not provide the tools to allow employees of Gamma Finland to deal with the cultural challenges. Cultural fit and distance could only be assessed after the two parties learned from each other, meaning that cultural integration could only really start after the acquisition. The parent company wanted to respect the culture of the acquired target, a successful and fast-growing company. The parent company did not want to impose changes which would disrupt the target's progress.

Consequently, the actual acculturation took relatively long because the contacts between the managers and employees of both companies were limited before and after the deal. Acculturation can only truly happen through interaction. Thus, in cross-border acquisitions where the national and/or organizational cultures are unfamiliar to the acquirer, the acculturation process starts slowly with the acquirer and the target getting to know each other. Accordingly, cultural differences can only be evaluated and assessed after the deal takes place, though this continues throughout the integration process. In line with Janson (1994), this study illustrates that the level of cultural distance or lack of cultural fit should not be an issue, per se. Instead the acquirer must carefully assess cultural fit and cultural distance during the pre-acquisition phase in order to plan the integration strategy and the acculturation process.

As Schweiger and Goulet (2005) suggest, cultural learning may prove to be decisive in facilitating integration. Findings also suggest that during the early stage of the post-acquisition integration, the acculturation process proceeds slowly as the acquirer and the target company get to know each other. During this time period both companies evaluate and assess each other's cultures and become more and more aware of the differences. Companies need to adopt a phased approach in cross-border acquisitions, and during the first year the acquirer should conduct a full-scale cultural audit and communicate the results to the employees (cf. Quah and Young, 2005).

Trust is a key factor for further cooperation between groups with different cultures, and regular dialogue is critical in trust building (Biljsma-Frankema, 2001). Trust building is part of the process when the two companies become acquainted with each other. This phase takes time and can slow down the acculturation process depending on the specific acquisition and level of cultural distance. Cross-border acquisitions in culturally distant countries enable companies to access diverse routines and repertoires that can be beneficial and could have the potential to enhance the combined firm's performance over time (Morosini et al., 1998). In line with Weber et al. (1996), the prevailing, unidimensional approach to researching culture in cross-border acquisitions reveals only a part of the very complex process taking place. Instead, by studying several dimensions – including local/global aspects, low/high cultural awareness and the required degree of integration – a more complete picture can be drawn. These factors should be considered in researching the acquisition process to obtain a better understanding of how culture really affects the integration process.

Even though some of the dimensions of integration are manageable, serendipidity still plays a role. In particular, various process-related issues are often outside the control of the manager (Jemison and Sitkin, 1986). In takeovers, the acquirer can be prone to impose its managerial and cultural practices. From a sustainable human resource management perspective, however, limited cultural integration might lead to better results, as the present case illustrates. Prior research on culture and M&As has been contradictory (e.g. Teerikangas and Very, 2006; Stahl and Voigt, 2008), and a recent meta-analysis raised a number of conceptual and methodological concerns (Stahl and Voigt, 2008). In addition, the nature of the research field is challenging, and the difficulties in obtaining data from several top executives of acquired firms tend to constrain a number of activities associated with traditional measurement development (Veiga et al., 2000; Larsson and Lubatkin, 2001).

Consequently, cultural integration in cross-border acquisitions needs to be operationalized. This study provides a synthesis of the related concepts and suggests a multi-dimensional approach for conceptualizing cultural integration. However, several measurement-related questions need still further clarification, and the unit of analysis needs to be carefully defined as nations and organizations are becoming increasingly heterogeneous (e.g. Usunier, 1998; Jacob, 2005; Schreyögg, 2005).

This research makes theoretical and methodological contributions. First, the study brings dynamics to cultural integration theory by combining analysis of cultural differences and change. Second, the use of a longitudinal, mixed-method research approach provides a methodological contribution to earlier research. Neither quantitative nor qualitative methods alone would have provided such a holistic picture of the phenomenon investigated (cf. Teerikangas and Very, 2006; Brannen and Peterson, 2009).

Nevertheless, a number of questions still remain. For example, in order to enhance cultural integration, managers should probably develop incentives for improved cultural awareness. What should these incentives be? Additionally, the question of experience is often highlighted in cross-border acquisitions, but whose experience should we take into account? After all, in many companies a centralized M&A team coordinates the beginning of the takeover, and then the target company is delivered to the responsible business unit. The M&A team might have a lot of experience operating in different cultures, but the situation in the business unit is completely different. For example, awareness varies in different parts of the organization. The top management that makes the strategic decision of acquisition may be aware of cultural differences, but these differences may not be as visible to the responsible business unit. This lack of awareness may explain some of the cases where the continuity of business after acquisition has not reached the expected objectives.

This study has also many managerial implications. The results emphasize the need of a culturally aware M&A team that can assess the cultural distance and fit prior to the deal but who can also choose an appropriate integration strategy based on findings from the due diligence process. Adequate training of managers can increase their cultural awareness in cross-cultural interaction so that they may reach a psychological position where 'my culture's OK, your culture's OK' (Park and Harrison, 1993; Cartwright and McCarthy, 2005). However, not all culture-related knowledge is easily transferred. In particular, a lot of culture-specific knowledge and understanding of appropriate behaviour is tacit in nature and deeply embedded in people (Johnson et al., 2006).

Furthermore, factors other than the individual determine the success of cross-border acquisition (Bonvillian and Nowlin, 1994). In summary, different national cultures pose both challenges and opportunities for the acquirer and the acquired (cf. Hitt and Pisano, 2004; Reus and Lamont, 2009). Cultural differences can be used to enhance the combination potential in the integration process (Björkman et al., 2007), but culture may impact on acquisition performance both negatively and positively.

Cultural differences matter in cross-border acquisitions, but more research is needed to understand how these differences affect the integration process, how they can be managed more effectively (Stahl and Voigt, 2008.) and which cultural differences matter (Janson, 1994). More research is needed regarding culture-related management characteristics (e.g. cultural awareness) that facilitate cultural integration. In managing cultural integration in cross-border acquisitions, culturally conscious management (cf. Pribilla, 2002) should be the emphasis instead of focusing on differences or similarities. This approach should also enhance sustainable human resource management in the long run.

Notes

1. Although the terms 'mergers' and 'acquisitions' are commonly used interchangeably in the literature, mergers remain a minority of the deals. Additionally, in terms of culture, the basis for integration is completely different. Whereas mergers occur often amongst equals and the result is a jointly negotiated consensus-based third culture, in acquisitions power and hierarchy (acquirer and target) define the roles. As a result, the degree and nature of cultural integration is determined by the dominant partner (cf. Olie, 1994a).
2. Related concepts include cross-cultural literacy (often used in anthropology, for example, when referring to awareness and understanding of cultural differences), cultural intelligence (Earley and Mosakowski, 2004) or cross-cultural competence (Johnson et al., 2006) as an individual characteristic.
3. The cultural distance between cultures was evaluated with the help of a calculator of Hofstede's dimensions found at Hofstede's website (www.geert-hofstede.com).
4. These responses represent the cross-sectional view in the acquired organization, Gamma Finland, though the respondents do not represent a panel but all the respondents of that specific questionnaire round.

References

Angwin, D. and Savill. B. (1997). Strategic perspectives on European cross-border acquisitions: a view from top European executives, *European Management Journal*, 15(4), 423–35.

Arnold, H.J. and Feldman, D.C. (1992). A multivariate analysis of the job turnover process, *Journal of Applied Psychology*, 67(3), 350–360.

Barkema, H.G., Bell, J.H.J. and Pennings, J.M. (1996). Foreign entry, cultural barriers, and learning, *Strategic Management Journal*, 17(2), 151–166.

Beckerman, W. (1956). Distance and the pattern of intra-European trade, *The review of Economics and Statistics*, 38(1), 31–40.

Bijlsma-Frankema, K. (2001). On managing cultural integration and cultural change processes in mergers and acquisitions, *Journal of European Industrial Training*, 25(2), 192–207.

Birkinshaw, J., Bresman, H. and Håkansons, L. (2000). Managing the post-acquisition integration process: how the human integration and task integration processes interact to foster value creation, *Journal of Management Studies*, 37(3), 395–423.

Björkman, I., Stahl, G.K. and Vaara, E. (2007). Cultural differences and capability transfer in cross-border acquisitions: the mediating roles of capability complementarity, absorptive capacity, and social integration, *Journal of International Business Studies*, 38(4), 658–72.

Blau, G.J. (1985). The measurement and prediction of carrier commitment, *Journal of Occupational Psychology*, 58(4), 277–288.
Bonvillian, G. and Nowlin, W. (1994). Cultural awareness: an essential element of doing business abroad, *Business Horizons*, November–December, 44–50.
Brannen, M. and Peterson, M. (2009). Merging without alienating: interventions promoting cross-cultural organizational integration and their limitations, *Journal of International Business Studies*, 40(3), 468–89.
Brewer, P.A. (2007). Operationalizing psychic distance: a revised approach, *Journal of International Marketing*, 15(1), 44–66.
Buono, A.F. and Bowditch, J.L. (1989). *The Human Side of Mergers and Acquisitions: Managing Collisions between People, Cultures, and Organization*. San Francisco, CA: Jossey-Bass.
Buono, A.F., Bowditch, J.L. and Lewis, J.W. (1985). When cultures collide: the anatomy of a merger, *Human Relations*, 38(5), 477–500.
Cartwright, S. and Cooper, C.L. (1992). *Mergers and Acquisitions, the Human Factor*. Oxford: Butterworth-Heinemann.
Cartwright, S. and Cooper, C. (1993). The role of culture compatibility in successful organizational marriage, *Academy of Management Executive*, 7(2), 57–70.
Cartwright, S. and McCarthy, S. (2005). Developing a framework for cultural due diligence in mergers and acquisition, in G. Stahl and M. Mendenhall (eds), *Mergers and Acquisitions: Managing Culture and Human Integration*. Palo Alto, CA: Stanford University Press, pp. 253–68.
Cartwright, S. and Schoenberg, R. (2006). Thirty years of mergers and acquisitions research: recent advancement and future opportunities, *British Journal of Management*, 17, S1–S5.
Chaudhuri, S. and Tabrizi, B. (1999). Capturing the real value in high-tech acquisitions, *Harvard Business Review*, 77(5), 123–30.
Child, J., Faulkner, D. and Pitkethly, R. (2001). *The Management of International Acquisitions*. New York, NY: Oxford University Press.
Cording, M. (2004). *Organizational Integrity and Acquisition Performance: The Role of Values in Chain Creation*, PhD Thesis, Charlottesville, VA: University of Virginia.
Datta, D.K. (1991). Organizational fit and acquisition performance: effects on post-acquisition integration, *Strategic Management Journal*, 12(4), 281–97.
Datta, D. and Puia, G. (1995). Cross-border acquisitions: an examination of the influence of relatedness and cultural fit on shareholder value creation in U.S. acquiring firms, *Management International Review*, 35(3), 337–359.
Datta, D.K. and Puia, G. (2005). Cross-border acquisitions: an examination of the influence of relatedness and cultural fit on shareholder value creation in US acquiring firms, *Management International Review*, 35(4), 337–59.
Den Hartog, D.N. (2004). Assertiveness, in R.J. House, P.J. Hanges, M. Javidan, P.W. Dorfman and V. Gupta (eds.) *Leadership, Culture and Organizations: The GLOBE Study of 62 Societies*, Thousand Oaks, CA: Sage, 395–436.
Dow, D. and Karunaratna, A. (2006). Developing a multidimensional instrument to measure psychic distance stimuli, *Journal of International Business Studies*, 37(5), 578–602.
Dubois, A. and Gadde, L.-E. (2002). Systematic combining: an abductive approach to case research, *Journal of Business Research*, 55(7), 553–60.
Earley, P. and Mosakowski, E. (2004). Cultural intelligence, *Harvard Business Review*, 82(10), 139–46.
Fang, T., Camilla, C. and Schultzberg, S. (2004). Why did the Telia-Telenor merger fail? *International Business Review*, 13(5), 573–94.

Fraser, C. and Zarkada-Fraser, A. (2002). An exploratory investigation into cultural awareness and approach to negotiation of Greek, Russian and British managers, *European Business Review*, 14(2), 111–27.

Ghauri, P. and Grønhaug, K. (2002). *Research Methods in Business Studies: A Practical Guide*, 2nd edn. Harlow, UK: Prentice Hall.

Golden, B.R. (1992). The past is the past – or is it? The use of retrospective accounts as indicators of past strategy, *Academy of Management Journal*, 35(4), 848–60.

Hair, J.F., Black, W.C., Babin, B.J., Anderson R.E. and Tatham, R.L. (2006). *Multivariate Data Analysis*, 6th edn. Upper Saddle River, NJ: Pearson Prentice Hall.

Haspeslagh, P.C. and Jemison, D.B. (1991). *Managing Acquisitions: Creating Value through Corporate Renewal*. New York: The Free Press.

Hitt, M. and Pisano, V. (2004). Cross-border mergers and acquisitions: challenges and opportunities, in A. Pablo and M. Javidan (eds), *Mergers and Acquisitions*. Boston, MA: Blackwell.

Hitt, M.A., Harisson, J. and Ireland, D. (2001). *Mergers and Acquisitions: A guide to Creating Value for Stakeholders*. New York, NY: Oxford University Press.

Hoecklin, L. (1995). *Managing Cultural Differences: Strategies for Competitive Advantage*. Boston, MA: Addison-Wesley.

Hofstede, G. (1997). *Cultures and Organizations: Software of the Mind. Intercultural Cooperation and Its Importance for Survival*. Columbus, OH: McGraw-Hill.

Hofstede, G. (1980). *Culture's Consequences: International Differences in Work-Related Values*. San Francisco, CA: Sage.

Hurmerinta-Peltomäki, L. and Nummela, N. (2006). Mixed methods in international business: a value added perspective, *Management International Review*, 46(4), 1–21.

Jemison, O.B. and Sitkin, S.B. (1986). Corporate acquisitions: a process perspective, *Academy of Management Review*, 11(1), 145–163.

Janson, L. (1994). Towards a dynamic model of post-acquisition cultural integration, in L. Janson and A. Sjögren (eds), *Culture and Management in a Changing Europe*. Stockholm : Institute of International Business, pp. 127–52.

Johanson, J. and Wiedersheim-Paul, P. (1975). The internationalization of the firm: four Swedish case studies, *Journal of Management Studies*, 12(3), 305–22.

Johnson, J.P., Lenartowicz, T. and Apud, S. (2006). Cross-cultural competence in international business: toward a definition and a model, *Journal of International Business Studies*, 37(4), 525–43.

Kanungo, R.N. (1982). *Work Alienation: An Integrative Approach*, New York, NY: Praeger Publishers.

Kim, S.W., Price, J.L., Mueller, C.W. and Watson, T.W. (1996). The determinants of carrier intent among physicians at a U.S. Air Force hospital, *Human Relations*, 49, 947–976.

King, D.R., Dalton, D.R., Daily, C.M. and Covin, J.G. (2004). Meta-analyses of post-acquisition performance: indications of unidentified moderators, *Strategic Management Journal*, 25(2), 187–200.

King, N. (1994). The qualitative research interview, in C. Cassell and G. Symon (eds), *Qualitative Methods in Organizational Research: A Practical Guide*. London: Sage, pp. 14–35.

Kogut, B. and Singh, H. (1988). The effect of national culture on the choice of entry mode, *Journal of International Business Studies*, 19(3), 411–32.

Kusstatscher, V. and Cooper, C. (2005). *Managing Emotions in Mergers and Acquisitions*. Cheltenham: Edward Elgar.

Kvale, S. (1996). *InterViews: An Introduction to Qualitative Research Interviewing.* Thousand Oaks, CA: Sage.

Larsson, R. and Lubatkin, M. (2001). Achieving acculturation in mergers and acquisitions: an international case survey, *Human Relations*, 54(12), 1573–607.

Larsson, R., Brousseau, K., Driver, M. and Sweet, P. (2004). The secrets of merger and acquisition success: a co-competence and motivational approach to synergy realization, in A. Pablo and M. Javidan (eds), *Mergers and Acquisitions> Creating Integrative Knowledge*. Oxford: Blackwell, pp. 3–19.

Laurent, A. (1989). A cultural view of organizational change, in P. Evans, Y. Doz and A. Laurent (eds.). *Human Resource Management in International Firms*, London: Macmillan Press, 83–94.

Lees, S. (2003). *Global Acquisitions: Strategic Integration and the Human Factor.* New York, NY: Palgrave Macmillan.

Leonard-Barton, D. (1990). A dual methodology for case studies: synergistic use of a longitudinal single site with replicated multiple sites, *Organization Science*, 1(3), 248–66.

Lodorfos, G. and Boateng, A. (2006). The role of culture in the merger and acquisition process: evidence from the European chemical industry, *Management Decision*, 44(10), 1405–21.

Luostarinen, R. (1979). *Internationalization of the Firm.* Helsinki: Helsinki School of Economics.

Mael, F. and Ashforth, B.E. (1992). Alumni and their alma mater: a partial test of reformulated model of organizational identification, *Journal of Organizational Behavior,* 13, 103–123.

Meglio, O. and Risberg, A. (2010). Mergers and acquisitions: time for a methodological rejuvenation of the field, *Scandinavian Journal of Management*, 26(1), 87–95.

Meyer, S.P., Allen, N.J. and Smith, C.A. (1993). Commitment to organizations and occupations: extension and test of a three component conceptualization, *Journal of Applied Psychology,* 78(4), 538–552.

Moorman, R.H. (1991). Relationship between organizational justice and organizational citizenship behaviors: do fairness perceptions influence employee, *Journal of Applied Psychology,* 76(6), 845–855.

Morosini, P., Shane, S. and Singh, H. (1998). National cultural distance and cross-border acquisition performance, *Journal of International Business Studies*, 29(1), 137–58.

Mowday, R.T., Steers, R.M. and Porter, L.W. (1979). The measurement of organizational commitment, *Journal of Vocational Behavior,* 14(3), 223–247.

Nadolska, A. and Barkema, H.G. (2007). Learning to internationalise: the pace and success of foreign acquisitions, *Journal of International Business Studies*, 38(7), 1170–86.

Navahandi, A. And Malekzadeh, A.R. (1988). Acculturation in mergers and acquisitions, *Academy of Management Review,* 13(1), 79–90.

O'Grady, S. and Lane, H.W. (1996). The psychic distance paradox, *Journal of International Business Studies*, 27(2), 309–33.

Olie, R. (1994a). Culture and its impact on mergers and acquisitions, in L. Janson and A. Sjögren (eds), *Culture and Management in a Changing Europe*. Stockholm: Institute of International Business, pp. 153–75.

Olie, R. (1994b). Shades of culture and institutions in international mergers, *Organization Studies*, 15(3), 381–405.

Park, H. and Harrison, J.K. (1993). Enhancing managerial cross-cultural awareness and sensitivity: transactional analysis revisited, *Journal of Management Development*, 12(3), 20–9.

Pettigrew, A. (1990). Longitudinal field research on change: theory and practice, *Organizational Science*, 1(3), 267–92.

Porter, L.W., Steers, R.M., Mowday, R.T., and Boulian, P. (1974). Organizational commitment, job satisfaction, and turnover among psychiatric technicians, *Journal of Applied Psychology*, 59(6), 603–609.

Pribilla, P.H. (2002). Personnel and cultural integration, in G. Picot (ed.), *Handbook of International Mergers and Acquisitions*, Houndmills, UK: Palgrave Macmillan, pp. 309–41.

Price, J.L. (2000). Reflections on the determinants of voluntary turnover, *International Journal of Manpower*, 22(7), 600–824.

Quah, P. and Young, S. (2005). Post-acquisition management: a phase approach for cross-border M&As, *European Management Journal*, 23(1), 65–75.

Ranft, A.L. and Lord, M.D. (2000). Acquiring new knowledge: the role of retaining human capital in acquisitions of high-tech firms, *Journal of High Technology Management Research*, 11(2), 295–319.

Reus, T.H. and Lamont, B.T. (2009). The double-edged sword of cultural distance in international acquisitions, *Journal of International Business Studies*, 40(8), 1298–316.

Risberg, A. (2001). Employee experiences of acquisition processes, *Journal of World Business*, 36(1), 58–84.

Rizzo, J.R., House, R.J. and Litzman, S.I. (1970). Role conflict and ambiguity in complex organizations, *Administrative Science Quarterly*, 14(2), 150–163.

Schein, E. (1989). *Organizational Culture and Leadership*. San Francisco, CA: Jossey-Bass.

Schoenberg, R. (2006). Measuring the performance of corporate acquisition: an empirical comparison of alternative metrics, *British Journal of Management*, 17(4), 361–70.

Schreyögg, G. (2005). The role of corporate cultural diversity in integrating mergers and acquisitions, in G. Stahl and M. Mendelhall (eds), *Mergers and Acquisitions: Managing Culture and Human Integration*. Palo Alto, CA: Stanford University Press, pp. 108–25.

Schweiger, D.M. and Goulet, P.K. (2005). Facilitating acquisition integration through deep-level cultural learning interventions: a longitudinal field experiment, *Organization Studies*, 26(10), 1477–99.

Shimizu, K., Hitt, M.A., Vaidyanath, D. and Pisano, V. (2004). Theoretical foundation of cross-border mergers and acquisitions: a review of current research and recommendations for the future, *Journal of International Management*, 10(3), 307–53.

Sinkovics, R.R., Zagelmeyer, S. and Kusstatscher, V. (2010). Between merger and syndrome: the intermediatory role of emotions in four cross-border M&As, *International Business Review*, 20(1), 27–47.

Sousa, C.M.P. and Bradley, F. (2006). Cultural distance and psychic distance: two peas in a pod? *Journal of International Marketing*, 14(1), 49–70.

Stahl, G.K. and Voigt, A. (2008). Do cultural differences matter in mergers and acquisitions? A tentative model and examination, *Organization Science*, 19(1), 160–76.

Taris, T.V. (2000). *A Primer in Longitudinal Data Analysis*. London: Sage.

Teerikangas, S. and Very, P. (2006). The culture-performance relationship in M&A: From yes/no to how, *British Journal of Management*, 17, S31–S48.

UNCTAD (2008). *World Investment Report: Transnational Corporations, and the Infrastructure Challenge*. United Nations Conference on Trade and Development. New York and Geneva: UNCTAD.

UNCTAD (2010) *World Investment Report: Investing in a Low Carbon Economy*, New York and Geneva: United Nations.

Usunier. J.-C. (1998). *International and Cross-Cultural Management Research*. London: Sage.

Vaara, E., Tienari, J. and Säntti, R. (2003). The international match: metaphors as vehicles of social identity building in cross-border mergers, *Human Relations*, 56(4), 419–52.

Vaara, E. ,Tienari, J. and Laurila, J. (2006). Pulp and paper fiction: on the discursive legitimation of global industrial restructuring, *Organization Studies*, 27(6), 789–810.

Veiga, J., Lubatkin, M., Calori, R. and Very, P. (2000). Measuring organizational culture clashes: a two-nation post-hoc analysis of a cultural compatibility index, *Human Relations*, 53(4), 539–57.

van de Ven, A. (1992). Suggestions for studying strategy process: a research note, *Strategy Management Journal*, 13, 169–91.

Very, P. and Schweiger, D.M. (2001). The acquisition process as a learning process: evidence from a study of critical problems and solutions in domestic and cross-border deals, *Journal of World Business*, 36(1), 11–31.

Very, P., Lubatkin, M. and Calori, R. (1996). A cross-national assessment of acculturative stress in recent European mergers, *International Studies of Management and Organization*, 26(1), 59–86.

Very, P., Lubatkin, M., Calori, R. and Veiga, J. (1997). Relative standing and the performance of recently acquired European firms, *Strategic Management Journal*, 18(8), 593–614.

Warr, P., Cook, J. and Wall, T. (1979). Scales for the measurement of some work attitudes of psychological well-being, *Journal of Occupational Psychology*, 52, 129–148.

Weber, Y. (1996). Corporate cultural fit and performance in mergers and acquisitions, *Human Relations*, 49(9), 1181–202.

Weber, Y., Shenkar, O. and Raveh, A. (1996). National and corporate fit in M&A: an explorative study, *Management Science*, 42(8), 1215–27.

Weick, K.E. (1979). Cognitive processes in organization, in B.M. Staw (ed.), *Research in Organizational Behavior*. Volume 1, Greenwich, CT: JAI Press. 41–74.

Welch, C., Marschan-Piekkari, R., Penttinen, H. and Tahvanainen, M. (2002). Corporate elites as informants in qualitative international business research, *International Business Review*, 11(5), 611–28.

Yin, R.K. (2003). *Case Study Research: Design and Methods*, 3rd edn. Thousand Oaks, CA: Sage.

Zander, L. and Lerpold, L. (2002). Managing international alliance and acquisition integration, in M. Tayeb (ed.), *International Management*. London: Pearson Education, pp. 132–55.

10

Does Export Marketing Engagement by Manufacturers Pay Off? Evidence from the Vietnamese Wood Furniture Industry

Bent Petersen and Song-Hanh Pham

Introduction

Presently, price-competitive manufactures from the emerging economies of Asia are flooding the world market. The welfare gains to the consumers in the mature Western economies are undisputed and the persistently high growth rates of emerging economies, such as those of China, Taiwan and Vietnam, are, to a large extent, driven by the successful export of manufacturers.[1] However, from the perspective of individual firms in these emerging economies the export blessings are questionable. Generally, the competition among the exporting firms is extremely tough (Kessing and Lall, 1992; Hobday, 1995; Piore and Ruiz Durán, 1998) and it is now standard procedure for global buyers to appropriate the productivity gains of local manufacturers by incorporating annual price reductions in their sourcing contracts (Gereffi, 1999; Ernst, 2001). A way to escape such a price and profit squeeze might be to 'move up the value chain' into more lucrative upstream and downstream activities (Schmitz, 2006). In contrast to manufacturing, research and development (R&D) and marketing, sales are assumed to be less competitive activities with better opportunities for monopolistic earnings because entry barriers to these upstream and downstream activities are high in general (Wise and Baumgartner, 1999; Powell and Snellman, 2004). Hence, by embarking on a catch-up process (Schmitz and Knorringa, 2000; Kaplinsky et al., 2003; Mudambi, 2008) or a functional upgrading process (Gereffi, 1999; Kaplinsky and Morris, 2001; Humphrey and Schmitz, 2004) in the direction of the two higher ends of the global value chain, emerging economy firms may improve their possibilities for appropriating the value they create in the global chain and thereby generate economic rent.

Against this industrial organization view, there is the capability/resource-based view (Barney, 1991; Hoetker, 2005; Diez-Vial, 2007). It might very well be that competition slackens when firms move up the value chain, but it does not disappear completely, and if entrant firms do not possess the resources needed for exercising the new activities in a capable manner, they are going to operate at a competitive disadvantage with incumbent firms. The liability of foreignness is particularly significant in physically and culturally distant countries. That is why export firms must pay specially attention when dealing with such contexts. Seen from the capability view perspective, exporting manufacturers from emerging economies are better off 'sticking to their knitting' (Peters and Waterman, 1987); in other words, they should keep focused on manufacturing and leaving the upstream and downstream activities to other, more specialized and capable, firms.

In conclusion, the literature offers two opposing theoretical views as to whether emerging economy manufacturers should embark on functional upgrading (as promoted by the industrial organization view) or in general are better off 'sticking to their knitting' (as recommended by the capability view). With these two, equally persuasive, views empirical evidence is imperative, but large-scale empirical studies addressing this issue are in short supply. Hence, Schmitz (2006:563) has summarized that there is limited information on whether other nodes of the value chain (such as logistics, design and marketing) offer higher returns than manufacturing.

The goal of this chapter is to contribute to filling the empirical research gap. The focus is on value appropriation of contract manufacturers in the emerging economy of Vietnam. A large-scale study of Vietnamese manufacturers of wooden furniture is analysed. As a result of the country's economic liberalization process called 'Doi Moi', introduced some 20 years ago, the country's wood furniture industry has globalized. As most manufacturers in this industry are finding their buyers overseas, the industry is well-suited for shedding light on the research question of this chapter, namely, does functional upgrading of marketing and sales activities pay off? The pay-off is measured in terms of export performance and it has been recognized that marketing and sales are a multi-faceted construct. Therefore, we look at the covariance between export performance and the individual marketing and sales activities that in total make up the marketing mix.

The chapter is organized as follows. We next provide a literature review, which leads to the development of six hypotheses about the effect of engaging in specific marketing activities on export performance. This is followed by the research methodology and the results of the survey study. We then analyse and discuss the results, draw policy and management implications, before concluding the chapter.

Literature review and development of hypotheses

The issue as to whether producers from emerging economies are better off by involving themselves in the downstream activities as an add-on to their own manufacturing has been theoretically debated among different literature streams. The capability view (Peters and Waterman, 1987; Barney, 1991; Hoetker, 2005; Diez-Vial, 2007) suggests that a firm should focus on what it does well and give away activities in which it has no or a weak competitive advantage. The argument for international specialization is based on the comparative advantage of nations which recommends that firms in countries with abundant labour should focus on producing labour-intensive products. Compared to sourcing firms from high income countries, emerging economy firms have more advantage in producing labour-intensive products due to the low labour cost, though they are not as advantaged in marketing since there is a lack of managerial skills, marketing knowledge and the capacity to brand in consumer markets. According to this reasoning, for economic efficiency, emerging economy firms should specialize in producing and delegating export marketing responsibility to their foreign partners.

In contrast, the literature on the global value chain recommends a move towards a design and marketing function. Gereffi (1999) argues that to get higher income, emerging economy firms need to move more towards value added activities, including marketing and design. Gereffi names the process in which a firm moves beyond the manufacturing function to other functions in the downstream and/or upstream end as 'functional upgrading'. Studies of the global value chain (Gereffi, 2001; Kaplinsky and Morris, 2001; Humphrey and Schmitz, 2004) have brought to the debate arguments on functional upgrading as a determinant of a firm's sustainable development. These claims lack strong empirical support as most of them are based on a small number of observations. Notably, recent studies (Bazan and Navas-Alemán, 2003, 2004; Schmitz, 2006) begin their inquiries by asking whether functional upgrading really makes emerging economy firms better off. In an empirical study on the Brazilian shoe industry, Bazan and Navas-Alemán (2003, 2004) have found that the profitability of manufacturers who embark on selling their own design and establishing their own marketing channel is not higher than the profitability of those who attached their activities to manufacturing only.

The competition in markets of traditionally manufactured products has become more and more severe. Moving beyond the manufacturing function into functions of high value is a current trend in international business. The question is, then, which functions along the value chain are high value added and bring higher returns? Kaplinsky (2000) argues that design, marketing and R&D often require intangible knowledge that is difficult to learn and imitate, hence have the potential to generate higher returns. Mudambi

(2007) depicted the pattern of value added along the value chain by the 'smiling curve of value creation' in which high value added activities are located at two ends of the value chain: high value added activities include R&D and marketing, while low value added activities are located at the manufacturing stage. Mudambi (2008:12) explains this pattern: 'Mechanization and standardization have reduced the costs of manufacturing and logistics processes. Processes supporting mass customization have become widely available and subject to rapid imitation. This, in turn, has reduced the scope for the use of such processes to generate the differentiation required to support value creation. It is difficult for firms to extract high value added from manufacturing of tangible and standardized products'. In contrast, marketing demands more tacit and experiential knowledge, and not the creation of standardized and intangible values, providing room for generating differentiation and thereby enabling high value added extraction, yielding higher economic returns than the manufacturing function.

Marketing function, more importantly, is a mechanism helping firms to achieve financial success. Mizik and Jacobson (2003) argue that a firm's ability to create value, such as by production or design, is necessary but insufficient to achieve financial success. They argue that marketing factors such as reputation, brand effects and advertising are necessary dividing mechanisms, enabling firms to appropriate more of the value created. Marketing, therefore, plays a key role in the process of extracting profits.

When a firm joins a global value creation system, the amount of value it appropriates depends on its bargaining power, which in turn is subject to not only the firm's value creation and appropriation ability but also its position in the global value chain. The more monopoly position a firm holds, the more bargaining power the firm has, and thereby the higher return it appropriates. For example, Chiu and Wong (2002) provide a case in which powerful buyers force the Hong Kong electronics suppliers to take the buyers' orders even at low economic returns. They argue that 'the weakness of local suppliers in marketing and the tight control of overseas buyers in distribution are just two sides of the same coin. Underlying this business arrangement is such power asymmetry that a buyer's approval is always prior to anything done on the part of a supplier, leaving most suppliers with few choices but to take buyers' orders' (ibid.: 11). Gereffi (1994) explains the distribution of wealth within a chain as an outcome of the relative intensity of competition within different nodes. Kaplinsky (1998:14) argues further that 'sustainable income growth can only be assured by developing the capacity to identify and then appropriate areas of value accretion that are protected to some extent from competition. These protected spheres are characterized by economic rents'. Thus, it is necessary for firms to locate their resources to the activities which provide a favourable position in the chain, protected to some extent from competition, and thus enabling high value appropriation.

Thanks to the advantages of first comers in the global market, firms from advanced market economies tend to retain control over the activities that can create and appropriate the most value and outsource all low value added activities to emerging economies (Mudambi, 2008). They keep the design and marketing function while delegating manufacturing functions to firms in emerging economies. Acting as chain leaders, such first comers coordinate value creation activities along the chain, deciding whom to outsource to and at what price. This governing power enables chain leaders to appropriate a large amount of value, even gaining more value than what they create. The gap between their value appropriation and value creation is what chain leaders seize from other members of the chain, for example from their suppliers in emerging economies. Improving production capability enables emerging economy producers to create more value, but such improvement does not guarantee that the producers will capture the whole value they create. Instead, the bargaining power of chain members decides the amount of value they can appropriate. Improving production capability is necessary but not sufficient for firms in emerging economies to appropriate more value. Meanwhile, moving into more skilled activities like marketing enables emerging economy firms to reach high value added positions and thereby catch more value. Appropriating more value provides a firm with positive cash flow which it can use for expanding its export business and gaining more profit due to economics of scale, thereby sustaining export development. In other words, value creation capability strengthens a firm's value appropriation capability, which in turn facilitates its export success in the long run. In the short term, there may be a downturn in export turnover when a firm moving towards the marketing function is blocked by its customers, as reported in Bazan and Navas-Alemán (2003, 2004). This downturn will disappear in the long run because producers with good marketing capability can approach other types of buyers rather than the captive chain buyer. A firm can overcome a blockage by powerful buyers against its engagement in a marketing function with a multi-chain strategy. Buyers in captive chains may block a producer's moving towards marketing, but it does not mean that buyers in market-based chains can also obstruct a producer's undertaking marketing. When undertaking a marketing function, firms can improve their bargaining powers in market-based chains to gain higher economic returns.

In conclusion, if a producer can move from a pure manufacturing function towards a marketing function, he or she can acquire new capabilities, breaking out of the captive relationship, obtaining a more favourable position to claim more economic returns. In other words, if an emerging economy manufacturer undertakes more marketing responsibility in export business, this can lead to better export performance.

Marketing is a broad concept, including many activities. It will be more meaningful if specific marketing activities are investigated in relation to export performance because marketing activities do not have the same effect on export performance. For example, order-searching activities may positively impact on export turnover immediately, while after-sale service activities fostering customer satisfaction do not boost export sales immediately but promote turnover in the long term. Therefore, for more precise prediction on how each marketing activity influences export performance, we decompose the marketing function into sets of activities along an export marketing process.

Based on the definition of marketing as being the business function identifying customer needs and wants, determining which target markets the firm can serve best, and deciding on the appropriate products, services and programmes to serve these markets (Kotler and Armstrong, 2005), the marketing process can be said to consist of such activities as market research, product development, promotion, pricing, distribution and after-sale service. In international marketing, the key determining factors affecting marketing strategy include the decision to standardize or adapt the approach to the conditions of foreign markets (Cavusgil and Zou, 1994). Hence, the export marketing process can be divided into six main groups of activities: export market intelligence, export product adaptation, export promotion, pricing of the export product, distribution in the export market and after-export-sale service.

Market intelligence includes market research activities such as market forecasting, competitor analysis, order searching, and so on. It is difficult for a firm to increase turnover if it passively waits for customers to knock on their door. Market forecasting and competitor analysis provide firms with knowledge of market conditions, thus helping them to understand better market demand and supply, as well as price; thereby, firms do not miss chances to appropriate high returns, leading to better performance in international markets. Cavusgil (1984) suggests that market intelligence is one of the organizational capabilities that determines export performance. Madsen (1987) notes that a firm's use of international marketing research positively affects export sales, growth and composite measures of export performance. Aaby and Slater (1989) assert that export market intelligence is a 'critical success factor', discriminating successful from unsuccessful small to medium-sized enterprise (SME) exporters. Therefore:

> Hypothesis 1. *Export market intelligence responsibility affects positively export performance.*

Product adaptation is defined in terms of the degree to which the firm's actual and augmented product elements are adapted to export markets to accommodate for differences in environmental factors, consumer behaviour, usage patterns and competitive situations (Leonidou et al., 2002). Product adaptation involves modifying products to be suitable for the habits and tastes of consumers in export markets. It includes such activities as identification and specification of product modifications needed to serve export market customers. Zou and Stan (1998) claim that product adaptation concluded by several studies is a significant determinant of export sales, profit and growth. However, some studies found insignificant effects of product adaptation, while others reported negative effects. It is recommended that product adaptation should be dedicated further research attention, though its overall effects seem to be positive. This research explains the few negative correlations reviewed in Zou and Stan's (1998) study based on cost of adaptation. It is argued that if negative correlations exist between export product adaptation and export performance, this happens in the short run, at the start of product modification for consumers in export markets. In the long run, the initial cost of adaptation may diminish because fixed costs often depreciate over time while turnover may increase because of customer satisfaction with the adapted products, leading to increase in not only export revenue but also profit. The review of export performance literature conducted by Leonidou et al. (2002) deals with the inconclusive issue relating to the negative correlation raised by Zou and Stan (1998) claiming that product adaptation is positively related to export performance. In line with the confirmation by Leonidou et al. (2002), this research investigates the argument that an adapted product can satisfy foreign consumers' needs and preferences better, and that a strong product allows a firm to transfer it more easily to the foreign markets. If a producer can supply products that meet customer demand better, this can lead to greater profitability because a better product–market match can result in greater customer satisfaction, which can give greater pricing freedom vis-à-vis competitors. Therefore, it is posed that:

> Hypothesis 2. *Export product adaptation responsibility affects positively export performance.*

Export promotion consists of such activities as advertising, personal visits and calls to potential customers, emailing, website communication, trade fair participation, and so on. The promotional activities make a firm and its product known to customers and distinguish it from other products. Promotion activities create image and brand and thereby strengthen a firm's bargaining power, leading to more value appropriation.

Zou and Stan (1998) maintain that promotion intensity seems to affect positively export sales, export profits and satisfaction with export. Leonidou et al. (2002) confirms that all six promotion-related variables, including advertising, sales promotion, personal selling, trade fairs, personal visits and promotion adaptation, were empirically confirmed for their effects on export performance. Therefore it is hypothesized that:

> Hypothesis 3. *Export promotion responsibility affects positively export performance.*

Pricing is the only marketing mix variable that generates revenue. It is a means to appropriate value and earn profit. Zou and Stan (1998) calculate that price adaptation seems to influence positively export sales, export profits and export growth according to some studies, but appears insignificant in others. They suggest that the weak and inconsistent research findings on pricing require more research. Leonidou et al. (2002) review studies that show that for six pricing-related activities, including price setting method, pricing strategy, sales terms, credit policy, currency strategy and price adaptation, examined in the export literature for their potential influence on a firm's export performance, only sales terms and currency strategy are not empirically supported for associating positively with any export performance measures. Thus it is argued that pricing, including such activities as price setting, quantity discounts and provision of export financing, is only a means to appropriate value and earn profit. Pricing affects directly export turnover and profit. The greater the extent that a firm can do pricing, the higher price the firm gains, leading to a better export outcome. Therefore, it is proposed that:

> Hypothesis 4. *Export pricing responsibility affects positively export performance.*

Distribution in export markets comprises such activities as operating sales outlets, communicating with local distributors in the export market and employing logistics in that market. These efforts may generate negative cash flow in the short run because resources are withdrawn from low margin contract manufacturing and assembly to build distribution channels in developed country markets; this requires a huge effort and financial investment, often beyond the resources and capabilities of emerging economy firms (Mudambi, 2008). The effort of emerging economy firms to create their own brands and distribution channels in advanced economies may also be blocked or retaliated by leading firms controlling the distribution in export market (see for example, Bazan and Navas-Alemán, 2003, 2004), causing a downturn in export turnover and profit. However, these short-run downturns can be considered investments in developing crucial competences and sustaining existing competitive advantages. Dealing directly with distribution channels in the export markets reduces the commission cost paid to agents, enabling emerging economy firms to capture more value, thus increasing profit. Leonidou et al. (2002) found that the use of export sales representatives/offices and direct buying were found to be related positively to export sales intensity, while the adoption of overseas distributors/agents and merchants showed weak associations with performance measures. Zhang et al. (2003) argued that the strong relationships of exporting manufacturers with their foreign distributors are an enduring source of competitive advantage because, in an increasingly competitive global economy, classical marketing tools, such as price and product quality, are susceptible to competition by strong rivals. Sustained channel relationships enhance international venture performance through reduced transaction costs, a rich market and process-information exchange (ibid.). Therefore, the greater the extent that a firm conducts distribution activities in the export market, the better export outcome the firm gains. Therefore:

> Hypothesis 5. *Export distribution responsibility affects positively export performance.*

After-sale services, including customer serving, warranty service, spare part delivery service, and so on, bring about customer satisfaction. After-sale services are value creation activities. Improving such value creation affects positively the image and brands of firms, thereby improving bargaining power, which enables more value appropriation. Warranty provision has been postulated to augment the value of products exported, since this can offset foreign customers' reservations regarding product performance and reducing risk perceptions pertaining to the purchase of such goods. This element is particularly important when a firm enters a new overseas market or exports to geographically and culturally remote markets. International customers are particularly concerned with an exporter's ability to offer necessary services (Terpstra and Sarathy, 1997). Leonidou et al. (2002) note that customer service has been a critical success factor in international markets. Therefore, it is posed that:

> Hypothesis 6. *After-sale service responsibility affects positively export performance.*

Research methodology

Empirical model

Reviews of the literature on the determinants of export performance (Leonidou, 1995a, 1995b; Zou and Stan, 1998; Leonidou et al., 1998, 2002; Katsikeas et al., 2000; Balabanis et al., 2004) converge to two distinct sets of predictors for export performance, namely background variables and intervening variables. It is believed that intervening variables affect directly export performance. The background group includes variables relating to managerial, organizational and environmental factors that serve as a background or antecedent indirectly affecting export performance. Because of their impact on export performance, background variables should be controlled when predicting the effects of intervening variables.

Firm size

This variable is traditionally used as a proxy for organizational resource availability (Pedersen and Petersen, 1998). It is widely accepted as a determinant of international expansion (Cavusgil, 1984; Johanson and Vahlne, 1977). Large firms are believed to have a greater ability to expand resources and absorb risks than smaller ones (Erramilli and Rao, 1993; White et al., 1998). They are thought to possess an above-average ability to seize profit, to leverage in a lower cost of capital and to diversify their operation portfolios and internationalize easily (Cavusgil, 1984; Calof, 1994).

Export experience

This variable is extensively cited in export performance literature as a determinant of export performance (Madsen, 1989). According to the stage internationalization theory (Johanson and Vahlne, 1977), the more international experience a firm has, the better the firm grows in international markets. Therefore, a firm's export experience can be a predictor of export performance and should be used as a control variable in the research model.

Firm location

This factor does not seem to have been used in control variables of export literature. However, firm location is closely linked to environmental factors such as infrastructures, business climate and government policy, which have been reviewed as background variables influencing export performance. Therefore, firm location should be considered as a predictor of export performance. A firm located in a good business environment with a good infrastructure, availability of raw materials and supporting industries certainly is in a more favourable condition than a firm in an unfavourable business environment.

Taking into account the above discussion, in this study we investigate firm size, export experience and firm location as its control variables. The empirical model will take the form of linear multi-regression correlation with three control variables and six independent variables.

Measurement

Export market intelligence responsibility

Market intelligence includes activities which help a firm to understand its market in order to navigate potential buyers. These market intelligence activities can be the analysis of market trends, competitor analysis, searching for customers, and so on. Practically, in export business, market intelligence mainly involves order searching rather than analysis of market trend or competitors. Therefore, in this research, export market intelligence responsibility is measured by the extent to which a firm conducts order searching.

Export product adaptation

Due to differences in culture, geographical location and climate, export markets may require variability of product specifications. These entail firms to make modifications to their exports to different markets. Therefore, in this research export adaptation responsibility is measured by the extent to which a firm conducts modifications for its export products.

Export promotion responsibility

Promotional activities help the execution of sales. They include advertising, personnel sales, calls to potential customers, and so on. However, not all of these activities are applicable in export markets. The most popularly used promotion method in export is advertising using media such as the internet or specialized magazines. Therefore, in this research export promotion responsibility is measured by the extent to which a firm conducts advertising in export markets.

Export pricing responsibility

Theoretically, any firm should be able to quote a price which is based on either market price or its cost structure. In export business, due to the different market price or cost structure, there exists an issue of information asymmetry in price setting. A buyer may not be well aware of a producer's cost structure and a producer may not be aware of price setting in end-user markets. Therefore, a firm's export profit margin largely depends on its ability to negotiate the price, which strikes a balance between the minimum price it is willing to sell a product for and the maximum price the buyer is prepared to pay. Therefore, in this research export pricing responsibility is operationalized as the extent to which a firm can set a contract price closer to the price it is willing to sell its products.

Export distribution responsibility

Distribution method shows the way a firm distributes its product to the end users. Distribution responsibility is reflected by the extent to which the firm distributes its products directly to its end users. Therefore, export distribution responsibility in this research is operationalized as the extent to which a firm sells directly to end users in its export markets.

After-export-sale service responsibility

After-sale services are services provided to end-user customers, such as customer service, warranty service, spare part delivery, and so on. For simple manufacturing products such as wooden furniture, after-sale service is mainly warranty service. Other after-sale services are less applicable or non-existent. Therefore, after-export-sale service responsibility in this research is operationalized as the extent to which a firm offers warranty service to end users in its export markets.

All the above measurement scales are on the 5-point Likert scale, ranging from 0 to 4, with 4 defining 'completely done by the firm' and 0 defining 'completely done by its business partners'.

Export performance

Reviews of the export performance literature summarize two principal ways of measuring export performance: economic (financial measures such as sales, profits and market share) and non-economic (non-financial measures relating to product, market, export experience , and so on). Most of the background and intervening variables are associated with economic measures of performance, particularly export sales intensity (export to total sales ratio), export sales growth and export profitability (Katsikeas et al., 2000).

Export sale intensity

In an emerging economy such as Vietnam, export turnover is calculated in a foreign currency while domestic turnover is calculated in the domestic currency. Hence, respondents are easily confused when asked to reveal the export to total sales revenue ratio. It is easier for respondents to figure out the export volume to total volume ratio than the ratio of export to total revenue. Therefore, the indicator on export sales intensity is modified in this research as the export volume to total sales volume ratio.

Export profitability

Financial outcomes can be measured objectively as well as subjectively. Objective financial data may provide exact values, but such data are not easily revealed. Subjective managerial perception may not provide exact value, but such data are readily accessible and also important because they affect future strategies. Cavusgil and Nevin (1981) and Schlegelmilch (1986) indicate that managerial aspirations about export profit and export profit relative to domestic profit will affect directly a firm's decision to involve itself further in exporting. The use of this subjective variable encourages more firms to respond because respondents need not provide confidential export profitability figures (White et al., 1998).

The direct question regarding absolute US dollar figures on sales or profits will lower response rates to an unacceptable level. A number of previous empirical studies did not use direct financial performance measures (see for example, Koh, 1991; Kundu and Renko, 2005) but asked questions that referred to the firm's export-profit aspiration level. Therefore, in this research, profitability is to be measured by subjective managerial perceptions which are export profitability fulfilment levels.

Export growth

Export growth is often measured by the ratio of the export turnover or profit of the studied year to that of the previous year. In this research, export growth is measured with the ratio of the export profit of the existing year to that of the previous year.

The use of a multiple item scale was popular in measuring export performance because different measures of this performance capture different facets of the strategic and operational phenomena that underlie it (Katsikeas et al., 2000). Export performance in this research is operationalized as a scale reflecting three indicators: export profit growth, export volume to total sales volume, and export profit fulfilment level.

Control variables

Firm size is measured in terms of the number of employees and is normalized as a logarithmic function of the number of employees. *Firm export experience* is measured by the number of years a firm is involved in the export business and is normalized as a logarithmic function of the number of exporting years. Regarding *firm location,* Vietnam wood furniture producers are in three main regions: the North (in and around Dong Ky), the Centre (in and around Quy Nhon) and the South (in and around Binh Duong). The three regions differ in historical and cultural conditions as well as economic infrastructure. These differences in environmental factors obviously lead to some differences in business performance among firms of different regions. The qualitative variable *firm location* has three categories.

Data collection

One key informant technique was selected as it consumes less time and resources than several others. To overcome the disadvantage of the one key informant technique, the research follows the requirements by Campbell (1955) and Phillips (1981) of selecting informants with specific knowledge regarding the unit of analysis, possessing the capability to describe and communicate the phenomenon of interest, and be independent from the phenomenon of interest. The sampling frame was sorted using sector, ownership and location taken from business directories.

Data were collected through a structured questionnaire (please see the Appendix), which was mailed to one key informant in a firm selected from a list of 1,047. A mail survey was selected because of the advantages it offers, including wider distribution, less distribution bias, better likelihood of thoughtful replies, no interviewer bias, central control, as well as time and cost savings (Erdos, 1974). To reduce the response rate, follow-up mailing and phoning to non-respondents were applied. Thus a total response rate of 28.8 per cent has been achieved, which is satisfactory, given that mail survey response rates vary from 10 to 65 per cent (Armstrong, 1975).

Reliability of data

To overcome unreliable and biased answers, key informants were managers who were in charge of wood furniture exporting. Informants would have no interest in not telling the truth to the researcher since they are independent of the researcher and the research outcome. All critical indicators do not involve any benefit to the informants. Thus it is believed that they provide objective answers. Moreover, according to Erdos (1974), by using a mail survey, the research will experience less distribution bias, a higher likelihood of thoughtful replies and no interviewer bias. In summary, the informants were knowledgeable, holding no motive not to tell the truth and were motivated to provide thoughtful replies. All these empirical settings promise an outcome of highly reliable data.

Statistical technique

The multiple regression method is employed. Latent variables are measured only through multiple indicators, hence confirmative factor analysis is conducted to check the validity of the latent constructs. SPSS 14 and AMOS version 6.0 have been used for data processing.

Results

Testing for the non-response bias

After data screening, testing for linear assumptions and passing, a standard test of non-response bias was conducted to detect and eliminate non-bias problems. In the sample, 54 per cent of respondents answered in the first phase while the rest of the answers were obtained after several additional attempts at data collection. It is assumed in empirical studies that late respondents are similar to non-respondents because both of them do not feel interested in the survey and tend to decline to respond (Armstrong and Overton, 1977). Therefore, the group of late respondents was tested against the early respondents group with respect to equality of means. The test applied is the T-test of null hypothesis that there is no mean difference between the two groups. Based on the significant level of the two tail T-test, the results of the independent samples test for equality of means between the early response group and the late response group shows that at 95 per cent confident level there is no difference between the two groups. Hence, non-response bias does not appear to be a problem.

Testing for the validity of measurements

Construct validity

Conducting confirmative factor analysis for EP, only item EP3 has factor loadings lower than 0.5. To get convergent validity, EP3 with the factor loading lower than 0.5 was excluded. The statistical result was that EP3 had factor loadings lower than 0.5, which indicated that EP3 was not statistically significant to represent construct export performance. The EP scale was finalized with two indicators, EP1 and EP2, with all factor loadings greater than 0.5; VE equalled 0.576 and Cronbach's alpha equalled 0.734, meeting all requirements for convergent validity. EP was validity measured by two indicators, EP1 and EP2, which was therefore computed as a summated scale of these two items.

Hypothesis testing

As suggested by Aiken and West (1991), multiple-regression analysis was used to test the hypotheses. The control variables (*lgIE, lgSi*) and dummy variables (*Lo1* and *Lo2*) were entered in step 1. The independent variables (*MI, Proad, Pro, Pri, Dis, Ass*) were included in step 2. Analysis of result testing had to be based on significances of coefficients of independent variables and model fit.

In the multiple regression model, model fit can be assessed upon five indexes including R square, adjusted R square and standard error of estimate (see Table 10.1). The F ratio and its significant level (Hair et al., 2005) are calculated, of which the adjusted R square is the critical index and should be at least 0.5.

The coefficients of *MI, Proad, Pro* and *Pri* on EP are significant at 0.01 (see Table 10.2), indicating that the effects of *MI, Proad, Pro* and *Pri* on EP are confirmed. Moreover, these coefficients are all positive, implying that Hypotheses 1, 2, 3 and 4 are all supported.

The coefficients of *Dis* and *Ass* on *EP* are not significant even at 0.05, indicating that hypotheses 5 and 6 are not supported. Table 10.3 gives a summary of the results from testing the hypotheses.

Discussion

The hypothesis testing results show that a positive relationship exists between engagement in export marketing and export performance. However, the testing results also suggest that not all marketing activities lead to export success. Engagement in export market intelligence, product adaptation, promotion and pricing significantly contribute to a firm's export success, while engagements in distribution and an after-sales service do not. The contribution of export pricing is the biggest among export marketing tools. This signals that a firm can upgrade in quality, but the most significant determinant of a firm's export performance is its pricing autonomy. A firm needs to increase its pricing autonomy to obtain better economic returns. This result fits well with the earlier theoretical discussion of bargaining power that

Table 10.1 Model fitness

R	R square	Adjusted R square	Std. error of the estimate
0.797	0.636	0.622	0.57527

Note: Predictors: (Constant), *lgIE, lgsize, Lo1, Lo2, MI, Pro, Pri, Proad, Ass, Dis.*

Table 10.2 Model coefficients

	Non-standardized coefficients		Standardized coefficients		
	B	Std. error	Beta	T	Sig.
(Constant)	0.520	0.212		2.447	0.015
lgsize	0.077	0.066	0.048	1.160	0.247
lgIE	0.142	0.110	0.049	1.294	0.197
Lo1	−0.441	0.083	−0.220	−5.318	0.000
Lo2	−0.252	0.114	−0.088	−2.207	0.028
MI	0.140	0.037	0.176	3.778	0.000
Proad	0.116	0.039	0.148	2.948	0.003
Pro	0.172	0.036	0.226	4.820	0.000
Pri	0.213	0.039	0.265	5.412	0.000
Dis	0.003	0.031	0.004	0.093	0.926
Ass	0.034	0.035	0.048	0.969	0.333

Note: Dependent variable: *Export Performance (EP)*.

Table 10.3 Summary of hypothesis testing results

Hypothesis	Content of hypothesis	Testing result
H1	Export-market-intelligence engagement affects EP positively	Supported at 0.01
H2	Export-product-adaptation engagement affects EP positively	Supported at 0.01
H3	Export-promotion engagement affects EP positively	Supported at 0.01
H4	Export-pricing engagement affects EP positively	Supported at 0.01
H5	Export-distribution engagement affects EP positively	Not supported
H6	After-sales-service engagement affects EP positively	Not supported

Note: *EP = Export Performance.*

pricing autonomy determines a firm's economic return. The value of the coefficient of export product adaptation is the smallest (0.148), suggesting that this is the least contributing factor to a firm's export outcome.

The hypothesis testing results support the view that moving towards the marketing function will make emerging-economy firms better off. Previous studies recommending functional upgrading do not clearly indicate how each specific marketing activity contributes to a firm's development in international markets.

It is worth mentioning that although the research findings generally support the view that involving more activities in the marketing function will make firms in an emerging economy better off, the research results suggest that the move towards a marketing function should be done with care. Firms should invest in responsibility which helps them to improve bargaining power rather than internalizing distribution activities in the export market. Assuming more responsibilities in distribution and after-sales service in export markets does not lead to accelerated export growth and increased profits.

Regarding managerial perspectives, the hypothesis testing results also suggest that firms should be more active in their export marketing development in international markets. Priority should be given to export pricing, then export promotion, export market intelligence and export product adaptation. A firm can delegate distribution and after-sales service in the export market to a partner.

Lastly, the hypothesis testing results indicate that, except for the control variable *firm location*, other control variables such as *firm size* and *export experience* are not significant. The findings challenge the popular beliefs that firm size and export experience affect a firm's export success.

Conclusions

Motivated by the debate on whether manufacturers from emerging economies should be involved in marketing functions or delegate them to their international partners, this chapter has provided theoretical arguments and empirical evidence to support the main theoretical proposition that if a producer can move from a pure manufacturing function towards marketing functions, such a producer can acquire new capabilities, breaking out from captive relationships and obtaining a more favourable positioning that allows the firm to claim for better economic returns.

The empirical findings show that taking more responsibility in export product adaptation, export market intelligence, export promotion and export pricing leads to better export performance. Moreover, the hypotheses testing results suggest that among four types of marketing responsibilities, including export product adaptation, export market intelligence, export promotion and export pricing, export pricing contributes the most while export product adaptation contributes the least to a firm's export success.

Although the research provides some notable theoretical and managerial implications, it is restricted by some limitations. These are mostly associated with the design of the measurements. The measurement of export performance was not fully reflected in the research. Export development is a dynamic process which is affected by a number of determinants. However, due to restricted data availability, the research incorporated a limited number of variables and could only conduct a cross-sectional analysis. Such an analysis does not adequately capture the dynamic nature of the examined variables. Although the research took into account the fact that undertaking export marketing responsibility in the year of the research may not contribute to export performance in that year but may be the year later, it only considered time lag for one year while the effectiveness of marketing investment may be time lagged for substantially more than a year. The research results could be improved if better measurement of export performance was developed. The research followed the current practice in the field of the export performance literature, which adopts a composite construct in assessing export performance, combining economic performance indicators with managerial perception. Although performance should be seen in terms of top management goals and ambitions, one could argue that an indicator with managerial perception of performance is not strong enough to measure and compare outcomes of different firms because each manager could perceive performance differently. We therefore suggest further research on export performance using more economic indicators, especially financial, including export profit growth rate and growth rate of profit per capital. Regarding the measurement of the six independent export marketing variables, based on the arguments for the most popularly used marketing activities, the research used a single item to measure each export marketing variable. The measurements of the six export marketing variables may be more precise if they are designed as multi-item scales.

Regarding the selection of statistical model, we chose a linear multi-regression model based on the assumption of no correlation among the six independent export marketing variables. In reality, there may be correlations among the six believed to be independent marketing variables. If this is the case, a structure equation model will be a more appropriate option than a linear multi-regression one.

This study was also limited to the context of wood furniture firms in Vietnam. The findings, if applied to other industries in Vietnam or firms in other emerging economies, should be interpreted with regard to the environmental context of the population. Vietnamese wood furniture firms have developed their internationalization in the period when the country's economy adopted an export orientation. The generalizability of the findings can be strengthened if other industries that developed their internationalization in different time periods are included. The generalizability of the findings can be also reinforced in a study with a population of firms from different emerging economies.

Appendix: Questionnaire

Please answer whether or not your company started exporting, including indirect exporting, before 2009. Information provided by you is to be used for academic research purposes only. Any details relating to identification of your firm is to be kept secret and undisclosed to any other people. Thank you very much for your answer.

Company name: (may not be provided if you do not want to reveal it) : ______________________

Headquarters' location : ______________________

Type of product : ______________________

Number of employees : ______________________

Registered capital : ______________________

Year of establishment : ______________________

Year of first export (including indirect export) : ______________________

Position of respondent : ______________________

Please indicate by circling one of the 0–4 numbers to what extent, in the period from 2007 to 2008, you are carrying out the following activities by yourself or handing them over to other parties. In case your company has several different export product lines please fill in the following questions only for your key export product line, i.e. the product line that in 2009 was generating the greatest export revenue.

0	1	2	3	4
Entirely by others	←		→	**Entirely by your company**

MI	The extent your company has handled export order searching.	0	1	2	3	4
Proad	The extent your company has handled export product modifications.	0	1	2	3	4
Pro	The extent your company has handled export advertising in your export markets.	0	1	2	3	4
Ass	The extent your firm offers warranty service to end-users in its export markets.	0	1	2	3	4

Pri	The extent your firm can set a contract price close to your willing to sell price.	0	1	2	3	4
Dis	The extent your company directly sells to end-users in your export markets.	0	1	2	3	4

Please indicate by circling one of the 0–4 numbers how you evaluate your company's export performance in 2009 (please do this for your key export product line in case your company has several different export product lines).

EP1 What was your company export growth rate in 2009?
EP2 To what extent has your company fulfilled export profit objectives?

Not fulfilled at all 0 1 2 3 4 Totally fulfilled

EP3 What was your company export to total volume ratio in 2009?

Note

1. However, Kaplinsky and Readman (2000) find the existence of immiserizing growth in a furniture sector where there are a number of countries that have experienced growing export volumes and falling aggregate receipts.

References

Aaby, N.-E. and Slater, S.F. (1989). Management influences on export performance: a review of the empirical literature 1978–88, *International Marketing Review*, 6(4), 7–26.

Aiken, L.S. and West, S.G. (1991). *Multiple Regression: Testing and Interpreting Interactions*. Newbury Park, CA: Sage.

Armstrong, J. (1975). Monetary incentives in mail surveys, *Public Opinion Quarterly*, 39, 111–16.

Armstrong, J.S. and Overton, T.S. (1977). Estimating nonresponse bias in mail surveys, *Journal of Marketing Research*, 14(3), 396–402.

Balabanis, G., Theodosiou, M. and Katsikeas, E.S. (2004). Export marketing: developments and a research agenda, *International Marketing Review*, 21(4/5), 353–77.

Bazan, L. and Navas-Alemán, L. (2003). Upgrading in global and national value chains: recent challenges and opportunities for the Sinos Valley footwear cluster, Brazil. Paper presented at the EADI's Workshop on Clusters and Global Value Chains in the North and the Third World, Novara, 30–31 October. (www.eco.unipmn.it/eventi/eadi/papers/bazannavasaleman.pdf).

Bazan, L. and Navas-Alemán, L. (2004). The underground revolution in the Sinos Valley: a comparison of upgrading in global and national value-chains, in H. Schmitz (ed.), *Local Enterprises in the Global Economy: Issues of Governance and Upgrading*. Cheltenham: Edward Elgar, pp. 110–39.

Barney, J. (1991). Firm resources and sustained competitive advantage, *Journal of Management*, 17(1), 99–120.

Calof, J.L. (1994). The relationship between firm size and export behavior revisited, *Journal of International Business Studies*, 25(2), 367–387.

Campbell, D.T. (1955). The informant in quantitative research, *American Journal of Sociology*, 60, 339–43.

Cavusgil, S.T. (1984). Differences among exporting firms based on degree of internationalization, *Journal of Business Research*, 12, 195–208.

Cavusgil, S.T., and Elvey-Kirk, L.A. (1998). Mail survey response behavior: a conceptualization of motivating factors and an empirical study, *European Journal of Marketing*; 32(11/12), 1165–92.

Cavusgil, S.T. and Nevin, J.R. (1981). Internal determinates of export marketing behavior: an empirical investigation, *Journal of Marketing Research*, 18(2), 114–119.

Cavusgil, S.T. and Zou, S. (1994). Marketing strategy performance relationship: an investigation of the empirical link in export market ventures, *Journal of Marketing*, 58, 1–21.

Chiu, S.W.K. and Wong, K.C. (2002). The hollowing out of Hong Kong Electronics: organisational inertia and industrial restructuring in the 1990s. Paper series, Hong Kong: Department of Sociology, The Chinese University of Hong Kong.

Diez-Vial, I. (2007). Explaining vertical integration strategies: market power, transactional attributes and capabilities, *Journal of Management Studies*, 44(6), 1017–1040.

Erdos, P.L. (1974). Data collection methods: mail surveys, in R. Ferber (ed.), *Handbook of Marketing Research*. New York, NY: McGraw-Hill, pp. 90 – 104.

Ernst, D. (2001). Small firms competing in globalized high-tech industries: the co-evolution of domestic and international knowledge linkages in Taiwan's computer industry, in P. Guerrieri, S. Iammarino and C. Pietrobelli (eds), *The Global Challenge to Industrial Districts: Small and Medium-Sized Enterprises in Italy and Taiwan*. Cheltenham: Edward Elgar, pp. 95–130.

Erramilli, M.K. and Rao, C.P. (1993). Service firms' international entry-mode choice: a modified transaction–cost analysis approach, *Journal of Marketing*, 57, 19–38.

Gereffi, G. (1994). The organization of buyer-driven global commodity chains: how US retailers shape overseas production networks, in G. Gerrefi and M. Korzeniewicz (eds), *Commodity Chains and Global Capitalism*. Westport, CT: Praeger, pp. 95–122.

Gereffi, G. (1999). International trade and industrial upgrading in the apparel commodity chain, *Journal of International Economics*, 48(1), 37–70.

Gereffi, G. (2001). Shifting governance structures in global commodity chains, with special reference to the internet, *American Behavioral Scientist*, 44(10), 1616–37.

Hair F.J., Black, C.W., Babin, J.B., Anderson, F.R. and Tatham, L.R (2005). *Multivariate Data Analysis*, 6th edn. Upper Saddle River, NJ: Pearson Prentice Hall.

Hobday, M. (1995). East Asian latecomer firms: learning the technology of electronics, *World Development*, 23(7), 1171–93.

Hoetker, G. (2005). How much you know versus how well I know you: selecting a supplier for a technically innovative component, *Strategic Management Journal*, 26(1), 75–96.

Humphrey, J. and Schmitz, H. (2004). Chain governance and upgrading: taking stock, in H. Schmitz (ed.), *Local Enterprises in the Global Economy: Issues of Governance and Upgrading*. Cheltenham: Edward Elgar, pp. 349–81.

Johanson, J. and Vahlne, J.E. (1977). The internationalization process of the firm: a model of knowledge development and foreign market commitment, *Journal of International Business Studies*, 8, 23–32.

Kaplinsky, R. (1998). Globalization, industrialisation and sustainable growth: the pursuit of the Nth Rent. IDS discussion paper, 365, University of Sussex, Institute of Development Studies, Brighton.

Kaplinsky, R. (2000). Globalisation and unequalisation: what can be learned from value chain analysis? *Journal of Development Studies*, 37(2), 117–46.

Kaplinsky, R. and Morris, M. (2001). *A Handbook for Value Chain Research*. Brighton: University of Sussex.

Kaplinsky, R. and Readman, J. (2000). Globalisation and upgrading: what can (and cannot) be learnt from international trade statistics in the wood furniture sector? Brighton: University of Sussex.

Kaplinsky, R., Memedovic, O., Morris, M. and Readman, J. (2003). *The Global Wood Furniture Value Chain: What Prospects for Upgrading by Developing Countries – The Case of South Africa*. Vienna: UNIDO.

Katsikeas, S., Leonidou, L. and Morgan, N.A. (2000). Firm-level export performance assessment: review, evaluation, and development, *Journal of the Academy of Marketing Science*, 28(4), 493–511.

Kessing, D. and Lall, S. (1992). Marketing manufactured exports from developing countries: learning sequnences and public support, in G. Helleiner (ed.) *Trade Policy, Industrialisation and Development*, Oxford: Oxford University Press, 176–193.

Koh, A.C. (1991). Relationship among organizational characteristics, marketing strategy and export performance, *International Marketing Review*, 8, 46–60.

Kotler, P. and Armstrong, G. (2005). *Principles of Marketing*, 11th edn. Upper Saddle River, NJ: Pearson Prentice Hall.

Kundu, K.S. and Renko, M. (2005). Explaining export performance: a comparative study of international new ventures in Finish and Indian software industry, *Advances in Entrepreneurship*, 8, 43–84.

Leonidou, L.C. (1995a). Export stimulation research: review, evaluation, and integration, *International Business Review*, 4(2), 133–56.

Leonidou, L.C. (1995b). Empirical research on export barriers: review, assessment and synthesis, *Journal of International Marketing*, 3(1), 29–43.

Leonidou, L.C., Katsikeas, C.S. and Piercy, N.F. (1998). Identifying managerial influences on exporting: past research and future directions, *Journal of International Marketing*, 6(2), 74–102.

Leonidou, L.C., Katsikeas, C.S. and Samiee, S. (2002). Marketing strategy determinants of export performance: a meta-analysis, *Journal of Business Research*, 55, 51–67.

Madsen, T.K. (1987). Empirical export performance studies: a review of conceptualizations and findings, *Advances in International Marketing*, 2, 177–98.

Madsen, T.K. (1989). Successful export marketing management: some empirical evidence, *International Marketing Review*, 6(4), 41–57.

Mizik, N. and Jacobson, R. (2003). Trading off between value creation and value appropriation: The financial implications of shifts in strategic emphasis, *Journal of Marketing*, 67, 63–76.

Mudambi, R. (2007). Offshoring: economic geography and the multinational firm, *Journal of International Business Studies*, 38(1), 206–10.

Mudambi, R. (2008). Location, control and innovation in knowledge-intensive industries, *Journal of Economic Geography*, 8(5), 699–725.

Pedersen, T. and Petersen, B. (1998). Explaining gradually increasing resource commitment to a foreign market, *International Business Review*, 7, 483–501.

Peters, T. and Waterman, R. (1982). *In Search of Excellence: Lessons from America's Best-Run Companies*. New York, NY: Harper & Row.

Peters, T.J. and Waterman, R.H. (1987). *In Search of Excellence*, New York, NY: Harper & Row.

Phillips, J.M. (1981). Assessing measurement error in key informant report: a methodological note on organizational analysis in marketing, *Journal of Marketing Research*, 18, 395–415.

Piore, M. and Ruiz Durán, C. (1998). Industrial development as a learning process: Mexican manufacturing and the opening to trade, in M. Kagami, J. Humphrey and M. Piore (eds), *Learning, Liberalisation and Economic Adjustment*. Tokyo: Institute of Developing Economies, pp. 191–241.

Powell, W.W. and Snellman, K. (2004). The knowledge economy, *Annual Review of Sociology*, 30, 199–220.

Schlegelmilch, B.B. (1986). Controlling country-specific and industry-specific influences on export behavior, *European Journal of Marketing*, 20(2), 54–72.

Schmitz, H. (2006). Learning and earning in global garment and footwear chains, *European Journal of Development Research*, 18(4), 546–71.

Schmitz, H. and Knorringa, P. (2000). Learning from global buyers, *Journal of Development Studies*, 37(2), 177–205.

Terpstra, V. and Sarathy, R. (1997). *International Marketing*, Seventh Edition, Orlando, FL: The Dryden Press.

White, S.D., Griffith, D.A. and Ryans, J. (1998). Measuring export performance in service industries, *Journal of International Marketing Review*, 15(3), 188–204.

Wise, R. and Baumgartner, P. (1999). Go downstream: the new profit imperative in manufacturing, *Harvard Business Review*, 77(5), 133–41.

Zhang, C., Cavusgil, S.T. and Roath, A.S. (2003). Manufacturer governance of foreign distributor relationships: do relational norms enhance competitiveness in the export market? *Journal of International Business Studies*, 34(6), 550–66.

Zou, S. and Stan, S. (1998). The determinants of export performance: a review of the empirical literature between 1987 and 1997, *International Marketing Review*, 15(5), 333–56.

11

Venturing Strategy and Growth Pattern of Malaysian Multinational Enterprises

Elaine Y. T. Chew, Lee Peng Ng and Chin Kian Low

Introduction

The international entrepreneurship research stream has challenged many of the traditional theories on internationalization and encouraged researchers to examine international business activities from new perspectives (McDougall et al., 2003). Over the years, several theories on international trade and international business have been developed to explain firms' activities outside their national boundaries such as the classical trade theories by Smith (1994 [1776]) and Ricardo (1978 [1817]). However, these two theories focus on the internationalization process at the national level, rather than at the firm level. Subsequent researchers (see for example, Hymer, 1976; Buckley and Casson, 1976; Dunning, 1988) have contributed significantly to the field of international business by explaining the growth of multinational enterprises (MNEs) and have provided insights into the reasons for foreign direct investment (FDI). The widely acclaimed Upsalla model (Johanson and Vahlne, 1977), which explained that MNEs engage in FDI incrementally and sequentially, has been criticized by entrepreneurship researchers as not being able to explain the emergence of international new ventures (INVs) – those that are new ventures and international from inception (Oviatt and McDougall, 1994, 2005).

Due to the advanced development of communication technology as well as transportation systems, international business activities today are not limited to large established MNEs any more. There is accelerated internationalization among the smallest and newest organizations (McDougall and Oviatt, 2000). Such a phenomenon has been driven by the increased competition as a result of the globalization process that has encouraged entrepreneurs to seek opportunities internationally rather than restrict themselves to the domestic market. Oviatt and McDougall (1994) suggest a model to address the phenomenon of INVs by integrating the theory of international business, strategic management and entrepreneurship.

Despite the increased importance of MNEs and new venture activities from developing countries, most of the research in this area is focused on the cross-border expansion of firms from Western developed countries. There are limited studies on MNEs from Asian newly industrialized countries such as Taiwan, Hong Kong, Singapore and Korea (e.g. Lu and Zhu, 1995; Zhang and Yuk, 1998; Erramilli et al., 1999; Sim and Pandian, 2002). A number of publications on these emerging market contexts focus on the determinants of FDI at the country or regional level (e.g. Chen, 1996; Zhang and Yuk, 1998; Zhang, 2001; Na and Lightfoot, 2006).

However, the knowledge about the operations and development of MNEs from developing and emerging economies in Asia and beyond remains scant. A review of the literature shows that few studies have comprehensively examined the venturing approach and growth patterns of MNEs from developing countries, with the exception of research published by Park and Bae (2004), who developed a typology to examine the dynamic patterns of new venture strategy and growth patterns of Korean firms.

In order to fill the gap in these areas, in this chapter we intend to explore the internationalization strategies and growth patterns of Malaysian manufacturers that engage in FDI. We will also explore the degree of relevance of Park and Bae's (2004) typology in examining new venture strategy in emerging markets. In contrast to Park and Bae (2004), who only focus on technology-intensive industries, we shall study Malaysian firms in different types of business. Park and Bae's typology is adopted as it offers a comprehensive framework for analysing strategic paths of internationalization from local to global markets based on product/market maturity and technological capabilities. The data obtained for the preliminary study will then be used to design questionnaires and develop propositions or hypotheses for testing in subsequent quantitative research to enhance our knowledge in this area.

This chapter proceeds with a more detailed literature review of theories on FDI, internationalization process and growth patterns of firms. Subsequently, the case studies of five Malaysian firms will be presented, followed by a discussion, an account of the research limitations, conclusions and directions for future research.

Literature review

Recently, internationalization has attracted research inquiries by international business and entrepreneurship scholars. Traditionally, research pertaining to international businesses has been focused on large and established multinationals, while entrepreneurship studies have been focused on venture creation and the management of small and medium-sized businesses within the domestic context (McDougall et al., 1994; McDougall and Oviatt, 2000). However, the dynamic changes of the environment, such as technological innovation and increased international exposure of individuals and firms, have enabled firms to operate globally from inceptions or shortly after their inception (Oviatt and McDougall, 1994). Such developments have brought about a greater overlap of international business and entrepreneurship research (McDougall and Oviatt, 2000).

Various theories have been developed to explain FDI and the internationalization process of firms (Morgan and Katsikeas, 1997). For instance, Buckley and Casson's (1976) internalization theory provides a rigorous explanation pertaining to the growth of MNEs and presents insights into the reasons for FDI. They argue that MNEs can gain economic benefits from the exploitation of various assets across a large number of international markets either by exporting or FDI (ibid.). For instance, market seeking firms that aim primarily to expand market share will be attracted to countries with a large, fast growing domestic market. Cost efficiency seeking firms will be interested in investing in countries with relatively cheap labour and raw material costs. To maximize economic gains, firms may be attracted overseas because of the low transaction costs of doing business in a foreign country. For instance, having similar knowledge and experience of business operations and familiarity with the local culture and language may be a source of low transaction costs. Getting involved in internationalization could enable firms to enjoy competitive incentives as a result of free trade agreements. For instance, firms may decide to penetrate a foreign market given a reduction in tariffs and relatively lower barriers. Efficiency seeking firms may internationalize their business activities in a particular country or location to exploit economies of scales through vertical integration so as to enhance the efficiency of regional activities such as production and markets that share similarity in products and services.

Besides the argument of economic benefits, Dunning's eclectic paradigm of international production (the OLI model) (Dunning, 1977, 1988) is one of the most widely referred-to conceptual frameworks for the analysis of international expansion patterns of business firms (Rugman and Verbeke, 2003; Sim and Pandian, 2007). The eclectic paradigm explains a firm's decision to invest abroad as being determined by a configuration of three sets of advantages (Dunning, 1988), namely ownership-specific (O) advantages, location-specific (L) advantages and internalization advantages (I). The O advantage refers to the core competencies that a firm possesses, such as high product quality and innovation, large financial capability, and expertise in marketing or management. The extent to which a firm can leverage its core competencies is closely related to the locational advantages. It is asserted that the core competencies possessed by a firm will be an advantage when they can be realigned so as to be applicable in the location of investment. The L advantages refer to the institutional and productive factors which are present in particular geographical areas; such as cheap labour costs, large market size, political stability, generous tax and other government incentives in a large and fast-growing market. The L in the framework explains the locational pattern of MNEs' investment activities abroad. Lastly, I advantages stem from the capacity of a firm to manage and coordinate activities internally. In short, the O advantages explain why firms engage in FDI in the first place, while L advantages explain why overseas production is preferred to exporting. Finally, I advantages explain why overseas production is preferred to other methods of transferring assets internationally, such as licensing.

The widely used Uppsala model explains internationalization, too. It argues that the internationalization of a firm is an incremental learning process (Johanson and Weidersheim-Paul, 1975; Johanson and Vahlne, 1977). The model suggests that firms would first establish themselves in a domestic market and only get involved in international activities gradually, which would increase the firms' foreign market commitment as they gain more experience and knowledge over time (ibid.). This model proposes that international business activities of firms tend to start with export via independent representatives/agents, followed by the establishment of sales subsidiaries and eventually an engagement in production in the host country. A firm's foreign operations across different countries are influenced by the psychological distance, which is the sum of factors preventing the flow of information from and to the market. The factors include differences in language, education, business practices, culture and industrial development. As such, firms' initial investment is focused on a foreign market with closer psychological distance, followed by markets with greater psychological distance as companies acquire more knowledge (Johanson and Vahlne, 1977).

However, the sequential approach to FDI as proposed by the Uppsala model has been challenged by a number of researchers (e.g. McDougall et al., 1994; Oviatt, McDougall and Shrader, 1994, 2003; Knight and Cavusgil, 1996; Fan and Phan, 2007; Mudambi and Zahra, 2007) as it fails to describe the phenomenon of INVs (McDougall and Oviatt, 2000). The advancement of technology in business communication, such as internet and video conferencing, has made international business venturing relatively easy as many of the conventional barriers are overcome. In other words, firms intending to venture abroad no longer need first to establish themselves in a domestic market. INVs are defined as firms that involve themselves in international business activities from inception and which seek to derive significant competitive advantages from the use of resources and the sale of their output in multiple countries (Oviatt and McDougall, 1994).

Realizing the limitations of the Uppsala model (Johanson and Weidersheim-Paul, 1975; Johanson and Vahlne, 1977), Johanson and Vahlne (2003) have proposed the revised internationalization-network model, which emphasizes learning through relationships. The revised model asserts that relationships enable firms to penetrate new country markets in which they can build new relationships and employ these as a basis for entering other country markets. Nevertheless, this revised model continues to assert the importance of experiential learning and resource commitment (Johanson and Vahlne, 1977, 1990) in addition to the element of network relationships. In 2009, Johanson and Vahlne further revised the Uppsala internationalization process model by adding recognition of opportunities, trust building and knowledge creation. This revised business network internationalization process model implies that internationalization depends on a firm's network relationships and its commitment to follow relationships with partners abroad where opportunities are spotted.

Different researchers have attempted to develop typologies in trying to understand the type and nature of INVs. For instance, Oviatt and McDougall (1994) suggest that different types of INVs can be distinguished by the number of value chain activities that are coordinated and by the number of countries entered. Gregorio et al. (2008) present a typology of INVs, delineating a variation in the extent to which new ventures span multiple markets and a variation in the degree to which new ventures entail the combination of individuals and/or other resources from different countries. The authors suggest that the emergence of INVs is the cross-border nexus of individuals and opportunities. INVs might emerge as there are opportunities for them to leverage domestically based resources across national borders. Some might emerge due to the opportunities to exploit foreign-based resources to serve the needs of domestic markets.

Park and Bae (2004) introduce a comprehensive new venture framework by using three dimensions to categorize different types of new venture strategies in developed countries, which include the level of technological capability (follower vs pioneer), product-market maturity (existing vs emerging) and target market (local vs global market). Consistent with Dunning's (1988) ownership advantage perspective, the asset endowments of a firm are one of the important factors for the firm's internationalization decisions. In addition, various studies support the view that firm-specific resources such as technological capabilities and product innovation will influence firms' performance (e.g. Zahra and Bogner, 1999; Bruton and Rubanik, 2002; Keskin, 2006). Product-market maturity, as described by Park and Bae (2004), is linked to the various stages of the product life cycle (PLC). The introduction and growth stages represent emerging markets, while the existing market is referred to as being in a maturity or decline stage. Lastly, the target market is defined as the geographical scope of the markets that new ventures enter and operate in.

Based on these dimensions, Park and Bae (2004) have developed seven types of new venture strategies as follows:

- Reactive imitation (local followers in the local existing market) – traditional SMEs that operate in an existing market, which is at the mature or declining stage. Such SMEs usually lack research and development (R&D) activities.

- Import substitution (local pioneers in the local existing market) – local firms with certain technological capabilities that provide products with a similar or slightly lower quality than MNEs and global innovators, but which are offered at a lower price to customers.
- Proactive localization (local followers in the local emerging market) – followers that imitate technology from market0 followers and perform modifications to match local customer needs.
- Creative imitation (local pioneers/global followers in the local emerging/global existing) – the firms possess technological capabilities in emerging industries in a local market and they are followers in the existing global markets.
- Global niche strategy (global pioneers in the global existing market) – new ventures focused on niche markets, offering specialized products at a premium price.
- Early market entry (global followers in the global emerging market). This strategy is followed by new ventures that are fast followers in global markets, combining existing knowledge and new technology development to provide their products in global emerging markets.
- Global innovation (global pioneers in the global emerging market) – new industries are created through the invention and commercialization of new technology and through the application of existing technology to new products.

The following is the diagram showing the new venture typology by Park and Bae (2004):

Park and Bae (2004) suggest that local new ventures with proper technological capabilities can pursue business opportunities in the global context. The initial conditions of the firms, their management and technological capabilities are found to influence the growth patterns and the speed of change of successful new ventures. The analysis also found that Korean

			Level of technological capabilities		
			Global follower		Global pioneer
			Local follower	Local pioneer	
Product/market maturity	Global emerging			Early market entry	Global innovation
	Global existing	Local emerging	Proactive localization	Creative imitation	Global niche
		Local existing	Reactive imitation	Import substitution	

Figure 11.1 New venture strategies framework

Source: Park and Bae (2004).

firms enter the global market by following a two-step internationalization process which is from creative imitation to global players.

Methodology

The five firms from different industries have been selected using purposive sampling. Their analysis helps us to identify the venturing strategies and the growth patterns of Malaysian multinationals. From the total of five firms presented in this chapter, two of the firms are publicly listed, while the remaining are SMEs. All the firms, except for one, are Malaysian new ventures which were established less than 20 years ago.

The case studies are mainly built on data collection through in-depth face-to-face interviews and open-ended questionnaires with the key decision-makers of the firms. Secondary data from company reports have also been collected. The in-depth personal interviews took place at locations in China and in the local premises of the firms. The interviews took two hours on average. The personal interviews and the administration of the questionnaires were conducted at different points of time due to the busy schedule of the key decision-makers in each firm. A copy of the questionnaire was emailed to the key personnel prior to the scheduled interview date.

Case summary

Case 1: Firm A

Firm A was established in the early 1990s. The company founder holds a degree in physics. He has more than 20 years experience in the rubber and latex manufacturing business. The founder seized the opportunity to start a business related to rubber products at a time when incentives were readily available from the local government. Through such timeliness, Firm A was able to benefit from its first-mover advantage. Its major product is a gloves, and the company began to export the product overseas from the time of its inception. It started operations with only one factory with less than five production lines. Currently, the firm is one of the world's leading glove manufacturers with a more than 20 per cent share of the world market. The firm was listed on the Kuala Lumpur Stock Exchange in the early 2000s. At the time of the interview, it had about 20 factories with more than 8,000 employees and exported to nearly 200 countries. The firm's factories were in Malaysia, Thailand and China.

Firm A faced fierce competition when it first introduced its brand to the international market. It was able gradually to acquire more market share by providing high quality products and reasonable pricing. In recent years, this firm has strengthened its R&D in order to develop more sophisticated products. It collaborates with a university in China to conduct research and laboratory testing with the aim of improving its existing products. As the development and manufacturing of gloves is not a technologically complicated process, the R&D costs of the firm are relatively low. The firm's continuous emphasis on R&D enables it to produce a diversified range of high quality and value-added glove products to cater for the ever increasing expectations of original equipment manufacture (OEM) clients. The firm's products have received numerous awards locally and internationally. The United States and Europe each account for 30 per cent of the firm's total exports. Sales offices have been set up in Germany and the United States as an ongoing effort to expand the firm's market share in Europe and North America. The firm's sales revenue for 2008 was above RM1 billion. The firm placed great emphasis on process innovation via a lean production system and invested substantially in modern manufacturing facilities in order to achieve cost efficiency.

Case 2: Firm B

Firm B was founded by two entrepreneurs, one of them with only a high school qualification obtained in the 1970s. At the time of its inception, the firm produced garments with three sets of second-hand sewing machines. Gradually, the firm diversified its business to embroideries, labelling and packaging to provide the relevant parts or services to finished garments. The diversification is part of the strategic vision of the founders to expand the business's reach. Firm B was listed on the Kuala Lumpur Stock Exchange in the mid-1990s. It is one of the pioneers in Malaysia of CAD automatic cutting machines and CAD-CAM marker planners. The adoption of the new technology enabled the firm to improve its efficiency and hence has created significant cost reductions and innovative designs. In the mid-2000s, the firm identified an opportunity and further diversified its packaging business to plastic packaging. As its major client in the textile business relocated its regional operation in Asia to Shanghai, China, the firm decided to accept its major client's invitation to invest in that country. Its plant in China is strategically located close to its major client so as to work logistically and closely by providing value-added services beyond those offered in Malaysia. It is a strategic move that has allowed the company to become vertically integrated in the value chain system. The saturation of the domestic market and stiff competition from local players in Malaysia also contributed to the firm's decision to seize the opportunity to follow its client by venturing abroad. The sales revenue for the firm in year 2008 was above RM400 million. As of July 2009, it had approximately 13,000 employees in Malaysia, China and Cambodia. To date, about 99 per cent of its apparel is exported overseas.

Case 3: Firm C

Firm C was established in the early 1990s. The founder of the firm is an entrepreneur with an accounting background. The firm started with producing metal stamping for furniture components. As the local furniture industry declined, it diversified its focus on metal stamping to the electrical and electronics industry. When its major IT clients shifted their production to China, in the mid-2000s, the firm shifted its focus to providing metal stamping for the disk drive industry. The firm has been market driven and the marketing team is aggressively looking for expansion opportunities that are complementary to its existing core business. Hence, the firm ventured into metal stamping for the automotive and telecommunications industries in 2007 and 2008 respectively. It has a group of experienced engineering staff who are able to design and build prototypes based on client needs as well as to provide cost saving advice to clients. The sales revenues for the firm in 2008 was above RM20 million. In 2008, around 60 per cent of its products were exported to overseas markets.

Case 4: Firm D

Firm D was founded by a group of engineering and economics graduates in the early 2000s. The major product or service provided by the firm is total cleanroom solutions for the semiconductor, electronics and medical industries. Given the unique business that provides technological solutions, Firm D locates itself close to its clients. Hence, the firm expanded its operations to China predominantly owing to the relocation of the manufacturing facilities of its major customers to that country. The firm is also the first Malaysian clean room solutions provider that ventured into China. Since the mid-2000s, the firm has aggressively expanded its business in foreign countries. Besides China, Thailand, Poland, Morocco, Singapore, Vietnam, the Philippines, Scotland, Sudan and Sri Lanka, the firm is in the midst of setting up operations in Paris and London. The firm's rapid expansion is made possible by its ability to provide effective cost saving solutions for its clients. The sales revenue of the firm was above RM30 million in year 2008.

Case 5: Firm E

Firm E was established in the mid-1990s. The founder of the firm had worked as a laboratory assistant in a local university for six years and received two months of training in Europe. He also worked briefly in Singapore in the same industry. Before the firm's inception, the founder leveraged his industrial skills by some involvement in the glass ornament business. This initial business venture faced a low return and a low debt collection. With the encouragement and support of a former colleague, the founder decided to venture into the laboratory glassware business. The firm started by capturing a share of the domestic market. The industry recognition for the firm's high quality products drew the attention of a Japanese firm, which then provided financially support for the purchase of sophisticated equipment and eventually a contract to produce for them. This was followed by exploring new business opportunities in Singapore. The founder also conducted his own market analysis to identify overseas markets and to set up sales offices in the Association of Southeast Asian Nations region.

The first step of the firm's market expansion in the region started with the founding of an affiliated firm in Thailand in 2003. In addition, a plant was set up in China in the same year in order to expand the firm's manufacturing capacity. The firm's major products are interchangeable laboratory glassware, condom formers and volumetric glassware. Its major clients include government agencies, universities and colleges, food and beverage manufacturing firms, hospitals, environmental institutions, biotechnology firms, testing and analytical laboratories, etc. The firm had imported a calibration machine from Germany in 2007 to produce volumetric glassware with an authorization to issue quality certificates which was recognized by the German authorities. The sales revenue of the firm for 2008 was above RM20 million.

Findings and discussion

The summary of strategies and growth of Malaysian new ventures as well as growth patterns and dynamic changes are presented in Tables 11.1 and 11.2.

Internationalization process, growth patterns and strategic change

The results support the view that the internationalization process of an organization does not necessarily experience sequential stages as proposed by the Uppsala model that stresses establishing positions in the domestic market and only then gradual advancement towards internationalization. For instance, Firm A has been involved in multinational activities since business commenced, while Firm D set up its subsidiaries overseas merely two years after its establishment (Table 11.1). The internationalization process of these two firms also differs from Park and Bae's (2004) conclusion that new ventures enter the global market by following a two-step process – migration towards creative imitation and transition towards a global player. Nevertheless, the path of internationalization of Firm B supports Park and Bae's view that creative imitation is a stepping stone between two different competitive markets, i.e. the local and global ones. Firm C and Firm E (Table 11.1), which use creative imitation as their current competitive strategy, have both evolved from a position of reactive imitation and import substitution (Figure 11.2).

Firms with strategic change growth patterns are firms that could accumulate technological capabilities and change their products and target markets (Park and Bae, 2004). The strategic change in growth patterns can be observed among Firms A, B and D (Tables 11.1 and 11.2). We can argue that the three firms are owned by founders who have the necessary knowledge and expertise. They play a significant role in their respective industry with a high domestic market share and high export ratio. The three firms constantly seek new opportunities, especially in the international markets. They have a strong business foundation and a strong hold of the domestic market. They have equipped themselves with a number of core competencies or firm-specific advantages that they can leverage when venturing abroad to adapt to market needs quickly (Table 11.2). Thus, these firms can grow through strategic change. For instance, Firm A's core competencies include its ability to achieve cost efficiency and economies of scale as a result of a lean production system, a huge production capacity and sustained demand. Years of experience and a fast learning curve also enable this firm to achieve cost efficiency through process innovation. Consistent with its market driven and cost efficiency strategies, Firm A has established two plants in China to benefit from its location advantage (Dunning, 1977, 1988). Setting up new plants in China is a strategic move to corporate growth given the access to cheap raw materials and labour, as well as the ability to cut costs by leveraging the strategic location in China for exporting to major clients in the US market. In recent years, this firm has strengthened its R&D to develop sophisticated products that are market driven. Firm A collaborates with a university in China to conduct research and laboratory testing with the aim of improving the quality and weight of its existing products. All continuous efforts have resulted in competitive advantages that have allowed Firm A to engage in aggressive market positioning in the global marketplace from an early market entry in the early 1990s to become a global innovator in the mid-2000s.

This study could identify a few common strengths of the interviewed firms that have been pivotal in overseas business venturing. One of the common strengths is the strong customer relationships that have been highlighted by Firms B and D. These firms have built close relationships with their major clients through their ability to provide consistently high quality products and prompt and reliable services. Their sustained high performance assists in building trust with their clients. Eventually, Firms B and D were invited by their major clients to set up plants in China so as to be logistically closer and integrated into the clients' supply chain, bringing quick improvement to on operational issues and efficient customization and/or collaboration in designing products and services. Operating and competing in the competitive and rapidly changing business environment of China exposed these firms to market trends, advanced technologies and latent needs for products and services. This exposure enabled the firms unexpectedly to take a big leap in accumulating technological capabilities and in expanding into markets with new products and services that are complementary to the core business. Firm B has a strong ability to fulfil the demand of its customers for more sophisticated products and it produced services that are complementary to

Table 11.1 Summary of strategies and growth of cases of Malaysian new ventures

	Firm A	**Firm B**	**Firm C**	**Firm D**	**Firm E**
Characteristics of firms					
Founding year	Early 1990s	Early 1970s	Early 1990s	Early 2000s	Mid-1990s
CEO	Founder/owner	Founder/owner	Founder/owner	Founder/owner	Founder/owner
Major product market	Powdered glove	Apparel	Metal stamping	Total cleanroom solutions	Interchangeable laboratory glassware, condom formers and volumetric glassware
Growth strategies and products	**Early market entry** (early 1990s to early 2000) powdered glove	**Proactive localization** (1970s) apparel	**Reactive imitator** (early 1990s) metal stamping for furniture components	**Import substitution** (early 2000s) total cleanroom solutions for clients in Malaysia	**Import substitution** (from mid-1990s) interchangeable laboratory glassware and condom formers
	Global innovator (from mid-2000s) powdered glove (production efficiency led to lower cost structure and hence became the global market leader)	**Creative imitation** (from mid-1980s) embroidery (apparel needs embroidery)	**Reactive imitator** (mid-1990s) metal stamping for electrical and electronics industry	**Global innovator** (from mid-2000s) total cleanroom solutions for global clients (China, Paris, London, North Africa, Poland, etc.)	**Import substitution** (from mid-1990s) scientific instruments
		Creative imitation (from 1990s) labelling (apparel needs labels)	**Creative imitation** (mid-2000s) metal stamping for disk drive industry		**Import substitution** (late 1990s) burettes

		Creative imitation (from 2000s) packaging (apparel needs packaging) **Early market entry** (from late 2000s) bottling (a form of packaging for a major client) and apparel; (from early 2000s) design and develop (for major clients)	**Creative imitation** (from mid-2000s) metal stamping for automotive industry **Creative imitation** (from late 2000s) metal stamping for telecommunications industry		**Creative imitation** (mid-2000s) volumetric glassware
Technical capabilities (%)					
Ratio of R&D to employee	0.5	4.0	4.0	6.0	7.5
R&D investment	1	8	16	1	5
Internationalization					
Export ratio	Range of 90%	Range of 90%	Range of 60%	Range of 90%	Range of 10%
Growth rate of export	Around 40%	Around 30%	Around 30%	Around 20%	Around 5%
Foreign subsidiaries	Less than 10	Less than 10	1	More than 10	Less than 5
Performance (2008)					
Sales (approximate)	RM1,500 million	RM500 million	RM30 million	RM30 million	RM20 million
Sales growth	Range of 20%	Range of 10%	Range of 20%	Range of 10%	Range of 10%
Number of employees (2009)	Around 8,000	Around 10,000	Around 200	Around 50	Around 50

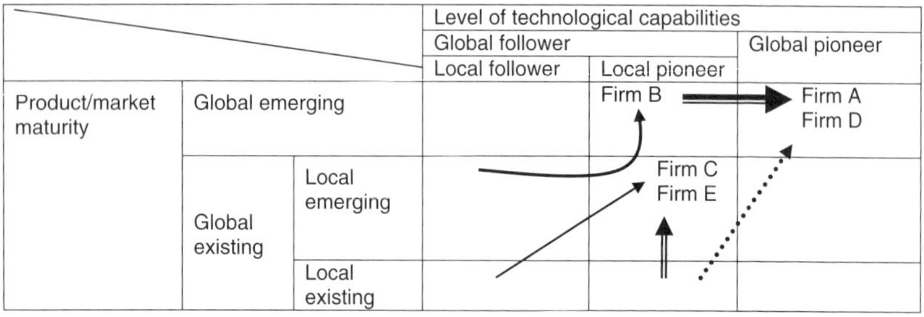

Figure 11.2 Different growth paths of Malaysian new ventures

the core apparel business by developing its unique apparel concept that is sold to existing customers. Despite its apparel being its main product, Firm B has ventured into the packaging and bottling business due to the higher profit margins from this segment. Firm D provides cost efficient and energy saving clean room services to customers. Apart from complying with international clean room standards, Firm D has also placed great emphasis on technical innovation and continuous improvements. Such strategic emphasis enables Firm D to provide high quality products and services that are effective in reducing the maintenance costs among the customers. Along with its customized and innovative clean room technology, the firm's strategic move to China has positioned it as a global innovator just two years after its establishment.

The growth pattern of Firms C and E is identified as strategic replication (Table 11.2). This means that new ventures pursue similar strategies even if they diversify into new markets with similar characteristics to previous ones in terms of three dimensions: technological capability, product-market maturity and the geographical target market (Park and Bae, 2004). Firm C ventured into metal stamping for the automotive and telecommunications industry as the growth in the electrical and electronics, as well as the disk drive industry, has slowed down. Firm E has emerged as a major manufacturer of interchangeable laboratory glassware and scientific instruments in the 1990s and is also currently involved in the manufacturing of volumetric glassware. Although Firm E innovatively created a cost-effective machine for the purpose of producing high quality volumetric glassware for high-end markets, its business venturing into Singapore and Indonesia replicates the same business approach and strategy.

Determinants of growth patterns and strategic changes

Park and Bae (2004) contend that three main factors affect the growth patterns and strategic changes of new ventures and which are the initial conditions of the new ventures: entrepreneurs' management capabilities, their technology strategy and efforts to accumulate technological

Table 11.2 Growth patterns and dynamic changes of case firms

	Firm A	**Firm B**	**Firm C**	**Firm D**	**Firm E**
Major product	Powdered gloves	Apparel	Metal stamping	Total cleanroom solutions	Interchangeable laboratory glassware, condom formers and volumetric glassware
CEO background	Physics major	high school qualification	Accountancy	Engineering major	Laboratory assistant/glass blower
Competitive strategy					
Initial	Early market entry	Proactive localization	Reactive imitator	Import substitution	Import substitution
Current	Global innovator	Early market entry	Creative imitation	Global innovator	Creative imitation
Strategic changes	Fast	Moderate	Moderate	Fast	Moderate
Growth patterns					
Replication vs change	Strategic change	Strategic change	Strategic replication	Strategic change	Strategic replication
Market vs technology	Market-oriented	Market-oriented	Market-oriented	Market-oriented	Market-oriented
Degree of globalization	High	High	Medium	High	Low
Performance	High to very high	Medium to high	Medium to high	High to very high	Medium to high

capabilities. Our analysis, using the Park and Bae framework, has been useful for explaining the growth patterns of Malaysian MNEs venturing from the domestic to the global business arena. However, the present study has found that the network capability of firms is another important factor in determining the growth patterns and firms' strategic changes. This finding implies that the aspect of network capability is necessary when evaluating internationalization processes and growth patterns of firms along with Park and Bae's framework. This finding also reinforces the importance of networks as an additional factor in Johanson and Vahlne's (2003) revised version of the internationalization-network model.

The initial conditions are related to the first product market and technological capabilities of new ventures that can critically affect the performance and future growth potential of new ventures (Park and Bae, 2004). Organizational and environmental factors will have a significant influence on a firm's potential and future direction. Two of the five firms in this study ventured abroad when they were invited by major clients. The invitation by clients and the pressure to sustain business opportunities from their main clients were the dominant driving forces that motivated the firms to take risks and decide on FDI. To a small extent, their decision was also partly spurred by internal/organizational factors such as declining sales and slow domestic growth. Furthermore, the firms also experienced high operating costs due to the increase in training expenses, especially for those workers who lacked skills. Domestic environmental factors over which the firms have less control have also prompted the companies to consider FDI. These include saturated domestic markets, little governmental focus on vocational training and difficulty in securing large projects. Meanwhile, the overseas environmental factors that have attracted the firms to engage in FDI include big untapped markets, a logistically close position to a major client in the supply chain system and relatively lower labour and material costs.

All interviewed firms had set market orientation as part of the strategy for enhancing growth. They are willing to invest in better technology to enhance organizational capability to provide value-added services which can enable them to move upstream in the value chain system. The ability to provide reliable services and high quality products according to customers' specification at a competitive price has enabled these firms to build trust and maintain good relationships with their customers.

Entrepreneurs' management capabilities have affected the strategic decisions and future directions of their businesses, thus contributing to their success or failure. The achievements of the five firms in the case studies have demonstrated the ability of the firms to respond and adapt fast to the changes in the environment. These firms have been able to capitalize on their technological and management capabilities to grow from reactive to creative imitation and to venture into global markets. All firms in this study perceive creativity and innovation as essential for continued growth of the business. Therefore, the continuous R&D efforts enable the firms to accumulate knowledge and technological capabilities that will enable them to produce better quality products and services. The R&D activities are performed in-house and/or in collaboration with universities, or by building strategic partnerships with other organizations to develop better technology.

In addition, this research has found out that networking is crucial for the development of new ventures. The network built through long-term customer relationships is the dominant driving force in motivating the firms to take risks in venturing abroad. Although the firms in this study have developed firm-specific advantages and technological and management capabilities to create a significant presence in their respective industry, it was their major clients' encouragement and support that prompted the firms to venture abroad. The network built over the years of business relationships assured most of the firms in this study that the many risks and transaction costs involved in FDI modes of operation could be minimized and managed.

Our findings on the importance of networks in the process of internationalization reinforce the findings in the network literature. The significant role of networks in the internationalization of born global firms has been widely recognized by various researchers (e.g. Madsen and Servais, 1997; Jaklic, 1998; Anderson and Wictor, 2003; Harris and Wheeler, 2005). Coviello and Munro (1995) posit that smaller firms' internationalization is frequently driven by their networks. They further argue that network partners influence a firm's choice of market and entry mode. Networks and relationships were found to have a significant impact on the internationalization of all firms, regardless of their size (Mort and Weerawardena, 2006). Networking capabilities have been found not only to be central to the growth of the firms in the hi-tech sector but also to play a similarly important role for firms in the low-tech sectors of the economy. In addition, business networks enable firms to proceed faster with international growth instead of adopting a gradual step-by-step approach (Chetty, 2003).

Conclusion

The results of this study provide better understanding of the development of new ventures and their internationalization process, which can serve as a reference and guideline for researchers and policy-makers. The findings of this chapter revalidate the framework suggested by Park and Bae (2004). A refined model needs to be developed given that Park and Bae's one is of a greater relevance to hi-tech firms. As such, more refined models can be developed for generalization purposes.

We should of course acknowledge the limitations of this study. First of all, the sample used comprises five firms from different industries, thus financial performance comparisons could not be made. Industry specific factors might have influenced the growth and internationalization process of the studied firms. More firms should be included to examine the new venture growth patterns by using Park and Bae's (2004) typology that could increase the generalizability of findings and their interpretation.

References

Anderson, S. (2003). Internalization in different industrial contexts. *Journal of Business Venturing*, 19, 851–75.

Anderson, S. and Wictor, I. (2003). Innovative internationalisation in new firms: born globals – the Swedish case. *Journal of International Entrepreneurship*, 1(3), 249–75.

Bruton, G.D. and Rubanik, Y. (2002). Resources of the firm, Russian high-technology startups, and firm growth. *Journal of Business Venturing*, 17, 553–76.

Buckley, J. and Casson, M. (1976). *The Future of the Multinational Enterprise*. London: Macmillan.

Chen, C.H. (1996). Regional determinants of foreign direct investment in mainland China. *Journal of Economics Studies*, 23(2), 18–30.

Chetty, S.K. (2003). Explosive international growth and problems of success amongst small to medium-sized firms. *International Small Business Review*, 21(1), 5–27.

Coviello, N.E. and Munro, H.J. (1995). Growing the entrepreneurial firm: networking for international market development, *European Journal of Marketing*, 29(7), 49–61.

Coviello, N.E. and Munro, H.J. (1997). Network relationships and the internationalization process of small software firms. *International Business Review*, 6(4), 361–86.

Dunning, J.H. (1977). Trade, location of economic activity and the multinational enterprise: a search for an eclectic approach, in B. Ohlin, P.O. Hesselborn and P.M. Wijkman (eds), *The International Allocation of Economic Activity*. London: Macmillan.

Dunning, J.H. (1988). The eclectic paradigm of international production: a restatement and some possible explanations. *Journal of International Business Studies*, 19(1), 1–31.

Erramilli, K.M., Srivastava, R. and Kim, S.S. (1999). Internationalisation theory and Korean multinationals. *Asia Pacific Journal of Management*, 16(1), 29–45.

Fan, T. and Phan, P. (2007). International new ventures: revisiting the influence behind the 'born global firm'. *Journal of International Business*, 38, 1113–31.

Gregorio, D.D., Musteen, M. and Thomas, D.E. (2008). International new ventures: the cross-border nexus of individuals and opportunities. *Journal of World Business*, 43, 186–96.

Harris, S. and Wheeler, C. (2005). Entrepreneurs' relationships for internationalization: functions, origins and strategies. *International Business Review*, 14 (2), 187–207.

Hymer, S.H. (1976). *The International Operations of National Firms: A Study of Direct Foreign Investment*. Cambridge, MA: MIT Press.

Jaklic, M. (1998). Internationalisation strategies, networking and functional discretion. *Competition and Change*, 3(4), 359–85.

Johanson, J. and Vahlne, J. (1977). The internationalisation process of the firm: a model of knowledge development and increasing foreign markets commitments. *Journal of International Business Studies*, 8(1), 23–32.

Johanson, J. and Vahlne, J.E. (1990). The mechanism of internationalization. *International Marketing Review*, 7, 11–24.

Johanson, J. and Vahlne, J.E. (2003). Business relationship learning and commitment in the internationalization process. *Journal of International Entrepreneurship*, 1, 83–101.

Johanson, J. and Vahlne, J.E. (2009) The Uppsala internationalization process model revisited: from liability of foreignness to liability of outsidership. *Journal of International Business Studies*, 40, 1411–31.

Johanson, J. and Weidersheim-Paul, F. (1975). The internationalization of the firm: four Swedish cases. *Journal of Management Studies*, 12(3), 305–22.

Keskin, H. (2006). Market orientation, learning orientation and innovation capabilities in SMEs: an extended model. *European Journal of Innovation Management*, 9(4), 396–417.

Knight, G.A. and Cavusgil, S.T. (1996). The born global firm: a challenge to traditional internationalisation theory. *Advances in International Marketing*, 8, 11–26.

Lu, D. and Zhu, G. (1995). Singapore foreign direct investment in China: features and implications. *ASEAN Economic Bulletin*, 12(1), 53–63.

Madsen, T.K. and Servais, P. (1997). The internationalization of born globals: an evolutionary process? *International Business Review*, 6(6), 561–83.

McDougall, P.P. and Oviatt, B.M. (2000). International entrepreneurship: the intersection of two research paths. *Academy of Management*, 43(5), 902–6.

McDougall, P.P., Shane, S. and Oviatt, B.M. (1994). Explaining the formation of international new ventures: the limits of theories from international business research, *Journal of Business Venturing*, 9, 469–87.

McDougall, P.P., Oviatt, B.M. and Shrader, R.C. (2003). A comparison of international and domestic new ventures, *International Journal of Entrepreneurship*, 1(1), 59–82.

Morgan, R.E. and Katsikeas, C.S. (1997). Theories of international trade, foreign direct investments and firm internationalization: a critique. *Management Decision*, 35(1), 68–78.

Mort, G.S. and Weerawardena, J. (2006). Networking capability and international entrepreneurship: how networks function in Australian born global firms, *International Marketing Review*, 549–72.

Mudambi, R. and Zahra, S.A. (2007). The survival of international new ventures. *Journal of International Business Studies*, 38, 333–52.

Na, L. and Lightfoot, W.S. (2006). Determinants of foreign direct investment at the regional level in China. *Journal of Technology Management in China*, 1(3), 262–78.

Oviatt, B.M. and McDougall, P.P. (1994). Toward a theory of international new ventures. *Journal of International Business Studies*, 25(1), 45–64.

Oviatt, B.M. and McDougall, P.P. (2005). Toward a theory of international new ventures. *Journal of International Business Studies*, 36, 29–41.

Park, S. and Bae, Z. (2004). New venture strategies in a developing country: identifying a typology and examining growth patterns through case studies. *Journal of Business Venturing*, 19, 81–105.

Ricardo, D. (1978 [1817]). *Principles of Political Economy and Taxation*. Harmondsworth: Penguin.

Rugman, A.M. and Verbeke, A. (2003). Location, competitiveness and the multinational enterprise, in A.M. Rugman and T.L. Brewer (eds), *The Oxford Handbook of International Business*. New York: Oxford University Press.

Pandian, R. and Sim, A. (2002). Internationalisation process: revisiting the Uppsala Model in the Asian context. University of Wollongong Research Online, Faculty of Commerce papers, http://ro.uow.edu.au/commpapers/795, accessed on 10 October 2011.

Sim, A.B. and Pandian, J.R. (2007). An exploratory study of internationalisation strategies of Malaysian and Taiwanese firms. *International Journal of Emerging Market*, 2(3), 252–73.

Smith, A. (1994 [1776]). *The Wealth of Nations*. New York: Modern Library.

Zahra, S.A. and Bogner, W.C. (1999). Technology strategy and software new ventures' performance: exploring the moderating effect of competitive environment. *Journal of Business Venturing*, 15, 135–73.

Zhang, K.H. (2001). What explains the boom of foreign direct investment in China? *International Economics*, 54(2), 251–74.

Zhang, X. and Yuk, H.P. (1998). Determinants of Hong Kong manufacturing investment in China: a survey. *Marketing Intelligence and Planning*, 16(4), 260–7.

12

Chinese Multinationals: Host Country Factors and Foreign Direct Investment Location

Diego Quer, Enrique Claver and Laura Rienda

Introduction

Until recently, China has been widely known as a destination for foreign direct investment (FDI). However, since 2002, Chinese outward foreign direct investment (OFDI) has increased substantially – by fourfold in the period from 2005 to 2009, and China was ranked as the sixth largest global outbound investor in 2009 (UNCTAD, 2010). It is also estimated that by the end of 2009 there were around 13,000 businesses with Chinese capital in 177 countries (MOFCOM, 2010). Table 12.1 shows the evolution of Chinese OFDI flows and stocks.

Chinese firms listed in Fortune Global 500 have been key players in the main Chinese cross-border mergers and acquisitions (M&As) carried out since 2002. The takeover of the Swiss–Canadian company Addax Petroleum and the partial acquisitions of Repsol YPF Brasil and Syncrude Canada by Sinopec, the acquisition of a 20 per cent stake in Standard Bank of South Africa by the Industrial and Commercial Bank of China (ICBC) or the takeover of Petrokazakhstan by China National Petroleum Corporation (CNPC) are the most outstanding examples. Table 12.2 shows the largest cross-border M&As carried out by Chinese companies listed in Fortune Global 500, ranked by transaction value.

Research into international business has not been unaffected by this rise of Chinese MNEs. After an initial few years when eminently descriptive papers predominated, recent studies have sought to explore further specific topics, such as the factors that determine Chinese OFDI location choice (Duanmu and Guney, 2009; Pangarkar and Yuan, 2009; Yuan and Pangarkar, 2010; Duanmu, 2011; Kang and Jiang, 2011; Kolstad and Wiig, 2011; Ramasamy et al., 2011). In this chapter we aim to contribute to the literature by analysing the influence of various host country factors on the location decisions of Chinese MNEs listed in Fortune Global 500. More precisely, we study how

Table 12.1 China's OFDI flows and stocks (US$ million)

	OFDI flow	OFDI stock
1982–90	495 (annual average)	4,455 (by the end of 1990)
1991–2000	2,195 (annual average)	27,768 (by the end of 2000)
2001	6,885	34,654
2002	2,518	35,206
2003	2,855	37,020
2004	5,498	38,825
2005	12,261	57,206
2006	21,160	73,330
2007	22,469	95,799
2008	52,150	147,949
2009	48,000	229,600

Source: UNCTAD, FDI Statistics (www.unctad.org).

factors such as the host market size, the host country's regulatory framework, political risk and cultural distance affect the number of FDIs in each country. Before that, we provide an overview of the distinctive characteristics of the internationalization process of Chinese MNEs.

The international expansion of Chinese MNEs: an overview

Motives of Chinese OFDI

Cost minimization is not a major objective of Chinese MNEs as China has been a low-cost production base itself (Cheng and Ma, 2007). The main motivations of Chinese MNEs are threefold (Wu and Sia, 2002; Wong and Chan, 2003; Deng, 2004; Hong and Sun, 2006): resource seeking, market seeking and diversification, and strategic asset seeking.

The search for resources, particularly natural resources, has been one of the traditional objectives of Chinese FDI. Until 1991, it was concentrated on Canada and Australia. Subsequently, FDI from China extended its reach to other countries during the 1990s with an increasing emphasis on fuel and industrial raw materials.

Initially, Chinese FDI often arose from the need to diversify markets and obtain foreign exchange. The establishment of trading subsidiaries promoted Chinese exports. Furthermore, Chinese companies have faced quantitative restrictions on exports to other countries which were even more severe than for non-Chinese companies, so manufacturing FDI has been in many cases the solution to continue accessing overseas markets.

Table 12.2 Top ten cross-border M&As by Chinese MNEs listed in *Fortune Global 500* (2002–10)

Rank	Year	Acquiring firm	Target firm	Industry	Target economy	Shares acquired (%)	Transaction value (US$ billion)
1	2009	Sinopec	Addax Petroleum	Oil and gas	Canada (Switzerland-based firm)	100	7.5
2	2010	Sinopec	Repsol YPF Brasil	Oil	Brazil	40	7.1
3	2007	ICBC	Standard Bank	Banking	South Africa	20	5.5
4	2010	Sinopec	Syncrude Canada	Oil	Canada	9	4.7
5	2005	CNPC	PetroKazakhstan	Oil	Kazakhstan (Canada-based firm)	67	4.2
6	2006	Sinopec	OAO Udmurtneft	Oil and gas	Russia	97	3.5
7	2010	CNOOC	Bridas	Oil	Argentina	50	3.1
8	2010	CNPC	Arrow Energy	Oil and gas	Australia	100*	3.1
9	2008	CNOOC	AWO	Oil and gas	Norway	100	2.5
10	2006	CNOOC	NNPC-OML 130	Oil and gas	Nigeria	45	2.3

* Joint bid with Royal Dutch Shell.

Note: CNOOC: China National Offshore Oil Corporation; NNPC-OML: Nigerian National Petroleum Corporation-Oil Mining Lease.

Source: Own elaboration based on Davies (2010) and news items from China Daily.

Some major Chinese state-owned enterprises (SOEs) have engaged in FDIs seeking to diversify risks. This strategy has been reinforced by the trade reforms started in the 1980s, which meant that some companies lost their monopoly in China. One such example is Sinochem, a foreign-trading SOE that held a monopoly over the import and export of oil and chemical fertilizers. As a result of the reforms, Sinochem had to find new lines of business, which have transformed it into a diversified company operating in industries such as oil, chemicals, tourism and property.

Many Chinese firms have also sought to exploit their comparative advantages in developing areas of South East Asia, Africa and Latin America. These are projects in which Chinese firms provide equipment, machinery and raw materials, through which they also contribute to increasing exports from China.

Finally, some Chinese companies, rather than exploiting an existing competitive advantage, are seeking to acquire strategic assets abroad. They are looking to access advanced technology and managerial know-how in developed countries. They also invest in developed markets seeking internationally recognized trademarks. One of the most outstanding examples of this is the acquisition of IBM's PC division by Lenovo.

As a concluding remark on the motivations of Chinese OFDI, it is worth mentioning a survey carried out by KPMG (2010), where 156 executives of mainland Chinese MNEs reported that the most popular objectives for outbound investment were geographic growth, building a global profile and reputation, diversification strategy, and climbing up or going down the value chain.

Facilitators of Chinese OFDI

The internationalization of Chinese companies has been favoured by factors such as the huge foreign currency reserves accumulated from exports or the knowledge acquired from foreign partners doing business in China (Child and Rodrigues, 2005; Hong and Sun, 2006). In any case, the real driving force behind the process has been the Chinese government, which considers the international expansion of Chinese companies as a key element that can ensure the country's economic growth.

The reasons that the Chinese government encourages OFDI are (Shoham and Rosenboim, 2009): resource exploration; projects that can promote Chinese exports; overseas research and development centres; M&As that can enhance the international competitiveness of Chinese enterprises and accelerate their entry into foreign markets; and encouraging international growth through OFDI which is considered consistent with China´s trade surplus and with the positive gap between savings and investments that characterizes the national accounts.

OFDI was first permitted in 1979, but it remained prohibited for private companies until 2003. During that initial period, the internationalization of Chinese companies was tightly controlled by the government (Buckley et al., 2007). In 2002, the Chinese government initiated a 'go out' policy, which aimed to boost the international competitiveness of Chinese companies by reducing the obstacles to OFDI. The setting up of overseas operations by Chinese firms then became one of the official policies for opening up the economy, with the leading role being played by SOEs, which were seen as instruments through which to achieve national objectives (Zhang and Van den Bulcke, 1996). Since then, the Chinese government has continued to provide incentives for the process such as tax relief, credit support, risk-safeguard mechanisms, information services and simplification of the process of approval (Luo et al., 2010). The Chinese government considers that forming large MNEs will help China to become a key player in the global economy. Helping Chinese companies to get onto the Fortune Global 500 list has thus become an objective in itself (Hong and Sun, 2006).

Anyway, FDI by any Chinese firm, either privately or state-owned, requires approval by the Chinese government, in order to ensure that all investment activities conform to government policies and goals. Taking into account this influence, Gugler and Fetscherin (2010) propose a conceptual framework outlining the interests of the government versus the interests of Chinese companies. They suggest that where both interests are high and aligned, it is expected that the scale and speed in which those investments will be conducted and executed will be great. This is the case for market-seeking and strategic asset-seeking investments.

Challenges for Chinese MNEs

Obviously, the emerging rise of Chinese MNEs is not without problems. As latecomers, they have a disadvantage compared to their Asian and Western counterparts. In particular, the main problems and challenges they must face are the following (Luo and Tung, 2007; Wu, 2007):

- Due to their limited experience in M&As, they have yet to demonstrate whether they have the skills required to face post-acquisition difficulties, in particular, those related to cultural differences;
- They lack international experience, in particular, specific market knowledge, which is only acquired through learning by doing;
- They need to improve their product and process innovation since it is difficult to survive in the long term only via acquisitions for knowledge development;
- The state ownership of many Chinese MNEs makes them vulnerable to political risk in countries where the assets they seek are considered strategic;
- The less developed status of the home stock markets and the lack of transparency derived from their state ties mean their corporate governance is generally weaker.

Foreign market entry modes of Chinese firms

Chinese companies have mainly employed three routes towards internationalization (Child and Rodrigues, 2005). The first of these is the original equipment manufacturing through joint ventures or licenses. It is an inward method of internationalization, i.e. within China itself. It consists of associating with a foreign MNE to obtain modern practices that help to strengthen international competitiveness with a view to eventual outward internationalization. An example of this strategy can be found at Huawei that is one of the world's leading suppliers of broadband internet access equipment, which initially established several joint ventures with foreign companies.

The second entry mode is acquisition. This has been chosen by large material processing SOEs, which have made major acquisitions to ensure the supply of raw materials. This mode has also been selected by Chinese firms belonging to other industries, with the aim of accessing technology, ensuring R&D skills or acquiring international branding. Acquisition provides a quick route to these benefits. Some of the above-mentioned acquisitions, such as Lenovo's acquisition of the PC division of IBM, are illustrative of this strategy.

The third route is that of organic international expansion, which involves the greenfield establishment of subsidiaries in other countries. The aim in this case tends to be to obtain advantages of differentiation in terms of, for example, adaptation to local needs, although it also facilitates managerial control and the possibilities for global integration. Domestic appliances manufacturer Haier may be deemed one of the best examples of a Chinese company that has gone international mainly along this route.

Host country factors and Chinese FDI: hypotheses development

As stated in the Introduction, our empirical research focuses on analysing the influence of host country factors on the number of Chinese FDIs in each destination country. In this section, we propose a series of hypotheses regarding the impact of host market size, market-supporting institutions, political risk and cultural distance.

Host market size

Characteristics of the host market are widely recognized factors that affect the flow of FDIs received by a country. Market access is one of the most acknowledged motivations of FDI (Duanmu and Guney, 2009). Empirical evidence has revealed a positive relationship between host market size and FDI inflows (Yu, 1990; Mascarenhas, 1992).

As markets increase in size, so do the opportunities for the efficient utilization of resources and the exploitation of economies of scale and scope via FDI (Buckley et al., 2007). Furthermore, a fast growing economy leads to a high level of aggregate demand for products and stimulates FDI inflows (Kang and Jiang, 2011). As a result, the larger the market size and the higher the economic growth rate, the more attractive the host country is and the more FDI is attracted to that country. Thus, we propose that:

> Hypothesis 1. *The number of Chinese FDIs in a country is positively associated with host market size.*

Market-supporting institutions

Institutional differences are particularly important for MNEs operating in more than one institutional context (Meyer et al., 2009). The formal and informal rules affect not only how a company chooses to enter an economy, but the very decision on whether or not to set up in a particular country.

Institutional factors play an increasingly important role in the location decisions (Zheng, 2009). Institutional changes in FDI regulations can have a major influence on geographic diversification decisions (Peng and Delios, 2006), and many countries have stepped up their bids to attract FDI by implementing favourable policies for foreign investors.

The strength of a country's institutional framework reduces business costs for foreign companies. In many emerging economies, institutional weakness may exaggerate the asymmetry of information, so companies face greater risks and need to spend more resources to find information (Meyer et al., 2009). In countries with no institutional restrictions, foreign investment companies are not subject to discriminatory policies regarding the percentage of ownership in the subsidiary, access to local resources or having to export part of their production. The presence of a favourable institutional framework in the host country can, therefore, be expected to attract FDI. As a result, we can propose that:

> Hypothesis 2. *The number of Chinese FDIs in a country is positively associated with the strength of market-supporting institutions in the host country.*

Political risk

Another institutional factor that has a strong influence on decisions to enter a certain country is the political environment; and political risk in the host country has taken up much space in the literature. Political risk can be considered alongside any other kind of external influence that affects the company's operations, whether that means the possibility of expropriation or nationalization of the investment, or other government actions or changes in the political and social situation that could have a negative effect on economic activity (Robock, 1971; Kobrin, 1979; Simon, 1984).

The differences in political risk between countries affect the stability of their markets, which affects foreign companies aiming to do business there. The high degree of uncertainty associated with foreign ownership or increased asset exposure in the event of eventual expropriation are some of the factors that can hinder FDI decisions (Brouthers, 2002; Pak and Park, 2004).

It is to be expected that political risk will be negatively related to FDI, given that MNEs will be more reluctant to invest in countries that are a high risk or have an unstable environment (Buckley et al., 2007; Zheng, 2009). These arguments would therefore suggest that:

> Hypothesis 3. *The number of Chinese FDIs in a country is negatively associated with rising levels of political risk in the host country.*

Cultural distance

Cultural distance refers to possible existing differences in terms of how individuals from different countries observe certain behaviours, which will affect the extent to which working practices and methods can be transferred from one country to another (Hofstede, 1980, 1991). It is another traditional factor in the literature on entry decisions (Madhok, 1997; Chen and Hu, 2002; Randoy and Dibrell, 2002; Pak and Park, 2004). It is argued that it can lead to additional costs in obtaining information and disrupt communication processes, as well as make it difficult for the local subsidiary to integrate, for the company's own routines to be applied and for the product to be adapted.

While institutions are crystallizations of culture, culture is the substratum of institutional arrangements (Hofstede et al., 2002). More precisely, culture can be considered part of the environment's informal institutions, which underpin formal institutions (Peng et al., 2008). When MNEs enter an institutional environment with a different set of rules, they must meet social expectations to demonstrate social responsibility and build social legitimacy in the host country. The difficulty in attaining this social legitimacy is related to the cultural distance between the country of origin and the host country (Cui and Jiang, 2009b, 2010). We can therefore expect that:

> Hypothesis 4. *The number of Chinese FDIs in a country is negatively associated with cultural distance between China and the host country.*

Empirical research

Data collection

The sample for this study is comprised of OFDIs made by mainland Chinese companies listed in Fortune Global 500. Overall, 44 different mainland Chinese firms were listed between 2005 and 2010.

The data on each FDI were obtained from news items published on the website of *China Daily* (www.chinadaily.com.cn), the largest English-language newspaper in China. Having searched all news items covering international operations by each of the 44 companies between January 2002 and December 2010, we identified 35 mainland Chinese firms that had invested abroad during this period. There were 189 FDIs in 63 countries, this being the sample for our study.

Descriptive statistics

Next, we provide some descriptive statistics of our sample. As Table 12.3 shows, the number of Chinese OFDIs grew substantially from 2004, with the last three years containing 107 out of the 189 FDIs covered by our sample, i.e. 56.6 per cent of the total: 2008 (40 FDIs), 2009 (33 FDIs) and 2010 (34 FDIs).

Table 12.4 shows descriptive data for location distribution of our sample. Australia leads the ranking of top destinations, with 17 FDIs.

Table 12.5 lists the top Fortune Global 500 mainland Chinese firms by OFDIs. The company that made most FDIs during the period analysed was CNPC (25 FDIs). The top 12 companies listed carried out 130 FDIs, representing 68.8 per cent of the whole sample.

Measures

The dependent variable in this study is the number of Chinese FDIs made in each country, a figure that was obtained directly from the *China Daily* website. The mean was three FDIs, with a standard deviation of 3.1.

We measured host market size by different indicators related to host country GDP (Li and Wu, 2006; Buckley et al., 2007; Bunyaratavej and Hahn,

Table12.3 Number of Chinese OFDIs, by year (2002–10)

Year	OFDIs	Per cent
2002	5	2.6
2003	7	3.7
2004	7	3.7
2005	19	10.1
2006	16	8.5
2007	28	14.8
2008	40	21.2
2009	33	17.5
2010	34	17.9
Total	189	100.0

Source: Own elaboration based on news items from *China Daily*.

Table12.4 Top destinations for Chinese OFDI (2002–10)

Rank	Country	OFDIs	Per cent
1	Australia	17	9.0
2	USA	13	6.9
3	Indonesia	11	5.8
4	UK	10	5.3
5	Canada	9	4.8
6	Russia	7	3.7
7	Singapore	6	3.2
8	Brazil	5	2.6
Other (55 countries)		111	58.7
Total		189	100.0

Source: Own elaboration based on news items from *China Daily*.

Table 12.5 Top Fortune Global 500 mainland Chinese firms, by OFDIs (2002–10)

Rank	Firm	Industry	OFDIs	Per cent
1	CNPC (China National Petroleum Corporation)	Oil and gas	25	13.2
2	Huawei Technologies	Telecommunications	15	8.0
3	ICBC (Industrial and Commercial Bank of China)	Banking and finance	14	7.4
4	Sinopec	Oil and gas	13	6.9
5	CNOOC (China National Offshore Oil Corporation)	Oil and gas	12	6.3
6	Bank of China	Banking and finance	10	5.3
7	Sinochem	Oil, fertilizers and chemicals	8	4.2
8	Lenovo Group	Computers	8	4.2
9	Sinosteel	Metals	7	3.7
10	China Telecom	Telecommunications	6	3.2
11	China Minmetals	Metals	6	3.2
12	Chinalco (Aluminium Corporation of China)	Metals	6	3.2
Other (23 firms)			59	31.2
Total			189	100.0

Source: Own elaboration based on news items from *China Daily*.

2007; Duanmu and Guney, 2009; Malhotra and Zhu, 2009; Duanmu, 2011; Kang and Jiang, 2011; Kolstad and Wiig, 2011;). More precisely, by using data from the UN Statistics Division (2010), we considered absolute host-market size (proxied by host-country GDP) and host-market growth (proxied by using the annual percentage increase in GDP). We used log transformation to normalize the distribution of both measures.

The strength of market-supporting institutions in the host country was proxied by the World Bank (2010) ranking on the ease of doing business. This annual report, which covers 183 economies, provides a quantitative measure of regulations for starting a business, dealing with construction permits, registering property, getting credit, protecting investors, paying taxes, trading across borders, enforcing contracts and closing a business. Based on each economy's mean score for these indicators, the World Bank produces a ranking of 183 countries, rated from the easiest country to do business in (1) to the most difficult (183). Previous research, such as the work by Meyer et al. (2009), has used a similar index to proxy the strength of market-supporting institutions.

Based on Buckley et al. (2007), Duanmu (2011) and Duanmu and Guney (2009), host country political risk was proxied by the political risk rating of the International Country Risk Guide (PRS, 2010). This rating assigns risk points to a preset group of factors, termed 'political risk components'. In every case the lower the risk point total, the higher the risk, and the higher the risk point total, the lower the risk. In order to obtain a measure of the relative political risk, we considered the political risk distance between mainland China and each target market.

We used two items to measure cultural distance. First, using the Kogut and Singh (1988) index, we calculated the cultural distance between China and each host country. Second, based on data reported by Ohio University (2010), we measured the cultural proximity to China using the percentage of ethnic Chinese in the host population (Buckley et al., 2007; Ramasamy et al., 2011). This variable takes value 1 when this percentage is higher than 1 per cent, and zero otherwise.

Results of the empirical research

The hypotheses were tested using an ordinary least squares regression to examine the impact of the independent variables (market size, ease of doing business, political risk and cultural distance) on the number of Chinese FDIs in each host country. Before conducting the regression analysis, we performed a multicolinearity diagnosis, examining the variance inflation factor (VIF) for all the variables. This test measures the extent to which the variances of the coefficients estimated in a regression are inflated when compared to the cases in which the independent variables are not linearly related. High VIF values can become indicators of the existence of multi-colinearity. The highest VIF was 2.99, which is well below 10, the cut-off

Table 12.6 Results of OLS regression analysis

Variables	β	*t*
Absolute host market size (H1)	0.52	3.70**
Host market growth (H1)	0.40	0.30
Ease of doing business (H2)	0.01	0.07
Political risk (H3)	–0.02	–0.12
Cultural distance (index) (H4)	0.08	0.49
Cultural distance (ethnic Chinese) (H4)	0.31	2.56*
R^2	0.41	
Adjusted R^2	0.33	
F	5.08***	

* p < 0.05; ** p < 0.01; *** p < 0.001.

Note: N = 63; variance inflation factors vary between 1.10 and 2.99.

point recommended by Neter et al. (1985). This allows us to rule out the presence of multicolinearity in our data. Table 12.6 shows the regression analysis results.

The regression equation is statistically significant (F = 5.08, $p < 0.001$). Hypothesis 1 predicted that host market size was positively associated with the number of Chinese FDIs. We obtained support for that hypothesis, but only for absolute host market size ($\beta = 0.52$, $p < 0.01$), since the positive effect of host market growth was not statistically significant ($\beta = 0.40$, $p > 0.1$).

Hypothesis 2 stated that strengthening institutions that make it easier to do business in the host country were positively related to Chinese OFDI. This hypothesis is not supported ($\beta = 0.01$, $p > 0.10$). Similarly, Hypothesis 3, which established an inverse relationship between political risk in the host country and the number of Chinese FDIs, is also not supported ($\beta = -0.02$, $p > 0.10$).

For Hypothesis 4, which stated that cultural distance would negatively affect Chinese OFDI, we obtained mixed results. By measuring the cultural distance using the Kogut-Singh index (1988), the observed effect is not statistically significant ($\beta = 0.08$, $p > 0.10$). However, when the cultural distance is proxied by the percentage of ethnic Chinese in the host country, a statistically significant result is obtained ($\beta = 0.31$, $p < 0.05$). This means that Hypothesis 4 can be partially supported.

Discussion and conclusion

In this chapter we aimed to study the influence of various host country factors on the location decisions made by large Chinese firms. We first hypothesized that Chinese MNEs were attracted by host market size. Our results support this view considering absolute host market size, which would coincide with the findings of previous research into Chinese MNEs (Li and Wu, 2006; Buckley et al., 2007; Bunyaratavej and Hahn, 2007; Duanmu and Guney, 2009; Duanmu, 2011; Kolstad and Wiig, 2011).

However, we did not obtain statistical significance when considering host market growth. This lack of significance has also been observed in previous papers on Chinese OFDI (Li and Wu, 2006; Kang and Jiang, 2011). Duanmu and Guney (2009) even found that GDP growth rate negatively and significantly impacted on Chinese OFDI. They argued that Chinese FDI may be more attracted by established economies, which have passed the phase of economic growth and may in some cases even experience an economic recession. Anyway, it should be pointed out that our findings are influenced by the global economic downturn over the last few years covered by our sample.

Regarding the strength of host market supporting institutions, our results did not support the predicted positive effect on the number of Chinese FDIs. Some previous studies on Chinese MNEs found that the managers of these companies gave considerable weight to regulations in the host country's institutional framework when deciding whether or not to enter that market (Cui and Jiang, 2009b, 2010).

One possible explanation for this result, which is against initial expectations, may be that although many Chinese companies do not have asset advantages such as technology and branding, they do have a transaction advantage: the ability to manage relationships within a complex environment such as China. This gives them an edge over MNEs from developed countries when it comes to investing in markets with these institutional characteristics (Morck et al., 2008). Therefore, in countries with a weak institutional framework, Chinese MNEs may have an advantage over Western competitors, given that the rules when doing business in China may be more similar to those of these host countries (Malhotra and Zhu, 2009). One example of this can be found in CNPC's entry in PetroKazakhstan, which had previously been controlled in that country by a Canadian firm.

Our third hypothesis, which established an inverse relationship between political risk in the host country and Chinese OFDI, is also not supported. This goes against the results of previous studies on Chinese MNEs (Duanmu and Guney, 2009; Duanmu, 2011). However, we did find empirical evidence in line with our result, suggesting that the risks of the host country do not affect Chinese MNEs in a conventional way. Cui and Jiang (2009a) find that country risk does not affect how Chinese MNEs commit FDI resources. Buckley et al. (2007) do not confirm that Chinese OFDI is negatively associated with high levels of political risk in the host country. Some papers even find that Chinese MNEs tend to invest in countries with higher levels of risk (Bunyaratavej and Hahn, 2007; Malhotra and Zhu, 2009; Kang and Jiang, 2011; Ramasamy et al., 2011).

Several explanations can be found for this result that contradicts the conventional influence of political risk on FDI decisions. Firstly, the size of the FDI may affect the influence of political risk. Thus, when making large investments Chinese companies can take advantage of the opportunity to acquire cheaper assets in countries with a politically unstable system (Malhotra and Zhu, 2009). Secondly, Chinese companies may attempt to take advantage of the opportunities presented by high-risk countries, whose markets may not be highly exploited or may even be unknown to large Western MNEs, such as first-mover advantages, less competition or a lower level of consumer sophistication (Bunyaratavej and Hahn, 2007). Thirdly, the very idiosyncrasy of China's own institutional framework may also go some way to explaining our result (Buckley et al., 2007). Because of imperfections in the Chinese capital market, the cost of capital is very low for Chinese SOEs. Furthermore, because they are conditioned by the institutional influences of the Chinese government, they may not be behaving purely as profit maximizers. Finally, an important part of the Chinese OFDI has been directed at countries with which China has close political and ideological ties, many of which have a high political risk.

Regarding our fourth hypothesis, which predicted a negative influence of cultural distance on Chinese OFDI, our results were able to provide partial support. By measuring the cultural distance using the Kogut-Singh index (1988), we did not obtain statistical significance. This result goes against observations made by certain previous studies. For example, using the same measurement tool, Li and Wu (2006) found that cultural distance had a negative influence on the number of Chinese FDIs in each country, and Kang and Jiang (2011) reported that Chinese firms tended to locate FDI operations in host countries with a smaller cultural distance. Cui and Jiang (2009a, 2009b, 2010) found, albeit using another approach, that cultural barriers also had a negative impact on Chinese companies committing FDI resources.

One possible reason for our result may be that the influence of cultural distance may depend on the Chinese company's objectives. While investments that sought markets might well have been initially aimed at countries in which this distance was smaller, investments that seek know-how have been mainly aimed at developed countries in North America and Europe, which are culturally more distant (Young et al., 1996). Also, many Chinese companies do not seem to shy away from cultural distance, perhaps aided by the alliances they have made in China with MNEs from developed countries (Luo and Tung, 2007).

However, using the proportion of ethnic Chinese in the host country as a measure of cultural proximity, an influence can be observed in line with Hypothesis 4. The proportion of ethnic Chinese in the host country seems to be a significant factor in attracting Chinese OFDI. This result coincides with findings by Buckley et al. (2007), who offer various explanations for the particular importance of Chinese people who are resident overseas. The Chinese diaspora has contributed to China's integration into the world economy, thanks in particular to the number of FDIs in China from Singapore, Hong Kong and Taiwan. However, Chinese overseas residents may also have a significant influence on the choice of host country for Chinese OFDIs. Contacts and social networks (known in China as *guanxi*) are one of the essential ingredients for the Chinese when doing business. The presence of overseas residents in a certain country may therefore reduce the risks and costs associated with identifying business opportunities by Chinese companies, thus favouring Chinese OFDI.

In conclusion, our findings suggest that the location patterns of Chinese MNEs show both conventional and less conventional features. Thus, a larger absolute market size in the host country is an attractive location factor, particularly for Chinese companies looking for markets as part of their international expansion. Moreover, the presence of overseas Chinese residents in the host country seems to be a factor that helps Chinese companies to overcome possible cultural barriers.

However, other findings from our work seem to go against the conventional logic that has been observed in location decisions made by MNEs from other, particularly Western, countries. A weak institutional framework in the host country, which makes it more difficult to do business and which involves a high political risk, does not act as a particular disincentive for Chinese MNEs. Furthermore, although we used a conventional measurement that is widely used in the literature on MNEs, we were unable to confirm that cultural distance is an important institutional barrier for Chinese companies.

On the other hand, we have provided new empirical evidence regarding a phenomenon that is acquiring ever-increasing economic importance: the arrival of emerging-market MNEs on the international scene. Even though in recent years more and more studies have focused on Chinese MNEs, given the recent nature of their internationalization process, this research topic has yet really to establish itself. Further research is therefore needed to extend our knowledge of a type of MNE that plays an increasingly relevant role in international business.

References

Brouthers, K.D. (2002). Institutional, cultural and transaction cost influences on entry mode choice and performance. *Journal of International Business Studies*, 33(2), 203–21.

Buckley, P.J., Clegg, L.J., Cross, A.R., Liu, X., Voss, H. and Zheng, P. (2007). The determinants of Chinese foreign direct investment. *Journal of International Business Studies*, 38(4), 499–518.

Bunyaratavej, K. and Hahn, E.D. (2007). Outward foreign direct investments from China: theory and determinants. Paper presented at the AIB 2007 Annual Meeting, Indianapolis, 25–28 June.

Chen, H. and Hu, M.Y. (2002). An analysis of entry mode and its impact on performance. *International Business Review*, 11(2), 193–210.

Cheng, L.K. and Ma, Z. (2007). China´s outward FDI: past and future. Working paper 2007706001E. China, Renmin University, School of Economics.

Child, J. and Rodrigues, S.B. (2005). The internationalization of Chinese firms: a case for theoretical extension? *Management and Organization Review*, 1(3), 381–410.

Cui, L. and Jiang, F. (2009a). FDI entry mode choice of Chinese firms: a strategic behavior perspective. *Journal of World Business*, 44(4), 434–44.

Cui, L. and Jiang, F. (2009b). Ownership decisions in Chinese outward FDI: an integrated research framework and research agenda. *Asian Business and Management*, 8(3), 301–24.

Cui, L. and Jiang, F. (2010). Behind ownership decision of Chinese outward FDI: resources and institutions. *Asia Pacific Journal of Management*, 27(4), 751–74.

Davies, K. (2010). *Outward FDI from China and Its Policy Context*. Columbia FDI Profiles. Vale Columbia Center on Sustainable International Investment. (www.vcc.columbia.edu). Deng, P. (2004). Outward investment by Chinese MNCs: motivations and implications. *Business Horizons*, 47(3), 8–16.

Duanmu, J.L. (2011). Firm heterogeneity and location choice of Chinese multinational enterprises (MNEs). *Journal of World Business*, forthcoming.

Duanmu, J.L., and Guney, Y. (2009). A panel data analysis of locational determinants of Chinese and Indian outward foreign direct investment. *Journal of Asia Business Studies*, 3(2), 1–15.

Gugler, P. and Fetscherin, M. (2010). The role and importance of the Chinese government for Chinese outward foreign direct investments. *AIB Insights*, 10(4), 12–15.

Hofstede, G. (1980). *Culture´s Consequences: International Differences in Work-Related Values*. Newbury Park, CA: Sage Publications.

Hofstede, G. (1991). *Cultures and Organizations. Software of the Mind*. London: McGraw-Hill.

Hofstede, G., Van Deusen, C.A., Mueller, C.B. and Charles, T.A. (2002). The business goals network. What goals do business leaders pursue? A study in fifteen countries. *Journal of International Business Studies*, 33(4): 785–803.

Hong, E., and Sun, L. (2006). Dynamics of internationalization and outward investment: Chinese corporations´ strategies. *The China Quarterly*, 187, 610–34.

Kang, Y. and Jiang, F. (2011). FDI location choice of Chinese multinationals in East and Southeast Asia: traditional economic factors and institutional perspective. *Journal of World Business*, forthcoming.

Kobrin, S.J. (1979). Political Risk: A review and reconsideration. *Journal of International Business Studies*, 10(1), 67–80.

Kogut, B. and Singh, H. (1988). The effect of national culture on the choice of entry mode. *Journal of International Business Studies*, 19(3), 411–32.

Kolstad, I. and Wiig, A. (2011). What determines Chinese outward FDI? *Journal of World Business*, forthcoming.

KPMG (2010). *World Class Aspirations: The Perceptions and the Reality of China Outbound Investment*. KPMG China. (www.kpmg.com/cn).

Li, Y. and Wu, C. (2006). Agglomeration effect, location advantage and location choice of FDI from developing countries: The case of China. Paper presented at the AIB 2006 Annual Meeting, Beijing, China, 23–26 June.

Luo, Y. and Tung, R.L. (2007). International expansion of emerging market enterprises: a springboard perspective. *Journal of International Business Studies*, 38(4), 481–98.

Luo, Y., Xue, Q. and Han, B. (2010). How emerging market governments promote outward FDI: experience from China. *Journal of World Business*, 45(1), 68–79.

Madhok, A. (1997). Cost, value and foreign market entry mode: The transaction and the firm. *Strategic Management Journal*, 18(1), 39–61.

Malhotra, S. and Zhu, P.C. (2009). Determinants and valuation impact of cross-border acquisitions by firms from China and India. AIB 2009 Annual Meeting, San Diego, CA, 27–30 June.

Mascarenhas, B. (1992). Order of market entry and performance in international markets. *Strategic Management Journal*, 13(7), 499–510.

Meyer, K.E., Estrin, S., Bhaumik, S.K. and Peng, M.W. (2009). Institutions, resources, and entry strategies in emerging economies. *Strategic Management Journal*, 30(1), 61–80.

MOFCOM (2010). *2009 Statistical Bulletin of China's Outward Foreign Direct Investment*. Beijing: Ministry of Commerce (MOFCOM). (http://english.mofcom.gov.cn).

Morck, R., Yeung, B. and Zhao, M. (2008). Perspectives on China's outward foreign direct investment. *Journal of International Business Studies*, 39(3), 337–50.

Neter, J., Wasserman, W. and Kutner, M.H. (1985). *Applied Linear Statistical Models: Regression, Analysis of Variance and Experimental Designs*, 2nd edn. Boston, MA: Irwin.

Ohio University (2010). *Distribution of the Ethnic Chinese Population around the World*. Ohio University Library and the Shao Center. (http://cicdatabank.library.ohiou.edu/opac/population.php). Pak, Y.S. and Park, Y.R. (2004). Global ownership strategy of Japanese multinational enterprises: a test of internalization theory. *Management International Review*, 44(1), 3–21.

Pangarkar, N. and Yuan, L. (2009). Location in internationalization strategy: determinants and consequences. *Multinational Business Review*, 17(2), 37–68.

Peng, M.W. and Delios, A. (2006). What determines the scope of the firm over time and around the world? An Asia Pacific perspective. *Asia Pacific Journal of Management*, 23(4), 385–405.

Peng, M.W., Wang, D.Y.L. and Jiang, Y. (2008). An institution-based view of international business strategy: a focus on emerging economies. *Journal of International Business Studies*, 39(5), 920–36.

PRS (Political Risk Services) (2010). *International Country Risk Guide (ICRG)*. The Political Risk Services Group. (www.prsgroup.com).

Ramasamy, B., Yeung, M. and Laforet, S. (2011). China's outward foreign direct investment: location choice and firm ownership. *Journal of World Business*, forthcoming.

Randoy, T. and Dibrell, C.C. (2002). How and why Norwegian MNCs commit resources abroad: beyond choice of entry mode. *Management International Review*, 42(2): 119–40.

Robock, S.H. (1971). Political risk: identification and assessment. *Columbia Journal of World Business*, July–August: 6–20.

Shoham, A. and Rosenboim, M. (2009). China's new approach to ODI in Africa: A model for a government seeking natural resources, in I. Alon, J. Chang, M. Fetscherin, C. Lattemann and J.R. McIntyre (eds), *China Rules. Globalization and Political Transformation*. Hampshire, UK: Palgrave Macmillan, pp. 216–30.

Simon, J.D. (1984). A theoretical perspective on political risk. *Journal of International Business Studies*, 15(3), 123–43.

UN Statistics Division (2010). *National Accounts Main Aggregates Database.* United Nations Statistics Division. (http://unstats.un.org).

UNCTAD (2010). *World Investment Report 2010. Investing in a Low-Carbon Economy.* New York and Geneva: United Nations Conference on Trade and Development.

Wong, J. and Chan, S. (2003). China's outward direct investment: expanding worldwide. *China: An International Journal,* 1(2), 273–301.

World Bank (2010). *Ease of Doing Business Rank.* (www.doingbusiness.org/rankings).

Wu, F. (2007). Corporate China goes global, in H. Wai-Chung Yeung (ed.), *Handbook of Research on Asian Business.* Cheltenham: Edward Elgar Publishing, pp. 445–65.

Wu, F. and Sia, Y.H. (2002). China's rising investment in Southeast Asia: trends and outlook. *Journal of Asian Business,* 18(2), 41–61.

Young, S., Huang, C.H. and McDermott, M. (1996). Internationalization and competitive catch-up processes: case study evidence on Chinese multinational enterprises. *Management International Review,* 36(4), 295–314.

Yu, C.M.J. (1990). The experience effect and foreign direct investment. *Weltwirtschaftliches Archiv,* 126(4), 561–80.

Yuan, L. and Pangarkar, N. (2010). Inertia versus mimicry in location choices by Chinese multinationals. *International Marketing Review,* 27(3), 295–315.

Zhang, H.Y. and Van den Bulcke, D. (1996). International management strategies of Chinese multinational firms, in J. Child and Y. Lu (eds), *Management Issues in China in the 1990s: International Enterprises.* London: Routledge, pp. 141–64.

Zheng, P. (2009). A comparison of FDI determinants in China and India. *Thunderbird International Business Review,* 51(3), 263–79.

13

Meanings and Understandings in the Formation of Born Global Firms: The Case of Trikke Tech Inc.

René Eugenio Seifert and Bruno Henrique Rocha Fernandes

Introduction

Internationalization has traditionally been understood as a process of a gradual expansion overseas that starts with the firm's engagement in low risk, low cost and low commitment foreign country operations, and gradually progresses to higher levels of cost, risk and commitment involvements. Nevertheless, recently, authors have increasingly recognized the emergence of firms that internationalize fast from inception to multiple countries manifesting high levels of international commitment (Oviatt and McDougall, 1995, 2005a; Parker, 1998; Rialp et al., 2005; Zhou et al., 2007). In the international business literature such firms have been recognized as born global, and typically considered to be outcomes of international entrepreneurship. Ultimately, the emergence of international entrepreneurship and born global firms has challenged the dominant view of internationalization as an evolutionary and gradual process of international involvement.

Despite the increasing research on the issue of born global firms, these authors contend that the phenomenon of international entrepreneurship is far from being fully understood (Rialp et al., 2005). Recent evaluations designate that the field is fragmented, lacks a common theoretical integration and is in desperate need of further theoretical development (Keupp and Gassmann, 2009). In particular, the authors address the need to understand better the role of cognition, perception and interpretation of international entrepreneurship (Crick and Spence, 2005; Zahra et al., 2005). On this view, Zahra et al. (2005) argue that despite the fact that the cognitive perspective seems to be a promising approach for analysing the international entrepreneurship phenomenon, studies with this focus are still scarce. Jones and Dimitratos (2005), after reviewing the major studies on this topic, supplicate for more studies attempting to bring better understanding of how born global entrepreneurs perceive and interpret organizational and business reality.

In this chapter we aim to contribute to this area of study by giving an account of an investigation focusing on the relationship between meanings and understandings that characterize entrepreneurs' interpretation of born global firms and the phenomenon of international entrepreneurship. The investigation is based on the premise that international entrepreneurship is a specific kind of organizational demeanour and therefore, drawing upon the Weberian understanding of social action (Weber, 1968), is informed by the meanings and understandings of the interpretation by entrepreneurs. Here, interpretation is assumed to be the instance whereby the meanings and understandings that inform organizational action are produced and reproduced (Alexander, 1988). On this view the study aims to: (a) recognize relevant meanings informing international action in the interpretation by entrepreneurs; (b) understand how such meanings and understandings oriented the early consolidation of a born global venture; and (c) explore the conditions by which relevant meanings and understandings orienting international entrepreneurship were formed.

In order to investigate these issues and bring a discussion to them, the firm Trikke Tech Inc. has been studied. This entity is regarded as a born global venture established by three Brazilian entrepreneurs in 1999. From its inception the firm manifested high levels of international commitment and involvement in overseas operations. The firm's main product, the 'Trikke', was selected as invention of the year by Time Magazine in 2002 (Time, 2002). The reason for investigating this firm can be traced to two aspects. First, it entails a business enterprise from an emerging economy, Brazil, which has not been in the focus of leading international entrepreneurship research previously. Second, this is a case that challenges dominant orientation towards domestic operations in Brazil. The firm has been investigated through a series of face-to-face interviews with the founder-owners of the firm, which were triangulated with available published secondary data. Moreover, in order to investigate how particular meanings informed international action we reconstructed retrospectively Trikke's internationalization process from its inception. This enabled us to recognize how different meanings and understandings informed international actions at different stages of the firm's development and further recognize the contextual conditions in which they were formed.

The next section presents the theoretical framework that has informed the analysis. This is followed by a section that points out the methodological procedures for data collection and analysis. Then the internationalization of the firm is presented and analysed, followed by a section that considers the advancing consolidation of Trikke as a born global firm. The following section explores how relevant meanings were formed, and which then informed international entrepreneurship. Finally, limitations of the investigation are addressed and avenues for future research are integrated.

Theoretical framework

Internationalization has been understood as a process through which firms engage in international operations (Welch and Luostarinen, 1988). It became an important feature of the world economic development in the 1960s. Since then, many theories have been proposed to explain this phenomenon. The internationalization theories are usually characterized into two principal perspectives, namely economic and behavioural (Johanson and Vahlne, 1990; Andersson, 2000; Jones and Coviello, 2005). Despite their theoretical specifics both tend to assume that firms internationalize a long time after their inception (McDougall et al., 1994). Throughout that period firms operate exclusively in their home market. The two perspectives presume that firm internationalization develops as a process that starts with operations assuming a low risk, and undertaking low cost and unimportant commitment to international involvement, and that progresses slowly towards operations of gradually increasing cost, risk and involvement (Jones, 1999) of international activities.

According to Oviatt and McDougall (2005b:5) an international new venture (INV) is 'a business organization that, from inception, seeks to derive significant competitive advantages from the use of resources and the sale of outputs in multiple countries'. Put forward by efforts of international entrepreneurship, such firms can be characterized as fast internationalizing ventures, bringing activities to several countries simultaneously, and conducting foreign operations with high levels of international commitment.

Explaining the underlying logic of international entrepreneurship has been a major challenge to traditional theories of internationalization. McDougall et al. (1994) pointed out some of the major limitations of international entrepreneurship. Table 13.1 presents a summary of these limitations.

Oviatt and McDougal (2005a) note the fact that traditional internationalization theories do not explain the phenomenon of international entrepreneurship despite its critical significance in the fast and early internationalization of firms. Taking into account international entrepreneurship, four aspects should be considered when attempting to adjust existing internationalization theories. These are: transaction cost analysis; evaluation of alternative governance structures; consideration of localization advantages; and taking into account the ownership of unique resources. Oviatt and McDougal (2005a) argue that the internalization of economic transactions distinguishes between transactions that happen in the organizations and those regulated by markets. The alternative governance structures discriminate the set of transactions associated to the new ventures from those that characterize traditional organizations. The advantage of external localization separates transactions related to INVs from those that constitute domestic new ventures. Finally, the ownership of unique resources differentiates sustainable INVs from those that

Table 13.1 The limits of traditional international business theories in explaining international new ventures (INVs)

Framework	Core characteristics of the internationalization process	Limitations related to non-explained facts of INVs
Monopolistic advantage theory (Hymer, 1976; Caves, 1971)	Firms internationalize because they have unique superior resources over foreign firms in their markets. Firms enter international markets after exploiting its advantage in national markets.	Companies with similar advantages, in which just one internationalizes and the other does not. Some INVs explore international markets before their domestic markets.
Product cycle theory (Vernon, 1966)	Companies internationalize due to their product cycle development. Investments abroad are made to protect markets initially served by exportation and only after the maturity of the products and competition based on costs.	Many INVs invest abroad before its products reach the standardization and cost based on competition phase. Many foreign investments of INVs are made before exportations start.
Internalization theory (Buckley and Casson, 1976; Rugman, 1980; Hennart, 1982)	Companies internationalize because market imperfections generate opportunities for the companies to reach better economic results. The core element for internationalization is to reduce costs.	Many INVs do not base their location and organizational structure according to the lower cost logic.
Oligopolistic reaction theory (Knickerbocker, 1973)	Companies internationalize to be equivalent to the actions of other members of an oligopoly. Companies emulate one another to reduce the risk of being different.	Many INVs are the first ones to invest internationally within an industry. Many INVs avoid direct competition and do not emulate their competitors.
Stages internationalization theory (Johanson and Vahlne, 1977, 1990)	Companies internationalize because there is a demand for their products abroad and national companies receive purchase orders from their foreign buyers. The internationalization follows a gradual, sequential and evolutionary pattern, from non-regular exportations up to the point of settling a production unit abroad. Companies do access new markets, slowly amplifying the psychological distance.	Many INVs skip important steps in internationalization and invest abroad quickly. Many INVs do not follow a sequence of incremental steps. Many INVs establish their first external operation in distant (psychological) markets.

Source: Adapted from McDougall et al. (1994).

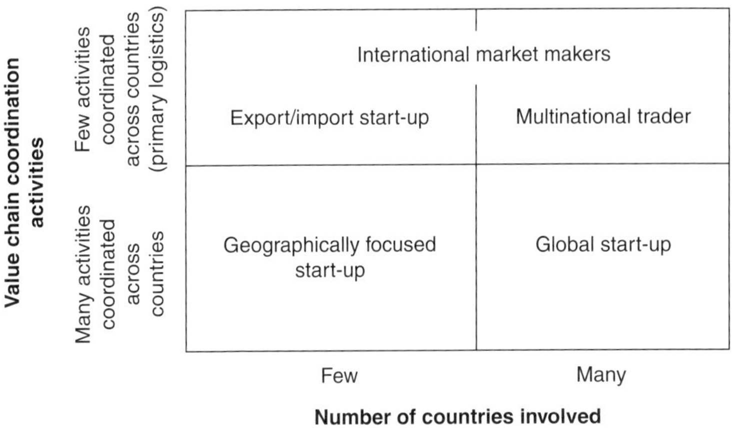

Figure 13.1 Types of International New Ventures
Source: Oviatt and McDougall (2005a: 37).

are short lived. As considered by Oviatt and McDougall (2005a) the first three elements define the necessary conditions for the existence of an INV, while the fourth establishes the necessary condition for the sustainability of international firms.

Oviatt and McDougall (2005a) also argue that once the necessary elements for the emergence of an INV are present, they can assume four basic forms. These are illustrated in Figure 13.1.

The typology presented in Figure 13.1 distinguishes four different types of INV according to the number of activities coordinated in the value chain and the number of countries served. New international market makers are those ventures that put into motion goods between nations. The most important activity in the value chain of these ventures is logistics. In general, such types of firm do not invest directly overseas, rather they have significant ability to discover and to create new markets without investing abroad. Depending on the number of countries served, such enterprises can be classified as being either export/import start-ups or multinational traders.

The geographically focused start-ups as well as the export/import start-ups normally serve particular international markets. However, the former coordinates substantially more activities than logistic operations in a particular region than the latter. Finally, the global start-ups are ventures that coordinate multiple activities of the value chain in multiple widely spread contexts.

Although Oviatt and McDougall (2005a) have contributed significantly to the clarification of the role of international entrepreneurship, this phenomenon still constitutes a major challenge in the field of firm internationalization (Rialp et al., 2005; Keupp and Gassmann, 2009). Pioneering the field, McDougall et al. (1994) argued that the formation of INVs is associated with traces and characteristics of venture founding managers, and to the reasons why they choose to compete internationally instead of acting exclusively in their home markets. They emphasize the fact that such entrepreneurs are observant of the existing realities worldwide and possibilities of combining resources with potential profitability that other people do not perceive.

Reviewing advances of ten years of research, Rialp et al. (2005) observed that studies aiming to explain the phenomenon of international entrepreneurship have focused on internal and external organizational aspects. On the one hand, main internal aspects considered are: the global vision of managers since the establishment of the firm; previous experience of the managers; commitment of management to international operations; personal and business-oriented relationships and networks; level of management market knowledge and commitment; available intangible assets based on the managerial knowledge; value creation through product differentiation, technological leadership, innovation and quality; development of proactive internationalization strategy focused on market niches spread throughout the world markets; customer orientation and relationship; and flexibility for quick adaptation to changes of the external environment. On the other hand, main external factors that require attention are: the type of industry in which the firm functions; the specifics of the geographic context of markets; market conditions among sectors of economic activities; and technological advancement of production, transportation and communication in the operational areas.

Keupp and Gassmann (2009) in a comprehensive review of 179 studies published in 16 journals over a 14 year period observed the following main explanatory factors focused on antecedent variables:

- Personal (manager's socio-cognitive skills and knowledge of demographics);
- Firm (R&D intensity, international experience, market share/size, firm ownership, advertising intensity);
- Industry (foreign and domestic industry structure, government policy, industry competition);
- Country (cultural distance, host country issues).

Moreover the research found that elements also important for international entrepreneurship are:

- Firm strategy (product-market strategy, planning, competitive strategy, international orientation);
- Competitive advantage (comparative advantage, intellectual property, innovatory capabilities);

- Resources and capabilities (resource stock, technology, factor endowments, resource constraints, firm capabilities);
- Organizational learning (learning capabilities, technological learning, knowledge growth and integration);
- Interfirm organization (use of collaborative agreements, interfirm networks, spillovers).

Based on the integration of the research findings Keupp and Gassmann (2009) have concluded that within the specialized literature concerning international entrepreneurship there are many inconsistencies, contradictions and knowledge gaps that have hampered significant advance of the field. Consequently, it can be recognized that various published research has rarely considered an interpretative perspective of international entrepreneurship. This perspective considers the idea that reality is a meaningful social construction and therefore responsible for producing and reproducing the meanings and understandings that give sense to and inform organizational choice and action (Bartunek, 1984; Daft and Weick, 1984; Child, 1997; Sandberg and Targama, 2007; Seifert and Machado-da-Silva, 2007). This perspective is further underlined by the assumption that what is known about the world is the result of complex cognitive processes which are collectively activated, sustained and transformed (Spender, 1998; Sandberg and Targama, 2007). It implies that multiple and different meanings could be given to any experience (Bartunek, 1984; Seifert and Machado-da-Silva, 2007) and that organizational choice and action are ultimately informed by interpretative meanings and understandings (Child, 1997; Silverman, 1978). This understanding draws upon the Weberian tradition of social action analysis (Weber, 1968). It considers that, in an attempt to understand social and organizational action, it is imperative to recognize and assess the meanings produced and reproduced by entrepreneurs' interpretative activity. Previous research suggests that by creating the meanings and understandings that inform organizational action, interpretation defines and limits at least three main vectors of organizational activity, namely: (i) the domain of operations; (ii) the appropriate principles of organization; and (iii) the appropriate criteria to evaluate performance inside organizations (Hinings and Greenwood, 1988; Machado-da-Silva et al., 2000). Accordingly, this study investigates how meanings and understandings produced and reproduced by interpretations are likely to inform international entrepreneurship activity.

Research methodology

Aiming to explore the relationship between interpretation and international entrepreneurship phenomena, we investigated the individual case of the firm Trikke Tech Inc., a Brazilian INV. Our choice for the qualitative design was considered to be adequate for an in-depth understanding of meanings associated with organizational action (Yin, 2003). Three main questions guided the investigation. The first one is: what are the meanings and understandings informing international action? The second is: how do particular meanings inform the internationalization process of the firm? The third is: how are meanings characterizing interpretation formed?

In view of the fact that internationalization is a process that develops over time (Melin, 1992), longitudinal analysis becomes an important aspect informing the investigation. Considering this, a historical reconstruct of the international expansion of the organization from its foundation has been applied. The study was carried out at the organizational level, having the entrepreneurial group as the main unit of analysis.

Secondary and primary data sources have been used. Secondary data focused on the firm's internal reports, institutional presentations, its website, as well as available publications about the firm in print media. Primary data were gathered through seven semi-structured interviews, of which six were personally conducted face-to-face and one via electronic communication.

Data analysis firstly considered the extent to which Trikke's internationalization could be regarded as such of a born global firm. Secondly, attention was devoted to relevant meanings and understandings informing international activities. Thirdly, the context where particular meanings were formed within the company's history was analysed.

The case study

By the end of the 1980s three young middle-class physicists invented a prototype of a small vehicle for human propulsion very similar to a scooter, but endowed with three wheels positioned in a triangle and mounted on a system of interchangeable axles known as 'three wheel carving (3 CV)'. Named Trikke (after the name of the company), the vehicle could reach speeds of up to 30 kmh without any need for putting the foot on the ground for propulsion, even when going uphill. Rather, the drivers had to just push the Trikke to the left or to the right to make it move. By keeping the three wheels in touch with the ground all the time, it offered greater stability than a bicycle or a scooter. Enthused by this invention, a small enterprise was established in Curitiba, Brazil, with the intention to produce and commercialize the Trikke.

Originally, the inventors' intention was to produce and sell the Trikke exclusively in the Brazilian domestic market. However, this attempt was hindered by the advent of 'Plano Collor', a government driven economic plan implemented by President Fernando Collor de Mello in 1990. The plan aimed to inhibit consumption in an effort to stem the high inflation at that time. It substantially reduced money circulation in the economy, and some of the early Trikke retailers were not able to pay for the goods they had purchased. Hence, a few months after starting up operations, the venture went into bankruptcy and the business was dissolved.

Despite this initial frustration, the group still believed in the product's potential and value. By the beginning of the 1999, one of the inventors decided to move to Los Angeles in the United States. With the help and support of his partners, his idea was to start producing the Trikke in Brazil and to sell the vehicle in the USA. The partners believed that US customers savvy for innovations would be interested and could easily buy the product due to their high purchasing power. In addition, venturing into the USA could benefit from a more stable economy than the Brazilian one.

They decided to open a new company in Brazil and register the product's patent in the USA. In the first months, the entrepreneur who had moved to the USA worked early mornings and nights as a pizza and newspaper delivery man. During the day he would ride his Trikke to promote the product. Through networking, he established relationships with some American investors who decided to partner in the venture. Trikke Tech Inc. was formally established in 1999 in the USA. Seven shareholders controlled the company, three Americans and four Brazilians (among them, the three inventors of the Trikke).

Not long after, the entrepreneurial team realized that the difficulties in selling the Trikke in the US market might be greater than initially thought. Despite the higher purchasing power of consumers, the company was unknown, the product was new and consumers were sceptical. Sales simply did not take off. Moreover, the strategy of producing in Brazil and exporting to the US was to a large extent limited by reduced financial resources. To complicate matters, the first Trikke shipment from Brazil to the USA disappeared on its way. Eventually, the shipment was found six months after the departure date from Brazil, which renewed the hopes of the entrepreneurs. More importantly, it enabled them to participate in specialized business fairs and events that were organized in the bicycle industry. It was in one of these events that the Trikke caught the attention of the CEO of China's (and the world's) biggest scooter manufacturer. A partnership was established and after some adaptations in the product using scooter technology, the first samples of the new Trikke prototype arrived in the USA. The main challenge now was to promote sales.

The Trikke attracted the interest of a business executive with much experience in the scooter industry. He became a shareholder in the venture and took the responsibility for marketing it. Using his background and network in the industry, he proposed a new product promotion strategy through Hollywood. For the 2002 Oscar award nomination, 60 Trikkes were given to actors and actresses competing for the statue. Some of them enjoyed the gift and started to use it inside the studios. Quickly the marketing strategy showed its results. Spontaneous media advertising showed some Hollywood stars using their Trikke. The interest in the product grew significantly and, by the end of 2002, it was voted invention of the year by *Time* magazine (Time, 2002).

The visibility of the product in the media opened opportunities for new partnerships for product representation and commercialization. However, as the Trikke became a market fad, it also attracted the interest of pirate companies, mainly from China. In the beginning of 2003, more than 50 pirate firms were copying, manufacturing and commercializing Trikkes. Notably, even the authorized Trikke manufacturer in China did not respect its outsourcing contract and started to sell the Trikke without paying royalties to the company. Facing this situation, Trikke shareholders decided to break the early outsourcing contract and establish a new partnership with another Chinese producer. At the same time they increased investments in international patents for the product.

Early marketing efforts led the sales to grow by 200 per cent in the first two years. However, during the third year sales decreased sharply. Managers argued that it was not enough to sell the product to retailers and wait for the final consumer to buy it. Rather, it became necessary to encourage final consumers to experience the Trikke. In the beginning of 2005, the company intensified the product promotion efforts. They invested massively in infomercials (long advertisements demonstrating the product which were shown on TV) in the US and internationally.

At that time, the company's global performance was consolidated. Half of the sales and distribution occurred through retail channels in 17 countries spread out on the five continents; another half was sold directly through the internet. Patents have been applied in 35 countries and, since 2005, the company has launched eight new models and versions of the Trikke, including one for practice in the snow and another one with a small adapted electrical power engine for commuting and mobility needs. Six years after its initiation in the USA, 13 people form the company board. The production is concentrated in one plant outsourced in China. Product research and development is located in Brazil, and institutional marketing and patent applications are concentrated in the USA. By 2011, with small changes, shareholder structure has remained roughly the same. Trikke vehicles are sold in over 40 countries. As a strategy for growth, the firm emphasizes a network and communities of Trikke users all over the globe.

The consolidation of a new international venture as a born global firm

As Oviatt and McDougall (2005a:31) defined it, an INV is 'a business that, since its foundation, looks to develop significant competitive advantages from the use of resources and the chances of sales in multiple countries'. The Trikke internationalization process fits that definition to the extent that from inception it engaged in operations, partnerships and sales in multiple countries. Contrary to what could be expected from dominant theories, the firm's internationalization process did not follow an incremental pattern starting from low international risk and commitment. Rather, international involvement and risk-taking have been significant from inception. The starting up of the venture in 1999 in a foreign country, followed by successive actions – such as international trade, production outsourcing, establishment of foreign partnerships and alliances, and the formation of an international distribution network – revealed that from inception the firm manifested an intense degree of international commitment. According to dominant theoretical approaches, international operations of this nature would only occur after the company had acquired significant experience from exports or operations of lower risk.

The case of Trikke fits well with the four criteria pointed out by Oviatt and McDougall (2005a) as necessary requirements for a firm to be considered an international new venture, namely:

- The internalization of some economic transactions, evident at the moment of the international foundation of the company in 1999 in the USA;
- The use of alternative governance structure, evident in Trikke's contracts and partnership agreements with suppliers, representatives and retailers;
- External localization advantage, demonstrated by early production in China, research and development in Brazil, institutional marketing and regulatory issues in the USA, and worldwide sales and distribution;
- Ownership of unique resources, expressed in an innovative product supported by international patents.

Interestingly, the case of Trikke is that of a born global firm that was not an outcome of deliberate planning. It emerged in the course of the firm's challenges and practical experience. Although the initial idea was to create an importer/exporter born international enterprise, it quickly evolved into an entrepreneurial venture coordinating multiple activities of the value chain in different countries, hence it became a born global firm.

Meanings, understandings and the formation of an international new venture

The theoretical perspective developed in this study considers that international entrepreneurship is a social conduct informed by the meanings and understandings of entrepreneurs' interpretations. The case of Trikke suggests that different meanings informed international action in different periods of the firm, and ultimately oriented the consolidation of the company as a born global venture.

Three major meanings or understandings were found to be relevant as informants of international action in the early attempt to start up a business venture in the USA. They were: (i) the understanding that the product embodied intrinsic values and potential for commercialization; (ii) the understanding that entrepreneurial success required persistence; and (iii) risk acceptance. The first considered that Trikke had an intrinsic value in terms of offering mobility, leisure and physical exercise. Such understanding underlined the belief that there would be a market for the Trikke whether in Brazil or abroad.

The understanding that entrepreneurial success requires persistence was mainly responsible for informing entrepreneurs' diligent insistence on venturing despite adversities such as the early failure in Brazil, trade difficulties in the USA or limited financial resources. Notably, it further informed the continuous search for alternative strategies and exploration of new business opportunities. Similarly, the understanding that entrepreneurship means accepting risks explains the option to venture with a new product into a new foreign market. The notion that international entrepreneurship is a risk-taking activity is at the core of this phenomenon (McDougall et al., 2003; Oviatt and McDougall, 2005a; Fan and Phan, 2007).

The analysis of the evidence shows that further understandings, in particular those informing action in multiple countries and the use of alternative governance structures, emerged in the course of the firm's practical experience. The understanding that the venture should engage in operations in multiple countries was associated with contingent experiences when starting up the business. The entrepreneurs' initial idea when entering the US market was to produce and manufacture in Brazil and sell in the USA. One of the entrepreneurs stated: 'We just wanted to sell in the USA, we never thought about creating a global company'. However, the same interviewee added: 'today, our objective is to have a company without borders, starting by ownership: we are eight partners, four Brazilians and four Americans, but we think about introducing Chinese, Europeans, people from everywhere in the partnership'. Such understanding is further corroborated by the firm's international operations on five continents.

Another emergent understanding considered the use of partnerships and alliances as a means of business organization and growth. Trikke's entrepreneurs observed that it was not their initial intention to establish a wide network of sales partners, outsource production or increase the number of shareholders in the venture. Such understanding mainly emerged given the limited resources available to the firm. Corroborating this understanding, one of the managers interviewed has noted that all the distribution of products now occurs through partners that 'usually, are Trikke heavy and passionate users'. Moreover, as further argued, future prospects for growth have been mostly based on the capitalization of opportunities through partnerships and strategic alliances.

These findings suggest that meanings and understandings have an important role in orienting and directing the consolidation of born global ventures. They indicate that in addition to the relevance of certain meanings driving international action, those informing action in multiple countries can be formed in the course of the firm's practical experience. This recognition indicates that the institutional context in which the firm is embedded, eventual contingencies and adversities in the course of social action, as well as social interaction and serendipity, are likely to condition the emergence of different meanings and understandings when venturing abroad.

Notably, the entrepreneurs in this case were based initially in the Brazilian market which faced restrictions that were overcome by reinitiating the business in the bigger and more innovation prone US market. The adversities the Brazilian entrepreneurs faced when trying to start up the business, the social encounters with eventual international partners, supported by a strong belief in the product, and persistence and risk-taking provided the elements for the consolidation of the venture as a born global company.

Conclusion

Trikke Tech Inc. is a born global venture from a big emerging economy, Brazil. We have considered how particular meanings and understandings have informed international entrepreneurship. The findings suggest that the inception of Trikke as a born global company has been informed by the entrepreneurs' understanding that the firm's innovative product had an intrinsic value and potential for commercialization and entrepreneurial success which required persistence and risk acceptance.

These understandings were critical in orienting international action, mainly after the entrepreneurs' frustrated attempt to start up the business in the Brazilian domestic market. Our analysis suggests that meanings and understandings orienting the use of alternative governance structures and action in multiple countries were not antecedents to the firm's inception but emerged in the course of the entrepreneurs' attempt to venture internationally. Put differently, the case evidences that although it was not the entrepreneurs' initial understanding and intent to become a born global firm, this understanding emerged as an alternative for their enterprising.

This study adds to the ongoing theorizing in international entrepreneurship in suggesting that meanings and understandings have a role to play here and that they inform action in multiple countries and are not static or present a priori in entrepreneurs' minds. Rather, they are outcomes of interpretation, namely the dynamic instance where meanings and understandings are produced and reproduced. Considering this, future research should investigate further how different meanings are likely to influence international entrepreneurship. In addition, we believe that more research is required to explore how such understandings are produced and reproduced within the dynamics of interpretation.

References

Alexander, J.C. (1988). *Action and Its Environments: Toward a New Synthesis*. New York, NY: Columbia University Press.

Andersson, S. (2000). The internationalization of the firm from an entrepreneurial perspective. *International Studies of Management and Organization*, 30(1), 63–92.

Bartunek, J.M. (1984). Changing interpretive schemes and organizational restructuring: the example of a religious order. *Administrative Science Quarterly*, 29(3), 355–72.

Buckley, P.J. and Casson, M. (1976). *The Future of the Multinational Enterprise*. London: Macmillan.

Caves, R. (1971). International corporations: the industrial economics of foreign investment. *Economica*, 38, 1–27.

Child, J. (1997). Strategic choice in the analysis of action, structure, organizations and environment: retrospect and prospect. *Organization Studies*, 18(1), 43–76.

Crick, D. and Spence, M. (2005). The internationalisation of 'high performing' UK high-tech SMEs: a study of planned and unplanned strategies. *International Business Review*, 14(2), 167–85.

Daft, R.L., and Weick, K.E. (1984). Organizations as interpretation systems. *Academy of Management Review*, 9(2), 284–95.

Fan, T. and Phan, P. (2007). International new ventures: revisiting the influences behind the 'born-global' firm. *Journal of International Busisness Studies*, 38(7), 1113–31.

Giddens, A. (1979). *Central Problems in Social Theory*. Berkeley, CA: University of California Press.

Hennart, J.-F. (1982). *A Theory of Multinational Enterprise*. Ann Arbor, MI: University of Michigan Press.

Hinings, C.R. and Greenwood, R. (1988). *The Dynamics of Strategic Change*. Oxford: Basil Blackwell.

Hymer, S. (1976). *The International Operations of National Firms*. Cambridge, MA: MIT Press.

Johanson, J. and Vahlne, J.-E. (1977). The internationalization process of the firm: a model of knowledge development and increasing market commitment. *Journal of International Business Studies*, 8, 23–32.

Johanson, J. and Vahlne, J.-E. (1990). The mechanism of internationalisation. *International Marketing Review*, 7(4), 11–24.

Jones, M.V. (1999). The internationalization of small high-technology firms. *Journal of International Marketing*, 7(4), 15–41.

Jones, M.V. and Coviello, N.E. (2005). Internationalisation: conceptualising an entrepreneurial process of behaviour in time. *Journal of International Business Studies*, 36(3), 284–303.

Jones, M.V. and Dimitratos, P. (2005). Future directions for international entrepreneurship research. *International Business Review*, 14, 119–28.

Keupp, M.M. and Gassmann, O. (2009). The past and the future of international entrepreneurship: a review and suggestions for developing the field. *Journal of Management*, 35(3), 600–33.

Knickerbocker, F.T. (1973). *Oligopolistic Reaction and the Multinational Enterprise.* Cambridge, MA: Harvard University Press.
Machado-da-Silva, C.L., Fonseca, V.S. and Fernandes, B.H.R. (2000). Cognição e institucionalização na dinâmica da mudança em organizações, in S. Rodrigues and M. Cunha (eds), *Estudos Organizacionais: Novas Perspectivas na Administração de Empresas (uma coletânea luso-brasileira).* São Paulo: Iglu, pp. 123–50.
McDougall, P.P.; Shane, S. and Oviatt, B.M. (1994). Explaining the formation of international new ventures: the limits of theories from international business research. *Journal of Business Venturing*, 9, 469–87.
McDougall, P.P., Oviatt, B.M., and Shrader, R.C. (2003). A comparison of international and domestic new ventures. *Journal of International Entrepreneurship*, 1(1), 59–82.
Melin, L. (1992). Internationalization as a strategy process. *Strategic Management Journal*, 13, 99–118.
Oviatt, B.M., and McDougall P.P. (1995). Global start-ups: entrepreneurs on a worldwide stage. *Academy of Management Executive*, 9(2), 30–43.
Oviatt, B.M., and McDougall P.P. (2005a). Toward a theory of international new ventures. *Journal of International Business Studies*, 36 (1): 29–41.
Oviatt, B.M., and McDougall P.P. (2005b). The internationalization of entrepreneurship. *Journal of International Business Studies*, 36(1), 2–8.
Parker, B. (1998). Evolução e revolução: da internacionalização à globalização, in S. Clegg, C. Hardy and W. Nord (eds), *Handbook de Estudos Organizacionais.* São Paulo: Atlas, pp. 400–33.
Rialp, A., Rialp, J. and Knight, G.A. (2005). The phenomenon of early internationalizing firms: what do we know after a decade (1993–2003) of scientific inquiry? *International Business Review*, 14, 147–66.
Rugman, A. (1980). A new theory of the multinational enterprise: internationalization versus internationalization. *Columbia Journal of World Business*, 15, 23–9.
Sandberg, J. and Targama, A. (2007). *Managing Understanding in Organizations.* London: Sage.
Schutz, A. (1967). *The Phenomenology of the Social World.* Evanston, IL: Northwestern University Press.
Seifert, R.E. and Machado-da-Silva, C.L. (2007). Environment, resources and interpretation: Influences in the internationalization strategies of the food industry in Brazil. *Brazilian Administration Review*, 4(2), 40–63.
Silverman, D. (1978). *The Theory of Organisations: A Sociological Framework.* London: Open University Press.
Spender, J.C. (1998) Pluralist epistemology and the knowledge-based theory of the firm, *Organization*, 5, 233–256.
Stake, R.E. (2005). Qualitative case studies, in N. Denzin and Y. Lincoln (eds), *The Sage Handbook of Qualitative Research*, 3rd edn. Thousand Oaks: Sage Publications, pp. 443–66.
Time (2002). The coolest inventions of 2002. 18 November, 160(21).
Vernon, R. (1966). International trade and international investment in the product cycle. *Quarterly Journal of Economics*, 80, 190–207.
Weber, M. (1968). *Economy and Society: An Outline of Interpretive Sociology.* New York, NY: Bedminster Press.
Welch, L.S. and Luostarinen, R. (1988). Internationalization: evolution of a concept. *Journal of General Management*, 14(2), 34–55.

Yin, R.K. (2003). *Case Study Research: Design and Methods*, 3rd edn. London: Sage.

Zahra, S.A., Korri, J.S. and Yu, J. (2005). Cognition and international entrepreneurship: implications for research on international opportunity recognition and exploitation. *International Business Review*, 14, 129–46.

Zhou, L., Wu, W.-P. and Luo, X. (2007). Internationalization and the performance of born-global SMEs: the mediating role of social networks. *Journal of International Business Studies*, 38(4), 673–90.

14

Internationalizing a Brazilian Software Development Firm

Daniela Buzzulini Prioste and Cesar Akira Yokomizo

Introduction

Internationalization has been a growth alternative for companies that allows them to reach new markets, gain scale and scope economies, increase firm security and profitability. In the last two decades, the globalization of economies, especially the emerging ones, has promoted a new competitive reality, which is more uncompromising, enabling the creation and implementation of previously unimaginable business models. Companies' initiatives regarding internationalization have boosted the growth rate of foreign direct investment (FDI). In the late 1980s, the average annual growth had the value of about US$100 billion, while the 2000s witnessed an average annual growth of approximately US$600 billion, which represents a six-fold increase. More than 30 per cent of the global FDI value is currently invested in emerging economies stimulating their economic advancement.

Over time, the relationship between FDI, international trade and innovation has become more interdependent. Firms with notable international operations are the ones that are leading overseas investment, participating in international trade and engaging in innovation. The most significant developments in innovation, especially those related to high technology, come from such firms. This fact renders cutting edge supremacy of these firms in highly competitive markets.

Nevertheless, it is not easy for such firms to outperform competitors in foreign countries. Internationalization requires companies: to possess competences which can be transferred overseas; to develop competitive advantages in their home country which can be used abroad; to create new advantages facilitating their operations in foreign markets (Vasconcellos, 2008a) where they face global and local rivals.

The internationalization of Brazilian firms is of critical importance for the advancement of the national economy. However, the country still lacks government policies, institutional support and initiatives that would facilitate the internationalization of Brazilian firms (Fleury and Fleury, 2011). Consequently, the number of international Brazilian firms is relatively small and their internationalization depends mostly on the persistence and efforts of the firms themselves.

Hence, although internationalization is a path that firms and countries should follow to increase their global competitiveness, enabling the process via the continuous creation of country and firm competitive advantages is a challenge to most emerging market firms and governments. This is especially the case in countries that need to compensate for many initial disadvantages (Child and Rodrigues, 2005) associated with firm capabilities and competences, the liability of foreignness and a late entry into the international business arena.

The goal of this chapter is to analyse and evaluate the internalization process of a Brazilian hi-tech firm in the software development industry in order to demonstrate the processes and mechanisms by which the firm has overcome a range of obstacles when internationalizing.

Literature review

Internationalization refers to selling products or services in markets other than the home one and engaging in activities facilitating a foreign market presence (Hitt et al., 2002; Paula, 2003). Grosse and Kujawa (1992) state that internationalization of businesses happens via several key type of activities, such as exporting, importing, investing directly, licensing, engaging in portfolio investment, obtaining unilateral loans and conducting transfers. Shi and Gregory (1998) define internationalization as the process by which a firm increases its engagement with international operations. Vasconcellos (2008a) characterizes business internationalization as any initiative conducted by a firm aiming to expand its operations outside its country of origin. According to Sousa et al. (2008:108) internationalization is 'the process of strategic planning and its implementation by a firm in order to operate in countries outside from the country where it was originally established'. Basu (2000:14) claims that 'the world of international business undergoes a transition in which companies are ignoring borders between countries and are considering the whole world as one single global marketplace. Such a break in geographic borders, time, and domestic barriers is converting current organizations into global organizations, which keep alliances and people worldwide'. Furthermore, Carneiro (2000:14) states that 'the phenomenon known as globalization is forcing some Brazilian companies to review their expansion strategies. In a supposedly more open economic system, these companies feel more and more threatened in the domestic environment by new and capable rivals and, at the same time, they consider better entry opportunities in the international marketplace'.

Regarding the classification of internationalized firms, Canals (1994) and Dyment (1987) suggest that they could be divided into several groups related to the phase of internationalization and the type of international activities in which they engage. These include:

- *Exporting firm*: during this primary phase of internationalization, the firm usually concentrates on exporting to one or several foreign countries.
- *Multinational firm*: the firm tries to exploit important competitive advantages, first, domestically, then in other countries. The multinational firm aims to transfer activities from its headquarters to foreign subsidiaries.
- *Global firm*: at the end of the 1970s, there emerged a trend in which firms started adopting coordinated strategies within all countries where they had operations, aiming to acquire global competitive advantages. Critical activities of such firms are concentrated in one or several countries.
- *Transnational firm*: such a firm combines adequately maximum economic efficiency, maximum capability to respond to local markets and extensive flexibility to transfer experiences from some countries of its operation to the whole organization functioning worldwide.

Models of the internationalization process

There are theoretical models of firm internationalization that try to 'explain the internationalization strategic decision, but can also describe internationalization phases or stages, indicating a continuous strategy view' (Vasconcellos, 2008a:134). The most important of these models are briefly referred to below. For example, Hymer's model confers that firms operate in more than one country because they have competitive advantages over rival foreign companies in their home markets. They exploit their advantages, first, in their home market, then they go international (Hemais and Hilal, 2004). The product life cycle model of Vernon (Buckley and Casson, 1998) suggests that firms begin their internationalization with exporting before shifting to direct investments. Moreover, established products are manufactured in emerging economies, because products manufactured with the application of stable technologies tend to be manufactured in countries where labour costs are low. The international product life cycle theory advocates that technology transfer is a means to reach and accelerate access to new markets (Vasconcellos, 2008a). Buckley and Casson's view of internalization suggests that firms pass through various steps in their internationalization process (Brasil and Ortega, 2006). The first one is indirect exporting, followed by direct exporting, which is then followed by the use of an agent, establishment of sales subsidiaries and finally of production subsidiaries in a foreign market. This model states that 'companies tend to internalize activities whose external transaction costs are high or whose transactions are inefficient' Vasconcellos (2008a:135). Buckley and Casson (1998) consider two interdependent reasons for a firm to launch operations in another country. The first one relates to location and the second to control systems. Location refers to where to internationalize, i.e. the choice of a country or region. Control systems refer to the organization and management of the internationalization process. It can be exporting, organized and controlled in the country of origin; licensing, organized in the country of origin and contractually controlled in the host destinations; and direct investment organized and controlled out of the country of origin. One of the most popular models is Dunning's eclectic paradigm. This was created to communicate the idea that the holistic explanation of international activities needs to have sound links with several economic notions. The model emphasizes the application of FDI as the most feasible alternative of a firm's international involvement (Vasconcellos, 2008a). The Uppsala stage model (Johanson and Vahlne, 1977) emphasizes non-economic values in a firm's decision to go abroad. Internationalization is developed gradually, with successive entries in new markets and gradual involvement and engagement within each of these markets. According to Mazzola (2006), this approach has three premises. It assumes lack of knowledge to internationalize as a key obstacle to internationalization; knowledge acquisition is achieved and augmented through international experience in previous markets; and the entry in a new distant market is the consequence of knowledge accumulation. Johanson and Vahlne (1990) propose a four-stage process for international involvement, including: non-regular exporting activities; exports through independent representatives; the launching of a foreign subsidiary; and the launching of operating units. As the process evolves, the firm would be more committed to international initiatives, which would include dedicated and specialized resources. Such incremental development is a response to perceived high risks associated with overseas markets. As the firm accumulates knowledge, risks get gradually lower. Bartlett and Ghoshal (1998) propose an internationalization model based on the notion of transnational corporation, which is a highly competitive firm worldwide with a multinational flexibility and global learning ability. The Nordic School model developed by Andersson places the entrepreneur as key to the internationalization process of the firm. This model also relates to the environment and the moment in which the entrepreneur would act and the resources deployed for internationalization (Andersson, 2000). The network theory emphasizes the relationships between headquarters and subsidiaries of the international firm, and between subsidiaries and external entities, such as suppliers and competitors. Competitiveness is associated with the performance of networks rather than with the performance of isolated organizations.

Table 14.1 presents a summary of the main features of the above stated models and theoretical approaches.

Table 14.1 Main features of the theoretical approaches

Theoretical approaches	Main features
Hymer's Model: power of market	Internationalization of a company occurs due to competitive advantages over foreign companies in its own market. Advantages are first exploited in the domestic market and then in international markets.
Vernon's Model: life cycle of product	Internationalization occurs sequentially: first exports, then FDI. Established products are manufactured in developing countries.
Buckley and Casson: internalization	Internationalization occurs when transaction costs are lower than market costs.
Dunning's Model: the eclectic paradigm	Internationalization occurs when the company perceives propriety, internalization or location competitive advantages.
Uppsala School's Model (Johanson and Vahlne)	Internationalization occurs gradually. Preference for countries with lower psychological distance in relation to the origin.
Bartlett and Ghoshal's Model	Organizational structures based on: companies' need to develop competences for strategic demands and administrative heritage.
Nordic School's Model (Andersson)	Focus on the role of the entrepreneur. Personal and professional networking.
Network Theory	Internationalization is viewed from the whole chain perspective, and not an isolated one.

Source: Vasconcellos (2008a).

Reasons for internationalization

Tanure (2005) suggests that firms are motivated to internationalize by the following reasons:

- Growth: domestic market saturation and search for new opportunities;
- Market: proximity with strategic clients and markets;
- Competition: competing with the worldwide best to be among the market leaders;
- Cost: products and processes economy of scale;
- Risk: reduction of country risk and reduction of capital cost;
- Other reasons: economy of scope and stockholders' ambitions.

In addition, Kotler and Keller (2006) posit that the majority of firms would prefer to remain in their domestic markets, if they were large enough. In this context, managers would not have to learn other languages and laws, cope with floating currencies, face political and legal uncertainties, or change the design of products to meet different needs and expectations of customers. It would be much easier and safer to conduct business domestically. Nevertheless, a myriad of factors forces more and more firms to the international business arena. They include:

- Firms realize that international markets may offer opportunities for higher profits compared to domestic markets;
- Firms need a larger base of clients to achieve adequate economy of scale;
- Firms require to be less dependent on one single marketplace;
- Firms realize that they can counter-attack strong rivals with better products or lower prices that invade their domestic market;
- Firms' clients conduct business abroad and need international attendance.

Brazil is a latecomer in the internationalization process and its participation in the international marketplace is still limited (Fleury and Fleury, 2007), even disproportionately smaller in comparison to the size and potential of the Brazilian economy. Da Rocha (2003) posits that Brazilian firms do not go international due to four main reasons. First, the country's geographic position: Brazil has borders representing insurmountable natural obstacles hampering internationalization. The second reason is associated with the environment. Third, the Brazilian market is huge and its size motivates firm to serve mostly the domestic market. Fourth, Brazilians consider themselves culturally distant from other nations, excluding to an extent the people living in the Latin American region and the Iberian Peninsula.

Approaches to internationalization

Considering the environment

Whenever a firm decides to go international, it has to define internationalization goals and a marketing strategy for foreign operations. Most firms start with a small international involvement. Some plan to remain small, while others have greater ambition in overseas markets (Kotler and Keller, 2006). Fleury and Fleury (2011: 204) suggest that 'once a firm decides to go international, the key issue is to define the markets to which it should dedicate efforts'. If the option is to enter a developed country, it is necessary to consider that there will be high barriers to entry, such as a high level of quality standards. Moreover, there will be aggressive competitors in those markets. Another potential setback is that companies do not master the language spoken in the country where they are planning to go. They do not know well the market structure, clients' preferences, legislation, technical norms or local business practices. Furthermore, managers need to synchronize different time zones.

Therefore, in order to reduce risks and increase chances for success, a firm may choose a foreign market with a high degree of institutional and cultural similarity to the home market (Fleury and Fleury, 2007). Findings from research conducted by Cyrino et al. (2005, cited in Fleury and Fleury, 2007) confirm that: 47 per cent of international Brazilian firms launched their first operation in Latin America; 21 per cent in Europe, of whom most selected the Iberian countries of Portugal and Spain; and 18 per cent in North America, mainly in regions with Latino populations. Fleury and Fleury (2007: 163) claim that 'as they learn in closer countries, companies diversify their geographic portfolio and start exporting to culturally distant locations. Regarding foreign investments, the trend is much the same'. Cultural distance can be defined as the difference between the culture of the country of origin and the culture of the country where internationalization is conducted (Hofstede, 1989). Cultural distance increases or reduces the effectiveness of the management of the internationalizing firm considering its specific advantages associated with a certain location (ibid.; Dunning, 1993). Firms need to be careful when choosing a market if the decision is made only on the basis the cultural proximity. They risk neglecting markets with better potential. Culture can lead to misperceptions about differences between countries and the potential opportunities they can offer. It can also lead to predictable marketing initiatives that constitute a disadvantage in terms of competitiveness (Kotler and Keller, 2006).

Abilities to deal with diverse cultures and promotion of international integration are conditions that are associated with political, economic and legal knowledge of the environment of the host countries, in which the firm launches international operations. In line with this, Vasconcellos (2008b:194) advocates that 'the structure of an organization focused on internationalization is intrinsically based on the development of human relations, may they be individual, group, inter-group, organizational, and inter-organizational. As a result, it is relevant to consider the cultural aspect, with focus on the analysis of the social group and the structures based on its routines and on its inter-relations'.

Partnership formation

Armando (2008:63) argues that 'there are many ways to establish relations with global networks. One possibility is through attracting and developing joint initiatives with multinationals. When multinationals launch an operation, they provide a channel ready to be used by local companies. They also bring incentives for local companies to reach the so-called world class standard to compete with or to sell to multinationals'. Another benefit is the transfer of technology through interaction with multinationals. Dedrick and Kraemer (1998) studied the Asian computer industry. They investigated the rewards that emerge from the relationships in the global production system: the most evident of which was the access to foreign markets through the distribution channels of multinational enterprises (MNEs) and direct exports to local distributors.

Brazilian institutions promoting internationalization

Brazilian firms willing to begin the process of internationalization can count on some Brazilian associations which serve as support systems for entering new markets. For the software industry, three associations deserve our attention. These are BRASSCOM, ABES and SOFTEX.

The Brazilian Association of Information Technology and Communication Companies (BRASSCOM) supports information technology and business process outsourcing firms. The member firms of this association account for 70 per cent of the contribution of IT and communication firms to Brazil's GDP. Founded in 2004, BRASSCOM works to position Brazil amongst the world's three leading strategic centres for information technology and business process outsourcing. To achieve this goal, it seeks to align public policies with private sector incentives, activities in domestic and international markets, as well as to encourage cooperation with employees and their employers. Its agenda is to promote Brazil's excellence and innovative capacity in IT, as this is essential for increasing the efficiency and productivity in every sector of the economy.

The Brazilian Association of Software Companies (ABES) was founded in 1986. Since then, it has contributed to developer, distributor and reseller software firms and service providers through legal consulting services, tax benefits, courses and seminars on leadership and management, improvement of national legislation, national awareness campaigns on the use of legal software, and legal protection of software. With members in 14 Brazilian states (out of 26), the ABES associates firms serving approximately 85 per cent of the Brazilian software market.

The Brazilian Association for Promoting the Software Export (SOFTEX) has the objective to carry out, promote, foster and support innovation, scientific and technological development through technology development and transfer. The association also promotes human capital development through education, training and the application of adequate technical and marketing training in the Brazilian software industry. The above stated applications are focused on serving foreign markets and upgrading Brazilian socio-economic development within the world economy.

Internationalization issues

Internationalization theory suggests that when a Brazilian firm goes international it should consider the following issues:

- Understand the culture of the countries in which the firm intends to internationalize;

- Set its marketing mix in accordance with the specifics of each target market;
- Use extensive professional networking to prepare for internationalization;
- Whenever possible, establish offices in or near key markets;
- Invest in qualified manpower with excellent command of foreign languages, mostly English;
- Seek for a good alignment with partners;
- Prepare and implement a plan to create and promote an international brand;
- Join associations which can assist and promote a firm's international operations (for example BRASSCOM and ABES);
- Seek government financing support for engaging in exporting;
- Use current multinational client firms to leverage international businesses;
- Exhibit products and services in national and international exhibitions, fairs and workshops.

Factors that may prevent Brazilian firms from entering international markets include:

- Organizational structure and managerial systems focused on domestic operations;
- Low levels of preparedness for international operations;
- Non-priority global products platforms;
- Lack of systematic investments to attract and retain people embedded with international expertise and mindset;
- Managerial staff composed mainly by employees with no international background;
- Good command of foreign languages considered not an issue;
- Lack of knowledge on international markets and their relationships;
- Difficulties regarding cultural issues.

Hence, Brazilian firms going international should address international markets as described in Table 14.2.

Methodology

Case study method was selected to conduct the study, which is essentially exploratory (Yin, 2001). Exploratory research aims at developing propositions that will be further investigated. Hair et al. (2007) advocate that the exploratory nature of a research stems from a good literature review, when the researchers identify there is little available information about the investigated subject, as is the case with this research. It can be considered exploratory because new relations, new patterns, new topics and new ideas are pursued.

Table 14.2 Main markets for a Brazilian company going international

Markets	Reasons
China, India, USA, Russia, Vietnam, Germany, Indonesia, Australia, Canada, Mexico and UK	In 2008, these were leading FDI countries. This measurement is promoted by the United Nations Conference on Trade and Development and is based on 12 economic and social variables.
Similar culture and institutions	Understanding the culture is important while defining the strategy because of external adaptation and internal coordination. This is the case for countries in Latin America, Portugal, Spain and catholic Europe because they have a similar culture and institutions when compared to those found in Brazil.
More compatible time zone	Not only does it facilitate communication between the Brazilian company and its clients and international partners but it also supports the required service.

Criteria applied to this case study are:

- A firm pertaining to the software development industry was selected, due to this sector's strategic importance in the development of the world economy;
- A firm with headquarters in an emerging economy is studied, due to the lack of studies addressing such contexts and also due to the lack of studies addressing the North–South internationalization;
- A firm internationalizing with already established international operations is studied, as the main purpose is an investigation of internationalizing strategies;
- Convenience in choosing the firm, in order to unlock access to the firm, both in terms of access to interviewees and of relevant internal documentation because of the authors' association with the research sector.

The selected firm wanted to stay anonymous as did the information providers.

Primary data collection included in-depth semi-structured interviews and analysis of official company documents. Vasconcellos (2008a) claims that the interview is a basic tool for all data collection process, mainly those with a qualitative nature. The criteria for selection of interviewees followed what Cyert and March (1963) called a 'dominant coalition', which means those empowered to make decisions. The interviewees were the key managers implementing the internationalization process of the firm.

The interview research document includes three sections. First, questions associated with provision of basic information on the internationalization process: how the process was started and what the first results were. Second, questions asking for information on the current internationalization situation, which comprises data on current partners and projects. Third, questions asking about the perceptions and forecasts on the future of internationalization, which includes the next steps planned to be implemented.

Analysis on the information provided was applied to enrich the understanding of the firm's internationalization process. Information sources include in-firm presentations on the internationalization process as well as website information. All face-to-face interviews were recorded and subsequently transcribed and analysed.

Results and analysis

The studied firm

The firm was founded in 1995. Its headquarters are in the São Paulo metropolitan region. About 300 people are employed, working in the headquarters and three branches of the firm, all located in Brazil. Main business activities include: system development, software licensing, training, infrastructure and development of information security products and services.

The firm is 100 per cent owned by Brazilian stockholders. In December 2007, it started receiving funds from Intel Capital, Intel's investment venture business. The purpose of this funding is to provide opportunities for growth of the internet economy via supporting the strategic interests of Intel in Brazil. Since its foundation in 1991, Intel Capital invested more than US$4 billion in approximately 1,000 ventures in more than 30 countries. Such investments aim at cooperating with the target firms, both in terms of marketing and in technological development, supporting them to reach new clients worldwide, to optimize new products and services and to expand its exposure to innovations and state-of-the-art technologies.

In 2000, the firm decided to open an office in Canada, aiming to reach the Canadian and US markets. This decision constituted the first initiative towards internationalizing. Recently, the firm has developed an initiative, jointly with a Portuguese partner firm, to enter the European market, focusing on the Portuguese and Spanish market, exploiting this partner's brand and its base of clients.

Why did the firm decide to go international?

Since its establishment, the firm has developed software solutions to major Brazilian banks, which provided it with rare know-how and expertise in developing solutions for the banking industry. When the firm management acknowledged that the firm had developed competitive advantages they started planning for internationalization. The foreign competitive landscape revealed the existence of banks with a smaller base of clients and a less complex type of services than the ones served by the firm. Competition in overseas markets was fierce, but the markets were not so concentrated and software solutions did not need to be as agile and complex as those in the Brazilian marketplace.

The internationalization process of the firm has been gradual. The first steps included the opening of an office in Canada, in 2000, and a partnership with a Portuguese firm. At present, the firm considered opening an office in Europe in order to discontinue sharing revenues with its Portuguese partner.

The founder of the firm is also its CEO and the key entrepreneur responsible for the internationalization process. Thus, the process depends strongly on his extensive professional networking.

The main reasons to go international include some of the ones proposed by Tanure (2005). Saturation of the domestic market does not stimulate growth. The firm decided to go international with leading technological solutions with the objective to become known as a firm selling solutions for developed countries, staying in the vanguard of software innovation.

Closeness to clients has been considered to be critical by the management when launching international operations in the target markets. For example, the opening of an office in Canada and engaging in a partnership agreement with a firm in Portugal was done so as to be close to potential users. Strategic markets include key clients in Canada and the US, and also customers in Portugal, a country with significant cultural proximity.

Vis-à-vis competition, the firm possesses know-how allowing it to serve the Brazilian banks, providing complex and sophisticated solutions. This is perceived by the firm's managers as its competitive advantage and potential to provide advanced solutions for banks, side by side with established, leading software firms.

Considering the financial risk, the firm's financial performance can be impacted on adversely as all current revenues are in Brazilian currency (the real). If foreign revenue is in other currencies, this will disperse the financial risk for the firm. It is also believed that international operations provide better pay-offs and that the cost of capital involved can be reduced. The entry of new competitors in the international marketplace has stimulated the search for new markets in order to diversify risks, strengthen business standing and, above all, learn the rules of globalization (da Rocha, 2003). To sum up, the main reason for the firm to go international was to exploit opportunities for higher profits, even though most of its gains came from economies of scale and cost reduction of products developed exclusively for the Brazilian market.

How did the firm go international?

Software development processes, management methods and controlling styles had been well advanced by the firm before the decision to go international was made. In the process of internationalization, the firm's positioning, recognition and brand appreciation were not only maintained but significantly enhanced in the domestic and overseas markets.

According to the classification of international firms (see for example, Dyment, 1987; Canals, 1994), the researched firm is an exporter who is still in the initial phase of its internationalization process with internationalization initiatives mostly concentrated in a single country. However, the firm is gradually expanding its international operations, as its aims are to explore opportunities for exploiting home country competitive advantages in a number of foreign markets.

From the perspective of the sequential approach to internationalization developed by Johanson and Vahlne (1990), we can argue that the firm is simultaneously in the second and third stage. The second stage refers to the firm's European international experience as it just exports software and other information technology products through a partner firm in Portugal. The third stage refers to the firm's Canadian experience, as it has created a subsidiary in this country. Nevertheless, it is important to emphasize that the value of sales generated and the efforts dedicated to the Portuguese and Spanish markets are significantly greater when compared to those associated with the Canadian and US markets.

The majority of firms launch a small venture when they go international. In our case, the main service sold in Brazil, software development for the banking system, was selected as the principal platform for launching the firm's internationalization. As the goal has been to export to developed countries, where the quality standards are the highest and where there are stronger and more aggressive well-established competitors, the option for offering high quality services already tested in the domestic market has been most important to the firm management. Moreover, Portugal has been chosen as the firm's key export market due to cultural proximity and language identity. The firm does not tune its marketing mix to the requirements of each market. Standardized products are offered to export markets. Localizing marketing initiatives is too predictable, which is regarded as a serious disadvantage in terms of dealing successfully with competition (Kotler and Keller, 2006).

Building strategic partnerships increases the strengths of the partners in terms of use of resources and sharing expertise. The partnerships built leveraged strengths and enabled the firm to fill in the gap between what it would like to accomplish and what its resources really would allow it to do. The Brazilian firm selected a partner in Portugal because it possessed no previous knowledge of the European market and also because it did not have a well-known international brand. The partner acknowledged that the Brazilian banking and information security systems were advanced and sophisticated and decided to offer these services in its own market.

Developing a partnership was of critical significance to the firm's internationalization process. Several factors were considered in the partner's selection process: current internationalization goals, timing for market penetration, partner's credibility, partner's image, ethical issues, investment capability, financial health, management of people and projects already implemented, and so on. Stockholders of the Portuguese partner were introduced to the Brazilian executives by a software multinational firm during an important international fair, where all three companies were exhibitors. Prior to engaging in the agreement, the main executive manager of the Brazilian firm travelled numerous times to Portugal. Nevertheless, as the partnership was legalized and the international operations were launched, a lack of alignment between the two companies became evident. In the preparation for their joint operations, they did not consider a key success factor, i.e. the availability of clients attractive to both companies. Each firm tried to choose the clients most suitable for itself, totally disregarding the interests of its partner. As a result, recently, the partnership agreement has been discontinued. Brazilian executives travel abroad in search of new partners.

The Portuguese partner securing access to its domestic market earned just a small part of the revenues from sales. Therefore, the cost structure in this case was very simple and lean. On the other hand, the Canadian office has a complex cost structure, because a significant part in this structure is the fixed cost necessary to support the firm's clients in the North American markets.

Internationalizing firms need to add several types of cost to production costs, and these vary from country to country. Generally, they encounter three options (Kotler and Keller, 2006). First, they need to determine a common price for all countries. Second, they need to price according to what the market can stand. Third, they need to determine a price in each country according to the costs generated in each country. The approach the researched firm adopted was to determine the price in each country according to what the market in that country can stand.

According to Kotler and Keller (2006), all internationalizing firms create divisions in their structure to cope with all internationalization activities. The studied firm created an international department in its early years of internationalization. This department has been responsible for the internationalization process, defining the goals to be reached in each country market, the budget, and the allocation of resources both for attracting new clients and for developing overseas projects.

The firm adopted its strategy as described by Kotler and Keller (2006:692): 'a local strategy that standardizes a number of essential elements and adapts others to local markets: this strategy is applicable to one industry (such as the telecommunications) in which each country requires a certain adaptation of its device, but the supplier can also standardize some of the core components'. The firm developed information security solutions for the Brazilian banking industry and adapted its software to meet the requirements of international clients and markets.

The internationalization process caused changes in the formal and interpersonal structures and responsibilities, apart from bringing changes in the attitude and mindset of people. Once changes were noted to be irreversible, the firm had to restructure itself, looking for new partners and opening new offices. Moreover, it was necessary to train people to acquire new skills, invest in technology, improve software development processes and obtain knowledge of each country where it intended to trade its brands. From a quality perspective, the main result from the internationalization process was the product quality improvement required by the need to meet international standards.

In line with Tanure (2005) the firm's managers cited some challenges that companies should overcome during their internationalization process. They included:

- Non-priority platform of global products;
- Organizational structure and managerial systems focused on domestic operation;
- Lack of systematic investments in attracting and training skilled people with an international mindset;
- A managerial board composed of Brazilians without prior international expertise.

According to Kotler and Keller (2006), before deciding whether to go international, it is necessary to weigh up several risks. Evidence shows that during its internationalization process, the firm faced the following problems:

- The firm had significant difficulties in understanding the preferences of foreign customers and it failed to offer competitive and appealing products;
- The firm could not easily understand the business culture in foreign countries or it did not know how to deal properly with foreign partners and clients;
- The firm acknowledged that the board of managers lacked international experience.

Another challenge faced by the investigated firm is internationalizing its human resources. According to a research conducted by Permutter and Heenan (1979), there are three types of firm mindset in internationalization. The first is ethnocentric, concentrating decisions in the country of origin and showing a high level of control over international operations.

The second is polycentric, which makes firms follow specific strategies for each market and shows autonomous and decentralized decision-making and control of international operations. The third is geocentric, where firms develop control strategies of domestic and international operations in one and the same way. The studied firm is ethnocentric, because all its decisions are centralized in Brazil and there is strict control of international operations. Home approaches and procedures of its headquarters are replicated in the firm's foreign operations.

According to Keegan (2006), there are some criteria for evaluating risk in international business operations. The primary type of risk is political, which involves analysing the risks that political changes may impact on businesses. Political risk was one of the determining factors for the firm when selecting its foreign markets. The markets of Portugal and Canada showed a low level of political risk that might have impacted on the firm's business. These countries have been selected because they have developed economies and offered access to the North American and the European markets.

The firm had expertise in the Brazilian banking market and a brand well-established in the home market, as well as a relatively large customer base in a large and sophisticated home market. It was agile with good relationships with clients and good networking capabilities. The firm offered products at a price lower than those of its competitors, as it relied on domestic labour. All these firm strengths were supported by a competitive wage structure, technical expertise, business growth and sound financial performance. Nevertheless, the firm had some weaknesses. It had no brand name recognized internationally; and, though it was involved in many pilot projects, it had only a few effective contracts. It did not apply an effective customer relationship management system and was developing software products only. Its employees lacked language proficiency in any other languages, but Portuguese.

The external environment provided opportunities that could be summarized as:

- Investment in knowledge management technologies to promote organizational knowledge;
- Opportunities for domestic and international partnerships;
- Investors interested in the firm's products and potential.

Meanwhile, the firm faced tough competition from other companies with aggressive job offers to skilful employees and from large firms seeking to consolidate their positions in Brazil via M&As. The firm experienced huge pressure to sustain its innovation levels due to fast technological changes, which needed increased financial commitment to ongoing innovation.

Final considerations and conclusions

When a firm launches operations in overseas markets, associated problems are complex. Differences regarding market needs, legislations, patterns and regulations, and the role of government demand a constant appropriate trade-off between adapting products and services to local priorities versus the benefits due to offering global products and services (Vasconcellos, 2008a). The goal of any internationalization process is to offer a company opportunities for greater competitiveness, better financial performance and improved understanding of internationalization destinations.

The top manager responsible for the internationalization was also responsible for domestic sales. Such an approach is probably inappropriate because commercial businesses already established had higher priority, which put the expansion into foreign markets at a disadvantage. Defining objectives for international markets, budgeting and allocating resources to prospective new clients and projects were given low priority.

Partnerships should address mutual goals and these goals must be clear for both sides from the beginning of the process. If not, after a while, the partner companies might come to realize they have just wasted efforts which would then lead to the disintegration of the partnership. This was the case of the analysed firm in relation to its Portuguese experience.

The main motives for going international were the desire of the management to spread risks (not to be dependent on a single market and single currency); to increase productivity (by technological renewal and gains from economies of scale); and to learn through operations in other markets (that were more developed than the Brazilian market).

The limitations of this study refer to the fact that only one firm was investigated in a relatively short time period. Moreover, only managers from the Brazilian headquarters were interviewed. Thus the perspective of the international managers of the firm operating in foreign locations is missing.

Future longitudinal studies could be conducted to capture the ongoing internationalization process over time. Similar research can be conducted for firms in other industries to discover any industry specific effects. Finally, it is worth mentioning that the results from this study are limited in terms of generalization, by the constraints set from the application of the case study method.

References

Andersson, S. (2000). The internationalization of the firm from an entrepreneurial perspective, *International Studies of Management and Organization*, 31(1), 63–92.

Armando, E. (2008). Estratégia Empresarial, Governança e Renda em Cadeias globais de valor: casos em tecnologia da informação, PhD Dissertation, University of São Paulo.

Basu, S.C. (2000). An empirical framework for transforming global organizations through business process reengineering, PhD Dissertation, University of Memphis.

Bartlett, C. and Ghoshal, S. (1998). *Managing Across Borders: The Transnational Solution*, 2nd edn. Boston, MA: Harvard Business School Press.

Brasil, F.L. and Ortega, L.M. (2006). Análise da estratégia da internacionalização: o caso Bematech. Paper presented at the Workshop sobre Internacionalização de Empresas, March, São Paulo: FEA/USP.

Buckley, P.J. and Casson, M.C. (1998). Analyzing foreign market entry strategies: extending the internalization approach, *Journal of International Business Studies*, 29, 539–62.

Canals, J. (1994). *La Internacionalización de la Empresa*. Madrid: McGraw-Hill.

Carneiro, P.S.M. (2000). Internacionalização das Empresas Brasileiras. MSc Thesis, University of São Paulo.

Child, J. and Rodrigues, S. (2005). The internationalization of Chinese firms: a case for theoretical extension? *Management and Organization Review*, 1(3), 381–410.

Cyert, R.M. and March, J.G. (1963). *The Behavioral Theory of the Firm*. Englewood Cliffs, NJ: Prentice Hall.

Dedrick, J. and Kraemer, K.L. (1998). *Asia's Computer Challenge: Threat or Opportunity for the United States and the World*. New York, NY: Oxford University Press.

de Lacerda, A.C. (2007). Internacionalização das Empresas Brasileiras: 2006. (http://terramagazine.terra.com.br/interna/0,,OI1092269-EI7095,00.html). Dunning, J.H. (1993). *Multinational Enterprises and the Global Economy*. London: Addison Wesley.

Dyment, J.J. (1987). Strategies and management controls for global corporations. *Journal of Business Strategy*, 17(4), 20–6.

Fleury, A. and Fleury, M.T.L. (2007). *Internacionalização e os Países Emergentes*. São Paulo: Atlas.

Fleury, A. and Fleury M.T. (2011). *Brazilian Multinationals: Competences for Internationalization*. Cambridge University Press: Cambridge, UK.

Grosse, R. and Kujawa D. (1992). *International Business: Theory and Managerial Applications*. Boston, MA: Irwin.

Hair Jr, J.F., Money, A.H., Samouel, P. and Page, M. (2007). *Research Methods for Business*. Bognor Regis: John Wiley and Sons.

Hemais, C.A. and Hilal, A. (2004). O processo de internacionalização da firma segundo a escola nórdica, in A. da Rocha (ed.), *A Internacionalização das Empresas Brasileiras: Estudos de Gestão Internacional*. Rio de Janeiro: Mauad, pp. 13–28.

Hitt, M., Raphael, A., Lucier, C. and Nixon, R. (2002). *Creating Value: Winners in the New Business Environment*. Oxford: Blackwell.

Hofstede, G. (1989). Organising for cultural diversity, *European Management Journal*, 7(4), 390–7.

Johanson, J. and Vahlne, J.-E. (1977). The internationalization process of the firm: a model of knowledge development and increasing foreign market commitments. *Journal of International Business Studies*, 8(1), 23–32.

Johanson, J. and Vahlne, J.-E. (1990). The mechanism of internationalization. *International Marketing Review*, 7(4), 11–24.

Keegan, W.J. (2006). *Marketing Global*, 7th edn. São Paulo: Pearson Prentice Hall.

Kotler, P. and Keller, K.L. (2006). *Administração de Marketing: A Bíblia do Marketing*, 12th edn. São Paulo: Pearson Prentice Hall.

Mazzola, H.J. (2006). Estratégias de internacionalização em serviços de engenharia intensivos em conhecimento. Paper presented at the Workshop sobre Internacionalização de Empresas, March, São Paulo: FEA/USP.

Paula, G.M. (2003). Estratégias corporativas e de internacionalização de grandes empresas na América Latina. Paper CEPAL-ECLAC 137, Santiago. (www.eclac.org/publicaciones/xml/7/12507/LCL1850P.pdf). Permutter, H.V. and Heenan, D.A. (1979). *Multinational Organization Development*. Reading: Addison Wesley.

da Rocha, A. (2003). Por que as empresas brasileiras não se internacionalizaram? in A. Da Rocha (ed.), *As Novas Fronteiras: A Multinacionalização das Empresas Brasileiras*. Rio de Janeiro: Mauad, pp. 81–105.

Shi, Y. and Gregory, M. (1998). International manufacturing networks: to develop global competitive capabilities. *Journal of Operations Management*, 16, 195–214.

Sousa, A.F., de Neto, A.B., Oliva, F.L. and Armando, E. (2008). *Melhores Trabalhos Práticos III*. São Paulo: Akademia.

Tanure, B. (2005). Os Desafios Principais das Young Multinationals Brasileiras. (www.coppead.ufrj.br/workshop/docs/conferencia_betania_tanure.pdf). Vasconcellos, E.G.P. (2008a). *Internacionalização, Estratégia e Estrutura*. São Paulo: Atlas.

Vasconcellos, EG.P. (2008b). *Internacionalização Competitiva*. São Paulo: Atlas.

Yin, R.K. (2001). *Estudo de Caso: Planejamento e Métodos*. Porto Alegre: Bookman.

Websites

Brazilian Association of Information Technology and Communication Companies: (www.brasscom.org.br).

Brazilian Association of Software Companies: (www.abes.org.br).

Brazilian Association for Promoting the Software Export: (www.softex.br).

15
Brand Strategies of Firms from Emerging Economies

Claude Chailan and Francis Ille

Introduction

During the first half of 2009, the FTSE International Emerging Markets Index was up 41.1 per cent, whereas the FTSE All World Developed Markets Index was up by only 7.2 per cent (Oakley, 2009). Still, most of the brands originating from emerging economies are practically unknown by the majority of Western consumers. In order to increase their profitability by 'climbing up the value chain', many headquarters of emerging-economy firms in Bangalore, Beijing, Moscow, Mumbai, São Paulo, Shanghai, Rio de Janeiro, St Petersburg, Shenzhen or Tianjin have realized that one of the critical success factors for their international reputation is related to their brand image. A number of new brand strategies have been developed and implemented by these firms in order to achieve a better status up the value chain. It is a understatement to state that the development of China in the last 20 years as a major economic power, mostly due to its enormous manufacturing capabilities, has been largely facilitated by the reputation of Chinese brands. It is a well known fact that the image of emerging economies in the West is not one of innovators and brand developers. Consequently this reality contributes to a deficiency in the country of origin (COO) effect in the internationalization of the firms from this part of the world. For this reason the definition of an international brand strategy is of core concern of many firms from emerging economies. The world business environment becomes increasingly competitive and more complex. Consequently, firms are no longer focusing only on production management, but also on defining the most adequate brand policy to achieve their strategic goals in the international marketplace (Kapferer, 2005; Whitelock and Fastoso, 2007). However, the ranking of brands from emerging economies by international branding organizations such as Interbrand (2010) shows that a small number of them have achieved international recognition allowing them to compete successfully in the global arena. This situation calls for an investigation of brands and brand strategies from emerging economy firms. Such an investigation will provide a better understanding of the influence of the level of economic development of emerging-economy brand strategies on their local firms. Therefore brand management in such firms is a key issue for the comprehension and facilitating of the development of competitive advantages (Sharma, 1999; Slater and Olson, 2001) and marketing strategies (Day, 1994; Ponsonby-McCabe and Boyle, 2006; Mattsson et al., 2006) by such firms.

Several key questions are related to the issue of branding in emerging economies. They concern: the impact of brands from emerging economy firms on the customers' perception of the portfolio of products; the branding policy which should be selected in their local and global market orientation; and the identification of the key factors that need to be considered at the launching or the developing of a brand originating from an emerging economy on foreign markets. Consequently, the purpose of this chapter is to investigate the brand strategy and policy of emerging economy firms in order to understand whether their brands are endorsed by their 'emerging' origin or not, in order to contribute to the understanding of the phenomenon of brand strategies in the emerging economy context.

From country-of-origin effect to brand equity

Country-of-origin effect on marketing

Throughout our lives we shape images of different countries through our education, our family background, our friends and relatives, the products from these countries and our numerous personal experiences. Several studies have revealed that consumers have stereotypes of countries and that these stereotypes affect the ways they perceive the products originating from such countries (see for example, Tan and Farley, 1987; Peterson and Jolibert, 1995; Verlegh and Steenkamp, 1999). The COO effect has been defined as 'the picture, the reputation, and the stereotype that businessmen and consumers attach to products of a specific country. This image is created by such variables as: representative products, national characteristics, economic and political background, history and traditions' (Nagashima, 1970:68). Established images in our minds of country of origin, together with such factors as brand and price, influence the way we as consumers evaluate products made in different parts of the world (Maheswaran, 1994; Gürhan-Canli and Maheswaran, 2000; Papadopoulos, 2004). The accumulated COO information could also be used as a heuristic to simplify consumer choice. For instance, consumers tend to perceive German cars as reliable and might use this information at the time they decide between two seemingly attractive cars having different origins.

Research shows that the COO effect is particularly important for some product categories. For instance the international study by Aiello et al. (2009) confirms that consumers worldwide associate correctly luxury brands with their COO. This fact puts more weight on the process of purchasing decisions of luxury goods than on the case of purchasing convenience or fast moving consumer goods. Many brands utilize the COO information as a point of differentiation within their product category. Part of Absolut Vodka value proposition is based on the statement that it is not Russian, but originating from Sweden, which aims to turning a handicap in the vodka market into a value-adding differentiating element. 'Made in Sweden' became the success-bringing slogan for IKEA when it started its business, in order to nurture the brand with positive associations linked to the distinguished Swedish school of design. Other brands have also built their positioning by exploiting solely or predominately such branding tactics. For instance, Dutch cheese is positioned in France as the only alternative to French cheese, with the claim that it originates from 'the other country of cheese'. Historically, branding aimed at identifying a product's manufacturer with its name and location (Kapferer, 2000; Chailan, 2008) in the minds of consumers. The use of country endorsement in a way helps to focus the brand in relation to its historical country based associations. It enhances the brand's *raison d'être*, its roots, its heritage and its authenticity, which are the major determinants of consumers' perceptions and decisively influence choices in certain industries such as wine, fashion or cosmetics.

The COO effect brings in critical information related cues, which play major roles in having the product accepted and purchased in the different world markets. Also, the development of clusters of industries, as identified by Porter (1998), and of people as examined by Florida (2008), has increased the role of COO effect in the positioning of countries in matters concerning international relations and economic development (Papadopoulos, 2004; Baker and Cameron, 2008). The COO effect remains essential for most companies although this effect may lead to biased perceptions of foreign products (Johansson et al., 1994). Also COO effect is decisively context-dependent, varies significantly across situations (for example in the case of various product categories or industries), and is impacted on by culture-specific factors (Klein et al., 1998; Gürhan-Canli and Maheswaran, 2000). Thus, one and the same country can bring about positive associations (for instance, Russia for caviar) or negative ones (for example, Russian for cars), depending on the product category considered.

The COO effect is, in its very essence, mainly based on the perceived characteristics associated with the population descriptors of a country. Thus, the French are 'refined', the Japanese are 'good at miniaturization', the Germans at 'reliability' and the Swiss at 'precision' (Anholt, 2000). Academic research has focused on the image transferred by the country's origin to a product category such as German cars, Swiss watches or English men's shoes. Origin brands will often express those personality traits attributed to the people and associated with their country of origin (van Gelder, 2003) or regional association within a particular country. For example, attributes such as 'competent and serious' are associated with the Germans, 'sophisticated and stylish' with the Italians, 'rugged and independent' with the American citizens of the United States, 'perfectionist and balanced' with the Japanese, 'passionate' with the Spaniards, 'mysterious' with the Indians, 'romantic' with the Parisians, 'exciting' with the New Yorkers, and 'cool' with the Londoners.

Links between country of origin and brand equity

Initially, a brand was considered to be a name or trademark associated with a product. In the last decades, marketeers have claimed that it helps identify one supplier's goods from the competition, hence broadening the mere concept of brands.

Brand equity reflects the additional benefits and values that consumers perceive they get by preferring one brand to another (Farquhar, 1989; Keller, 1993; Baker and Cameron, 2008). While it is difficult to measure it precisely, brand equity comprises a set of associations which help establish a relationship between a particular brand and its clientele by generating a value proposition providing credibility and involving benefits to the customer.

As countries have been more and more considered as brands (see for example Bennett, 1999; Howie, 2003; Pike, 2004), they need to enforce their equity. Papadopoulos and Heslop (2002:295) describe place equity as 'the value that may be embedded in perceptions by various target markets about the country, and the way in which these perceptions may be used to advance its interests and those of its constituents'. References to countries are everywhere around us in our daily life and issues of country equity and brand image have become vital in developing effective strategies and sustainable competitive advantages for firms from respective companies (Baker and Cameron, 2008). For Roth and Romeo (1992:480) 'country image refers to the consumers' perceptions of products from a particular country, based on their prior perceptions of the country's production and marketing strengths and weaknesses'.

As a country is a very complex concept based on a myriad of different products, services and experiences, branding involving countries is multifaceted and offers cross-sector stakeholder cooperation (Ashworth and Voogd, 1990; Therkelsen and Halkier, 2008). Countries are more likely than conventional products and corporations to have an image and which brings an identity in the minds of consumers prior to or irrespective of any marketing efforts (Therkelsen and Halkier, 2008). Also, due to globalization associated with developments, changes in the production processes have also altered the way commercial brands employ the concept of territory. Presently COO has become a core attribute for many commercial brands. Consequently, the assertion of country uniqueness has become an institutionalized global practice for celebrating brand identity. This uniqueness often emphasizes the historical, social and cultural values and, as such, country uniqueness can be communicated as a brand specific identity, a foundation on which brand equity can capitalize in order to boost consumer loyalty and generate better revenue, increasing possibilities for profit augmentation.

New perspectives on emerging economies related to brand equity

Recently, marketeers have started to consider that ideas, celebrities and places could be managed as brands. Research has investigated particularly consumers' perceptions across different competing geographically based brand models (van Gelder, 2008). Geographical locations employ practices, developed by marketing, transfer knowledge to specific location environments and translate concepts according to environmental needs and characteristics (Kavaratzis, 2005).

A vast majority of studies have addressed and examined the geographical marketing concept from a twofold perspective. The first one focuses on the place as a potential tourist destination. Then, the primary marketing objective is to valorize the place in order to render it an attractive destination to visitors and/or investors. The second perspective considers the place as a source. A long standing line of research has investigated how the COO of a product or a firm impacts on consumers' evaluation of the performance or perception of the product or firm personality.

Although not to the same extent, most brands possess common features of being associated with a particular country. The place endorsement approach is widely put in practice by Western firms. However, studies based on research of firms from emerging economies reveal that their marketing strategies associated with brand endorsement approaches are still in their infancy. Seisdedos and Mateo (2008) assert that the processes for managing place endorsement have not grown at the same pace as the development of emerging countries in the world economy. Yet, several strategic questions are connected to the idea of place endorsement, such as: Is there a specific impact of the names of emerging economies on products, beyond the mere COO effect? How does the consumer interpret this information? Which criteria are taken into account by the customers to value the endorsement of emerging economies? Or, say, how transferable are the key features of emerging economies?

Managing brands by firms from emerging economies: conceptual framework

Brands are viewed as key value-creating resources and useful sources of sustainable competitive advantage because they are firm-specific, protected by law and inimitable (Urde, 1999; Teece, 2000; Barney, 2001). Thus, a key challenge facing emerging economies' firms is how to manage brands more effectively than their competitors (Johnson and Selnes, 2004). A possible route to be followed is by drawing on a firm's specific internal and inimitable capabilities. However, a review of the literature illustrates that scant attention has been devoted to the investigation of the specific drivers of firms from emerging economies in the process of their internationalization as well as in the process of creation and implementation of their brand policy options when performing internationally (Whitelock and Fastoso, 2007; Guzmàn and Paswan, 2009).

Several articles have addressed the branding approach of firms from emerging economies. Schultz (2008) differentiates between the old 'Chinese' model, in which the transformation of raw materials into manufactured goods was not applied when selling Chinese branded products, and the 'Indian' model, in which the primary materials are turned into Indian branded goods. This has changed dramatically in recent years (Magnusson et al., 2008) with the objective of enterprises from emerging economies striving to be independent of Western developers. In the automotive industry, for example, a recent study compares the perception of brand personality by US buyers of automobiles with Chinese or Indian brands (Fetscherin and Toncar, 2009). The study shows that the cars with the Chinese brand name were perceived as more daring, up-to-date and outdoorsy; Indian cars were perceived as being less intelligent, successful and upper class.

Through the process of brand image building, firms from emerging economies realize that brands must face and respond to two brand-specific questions, typical for emerging economies. The first one is related to clarifying the role of brand functions, and the second regards the choices linked to the global and local dimensions of positioning. According to the literature brand functions refer to the three key reasons for which a brand is chosen by a customer (Kapferer, 1991; Keller, 1993; Riezebos, 2003). Firstly, the brand provides an indication of the origin of the product, which guarantees a certain standard of quality and performance, and leads to creation of consumer confidence. Secondly, brands mark the difference and facilitate the spotting of a product. Thirdly, the brand disseminates a specific value with which consumers identify.

Facing such complex consumer expectations, a main obstacle to the success of brands from emerging economies may be the negative perception that consumers in developed countries have towards products originating from that part of the world. This fact results in lower customer expectations in terms of the quality, absence or low level of trust in such brands, and overall low loyalty levels. Therefore, most consumers are not willing to pay high prices for products originating from emerging economies (Magnusson et al., 2008).

The local versus global brand dimension refers to the type of international orientation which defines the degree of localness a company should emphasize when choosing its brand and their features. The brand choice may, or may not, contribute to transmitting the values of its origin, especially when it develops abroad (Theodosiou and Katsikeas, 2001). The brand could be an indicator of the degree of the product's localization/globalization and as such adds or removes value to the customers. The international orientation of a brand is a choice of strategy that would determine the specificity of the competitive advantage of a firm, as well as the firm's performance characteristics.

Firms from emerging economies must make the best of any distinctions linked to the uniqueness of their geographical situation. Western consumers often associate it with low product quality, misleading/disappointing products, or products that do not comply with international standards. This situation represents a double paradox associated with brands from emerging economies. The first one is the paradox of trust and the second is the one of localness.

The trust paradox of brands from emerging economies

The first paradox associated with brands from emerging economies is that of the intense contradiction between the trustworthiness that consumers come to expect from brands and the mistrust generated by a brand from an emerging country. A brand not only allows for differentiation between competing products (Kapferer, 2000; Riezebos, 2003), but also transfers a benefit to the client, based on their confidence in the quality and uniqueness of the brand. A brand is a tool for reducing risk and serves as a guarantee for the consumer. A brand identifies the source of the product or service and as such it represents a performance standard for which it is purchased. This standard is founded on a combination of criteria which function like a trust pact and guarantee of consistent quality regardless of the intermediary between the producer and the end consumer (Aaker, 1992; Keller, 1998). The decrease in the perceived risk linked to the purchasing of a brand is set forth as the consumer's first expectation of this brand (Farquhar, 1989; Berthon et al., 1999; Azoulay and Kapferer, 2003). The higher the perceived risk, the higher the need for the brand as a tool of reinsurance at the moment of purchasing, regardless of whether this risk is financial, physical, technological, psychological or social (Kapferer, 1991). For this reason, the value of a brand for both the company and the consumer is emphasized on numerous occasions. Thus, firms consider brands as capital which must be optimized (Kapferer, 1991; Aaker, 1992; Keller, 1998; Riezebos, 2003).

Contrary to consumer expectations, the identification of an 'emerging' origin of a brand or a brand that carries with it the notion of an emerging economy as its origin, mostly linked to negative connotations, can often be perceived as a risk indicator rather than a risk reducer. In fact, numerous prejudices may be associated with a product's country of origin. These prejudices have been reinforced by a considerable number of scandals linked to certain socio-economic experiences associated with brands, for example Nike in Vietnam and Pakistan, or cases related to the compromising of fundamental rights (such as exploitation of child labour, implementation of extended shifts, introducing working conditions without breaks, and so on). Comparable to the above are the examples with the implementation of low-cost production approaches and the implementation of hazardous ingredients (for instance, Mattel toys made in China with the use of lead paint). Similarly, Iams, the famous Procter & Gamble pet food brand, had to issue a market recall of its products because they were dangerously contaminated by raw materials coming from China.

In 2008, the Chinese Ministry of Health (World Health Organization, 2008) acknowledged that 294,000 infants had been poisoned by Chinese-made melamine-contaminated milk, which resulted in 50,000 being hospitalized with at least six deaths. Many of the affected victims had stones or calculi in their kidneys, urethras or bladders. The image of Chinese production of manufactured food was tarnished by this occurrence.

The above examples show that production from emerging economies could often be associated with a supplementary risk while in fact the *raison d'être* for brands is to reduce the consumer's perception of risk. Every firm from an emerging economy must confront this paradox when they begin to envision their brand policy and develop a brand strategy.

Brand confidence also allows for the overcoming of doubts when considering innovation. A well-established brand serves as a means for consumers not to take risks, such as purchasing low-priced products with unknown quality and features, or trying new product categories or new consumer methods (Kapferer, 2000). Yet, emerging economies generally are followers rather than innovation leaders. They are not characterized by a high degree of innovation or supported by strong brands that would attract consumers to their products.

The local versus global paradox of brands from emerging economies

Of key consideration in international business operations is the definition of the marketing strategy of a firm related to the decision of whether it should be standardized or localized (Theodosiou and Katsikeas, 2001). Whitelock and Fastoso (2007) remind us that some researchers (for instance, Steenkamp et al., 2003) have found that a consumer preference for global brands could exist, due to higher quality and prestige, while other researchers (see for example, Schuiling and Kapferer, 2004) claim that local brands have an advantage over global brands in terms of brand awareness and trustworthiness. The issue related to the differences between local and global branding according to consumer perception is the key in defining how to create value and how to influence consumer choice to favour brands from emerging economies.

Consequently, the second paradox of brands from emerging economies is that of the dilemma between their local orientation (most of them are local from inception) and their aspiration to go global. The issue is to decide to what extent globalization or localization should be emphasized, and specifically to what extent rooting the brand in local operations may represent a positive or negative value added. The association with a country of origin can have a strong impact on a firm's ability to succeed in international markets. Particularly worrisome for firms from emerging economies is the fact that the identification-of-origin effect tends to be especially adverse in the case of firms from emerging economies (Magnusson et al., 2008).

Most brands from emerging economies have little or no name recognition outside of their own country and as such provide low brand equity both to customers and firms. Branded products are more valued by consumers than a product without a brand name (Sappington and Wernerfelt, 1985; Farquhar, 1989; Keller, 1993; Baker and Cameron, 2008), even more so in certain product categories than in others (Riezebos, 2003). Emerging countries' brands are known for their lack of differentiation which puts creating strong brand associations from such countries at a serious disadvantage, because they are still similar to 'me-too' products without any real distinction. Consequently, the equity value of brands from emerging economies is more related with a local significance that may represent a strong differentiation point for these brands, conditional on their ability to transfer the strong point of differentiation into dealing successfully with international competitors in gaining customer base and generating profits.

Conceptual framework

To create a response to these two fundamental paradoxes related to risk reduction and global versus local dimension firms from emerging economies must address foreign market specifics and establish appropriate brand strategies on the basis of criteria other than solely production considerations. The general approach to brand strategy formulation by firms from emerging countries can consequently be conceptualized in a matrix across two axes representing in one direction the customers' perception of a foreign brand and in the other direction the level of 'Westernization' vs 'localization' of brand characteristics emphasized by the firms.

The conceptual model of this investigation is presented in Figure 15.1. It provides a graphic representation of the possibilities for firms from emerging economies to generate brand strategy choices. These choices are defined by the way in which a firm positions itself vis-à-vis its own roots and its attitudes towards risk, linked with the serving of foreign customers. This framework is based on factors related to the elaboration of the two paradoxes and it integrates the degree of risk reduction with brand orientation towards local or global markets.

The horizontal axis represents the degree of localness or globalness that a firm wants to adopt when branding its products. The vertical axis represents the degree of risk perceived by the consumers. The lower the cognitive

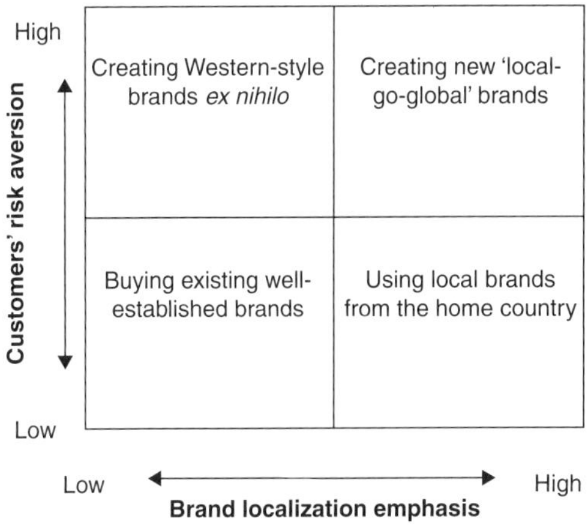

Figure 15.1 International brand policy options for the companies of emerging countries

effort, the less the consumers are willing to take a purchase risk (Kapferer, 2000). Also when consumers have a static attitude with a brand expectation risk will be at its maximum.

To obtain brands, firms from emerging markets use various approaches:

- Firms buy existing Western brands with a strong and well-established image (for example, the computer firm Lenovo bought IBM PC Division with its brand Thinkpad; the Indian giant Tata bought the Jaguar and Land Rover brands, Chinese television maker TCL bought the Thomson brand, Turkish firm Ülker bought the Godiva brand, and so on);
- Creating global brands from scratch by using Western marketing principles and performing in markets of developed economies (for instance, Haier and Huawei brands from China; Reliance and Infosys brands from India; Gorenje brand from Slovenia, and so on);
- Firms which have developed their local brands based on a favourable COO effect in their domain of expertise, to reach primacy in their field (for example, Tsingtao beer brand from China, the brands of Zain Telecom and Teva Pharmaceutical Industries in the Middle East, Ararat brandy brand from Armenia, Pliva pharmaceutical brand from Croatia);
- Creating global brands by using a local image and marketing techniques related to local language, culture and even possibly ethnic or religious belongingness (for instance, Baidu brand from China, Televisa and TV Azteca brands from Mexico, Mecca Cola brand launched in France and presently based in Dubai, the Fulla doll from the United Arab Emirates, and so on).

The above typology is used to compare the chosen brands on the basis of their marketing strategy and more precisely their approach to global recognition. This will be complemented by the study of other factors such as the influence of the company leader.

Brand practices of companies from emerging economies

The cases that are described below are from emerging countries in which one or several brands are becoming known at the international or global level.

Firms from emerging economies that bought existing well-known brands

Emerging economies' firms counteract the negative effects of COO perceptions by acquiring well-established brand names from developed economies. This opportunistic approach is applied so as to benefit from the image of some already existing appreciated and well-known brands and to improve the perceived quality of the emerging countries' products. Such an approach could broaden their market presence and deepen the emerging countries' marketing expertise. This option allows acquiring firms to gain immediate access to a set of already existing brand associations in the consumers' mind and so to earn time as well as to limit or at least make manageable the risk of negative associations.

The Chinese firm Lenovo is a perfect example of an emerging country company, which tried to establish global brand position by purchasing an existing world famous brand in the PC business. The company was created in 1984 under the name of Legend (Quelch and Knoop, 2006). It was very successful in China but blissfully unknown outside the country. The firm bought the PC Division of IBM in 2004 to strengthen their brand image, after switching their name from Legend to Lenovo. Hence they acquired major competitive advantages coming from the application of the co-branding strategy in adopting the Lenovo-IBM logo on its products (Ille, 2009). They also extended the Thinkpad brand image by sponsoring the Winter Olympics in Turin in 2006 and the Summer Olympics in Beijing in 2008. According to the contract Lenovo signed with IBM, the Chinese firm obtained the right to use the IBM logo on its products for five years while keeping ownership of the Thinkpad brand forever. Recent years have presented Lenovo with some difficulties to live up to its expectations, showing that acquiring a global brand was probably not enough to guarantee full success (Kotler and Pfoertsch, 2007).

The Indian Tata Group bought the Jaguar and Land Rover brands for US$2.3 billion in 2008, illustrating the strategy defined by the CEO, Ratan Tata: 'the only way I can enter the U.S. market is through mergers and acquisitions, so if I get an opportunity, then I will look at it very actively' (Khanna et al., 2008:12). Tata hopes to boost the Jaguar brand image and benefit from this development in order to acquire a global reputation. It is probably too early to see the result of these acquisitions and whether they will avoid brand dilution by selling simultaneously the low priced Nano car.

In the luxury business, brand image is even more important. The Indian watch and jewellery brand Titan also belongs to the Tata group. Apart from being extremely successful in its large domestic market, the brand is also rather successful in the Middle East. However, so far it has not been able to achieve global presence in the world's major watch branded markets. To achieve such a goal Tata group may have to consider buying an existing brand with a more favourable COO image.

On 2 August 2010, Zhejiang Geely Holding Group Co. Ltd, one of the fastest-growing automotive manufacturers in China, announced it had completed the 100 per cent acquisition of the Volvo Car Corporation, the iconic Swedish car brand, previously owned by the Ford Motor Company, synonymous with extreme security and durability. Mr Li Shufu, Chief Executive of Geely Holding Group, was delighted to celebrate a 'historical day' for his firm, giving it the image and the prestige to penetrate Western markets. The transaction was worth US$1.5 billion.

Firms from emerging economies that have created 'Western-style' brands *ex nihilo*

In this category, the firms have developed a local brand by using the marketing strategies applied in the creation of Western brands. Such brand policy may reduce the negative effects of the product origin by adopting brand names that conjure positive images for the customer. Behaving this way, these firms can offset the negative effect from their home countries associated with perceived images and make consumers distinguish the branded product as being from a different country. This approach allows consumers to be reassured by avoiding any claims or carrying across negative prejudices associated with the origins of the initial brand.

Haier is a Chinese household appliances brand whose name was created in 1984 by Zhang Ruimin, then a young assistant city manager in Qingdao. The brand implied technology competence associated with the motto 'patently geared for global stardom' (Batey, 2002). Ruimin established the base line: 'if we can effectively compete in the mature markets with such brand names as GE, Matsushita and Philips, we can surely take the markets in the developing countries without much effort' (Palepu et al., 2005:11). Haier's brand image was even strengthened through the Beijing Olympics sponsorship by applying Western style recipes for success; and the brand is currently one of the most well known Chinese brands outside the country. In this case there was no need to 'borrow' an outside name in order to achieve international reputation. Haier realized the importance of convincing the Western consumer about its quality (Larçon, 2010) and, in order to become more global, they have staffed the European headquarters of the firm with European executives (Latessier, 2010).

Reliance is an Indian firm created by Anil Dhirubai Ambani. It ranks among India's top three private sector business enterprises in terms of net worth and is ranked in the World Top 500 Most Valuable Brands. The Reliance name is all over India and neighbouring countries and is synonymous with quality in the fields of communication, energy, insurance and portfolio management for enterprises and individuals. Although the fight between the Ambani brothers has made the headlines of the financial press, the Reliance Communication brand has become a symbol of the success of Indian technology in the field of telecommunications services, namely through Reliance Infocomm. Reliance has become India's biggest private sector company and is now in the process of completing a joint venture with Atlas Energy.

Infosys Technologies Ltd, a globally admired knowledge enterprise, has been a pioneer of knowledge management and one of the first brands to demonstrate Indian software expertise (Mehta et al., 2007). This software giant, created in 1981 (Capelli et al., 2010), had to face the challenge of building a global brand out of a service industry and built its strategy on their Global Delivery Model for multilocation engagement teams (Murty and Desai, 2005). Infosys realized that it could not compete with IBM, Accenture or the major IT consulting firms in terms of recognition and therefore capitalized on the predictability in the fields of banking and insurance applications.

Huawei, the Chinese's most successful hi-tech company in the telecommunications industry, competing with CISCO in the router market, nurtures its capability in the domestic market (Sun, 2009) as a base for internationalization. Huawei uses inward and outward links to strengthen their firm's image. Huawei, just like its Western counterparts in the Silicon Valley, invests in R&D and in 2008 the firm became the largest patent applicant in the world under the World International Patent Organization's Patent Cooperation Treaty. It now appears in the *Business Week* list of the World's Most Influential Companies, on a par with Apple, J.P. Morgan, Wall Mart and News Corporation (McGregor, 2008).

Firms from emerging economies that used existing local brands

In the case of these firms, the brand name normally has had a strong local image prior to its internationalization. It may not have been portable abroad. There are difficulties such as the pronunciation of the foreign brand names, or even their identification when written in an alphabet different from Latin, such as Cyrillic, ideograms or Chinese characters, or because the word may have an unacceptable meaning in other languages. An option for firms from emerging economies is to make use of already existing and locally powerful brands. The company chooses to export (part of) its domestic culture with its products. This approach nurtures the differentiation from competitors although it may limit the brand audience.

Tsingtao beer brand is associated with a brewery created in 1903 to produce German style beer for the German troops occupying the Shandong Peninsula after the Boxer War. It has the name of the town now spelled in Pinyin transcription as Qingdao, situated in the Shandong Province. Tsingtao brand is so powerful in its home market that this fact attracted Anheuser-Busch to buy a 27 per cent share of the brewery. The Anheuser-Busch shares were later bought by Asahi Breweries in 2009. The Chinese government has a 32 per cent stake in the brewery. The 2008 Beijing Summer Olympics were a perfect opportunity for Tsingtao Brewery to promote its brand using the motto: 'passion, dream and success'. China was totally cut off from the Western world between 1949 and 1979. During this period the brewery was state owned (Hill, 2004) and was able to keep its local competitiveness. The brewery rejuvenated in the 1980s, attracting the attention of foreign investors. Following sponsorship activities throughout the Beijing Summer Olympics, Tsingtao gained its reputation and became a global beer brand.

Another possible justification in the strategy of some brands from emerging countries is to reach some of the 200 million people who, according to the United Nations, are living outside their home country. Guzman and Paswan (2009) give the example of two Mexican cultural brands, Televisa and TV Azteca, both of which are Spanish language broadcast brands. When comparing the perception of brand personality for both brands, the researchers found that Mexicans living in the Dallas-Fort Worth area in Texas associated it with sincerity, excitement, sophistication, and competence much more than the Mexicans living in Mexico. This implies that a kind of nationalistic support to the brand is more powerful with people living outside their homeland and could be a strong justification for populations that have large diasporas (for example, Chinese, Indians and Mexicans living in the US) in supporting the products from their COO when living abroad.

In the late 19th century, in what later became the Soviet Union, Nerses Tairyants established a brandy production plant in Erevan, Armenia, associating it with the most prestigious mountain of Caucasia, Mount Ararat. Ararat cognac became so famous that the French spirit giant Pernod-Ricard bought the Yerevan Brandy Company with the Ararat brand name. The Shustov family, who owned the Armenian factory, applied some marketing techniques as early as 1912 when they were named 'Official Purveyor to the Russian Imperial Court'. The COO effect was a critical positive factor for the success of the Ararat brand being linked to the image of Armenia as a famous spirit-making country.

Firms from emerging economies creating new brands *ex nihilo*

In the case of the creation of a brand from scratch, capitalizing on some positive local aspects was related to the local language, culture or religion. The 'local' brand is likely to generate an element of differentiation as a creator of added-value in overseas markets. In this approach, an emphasis may be placed on developing the perception of brand localness by associating the positive values of the place of origin with the brand itself. The objective is to create new brands rooted in the local environment so as to capitalize on that environment and strengthen the differences. This practice highlights the positive components linked to the brand's history while simultaneously promoting its local origin.

The firm Baidu was founded in 2000 in the Beijing Zhong Guan Cun, the 'Chinese Silicon Valley'. It is an example of a brand developed as a search engine for the Chinese market. It has become the core engine used in any advertising campaign in the country. Google may have to leave China due to censorship issues, but observers point out that it was not going to be successful in the country in any case (Madden, 2010). Since Chinese branded companies are supposed to lack their own innovations (Bell, 2008) some are combining the characteristics of Western brands (such as quality, service, trustworthiness and modernity) with the consumer's need for low prices. Sasserath (2006) calls them 'clever brands'. Baidu has achieved the clever brand compromise, namely by using its knowledge of Chinese users' specific needs selling at a low price.

In the Middle East, Zain Telecommunications, headquartered in Kuwait, is aiming at becoming one of the top-ten global mobile operators worldwide by providing a world class service to customers in the Middle East and Africa. It started as a modest, single operator serving around 600,000 customers in the State of Kuwait to become a conglomerate with a commercial presence in 23 countries from Nigeria to Bahrain and from Jordan to Zambia with a 13,000 dedicated workforce serving more than 70 million customers in Africa and the Middle East. Just like Nestlé, which at the beginning of its business activities realized that the territory of Switzerland was too small for its success, Zain very soon decided it had to work outside the tiny State of Kuwait. The success of Zain has stimulated some other Middle Eastern telecommunications operators, such as the Qatar Telecom Co. (Qtel), which continues its development in the Gulf region as well as in Indonesia. Zain's CEO, Saad Al-Barrak, (Tiefel, 2009) has emphasized the importance of being a 'good corporate citizen' in all the countries in which Zain operates, something quite difficult to achieve and sustain in the Middle Eastern context.

An interesting brand strategy in some emerging economies is the one appealing to nationalist or religious feelings in order to create support for some ideology or religious faith. A good example is Mecca Cola, the firm of Tawfik Mathlouthi, a Tunisian entrepreneur, who has created a soft drink aiming at supporting the Palestinian cause. The brand is a 'drinkable manifestation of hostility toward America', and it appears to be taking off (Hanft, 2003). The company is headquartered in Dubai, United Arab Emirates, and although competing with Coke and Pepsi it takes advantage of its representation in the Arab world in which a part of the people are ready to sympathize with the Palestinians. Likewise, Bénedictine liquor, produced in the French region of Normandy since 1510, produced by monks, uses religion as a promotional tool.

Factors influencing the brand strategy of firms from emerging economies

Besides the strategic choice analysed above between developing your own brand or buying an existing one, it has been found that some other important factors have strongly influenced the success of brands coming from emerging countries in general and China in particular (Lou and Davies, 2006). These are addressed below.

Country of origin effect

It is easy for Germany to develop a brand in the manufacturing industry or for France in the luxury goods category. However, it is difficult for India to establish a brand for the precious stones industry or an African country in manufacturing. Likewise a brand from China may suffer from the image of its political orientation, or poor quality. However, Japan, between the early 1960s and 1980s, demonstrated that its COO effect could be changed, as was demonstrated by firms such as Toyota, who moved from 'junk status' to the zenith of quality within three decades. Therefore emerging countries have to engage in innovating to improve the image that influences negatively their COO (Ramo, 2007). The product and brand perception of emerging economy firms and their produce show that only 17 per cent of Americans expressed a high interest in buying products imported from China (Tucker, 2006). The efforts to improve the image associated with a negative perception of COO has been demonstrated in several studies (Akotia, 2005) conducted in Africa where the local brands lack foreign recognition.

Product category effect

Russian giant firms in the field of natural resources (for example Gazprom, Lukoil and Rosneft) and South African diamond producers do not require the same level of branding as the producers of goods for which know-how and expertise are of key significance (products such as fine watches, software products or financial products), which infers that the brand strategy of emerging countries' products depends on the type of industry and that it is easier for non-sophisticated products.

Degree of 'marketing maturity' of the country of origin

The countries which went through a planned economy period of development 'discovered' marketing in the late 1980s and throughout the 1990s.

Companies from these countries started developing their brands much later than the firms originating from advanced market economies. The same is valid for the marketing campaigns. For example the Soviet car manufacturer Lada did not use marketing campaigns (Day and Brad, 2009). Among the Chinese brands Haier, Tsingtao beer and Lenovo were among the first ones to develop their marketing communications strategies, but they are still far behind Western firms in terms of promotional budgets. We can hence infer that brand strategies of firms from emerging countries depends on the degree of their marketing 'maturity', including the cultural background and the stage at which they have been involved in marketing exposure.

Use of personality of firm founders as a promotional tool

Zhang Ruimin for Haier, 'Captain Wei' Jiafu for Cosco, Yang Yuanqing for Lenovo, Lakshmi Mittal for Arcelor Mittal, Nandan Nilekani for Infosys, Azim Premji for Wipro, although all coming for emerging economies, just like Bill Gates for Microsoft, Jack Welch for GE, Steve Jobs for Apple, Tom Watson for IBM or Bernard Arnault for LVMH, all had at the same time the charisma and the reputation to bring their brands to the highest level, allowing them to achieve world recognition. Every year, all marketing professionals read with great interest the list published by the *Financial Times* of the 'Most Respected Businessmen' because they know that these people have strong influences on brand image creation and development. This leads us to another possible explanatory factor for a brand's business success: the human personality of the leader, which strengthens the efficiency of emerging country brands.

The standardization versus adaptation debate

This has been a contentious issue for more than three decades (Theodosiou and Katsikeas, 2001). On the one hand technical driving forces in the areas of transportation and communications as well as significant economies of scale justify standardization policies. On the other hand, critics of standardization have questioned the significance of economies of scale and the cost savings underlying this approach. This debate is reinforced by considering the contingency perspective of international marketing (Cavusgil et al., 1993), according to which the difference between standardization and adaptation is in the degree of application rather than in the choice of the one or the other. Therefore the challenge facing companies, including those from emerging economies, is to decide which marketing-mix elements (brand included) they should adapt in regards to their foreign market presence objectives and to what extent.

Our analysis tends to support the recent research by Brown (2010) who predicts that the number of brands from emerging countries will grow very rapidly and will reach the top 100 of the Interbrand 'league' to join the only eight Asian companies appearing in the 2010 ranking. The odds are that more firms from emerging countries will acquire Western brands; but we have seen that this did not always guarantee success. As argued by Wang Fengying, CEO of Great Wall Motors, the first Chinese car manufacturer to get approval to sell its cars in the markets of the European Union (Waldmeir, 2010), 'it could take twenty years before the Chinese brands can reach true global competitiveness'.

Managerial perspectives and implications

In this chapter we have examined the reasons leading a firm from an emerging country to develop a specific brand approach. We have also recognized the role of brand strategy in creating a lasting and sustainable competitive advantage. The case study analysis shows that the building of the brand policy is above all the outcome of an initial managerial choice mixed with cumulative experience, with certain 'triggering' events serving as catalysts. The research findings suggest three important considerations concerning branding in emerging economies with direct implications for managers of firms from these countries trying to enter the markets of developed countries.

The first suggestion is that the local (but internationally oriented) brand of an emerging-country firm may be highly successful when developed within a framework which matches customers' expectations. When the local brand aims to provide quality and safety to the customer, in other words conveys a reliable relationship with the customer, it may reach this goal even when the brand is rooted in an emerging economy. An emerging company may be able to raise the perception of its products by capitalizing on a local brand image, conditional on respecting the brand standards concerning quality, consistency and supply as expected by the customers. The managerial decision of firms from emerging economies should be made regarding their brand policy and be based on a thorough analysis and assessment of the degree of similarity between their brand's profile and foreign-market customers' expectations.

The second suggestion is that overall consistency is the most important key factor, from the supply function via production to the delivery of the product to the marketplace. Managers must therefore recognize the importance of the role of quality consistency to all members of the value chain associated with the firm's activities. The brand can thus become a tool for internal cohesion because it is the vehicle of a value grouping which can be shared by employees and company stakeholders alike. A brand originating from an emerging economy must conform to the standards of perception which are expected by its international consumers because those consumers are not likely to compromise or forgive any quality defects just because the brand is not established or for any other reason. There will be no special indulgence on the part of consumers just because a brand comes out of an emerging country. In this regard, overall consistency of the brand and particularly consistency between the regularity and continuity in quality and supply are regarded as key factors.

The third suggestion concerns the accentuation of the local or global dimension. An emerging country's company can benefit from choosing to emphasize a local branding strategy, conditional on the creation and maintaining of the same quality standard of brands originating from developed countries. There is no danger here for locally rooted emerging-country brands. On the contrary, emerging countries' firms may successfully adapt a local branding strategy that consumers should associate with a positive country image. While some are looking for ways to neutralize negative images of emerging countries as it transmits to brands, research shows that a relevant option could be to emphasize the country and origin information in order to differentiate the product more easily.

Because the local versus global brand decision is situation-specific and has a long-term orientation, managers should carefully avoid following a trend. On the contrary, they ought to perform an in-depth assessment of the values linked to their brand localness and the way in which they can enhance these values as a major differentiating point from more conventional international competitors.

But the determination of some clever and charismatic CEOs from big emerging economies such as Brazil, Russia, India and China can contribute substantially to the change in perceptions related to the COO effect, similarly to the case of the developing Japanese brands between the early 1960s and the 1980s with people like Akio Morita for Sony, Konosuke Matsushita for National Panasonic and Kiichiro Toyoda for Toyota. Therefore, based on the examples of the case study firms, we have found that companies from emerging countries attempt to improve their competitiveness by implementing innovative brand strategies. Some of them have bought existing Western brands to benefit from a well-established brand image, others have developed their own brands, either by using some Western approaches or by capitalizing on their own local idiosyncrasies.

References

Aaker, D. (1992). The value of brand equity, *Journal of Business Strategy*, July–August, 27–32.

Aiello, G., Donvito, R., Godey, B., Pederzoli, D., Wiedmann, K.-P., Hennigs, N., Siebels, A., Chan, P., Tsuchiya, J., Rabino, S., Ivanovna, S.I., Weitz, B., Hyunjoo, O. and Singh, R. (2009). An international perspective on luxury brand and country of origin effect, *Brand Management*, 16(5/6), 323–37.

Akotia, M. (2005). Country branding: an imperative for developing countries; *IFE Psychologia*, 13(2), 150–63.

Anholt, S. (2000). The nation as brand, *Across the Board*, 37(10), 22–8.

Ashworth, G. J., and Voogd, H. (1990). *Selling the City: Marketing Approaches in Public Sector Urban Planning*. London: Belhaven Press.

Baker, M.J. and Cameron, E. (2008). Critical success factors in destination marketing, *Tourism and Hospitality Research*, 8(2), 79–97.
Barney, J. (2001). Resource-based theories of competitive advantage: a ten-year retrospective on the resource-based view, *Journal of Management*, 27, 643–50.
Batey, I. (2002). *Asian Branding: A Great Way to Fly*. London: Prentice Hall.
Bell, S. (2008). *International Brand Management of Chinese companies*. Heidelberg: Physica Verlag.
Bennett, O. (1999). Destination marketing into the next century, *Journal of Vacation Marketing*, 6(1), 48–54.
Berthon, P., Hulbert, J.M. and Pitt, L.F. (1999). Brand Management Prognostications, *Sloan Management Review*, 40(2), 53–65.
Brown, K. (2010). The long road to recognition, *Financial Times*, 1 June, p. 6.
Capelli, P., Singh H., Singh J. and Huseem M. (2010). Leadership lessons from India, *Harvard Business Review*, 88(3), 97–9.
Cavusgil S.T., Zou S. and Naidu G.M. (1993). Product and promotion adaptation in export ventures: an empirical investigation, *Journal of International Business Studies*, 24(3), 479–506.
Chailan, C. (2008). Brands portfolio and competitive advantage: an empirical study, *Journal of Product and Brand Management*, 17, 254–64.
Chailan, C. (2010). Building brands from emerging countries: why and how? A case study in an Arab country, Paper presented at the Global Brand Management Conference, Koç University, Istanbul, 21–22 June. (http://home.ku.edu.tr/~globalbrand/files/Chailan.pdf). Day, D. and Brad, E. (2009). The impact of culture on branding, *Branding Strategy Insider*, 8 May. (www.brandingstrategyinsider.com). Day, G.S. (1994). The capabilities of market-driven organizations, *Journal of Marketing*, 58, 37–52.
Farquhar, P. (1989). Managing brand equity, *Marketing Research*, 1(3), 24–33.
Fetscherin, M. and Toncar, M. (2009). Country of origin effect on U.S. consumers' brand personality, perception of automobiles from China and India, *Multinational Business Review*, 17(2), 111–271.
Florida, R. (2008). Megaregions: the importance of place, *Harvard Business Review*, 86(3), 18–19.
van Gelder, S. (2008). How to improve the chances of successfully developing and implementing a place brand strategy. (www.placebrands.net/_files/Successful_Place_Branding.pdf). Gürhan-Canli, Z. and Maheswaran, D. (2000). Cultural variations in country of origin effects, *Journal of Marketing Research*, 37(3), 309–17.
Guzman, F. and Paswan, A.K. (2009). Cultural brands from emerging markets: brand image across host and home countries, *Journal of International Marketing*, 17(3), 71–6.
Han, M.C. (1990). Testing the role of country image in consumer choice behaviour, *European Journal of Marketing*, 24(6), 24–40.
Hill, D. (2004). Tsingtao and Taiwan beer: trademark dispute between Beijing and Taipei, TED case study, case number 750. (www1.american.edu/TED/tsingtao.htm). Howie , F. (2003). *Managing the Tourist Destination*. London: Thomson Learning.
Ille, F.R. (2009). Building Chinese global brands through soft technology transfer, *Journal of Chinese Economics and Foreign trade Studies*, 2(1), 47–61.
Interbrand (2010). Best Chinese Brands 2010, *Business Week*. (www.interbrand.com/Libraries/Files/328_Best_China_Brands_2010_Release_pdf.sflb.ashx), Accessed 11 May 2011.
Johansson, J.K., Ronkainnen, I.A. and Czinkota, M.R. (1994). Negative country of origin effects: the case of the New Russia, *Journal of International Business Studies*, 25(1), 157–76.

Johnson, B. (2009). Ararat brandy to reposition, *Marketing Week*, 32(11), p. 41.

Johnson, M.D. and Selnes, F. (2004). Customer portfolio management: toward a dynamic theory of exchange relationships, *Journal of Marketing*, 68 (April), 1–17.

Kapferer, J.-N. (1991). *Strategic Brand Management*. New York: The Free Press.

Kapferer J.-N. (2000). *Remarques*. Paris: Les Editions d'Organisation.

Kapferer, J.-N. (2005). The post-global brand, *Brand Management*, 12(5), 319–24.

Kavaratzis M. (2005). Place branding: a review of trends and conceptual models, *The Marketing Review*, 5, 329–42.

Keller K.L. (1993). Conceptualisizing, measuring and managing customer-based brand equity, *Journal of Marketing*, 57, 1–22.

Keller, K.L. (1998). *Strategic Brand Management*. Upper Saddle River, NJ: Prentice Hall

Khanna, T. and Palepu, K.G. (2009). *Emerging Giants Going Global: How Emerging Market-Based Companies Can Overcome Barriers in Competing Abroad*. Boston, MA: Harvard Business School Publishing.

Khanna, T., Palepu, K., and Bullock, R. (2008). House of Tata: Acquiring a Global Footprint, Harvard Business School Publishing, Boston, MA, Case 9-708-446.

Khanna, T., Palepu, K., and Madras, C. (2006). Teva Pharmaceutical Industries, Ltd, Harvard Business School Publishing, Boston, MA, Case 9-707-441.

Khanna, T., Palepu, K.G. and Bullock, R. (2008). House of Tata: Acquiring a Global Footprint., Case 9–708–446, Boston, MA: Harvard Business School Publishing.

Klein, J.L., Ettenson, R. and Morris, M.D. (1998). The animosity model of foreign product purchase: an empirical test in the People's Republic of China', *Journal of Marketing*, 62(1), 89–100.

Kotler, P. and Pfoertsch, W. (2007). *Lenovo, Bridging East and West to Build a Global Brand*. Shanghai: CEIBS.

Kotler, P. and Pfoertsch, W. (2007). Being known or being one of many. The need for brand management for business-to-business (B2B) companies, *Journal of Business and Industrial Marketing*, 22(6), 357–62.

Larçon, J.P. (2010). Haier la nouvelle stratégie européenne, *Chine Plus*, 15, 43.

Latessier, I. (2010). Haier sacré empereur chinois du réfrigérateur, *Le Figaro*, 8 June, p. 22.

Lou, T. and Davies, G. (2006). Branding China: the ultimate challenge in reputation management, *Corporate Reputation Review*, 9(3), 198–210.

Madden, N. (2010). Whether it stays or goes, Google wasn't winning in China anyway, *Advertising Age*, 81(3), 2.

Magnusson, P., Haas, S.M. and Hongzin Z. (2008). A branding strategy for emerging market firms entering developed markets, *Journal of International Consumer Marketing*, 20(3/4), 95–107.

Maheswaran, D. (1994). Country of origin as a stereotype: effects of consumer expertise and attribute strength on product evaluations, *Journal of Consumer Research*, 21(2), 354–65.

Mattsson, J., Ramaseshan, R. and Carson, D. (2006). Let marketers reclaim corporate strategy, *Journal of Strategic Marketing*, 14, 165–73.

McGregor, J. (2008). The most influential companies in the world, *Business Week*, 11 December, pp. 5–6.

Mehta, N., Oswald, S. and Mehta, A. (2007). *Journal of Information Technology*, 22(4), 456–64.

Murty, P. and Desai, V. (2005). Infosys: the challenge of global branding, *Ivey case 905 A01*, London and Ontario: University of Western Ontario.

Nagashima, A. (1970). A comparison of Japanese and U.S. attitudes toward foreign products, *Journal of Marketing*, 34(1), 68–74.

Oakley, D. (2009). Emerging market equity outperform west, *Financial Times*, 7 June. (www.ft.com/cms/s/0/45cba328–5386-11de-be08–00144feabdc0.html#axzz1 MRNTFJme). Palepu, K., Khanna, T. and Vargas, I. (2005). Haier, *Case 9–706-401*, Boston, MA: Harvard Business School Publishing.

Papadopoulos, N. (2004). Place branding: evolution, meaning and implication, *Place Branding*, 1(1), 36–49.

Papadopoulos, N. and Heslop, L.A. (2002). Country equity and country branding: problems and prospects, *Journal of Brand Management*, 9,(4/5), 294–315.

Pike , S . (2004). *Destination Marketing Organisations*. Oxford: Elsevier.

Peterson, R.A. and Jolibert, A. (1995). A meta-analysis of country of origin effects, *Journal of International Business Studies*, 26(4), 883–900.

Ponsonby-McCabe S. and Boyle E. (2006). Understanding brands as experiential spaces: axiological implications for marketing strategists, *Journal of Strategic Marketing*, 14, 175–89.

Porter, M. (1998). Clusters and the new economics of competition, *Harvard Business Review*, 76(6), 77–90.

Palepu, K., Khanna, T., and Vargas, I. (2005). Haier, Harvard Business School Publishing, Boston, MA, Harvard BSP Case 9-706-401.

Papadopoulos, N. and Heslop, L. (2002). Country equity and country branding: Problems and prospects, *Journal of Brand Management*, 9(4/5), 294–314.

Publicis Sasserath (2006). *Deutschland und China: Chances aus der Marken Perspektive*. Frankfurt am Main: Vergleich um deutschen Recht.

Quelch, J. and Knoop, C. (2006). Lenovo case study, *Case 9–507-014*, Boston, MA: Harvard Business School Publishing.

Ramo, J.C. (2007). *Brand China*. London: Foreign Policy Centre.

Reed, J. (2010). Geely completes purchase of Volvo for $1.5bn, *Financial Times*, 2 August. (www.ft.com/cms/s/0/b25238b6–9e1e-11df-b377–00144feab49a.html#axzz1MRNTFJme). Riezebos, R. (2003). *Brand Management: A Theoretical and Practical Approach*. Harlow: Prentice Hall.

Roth, M.S. and Romeo J.-B. (1992). Matching product category and country image perceptions: a framework for managing country of origin effects, *Journal of International Business Studies*, 23(3), 477–497.

Sappington, D.E. and Wernerfelt, B. (1985). To brand or not to brand? A theoretical and empirical question, *Journal of Business*, 58(July), 279–293.

Sasserath Publicis (2006). Deuschland und China; Chances aus der Markenperspektive, Sasserath Publicis, Frankfurt, (in German).

Schuiling, I. and Kapferer, J.-N. (2004). Executive insights: real differences between local and international brands: strategic implications for international marketers, *Journal of International Marketing*, 12(4), 97–112.

Schultz, D.E. (2008). Branding from emerging markets, *Marketing Management*, 17(5), 10–11.

Seisdedos, G., and Mateo, C. (2008). The two-way relationship between a brand and its place of origin. (www.wharton.universia.net/index.cfm?fa=viewfeature&id=1464&language=English). Sharma, S. (1999). Trespass or symbiosis? Dissolving the boundaries between strategic marketing and strategic management, *Journal of Strategic Marketing*, 7(1), 73–88.

Slater, S. and Olson, E. (2001). Marketing's contribution to the implementation of business strategy: an empirical analysis, *Strategic Management Journal*, 22(11), 1055–67.

Steenkamp, J.-B., Batra, R. and Alden, D.L. (2003). How perceived brand globalness creates brand value, *Journal of International Business Studies*, 34(1), 53–66.

Sun, S.L. (2009). Internationalization strategy of MNEs from emerging economies: the case of Huawei, *Multinational Business Review*, 17(2), 129–30.
Tan, C.T. and Farley, J.U. (1987). The impact of cultural patterns on cognition and intention in Singapore, *Journal of Consumer Research*, 13(4), 540–4.
Teece, D.J. (2000). Strategies for managing knowledge assets: the role of firm structure and industrial context, *Long Range Planning*, 33(1), 35–54.
Therkelsen, A. and Halkier, H. (2008). Contemplating place branding umbrellas. the case of coordinated national tourism and business promotion in Denmark, *Scandinavian Journal of Hospitality*, 8(2), 159–75.
Theodosiou, M., and Katsikeas, C.S. (2001). Factors influencing the degree of international pricing strategy standardization of multinational corporations, *Journal of International Marketing*, 9(3), 1–18.
Tiefel, J. (2009). An interview with Saad Al-Barrak, *McKinsey Quarterly*, 3, 18–19.
Tucker, P. (2006). Made in China: branding a new image: from manufacturer to major marketer: Brand China is set to boom, *The Futurist*, January/February. (www.wfs.org). Urde, M. (1999). Brand orientation: a mindset for building brands into strategic resources, *Journal of Marketing Management*, 15(3), 117–33.
Verlegh, P.W.J. and Steenkamp, J-B.E.M. (1999). A review and meta analysis of country of origin research, *Journal of Economic Psychology*, 20(5), 521–46.
Wagstyl, S. (2010). A change in gear, fast-recovering emerging world companies form a growing number of the largest global groups, *Financial Times*, 12 May, p. 7.
Waldmeir, P. (2010). Global marque still eludes the Chinese', *Financial Times*, 1 June.
Wei, X. and Li, H.R. (2009). What will make China an innovation-oriented country? *Journal of Knowledge-Based Innovation in China*, 1(1), 8–15.
Whitelock, J. and Fastoso, F. (2007). Understanding international branding: defining the domain and reviewing the literature, *International Marketing Review*, 24(3), 252–70.
World Health Organization (2008). Expert meeting to review toxicological aspects of melamine and cyanuric acid, Ottawa, 1–4 December. (www.who.int/foodsafety/fs_management/infosan_events/en/index.html).

16
What Explains Asian Investments in Denmark?

Michael W. Hansen, Jens Erik Torp and Henrik Schaumburg-Müller

Introduction

In the spring of 2011, the Danish press announced that the Indian billionaire Shrinivas Dempe would invest between DKK 75 and 100 million in the Danish Soccer club FC Midtjylland. FC Midtjylland was chosen out of 58 football clubs from 20 countries. The investment would allow the Indian investor to get a foothold in the Danish soccer league. But it was not only to get into the Danish soccer league that the investment was contemplating. FC Midtjylland had over the years built a unique and outstanding ability to develop soccer talent. Indeed, the investment was reported mainly to be motivated by acquiring knowledge about training and organization which eventually could be transferred over to the Indian soccer league. This would develop and enhance Indian talent and raise the standards in Indian football.

This investment was the latest of a long list of Chinese and Indian investments in Denmark, which is a small, highly open, European economy with a long tradition for international trade and foreign direct investment (FDI). Other examples of Asian investments in Denmark can be seen within the Danish wind turbine industry, the shipping industry, the bio-tech industry, the IT industry, etc. The growing Asian investments are received with ambiguity by the Danish society. On the one hand, they represent a welcome influx of capital and they offer new opportunities for job creation and trade. On the other hand, concerns are raised that these investments may have an adverse impact in Denmark, for example by transferring Danish knowledge assets out of the country to the knowledge savvy Indian and Chinese companies.

As of yet, little is known about Asian investments in Denmark. Hence, this chapter will consolidate and update our understanding of Chinese and Indian investments in Denmark, focusing on the motivations behind these investments.[1] The analysis of the Chinese and Indian investments in Denmark will be embedded and informed by the literature on developing country multinational corporation (DCMNCs). This literature essentially discusses whether the upcoming DCMNCs can be adequately understood through the application of conventional FDI theory or whether they require the development of new conceptual and theoretical-analytical perspectives.

The chapter will start out with a description of the scope and content of Chinese and Indian investments in Denmark. A number of case studies will provide details about the strategies of Indian and Chinese investors. We will move on to present the two main positions within the DCMNC literature, namely the conventional perspective and the latecomer perspective. We will then discuss the extent and ways in which Indian and Chinese investments in Denmark corroborate either perspective. In conclusion, we shall discuss the impact of Asian investment in Denmark on Danish investment promotion in Asian emerging economies.

Scope and content of Chinese and Indian investments in Denmark

Scope of Chinese and Indian investments

If we look at Danish FDI statistics, it is only from around the year 2000 that we can trace an FDI inflow of a detectable size from China and India (Table 16.1). Between 2000 and 2005, a significant increase in Chinese and Indian investments took place, and Asian investment stock grew from DKK 0.1 billion to DKK 1.7 billion. The growth in Asian investments apparently stagnated for the period 2006–07, but, from 2008 onwards, the stock once more increased to a level of DKK 3.4 billion. Most recent flow numbers suggest that a large increase took place in 2010. The growth in FDI stock numbers should however not cloud the fact that Chinese and Indian investments as a percentage share of overall Danish IFDI are miniscule: less than 0.5 per cent of Danish inward stock comes from these countries. In comparison, Chinese and Indian outward stock accounted for 0.61 and 0.19 per cent respectively of global stock in 2007.

Looking at the flow statistics (Table 16.2), a similar picture emerges. India is hardly detectable in FDI flow statistics and only in 2008 and 2010 are there sizable investments taking place, in both cases due to large Chinese acquisitions. In general, the Chinese stock of FDI in Denmark has constantly been six to eight times higher than the stock of Indian FDI. This compares to the fact that Chinese and Indian OFDI stock by 2007 were US$96 billion and US$29 billion respectively (Pradhan and Patel, 2011), implying that Chinese investments, when compared to Indian investments, are overrepresented in Denmark.

If we compare inward stock from China and India in Denmark to the Danish outward stock in the two countries, we see that Denmark is investing five to seven times as much in the Asian giants (Figure 16.1). Rather

Table 16.1 Stock of foreign direct investment into Denmark (2000–09)

	2000	2005	2006	2007	2008	2009
Total Danish inward FDI stock (DKK billion)	359.0	503.3	580.5	632.0	686.4	692.1
Inward FDI stock from China (DKK billion)		1.5	2.3	2.5	3.1	3.0
Inward FDI stock from India (DKK billion)	0.0	0.2	0.3	0.3	0.3	0.4
Inward FDI stock from India and China (DKK billion)	0.1	1.7	2.6	2.8	3.4	3.4
India's and China's inward stock in total Danish inward FDI stock (per cent)	0.03	0.34	0.45	0.44	0.50	0.49

Source: Danish National Bank Statistics.

Table 16.2 Flow of FDI by economic activity (2005–10)

	2005	2006	2007	2008	2009	2010
Total inward FDI flow (DKK billion)	57.4	50.8	53.4	28.4	24.9	31.9
Inward FDI flow from China (DKK billion)	0.1	0.0	0.0	0.7	0.0	0.6
Inward FDI flow from India (DKK billion)	0.0	0.0	0.0	0.0	0.0	0.1
Inward FDI flows from India and China (DKK billion)	0.1	0.0	0.0	0.7	0.0	0.7
India's and China's inward FDI flow in total Danish inward FDI flows (per cent)	0.17	0.00	0.00	2.47	0.00	2.19

Source: Danish National Bank Statistics.

than moving towards a greater balance, the ratio seems to be increasing in recent years.

If we look at subsidiary statistics, a similar picture of modest Chinese and Indian engagement in Denmark emerges. There are no complete publicly available statistics on Indian and Chinese subsidiaries in Denmark. Through various sources such as embassy lists, dialogue with investment promotion agencies, newspaper clippings, interviews with company representatives, etc., we identified 18 Indian and 20 Chinese subsidiaries in Denmark in 2010. Tentatively, this number can be related to the 3,800 foreign subsidiaries in the country registered by Statistics Denmark in 2008, suggesting that Chinese and Indian investment account for less than 1 per cent of foreign owned firms in Denmark.[2]

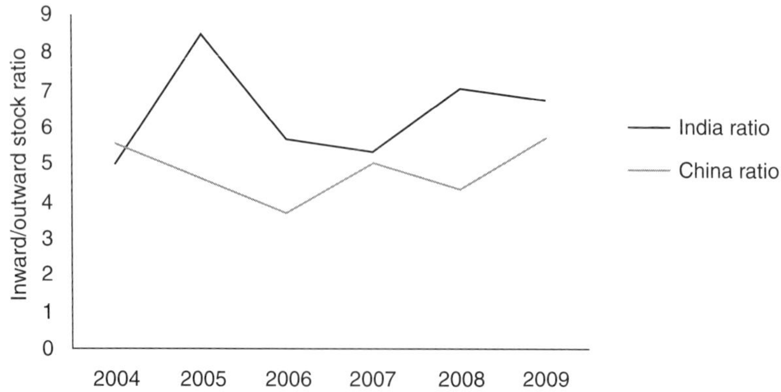

Figure 16.1 Relation between IFDI and OFDI from Asia
Source: Danish National Bank Statistics.

Content of Chinese and Indian investments

The Chinese portfolio of 20 subsidiaries is broadly distributed within manufacturing, (electronics, clean tech), transport and bio-technology (Table 16.3).

Four subsidiaries from the electronics industry represent large global Chinese-owned companies: Lenovo, producing PCs and laptops based on IBM technology and owned by the Chinese Legend Holding Company, has a marketing and sales affiliate in Denmark. Huawei Technologies, a leading telecommunication solutions provider, has established Telcom Network Infrastructure Application & Software, with strengths in wire line, wireless and IP Technologies (in competition with the Finish Nokia and the Swedish Ericsson) and smartphones (in competition with Cisco). Zhejiang New Jialian in the acoustics component industry has established a subsidiary in Denmark to develop R&D units in Denmark, aimed at tapping into the strong Danish competencies in this area. Through its investment in Denmark, LITS is interested in manufacturing and developing energy saving products such as LEDs controlling digital illumination.

Four Chinese firms are engaged in the Danish Clean tech sector, including two companies involved in the wind turbine industry, e.g. Envision Energy established R&D activity in 2008 in the Danish windmill cluster in Jutland, close to the global market leader Vestas. By 2012, Envision expects to have developed a new wind turbine prototype. Ming Yang Wind Power European's R&D Centre is also linked to R&D in the Danish windmill industry. It had considered locating its R&D in Germany, where it had major customers, but chose Denmark in order to access Danish R&D competencies. Finally, the Danish affiliate of Build Your Dreams (BYD) – a major

Chinese producer of batteries and electrical cars – has a sales and development subsidiary in Denmark to test the market for BYD's electrical vehicles, such as cars, hybrid electric auto models and buses. BYD Denmark is also working with Nokia to develop solutions for new phones (see Box 16.1)

Box 16.1 BYD: Build Your Dreams for electrical cars

Founded in 1995, the Chinese company BYD (Build Your Dreams) became the world's second largest battery company in 2002, producing 65 per cent of the global rechargeable nickel-cadmium batteries and 30 per cent of the lithium-ion mobile phone batteries. The company diversified into automotive in 2003 and in 2008 it started producing hybrid electric cars and later pure electric cars. In Denmark BYD Denmark ApS was established as a sales office in 2005 through a DKK 125,000 greenfield investment by BYD Europe BV. As Denmark has favourable tax schemes for electrical cars and as huge resources are invested by Danish utilities, municipalities and transport companies to develop electricity-based road transportation, Denmark is an attractive test case for BYD. Through Invest in Denmark's service, BYD and the Danish Transport company Movia underwent a partnership for developing and testing electrical buses in Denmark. BYD and other producers of electrical car solutions (such as Better Place Denmark), together with Danish public authorities and Danish industrial associations, are developing solutions as to how best to organize the introduction of electric cars into Denmark. Of particular interest is how to make it as easy as possible for the car user to recharge or change car batteries, either in special recharging stations or alternatively to exchange a fully discharged battery with a recharged one. While BYD has announced the introduction of its electric car in 2011 using the platform from Better Place Denmark, the technical discussions, inter alia, on how best to recharge batteries for electric cars within the Danish and broader European market appear at the time of writing to be inconclusive. Hence, it is not possible yet fully to assess the outcome of BYD's investment. However, BYD's interest in investing in Denmark has as a side effect stimulated producers of components for electric cars such as Taiwanese Amita to consider the option of undertaking their own investments in Denmark in relation to the introduction of electric cars.

There are four Chinese transport firms located in Denmark. Three of them are servicing air transport and tourism. Generally, these investments appear to be small, and it has not been possible to trace specific information on their activities. The last investment is in Penta Shipping. Penta Shipping is a joint venture between Cosco and the original Danish owners of Penta Shipping established in 1996. Since then, Penta Shipping has evolved into a Cosco Group company that essentially serves as a Scandinavian 'feeder' for Cosco's container centres in Hamburg and Rotterdam. Moreover, Penta Shipping has been assigned tasks for developing new business areas for the Cosco Group (see Box 16.2).

Table 16.3 Key industry sectors and Chinese investors

Sector	Name of investor company	Name of company in Denmark	Company activity	Activity in Denmark
Transport	Air China	Air China	Airline industry	Sales office
	Air China Cargo Co. Ltd	Air China Cargo Denmark	Logistics	Services
	COSCO Group	Penta Shipping A/S	Shipping	Services
	China International Travel Service	CITS Travel Denmark A/S	Tourism/travel	Sales & services
Electronics	Huawei Technologies Co.	Huawei Technologies Denmark ApS	Telecom industry; mobile network; Smartphones	Sales office; R&D: developing into design with Nokia Denmark
	Zhejiang New Jialian Electronics Co.	NJL Acoustics ApS	Electronics	R&D
	Lenovo	Lenovo Danmark ApS	IT hardware	Sales office
	LITS	?	LEDs	R&D
Clean tech	Envision Energy	Envision Energy Denmark ApS	Renewable power industry	R&D
	BYD	BYD Denmark ApS	Automotive industry;mobile phones	Sales cars;mobile phone design
	Dragon Power Co. Ltd	DP CleanTech Europe A/S	Bioenergy	Manufacturing and services
	Guangdong Mingyang Wind Power Industry Group Co. Ltd	Ming Yang Wind Power European R&D Centre ApS	Renewable power industry	R&D

Other manufacturing	Shanghai Worldbest Investment Development Group Co. Ltd	Everbest ApS	Textiles	—
	Bright Star Fireworks	Bright Star Fireworks Import A/S	Fireworks	Import
	China International Marine Containers Group Ltd (CIMC)	Holvrieka Danmark A/S	Manufacturing of stainless steel tanks/ containers	Manufacturing and services
	Brothers Pyrotechnics Inc.	LCH Fireworks A/S	Fireworks	Import
Consultant	NCO China Consult	NCO China Consult ApS	Consulting	Sales & services
	BMC SYS China	Dancom IT solutions ApS	IT software and solutions	Sales & services
Biotech	Shanghai ChemPartner Co. Ltd	ChemPartner Europe	Pharmaceutical and biotech	Contract R&D (European HQ)
	BGI	Beijing Genomics Inst.	High Technology/JV	Genetics; R&D

Box 16.2 Cosco: acquiring a regional hub for shipping services

Chinese shipping firms are among the world leaders. As the markets for Chinese manufacturing are in Europe, Chinese shipping firms also need to be present here. In 1996, Cosco (China Ocean Shipping Company) acquired a majority share in the Danish shipping company Penta Shipping. Cosco is a Chinese state-owned shipping company group and is the eighth largest shipping company in the world, which in 2011 included more than 1,200 companies and 120,000 employees worldwide. Cosco's main goal is to be the largest shipping company in Asia. They are the largest ship owners in the world, outbeating Danish Mærsk Shipping. Penta shipping was established in 1985 with the aim of focusing on the Chinese market. It quickly opened a sales office in Beijing and entered into an agency agreement for Scandinavia with Cosco. In 1996, Penta Shipping became a joint venture with Cosco. For Cosco it was important to be present in Scandinavia either through an agent or a sales subsidiary, since Scandinavia represents an important and stable 'out of port' market for container shipping, which could provide Cosco with container cargo for its vessels in the ports of Hamburg and Rotterdam. Penta Shipping, on the other hand, needed a partner company that could provide financial muscle during downturns of markets and secure stability in its business activities. In the ensuing joint venture, Cosco holds 75 per cent of the JV shares and the Danish partners 25 per cent. One of the main synergies from acquiring Penta Shipping has been that it could assist Cosco in developing new business areas with logistics for larger projects. At the same time, a previous business area of air freight was abandoned after the formation of the JV. Since its foundation, Penta Shipping has developed into a group company and has an office in Denmark, Sweden and Oslo. The volume of Penta Shipping's container shipping has increased from an annual 3,000–4,000 teus before the formation of the JV to a present level of an annual 100,000 teus, which means that Penta Shipping now ranks among the four top container shipping companies in Scandinavia. Penta had difficulties in the financial year of 2009; however, in 2010 the company was expecting a profit.

Finally, the Danish biotech competencies have attracted Chinese investors. The Beijing Genomics Institute (BGI) is a large genetics research project investigating genealogy and its connections with inheritance diseases such as cancer. The project draws on the excellent data bases on disease and population that is available in Denmark. The vision is to mark BGI Denmark as one of the largest centres of sequencing and bio informatics analysis in Europe. Another bio tech company is ChemPartner Europe which has established its European office in Denmark to undertake contractual preclinical R&D.

Looking at the Indian subsidiaries in Denmark, a different picture emerges. A few years ago, the Indian branch of the Danish investment promotion agency, Invest in Denmark, expected a surge of Indian investments in hi-tech sectors such as telecommunications, energy and biotechnology. However, these expectations were far from met and eventually only around 18 Indian firms have been established in Denmark (see Table 16.4), almost all of them in IT.

Table 16.4 Key industry sectors and Indian investors

Sector	Name of investor company	Name of company in Denmark	Company activity	Business activity in Denmark
IT and software	Four Soft	Four Soft Nordic A/S	Logistics software	Sales office
	Infosys	Infosys Technologies Ltd	Software services	Sales office
	ITC Infotech India Ltd	ITC Infotech Denmark	IT services & solutions	Sales & services
	Larsen & Toubro Limited (L&T)	Larsen & Toubro Infotech Denmark	Software services	Sales office
	Polaris Software Lab.	Polaris Software Lab. Ltd	IT services & consulting	Regional manager
	Tata Group	Tata Consultancy Services Denmark Ltd	IT services & consulting	Regional office
	Cognizant Technologies	Cognizant Technologies	IT services & consulting	Sales office
	Mahindra Tech	Mahindra Satyam	IT services & consulting	Sales office
	Polaris Software Lab Ltd	Polaris Software	IT services & consulting	Sales & services
	Infinite Computer Solutions	Infinite Computer Solutions	IT services & consulting	n/a
	Wipro Technologies	Wipro Technologies	IT services & consulting	n/a
	M/s Ubiqu7e System UK Ltd	IT and software development consultancy	IT services & consulting	n/a
	HCL Technologies	IT technology	IT services and consulting	Sales and service; regional office
	Lister Technologies	Lister Technologies	Software services	Sales & services
Manufacturing and engineering	Tooltech Solutions	Tooltech Denmark	Engineering services	Manufacturing; sales & services
	Indorama Ventures PCL and Sinterama SpA	Trevira Neckelmann A/S	Petrochemical products	R&D and production subsidiary
	Suzlon Energy	Suzlon Wind Energy A/S	Renewable power industry	Regional HQ; R&D
	Hikal Ltd	Hikal Marsing Pharma	Pharmaceutical	Marketing & distribution

Thus, 14 out of the 18 Indian companies are in IT software. They have typically arrived in Denmark in connection with Danish firms' strategies of outsourcing and off-shoring IT activities to India. Indian providers of IT and software services have invested in Denmark to be close to their new clients. A representative office also facilitates the task of bringing Indian staff to work at the site of the Danish clients. The larger Indian IT companies like Tata Consultancy Services, HCL, Infosys, ITC Infotech and Larsen & Toubro partly established themselves for these reasons. Satyam, which was smaller and came later than the other companies, went into an alliance with KMD. It targeted smaller Danish clients who could have an interest in outsourcing specific IT tasks, being too small to build up their own IT organization. Since its entry, Satyam has been acquired by the Mahindra Group.

The exception to this sales supportive business model in IT is Four Soft Nordic. In 2003, the Indian IT company Four Soft acquired the Danish provider of software services for the shipping industry Transaxiom. This acquisition not merely supported trade services from India, but brought a large new market portfolio to Four Soft together with strong capabilities for developing IT services for the shipping industry (see Box 16.3).

Box 16.3 Four Soft: Acquiring a Nordic lead firm in shipping services

In the year 2000, a former senior employee of United Parcel Service America had observed a need for mainframe enterprise resource planning systems in the market. In order to cater to that market, Four Soft Ltd was formed. During the first years of its existence, Four Soft based its growth strategy on acquisition of companies with technological know-how and a presence in geographical areas perceived to represent new business opportunities for Four Soft's products. In 2005, Danish Transaxiom (established in 1992) became a target for Four Soft's acquisition strategy. The Danish company possessed what Four Soft considered to be strategically important assets as Transaxiom had developed one of the IT systems most widely used within the industry and had obtained a global market share of more than 50 per cent for some products. In parallel, Four Soft also acquired some of Transaxiom's competitors in Holland and the UK, thereby providing it with a globally dominant position for some segments within the industry and a notable presence in others. The acquisition strategy was not without drawbacks. The initial expectations that the acquisition would benefit from synergy between the Indian HQ and the Danish subsidiary did not materialize and serious difficulties in the day-to-day cooperation between these two parts of Four Soft's organization emerged. On this basis, Four Soft focused more on consolidating its acquisitions with emphasis on technological development and market-seeking based on in-house know-how. As part of this new strategy and in order to make better use of the assets of Four Soft Nordic, groups of engineers were sent for longer stays at Four Soft HQ. The global R&D centre for internet-based solutions will be consolidated in India, whereas the older mainframe technology development will be based in Denmark. Moreover, from a similar intention to capitalize on sales and marketing competencies in Denmark, Four Soft HQ has begun sending some of its key commercial staff to stay at Four Soft Nordic's offices in Denmark for longer periods so that they can learn about Western sales and marketing practices. Approximately 95 per cent of Four Soft's business comes from international operations outside India, and Europe has become the major contributor to Four Soft's revenues, generating more than 50 per cent of turnover. Four Soft Nordic itself generated yearly revenue of DKK 44.87 million, with a net profit of DKK 9.2 million. Four Soft Nordic was furthermore able to maintain most of Transaxiom's key costumers to the degree that some clients, including DHL, in some areas have all of their logistics and freight transport IT systems developed by the company. Nevertheless, some other previously important clients, such as Maersk, have developed their own capabilities. In 2010 Four Soft successfully achieved a CMMI Level 5 Certification which recognizes the firm for best-in-class processes related to design, development and maintenance of software that enables the best user experiences for their customers.

Four Indian companies outside the software industry have been established in Denmark where the investments by Suzlon in the wind turbine industry and Reliance Industries in the textile industry are the more significant ones. Suzlon, the world's third largest wind turbine producer, is by far the largest Indian engagement in Denmark. This company has since 2004 located global coordination and management functions in Denmark, including global sales and marketing, and more recently the company has also embarked on R&D investments in Denmark (see Box 16.4).

Box 16.4 Suzlon: Tapping into the Danish wind turbine cluster

Based on a business platform to develop wind turbines, manufacture all key components, install them and undertake maintenance, Indian wind turbine producer Suzlon Energy Ltd has become a major player within the global wind turbine industry. Until 2001, Suzlon was overwhelmingly an Indian player, but since then it has embarked on rapid international expansion and is now the third largest global player in the industry. In August 2004, Suzlon India undertook a greenfield investment in Denmark in order to establish its international business headquarters, named Suzlon Energy A/S, with the mandate to develop and manage an expansion of the firm's activities outside India. By November 2005, Suzlon India's investments in the Danish headquarters reached US$24 million. Furthermore, in 2009, Suzlon India created 30 jobs in an R&D centre for new technologies, which is located at the vicinity of the international business headquarters. The Danish R&D activity is working closely with Suzlon's technology centre in Rostock Germany with over 100 employees. The choice of Denmark as the hub for Suzlon's international expansion was based on several considerations: many years of experience with wind turbine technology on the manufacturing and supplier side; the extensive research carried out at Danish universities; and management competences within wind engineering, project execution, operations, financial engineering, service and maintenance. All Suzlon's investments in Denmark are all greenfield investments, although the 2004 entry was partly motivated by acquiring staff that had been made redundant in the merger between NEG Micon and Vestas. The advantages of locating in Denmark are numerous. First, it has proven useful for Suzlon to initiate cooperation with Danish technological universities in order for them to include wind turbine technology in their curricula research and teaching. Another perceived advantage of a location in Denmark has been the opportunity to outsource research on new technology to Danish technological institutes and technical universities on a consultancy contract basis. Third, the present economic crisis has led to a situation in which some clients have difficulties in honouring their contractual payments. In this regard the location in Denmark has given Suzlon access to the Danish export credit guarantee system, which guarantees payments to Suzlon in the case where clients fail to meet contractual obligations.

Reliance Industries, a huge Indian conglomerate with its main business in petrochemicals and materials, in 2004 took over one of the last remaining entities of the once sizable Danish textile and garment manufacturing industry, Trevira Neckelmann. In 2007, most of the production was moved to Poland with the loss of 300 Danish jobs. For a while, Reliance maintained and developed the R&D activity of Trevira Neckelmann, but eventually this was also divested (see Box 16.5).

Box 16.5 Reliance Industries Ltd: Investing and divesting in the last remnants of Danish textile production

In 2004, Reliance Industries Ltd, India's largest private sector enterprise, acquired the large German firm Trevira Group. Trevira produces branded polyester fibre and yarn products, supplying among others the auto industry, and has its own R&D facilities. The acquisition led to the creation of the world's largest polyester fibre and yarn producer. As an incidental outcome of the acquisition, Reliance also acquired the Danish company Treviara Neckelmann in Silkeborg, Denmark. This company was involved in the production of polyester based textile products and was, as such, labour intensive with more than 300 employees. However, the subsidiary also had important R&D activities. For Reliance, the plan was to tap into the knowledge- and R&D-intensive part of the group and to reorganize to make it more effective. But, in the case of the Danish acquisition, these great hopes never materialized: In 2007, production activities in Silkeborg were moved to the group's plant in Poland, leading to 300 jobs being lost. The reason cited by management was high-production costs compared to low-cost locations, and growing pressures from the group's main customers in the car industry to reduce costs. The R&D part was maintained as a Trevira Competence Center in Silkeborg, accounting for 60–70 jobs by the middle of 2009. Reliance undertook additional investments of DKK 50 million to develop the unit. In 2009, the financial crisis and in particular the downturn in the auto industry led to Reliance declaring the Trevira Group insolvent and that it had to sell it off. In the ensuing restructuring, the plants in Germany and Poland acquired new owners and Reliance sold the remaining R&D facility in Silkeborg to Sinterama SpA which formed Indorama Ventures.

Both India and Denmark have competitive advantages in biotechnology. Hence it was expected that many Indian biotech firms would benefit from establishing themselves in the Øresund biotech cluster. However, eventually only two such investments materialized. One was the Hikal's acquisition of a majority stake in the Danish pharmaceutical trading company Marsing, which trades in active ingredients for the pharmaceutical industry. The Danish acquisition allowed Hikal to find a European outlet for its generic drugs. The other example of a biotech investment is the start-up Indian biotechnology firm Avesthagen from Bangalore. In 2004, this company opened the Avesta Nordic Research office in Copenhagen in a strategic joint venture with the Danish Centre for Clinical & Basic Research. This also led to the establishment of a joint venture company in India, together with the Danish Industrialization Fund for Developing Countries. Through its Danish investment, Avesthagen wanted to assist Nordic firms in outsourcing R&D activities to India. However, the office in Copenhagen and the joint venture in India closed down in 2007.

Theoretical perspectives on developing country MNCs

In recent years, a burgeoning literature on DCMNCs has evolved (see for example, Hobday, 1995; Beausang, 2003; Mathews, 2006; Ramamurti and Singh, 2008; Tolentino, 2008). Essentially, this literature debates whether DCMNCs are distinct from developed country MNCs and thus require special theoretical and conceptual tools, or whether they can be captured by standard FDI theory (Mathews, 2006; Narula, 2006; Dunning et al., 2008).

The conventional view

At the most general level, the conventional FDI literature explains OFDI from developing countries from what is essentially a modernization perspective. According to this view, FDI patterns become increasingly complex with economic development. As countries modernize their economies, the FDI profile changes in terms of the balance between inward and outward investment and in terms of the nature of FDI. Hence the Investment Development Path (IDP) theory (Dunning, 1981; Dunning and Narula, 1996, 2004) argues that FDI patterns interact with locational factors in a dynamic fashion. The model makes a distinction between five stages of the IDP, going from the least developed countries to the most advanced countries. Each stage is characterized by a particular IFDI and OFDI pattern. In regard to developing countries, the theory predicts that IFDI will dwarf OFDI until developing country firms have built ownership-specific advantages that allow them to embark on FDI. Initially, OFDI from developing countries will be directed towards other developing countries as this is where developing country firms will have competitive advantages vis-à-vis local firms. FDI in developed countries will be small and will generally be aimed at complementing trade.

A similar logic can be found in Vernon's (1966) classical product-cycle theory of FDI. According to this theory, developing countries will become outward investors only as products and technologies developed and introduced in developed countries mature. This process takes place partly through imitation, partly through diffusion. From a product cycle perspective, we can expect developing country investments in developed countries to exploit an advantage obtained in technological sunset industries, where developed countries are no longer competitive. This could be heavy industry such as steel and cement, or it could be labour intensive industries such as textile and garment production or electronics. This is roughly what Ramamurti (2009) calls 'mature mid-technologies'.

Generally speaking, conventional FDI literature stresses the resource and capability disadvantages of DCMNCs and argues that weak ownership-specific advantages is a serious constraint on developing country FDI in developed countries. Rugman and Li (2007) make a distinction between 'firm-specific advantages' (FSAs) and 'country-specific advantages' (CSAs).[3] They argue that OFDI from developing countries is mainly based on CSAs such as natural resources, cheap capital and low labour costs, whereas Western MNCs mainly base their FDI on FSAs such as propriety technology, strong organizational capabilities or unique capabilities to manage complex network organizations across borders. Due to weak internationalization capabilities, it can be expected that DCMNCs will move into internationalization through a gradualist path, where they use internationalization into geographically and culturally nearby locations to build capabilities (experiential knowledge) that they can use in new internationalization attempts (Johanson and Vahlne, 2003; Kuada, 2004). Moreover, as DCMNCs have not yet developed FSAs related to managing operations at a global scale, it is expected that their CSA driven investments, especially in developed countries, eventually will experience problems of performance and integration.

The latecomer perspective

Spurred by the surge in FDI from developing countries in the 1990s and 2000s, and echoing Gerschenkron's (1962) notion of 'latecomer' advantage of 'backwardness', a literature has recently evolved which tries to explain why growing numbers of firms from developing countries evidently are successful in competing with developed country firms in their own markets, in spite of, or maybe because of, their latecomer status. This literature argues that, in light of the rapidly growing presence of DCMNEs in global industries, we need to revisit and revise our theoretical tools and conceptions of FDI (Hobday, 1997; Ernst, 2000; Mathews, 2006; Li, 2007). Where previous theories of FDI are rooted in trade theory, industrial organization and transaction costs economics, the latecomer theories are rooted in resource- and knowledge-based theory (Barney, 1991; Grant et al., 2000), network theory (Anderson et al., 1997) and theories of learning and dynamic capabilities (Teece, 2000).

In particular, four aspects of latecomer firms are emphasized by this literature: First, DCMNCs have strong abilities to compensate for their disadvantage of backwardness by accessing complementary assets through acquisitions (Buckley, 2009), through learning (Mathews, 2006), through linking up to foreign MNCs in global value chains (Gereffi et al., 2001; Buckley, 2009) or through acquiring assets in the market (Teece, 2000). Thus, DCMNCs are exceptionally agile in closing gaps in the resource base through what Mathews (2006) calls 'linkage', 'leverage', and 'learning' capabilities. Second, DCMNCs have superior abilities to undertake organizational, strategic and technological innovation. Contrary to incumbent MNCs, latecomer firms are not constrained by Western management orthodoxies. Therefore they are better positioned to take in new ideas and innovations. 'Frugal innovation' – innovation processes that cater specifically to the needs of developing country consumers, that are kept simple and that observe low costs and efficiency at all stages of the innovation cycle – is an example of an innovation practice that provides DCMNCs with unique advantages. Third, DCMNCs possess advantages distinct to their developing country home base, advantages such as flexibility, low overheads, cost effectiveness and network-based business models (Buckley et al., 2007; Ramamurti, 2008; Ramamurti and Singh, 2008). Fourth, and partly as a consequence of the above, DCMNCs are capable of embarking on born global paths of internationalization (Oviatt and McDougall, 1994) that defy the gradualist patterns of developing country FDI predicted by the conventional FDI literature (Johanson and Vahlne, 1977).

Contrasting the conventional and latecomer perspectives

Based on this brief excurse of the DCMNC literature, we can identify a number of dimensions on which the predictions of the two literatures differ in regard to DCMNC engagement in developed countries:

- *The size of developing country FDI.* The conventional perspective will predict that developing country FDI in developed countries will be small relative to inward investment from developed countries. Only in the latter stages of the IDP will significant OFDI from developing countries take place. The low FDI from developing countries is mainly due to DCMNCs' lack of ownership specific advantages. In contrast, the latecomer perspective holds that DCMNCs, contrary to earlier internationalization incidents, can short-circuit the IDP and quickly move into developed countries and/or advanced types of activities. This is due to the linkage, leverage and learning capabilities of latecomer firms, in combination with new opportunities offered by global economic integration.

- *The industry profile of developing country FDI.* According to conventional FDI theories, DCMNC investments in developed countries will be rare and, when they occur, they will tend to support the exploitation of the comparative advantages of their home base, e.g. low cost production and/or production in technological sunset industries. In contrast, the latecomer literature holds that DCMNCs may have advantages that are superior to those of developed country MNCs, not only in technological sunset industries but also in frontier technologies. This is due to their special innovation practices and their strong linkage, leverage and learning capabilities.
- *The motivations behind developing country investments.* Typically, the FDI literature makes a distinction between four types of investment motives, namely resource seeking, market seeking, efficiency seeking and strategic asset seeking (Dunning and Lundan, 2008). From a conventional perspective, DCMNCs in developed countries will mainly be motivated by market access in technologically less advanced industries. In contrast, the latecomer perspective stresses that DCMNCs typically will be aimed at accessing strategic assets that can assist them in their catching up strategies and/or exploiting superior positions in low cost production. Neither literature expects much efficiency or resource-seeking investment in developed countries.
- *The sustainability of developing country FDI.* From a conventional perspective, DCMNCs are likely to experience problems with securing long term sustainability and performance of their investments in developed countries. This is due to their limited capabilities and resources related to international production. In contrast, the latecomer perspective argues that DCMNCs not only possesses the ownership advantages that allow them to overcome the liability of foreignness in developed countries, they also possess dynamic capabilities that allow them to succeed in these countries in spite of their initial disadvantages.

What explains Asian investments in Denmark?

In the previous sections we have presented two generic positions on developing country FDI, the conventional perspective and the latecomer perspective. We will not attempt to resolve the debate between these two perspectives here but, more modestly, discuss the Danish case in light of the conventional and late comer perspectives, respectively.

The size of developing country FDI

As mentioned, from a conventional perspective, the FDI balance between a developed country and developing countries is expected to be skewed, with large FDI outflows from the developed country compared to the inflows from the developing country. In accordance with this, we found that Danish

FDI stock in China and India is seven to eight times higher than Chinese and Indian stock in Denmark and that, overall, less than 0.5 per cent of Danish IFDI comes from these countries. From a conventional perspective, the skewed FDI pattern is simply a reflection of the two Asian giants' and Denmark's position in the IDP. These countries have locational advantages that attract efficiency seeking and market seeking Western/Danish investors, but the ownership specific advantages of Chinese and Indian firms are not yet developed enough to make reciprocal investments in Western markets feasible. If there is any indication of latecomer theory in the level of IFDI into Denmark, it would be that the Asian investments recently appear to have been on the rise, a reflection of the fact that Indian and Chinese firms are improving their ownership specific advantages.

Another issue is that the surge in Chinese and Indian investments in Europe appears to have circumvented Denmark. For instance, while Chinese investments in Europe increased 14 times between 2003 and 2009, Chinese investment in Denmark only doubled between 2004 and 2009. Moreover, Sweden, an economy 1.4 times larger than the Danish, hosted four times as much investment stock from China in 2007 (MOFCOM) and four times as many Chinese subsidiaries in 2010 (*Berlingske Tidende*, 2010). The relatively low level of Asian engagement in Denmark is surprising as the country has one of the world's best business environments. It could be related to the fact that a small EU country such as Denmark may have greater problems coming 'onto the radar screen' of Asian investors looking for investment opportunities in Europe than countries with larger home markets. Moreover, the low level of investment could be attributed to a bad match between China's and India's industrial strengths in large-scale production within manufacturing and services, and Denmark's industrial strengths in niche and high-quality-oriented activities conducted to a large extent by SMEs. Finally, it has been argued that Danish investment promotion has been less geared to accommodate Asian investors than for example the investment promotion of their Swedish counterparts (ibid.).

The industry profile of developing country FDI

The conventional view holds that DCMNCs will mainly invest to support the market entry and global consolidation of their dominant industries such as heavy industries or low cost labour intensive industries. Indeed, many of the Chinese and Indian investments in Denmark appear to be reflecting the received comparative advantages of China and India in such industries. The electronics investments by Chinese firms and the IT and software investments by Indian firms are essentially about exploiting Chinese and Indian strengths in such industries by creating sales, marketing and distribution outlets in Denmark and beyond. Also, the Indian textile and garment investment by Reliance seems to be a reflection of Indian industrial strengths in this type of activity.

However, a surprisingly large part of the Indian and especially Chinese portfolio appears to be in technologically and organizationally advanced industries within services and manufacturing. For instance, Indian investors are active in R&D intensive industries such as renewable energy and pharmaceuticals, and several of the Indian IT firms appear to base their investment strategies in Denmark on advanced technologies, high knowledge intensity and on cutting-edge organizational modes. Likewise, Chinese investors such as BYD, with their investment in developing and testing battery-driven cars, Envision and Guangdong Mingyang Wind Power Industry, with their investment in wind turbine R&D, or BGI with a large genetic research investment in Denmark, all seem to be firms that are moving towards the technological frontier. Thus, there is indication that many of the Chinese and Indian investments in Denmark, in line with the latecomer theory, are embarking on FDI in technological frontier industries at much earlier stages than we would expect from a conventional perspective.

The motivations behind investments

As a point of departure we found that almost all Chinese and Indian investments in Denmark were market or strategic asset seeking and that virtually no investments were aimed at producing in Denmark or at accessing resources.

The market seekers are of two types. One is the traditional market seeker, who invests mainly to support trade with Denmark; the other is using Denmark as a regional hub for entering North European markets – the Chinese investors in electronics, Lenovo and Huawei Technologies, are examples of the former type, opening sales and service offices in Denmark to support exports from China. Another example is most of the Indian IT firms such as Infosys, ITC Infotech, Wipro and Tata. These IT giants support their export of IT services by creating sales and service offices close to their Danish and Scandinavian customers. Only by having close proximity to customers is it possible for these firms to exploit effectively their home country advantage in offering IT services based on qualified but comparatively low-paid Indian software engineers.

Examples of investments using Denmark as a regional hub for expanding trade into the North European and Baltic markets are for instance Cosco which developed Penta Shipping into a hub for its Scandinavian activities, or Four Soft which used Danish investment to strengthen its overall European platform in IT solutions for the shipping industry. Suzlon not only created a regional hub for its European wind turbine activities via its investment in Denmark, it also established its global sales and a marketing hub there.

A very large proportion of Asian investors are strategic asset-seekers, that is investors seeking to build new ownership-specific advantages through FDI (as opposed to exploiting existing ownership-specific advantages). Apparently many Asian investors see opportunities of acquiring complementary assets in Denmark that can support them in their catch-up strategies and enhance their global and regional presence and capabilities. The strategic asset-seeking investments in Denmark were typically aimed at accessing high-end, high-value-added activities, upstream and downstream in the value chain. Examples of investments aimed at acquiring upstream capabilities are for instance Reliance expanding its R&D activities in Denmark (but out-sourcing everything else), Suzlon investing in building a global R&D centre in Denmark, or BYD, which, through its Danish investment in the development and testing of battery-driven cars, attempts to move from a low-cost imitator to a technological lead company in a niche sector within the automotive industry. At least 8 of the 20 Chinese investments were explicitly R&D oriented, as were at least 3 of the 18 Indian investments. Examples of investments aimed at acquiring downstream capabilities are for instance that Suzlon head-hunted previous Vestas/NEG staff to build its global sales and marketing HQ in Denmark, or Four Soft which tapped into the Danish partner's strong sales and marketing capabilities in the European market, eventually making the Danish subsidiary a main revenue centre of the corporation. Also Hikal's acquisition of a majority share in the Danish pharmaceutical trading company, Marsing, is indicative of an investment aimed at acquiring downstream sales, marketing and distribution competencies in Denmark. Thus, it is evident that several of the investments in Denmark helped Asian investors overcome the often huge market entry barriers in European markets and beyond. Interestingly, whereas Asian investors in other European countries have embarked on a strategy of acquiring brands, there are really no such examples from Denmark. This is partly a reflection of the fact that Danish industry has its main strength in business-to-business markets, and partly to the fact that most Danish brands are related to industries where only a few Asian firms invest.

It is evident that most of the strategic asset-seeking investments are made in activities closely related to well-known Danish clusters such as shipping, green tech, biotech and acoustics. Through their investments in the Danish green tech cluster, Indian Suzlon and Chinese Envision Energy not only obtained access to experienced sales, marketing and R&D people, they also accessed Danish export subsidies, knowledge at Danish universities and a well-developed supply and service industry. Similarly, BYD located its test facility in Denmark mainly due to Danish subsidies for electrical cars, favourable tax policies and an excellent infrastructure. Through their acquisitions in Denmark, Cosco and Four Soft have been able to tap into the excellent physical, commercial, regulatory and human infrastructure supporting the Danish shipping cluster. And Indian Hikal and Chinese BGI and Chempartners in various ways invested in the Danish biotech cluster.

So are the Asian investments in Denmark conventional or latecomer types of investments? Essentially, we found evidence of both. But it is evident that a disproportionate share of the Asian investors are investing in Denmark to support a technological and organizational leapfrogging strategy into higher-value-added activities related to sales, marketing and R&D, an observation aligned with the predictions of latecomer theory.

Sustainability of developing country FDI

From a conventional perspective it is sometimes argued that developing country FDI somehow should be relatively less sustainable due to weak ownership-specific advantages of DCMNCs. These firms may possess some advantages generic to firms coming out of developing country locations, but they lack firm specific advantages that would allow them to sustain their performance in foreign locations. Thus, these investors may have ample finance and trained personnel to undertake FDI in developed countries, but they will lack the organizational and managerial skills that are required to integrate effectively the foreign operations in their global organizations.

As Chinese and Indian investments have only a very brief history in Denmark, the question of their sustainability is very difficult to clarify, based on the available evidence. But we do find that several Asian investment projects never got off the ground and that many others were divested. Some of the surviving investments proved difficult to integrate and experienced internal tensions as Danish and Asian cultures met. It seems that especially those investors that are strategic asset seeking require strong integration, partly through full ownership control, and partly through direct management oversight by the Asian owners. The market-seeking investments appeared less integrated, at least initially. Thus, market-seeking acquisitions such as Four Soft and Penta Shipping seemed initially to be running rather independently. However, as the acquisition matured, the Asian owners clearly attempted to integrate the acquisitions into their global operations, for example by devising internal divisions of labour or by facilitating global learning and knowledge spillovers. This integration process heightened tensions inside the organization due to internal cultural and strategic differences, as seen in the Four Soft case.

Conclusion

This chapter has provided an overview of Chinese and Indian investments in Denmark and has discussed whether these investments were new or 'just' conventional types of investment. Holding the patterns of Chinese and Indian FDI in Denmark up against the two theoretical positions, novel insights into the drivers of Asian investments seen from the point of view of a small, open economy were gained. We have found that the Asian investors in Denmark are indeed unconventional in several respects: Rather than just being staged market-seeking entries in mature industries, many are strategic asset-seeking investments in technological frontier industries, evidently aimed at augmenting capabilities upstream or downstream in the investing firms' value chain. In accordance with the conventional view, many seemed to be traditional trade support investments in industries where developing countries traditionally have their comparative advantages, mainly in low cost IT and software, and in the textile and garment and electronics industries. We also found that the strategic ambitions of the Chinese and Indian investors in some cases were undermined by problems of integrating the Danish acquisitions and thus reaping the strategic rents of the investment. Moreover, many planned investments never materialized. These findings could indicate that at least some of the Asian investors lack the organizational and managerial capabilities to organize and integrate activities in developed countries.

The study holds important policy implications. The examined Chinese and Indian investments in Denmark may be few and far between, but they are almost certainly the vanguard of a much larger inflow of Asian investment in the future. As the Indian and especially Chinese economies become dominant global economies, it will be increasingly important for a small, open economy like the Danish one to secure investments from these countries. This is partly because Asian investments in Denmark are a prerequisite for accessing the low cost and resource rich bases of the Asian markets, in particular India's knowledge base and China's manufacturing base. It is also because many of the Asian MNCs are destined to become global leaders within their industries within the next few decades. Although their initial motive for investing in Denmark evidently has been to upgrade existing ownership-specific advantages by tapping into Danish skills and assets, they may in the future contribute to a further development of those assets through injection of capital and know-how, thus contributing to building Danish competitiveness.

Attracting investments from the Asian giants poses huge challenges for Danish investment promotion. For a small country like Denmark it is insufficient to rely on received advantages such as market size and resources to attract Asian FDI. Denmark needs to differentiate itself amongst other large and small European countries. In this situation, investment promotion and facilitation that caters specifically to the particular needs of Asian investors becomes essential. This implies providing effective and appropriate general policies and framework conditions such as tax policies, infrastructure, education and research and training initiatives. But it also requires effective development and promotion of specific Danish strengths. Thus, it is clear that the first wave of Indian and Chinese investments in the country was mainly motivated by accessing the well-known Danish clusters in renewable energy, biotech, acoustics and shipping. If Denmark in the future is to become an attractive destination for Asian investors, it is essential that the advantages that the country has in such areas are further developed and that Danish investment promotion focuses its services on facilitating the Asian investors' entry into these areas.

Notes

1. This chapter consolidates and updates the authors' previous research on Chinese and Indian investment in Denmark (see e.g. Torp et al., 2011).
2. Statistics Denmark in 2006 (Statistics Denmark, 2009) estimated that investment from BRIC countries accounted for 'significantly less' than 1 per cent of the then approximately 3,500 foreign firms in Denmark.
3. These are roughly equivalent to Dunning's (1988) ownership-specific and location-specific advantages in the OLI framework.

References

Anderson, U., Johanson, J. and Vahlne, J.-E. (1997). Organic acquisitions in the internationalization process of the business firm, *Management International Review*, 37(2), 67–84.

Barney, J. (1991). Firm resources and sustained competitive advantage, *Journal of Management*, 17, 99–120.

Beausang, F. (2003). *Third World Multinationals: Engine of Competitiveness or New Form of Dependency?* Basingstoke: Palgrave Macmillan.

Buckley, P. (2009). The impact of the global factory on economic development, *Journal of World Business*, 44(2), 131–43.

Buckley, P., Wang, C., and Clegg, J. (2007). The impact of foreign ownership, local ownership and industry characteristics on spillover benefits from foreign direct investment in China, *International Business Review*, 16(2), 142–58.

Danish National Bank Statistics. (http://nationalbanken.statistikbank.dk/statbank5a/default.asp?w=1280).

Dunning, J. (1981). Explaining the international direct investment position of countries: towards a dynamic or developmental approach, *Weltwirtschaftliches Archiv*, 117(1), 30–64.

Dunning, J. (1988). The eclectic paradigm of international production: a restatement and some possible extensions, *Journal of International Business Studies*, 19(1), 1–31.

Dunning, J. and Lundan, S. (2008). *Multinational Enterprises and the Global Economy*. Cheltenham, UK: Edward Elgar.

Dunning, J. and Narula, R. (1996). The Investment Development Path revisited: some emerging issues, in J. Dunning and R. Narula (eds), *Foreign Direct Investment and Governments: Catalysts for Economic Restructuring*. London: Routledge, pp. 1–38.

Dunning, J. and Narula, R. (2004). Industrial development, globalization and multinational enterprises: new realities for developing countries, in J.H. Dunning and R. Narula (eds) *Multinational and Industrial Competitiveness*. Cheltenham, UK: Edward Elgar, pp. 38–77.

Dunning, J., Kim, C. and Park, D. (2008). Old Wine in New Bottles: A Comparison of Emerging Market TNCs Today and Developed Country TNCs Thirty Years Ago, SLPTMD Working Paper Series No. 11, Department of International Economics, University of Oxford.

Ernst, D. (2000). Inter-organizational knowledge outsourcing: what permits small Taiwanese firms to compete in the computer industry? *Asia Pacific Journal of Management*, 17(2), 223–56.

Gereffi, G., Humphrey, J., Kalinsky, R. and Sturgeon, T. (2001). Introduction: globalization, value chains, and development, *IDS Bulletin*, 32(3), 1–8.

Gerschenkron, A. (1962). *Economic Backwardness in Historical Perspective*. Cambridge, MA: Belknap Press.

Giddy, I. and Young, S. (1982). Conventional theory and unconventional multinationals: do new forms of multinational enterprise require new theories? in A. Rugman (ed.), *New Theories of the Multinational Enterprise*. London: Croom Helm, pp. 55–78.

Grant, R., Almeida, P. and Song, J. (2000). Knowledge and the multinational enterprise, in C. Millar, R. Grant and C. Choi (eds), *International Business: Emerging Issues and Emerging Markets*. London: Macmillan, pp. 102–29.

Hobday, M. (1995). *Innovation in East Asia: The Challenge to Japan*. Aldershot, UK: Edward Elgar.

Hobday, M. (1997). Latecomer catch-up strategies in electronics: Samsung of Korea and Taiwan, *Asia Pacific Business Review*, 4(2–3), 48–83.

Johanson, J. and Vahlne, J. (1977). The internationalization process of the firm: a model of knowledge development and increasing foreign market commitments, *Journal of International Business Studies*, 8(1), 23–32.

Johanson, J. and Vahlne, J.-E. (2003). Business relationship commitment and learning in the internationalization process, *Journal of International Entrepreneurship*, 1(1), 83–101.

Kuada, J. (2004). Internationalization of firms from developing countries: towards an integrated conceptual framework, paper presented to the conference on Globalization, Internationalization of Companies and Cross Cultural Management, Aalborg, October.

Li, P. (2007). Toward an integrated theory of multinational evolution: the evidence of Chinese multinational enterprises as latecomers, *Journal of International Management*, 13, 296–318.

Mathews, J. (2006). Dragon multinationals: new players in 21st century globalization, *Asia Pacific Journal of Management*, 23, 5–27.

Narula, R. (2006). Globalization, new technologies, new zoologies, and the purported death of the eclectic paradigm, *Asia Pacific Journal of Management*, 23(2), 143–51.

Oviatt, B. and McDougall, P. (1994). Toward a theory of international new ventures, *Journal of International Business Studies*, 25(1), 45–64.

Pradhan, J. and Patel, S. (2011). Emerging multinationals: comparison of Chinese and Indian outward foreign direct investment, *International Journal of Institutions and Economies Chinese*, 3(1), 113–48.

Ramamurti, R. (2008). What have we learned about emerging-market MNEs? Insights from a multi-country research project, Copenhagen Business School, Copenhagen, Denmark, 9–10 October, 2–27.

Ramamurti, R. (2009). FDI from developing countries, paper presented to the 3rd Vale Conference on Sustainable Investment, November.

Ramamurti, R. and Singh, J. (2008). Indian multinationals: generic internationalization strategies, in R. Ramamurti and J. Singh (eds), *Emerging Multinationals from Emerging Markets*. Cambridge: Cambridge University Press.

Rugman, A. and Li, J. (2007). Will China's multinationals succeed globally or regionally? *European Management Journal*, 25(5), 333–43.

Statistics Denmark (2009). *Udenlandske firmaer i Danmark*. Copenhagen: Danmarks Statistik.

Teece, D. (2000). Firm capabilities, and economic development: implications for NIEs, in L. Kim and R. Nelson (eds), *Technology, Learning and Innovation*. Cambridge, MA: Cambridge University Press, pp. 105–28.

Tolentino, P.E. (2008). Explaining the competitiveness of multinational companies from developing economies: a critical review of the academic literature, *International Journal of Technology and Globalization*, 4(1), 23–38.

Torp, J., Hansen, M. and Schaumburg-Müller, H. (2011) Chinese and Indian multinationals in Denmark: is there anything special about them? in L. Brennon (ed.) *The Emergence of Southern MNCs and their Implications for Europe*. Basingstoke, UK: Palgrave Macmillan, pp. 165–94.

Vernon, R. (1966). International investment and international trade in the product cycle, *Quarterly Journal of Economics*, 80(2), 190–207.

17

New Challengers in a Global Game: Reflections on the Internationalization of Emerging Economies and Firms

Svetla Marinova and Marin Marinov

Internationalization at the country and firm level has assisted the growth and sustained expansion of developed economies and their firms over the last couple of centuries. Consequently, the understanding of internationalization patterns and theories explaining the causes, process and effects of firm internationalization have reflected the perspectives of advanced economies. In recent years, the internationalization process has engaged, on an ever growing basis, countries at a lower level of economic development that are driven by varying political agendas and state involvement in international activities with the objective to advance their national economy. On the one hand, the internationalization of emerging economies and firms has brought about imitative behaviour through the application of some conventional internationalization approaches and practices. On the other hand, many emerging economies and firms have reshaped the global business arena by applying new, unexpected strategies and tactics towards internationalization, accelerating its pace and getting international recognition over a short period of time. This development has challenged international business scholars to explain the phenomenon of the internationalization of emerging economies and firms. There is strong evidence that the recent achievements of many emerging economies has been continuously affecting the positions of developed countries in the world's economy. Thus the internationalization of emerging economies and firms has posed questions concerning the omnipotent significance of internationalization patterns and models pertaining to developed economies and their firms.

Internationalization of national economies and the role of markets and states

The social sciences have long debated the interplay between market and state in the economic development of nation states and the world economy. There have been competing arguments about the importance and contribution of these counterbalancing forces in ensuring long term sustainable economic prosperity. Proponents of the free market vehemently promote the idea that states should not regulate markets and that market forces are the only viable power that can ensure economic growth based on increased competitiveness. Supporters of the variations of state capitalism profess that markets cannot regulate themselves alone and that the state should play a role in ensuring economic stability, viability and continuity. It could be argued, though, that the role of the market and the state in the process of development and internationalization of national economies can be presented on a continuum. At one end of that continuum is the state exercising full control over all economic activities, determining the internationalization of a country and its firms. At the other end stands the market as the only regulator, with no state interference to provide guidance, control and assistance. However, considering the variations between these two extremes, only few countries can be found tending towards either of the polar ends. Examples of where the state decides and controls economic activities almost totally are North Korea and Cuba. Russia, at the time of Yeltsin's presidency, when the state withdrew fully as an owner, regulator and guidance provider of economic activities and internationalization, could be cited as an example tending towards the other end of the continuum. Such extremes inevitably lead either to isolation of national economies from international activities and to stagnated economic performance, as in the former examples, or to an economic chaos without rules in which omnipotent oligarchs dictate, rip off all the economic benefits and neglect the interests of society at large, as in the latter example. Yet, most countries in the world find themselves in positions along the continuum where markets and states complement one another to a varying extent. Some developed economies are in positions mostly regulated by market mechanisms. This is generally valid for the countries with Anglo-Saxon capitalism, good examples being the USA and the UK. Other developed economies, for instance in Scandinavia, tend to give priority to the role of the state in the functioning of their economies. Such countries aim at balancing the impact of the state with market forces, and this has given rise to various forms of state capitalism. Indeed, one could argue that, under the conditions of greater market dominance in a national economy, there are greater requirements for a stronger and better system of state governance (Rodrik, 2011) that controls and regulates the effects of market forces.

Emerging economies are found at different positions along the market–state continuum. In some of them, the state has almost withdrawn itself from guiding, controlling and regulating economic activities. However, others, China being a good example, have engaged in activities aiming at participation in globalization under new rules, whereby the state plays the role of a partial owner of productive assets, a planner, a controller and a regulator of internationalization of the country and its overall economic development – yet allowing a preplanned and somewhat restricted independence of market forces.

In Chapter 2 Karl Sauvant argues that emerging economy governments engaged in outward internationalization are presently paying more attention to their country's institutional structures and status as capital exporters, while some of their firms invest abroad as major international players. This situation is particularly true for the internationalization of state-owned and state-controlled firms from the emerging economies of China and Russia. It might be posited that in the case of emerging economies a country-specific interplay between the market and the state can bring better results for internationalization and economic development when new rules of participation in the global economy are established.

In Chapter 3, Witold Wilinski supports the notion that government intervention in and government support for the internationalization of firms from transition economies has generally brought better results for country and firm level internationalization than in the cases when the government has been indifferent towards the provision of guidance and regulation regarding such processes.

Taking an investment development path perspective in Chapter 4, Marian Gorynia, Jan Nowak, Piotr Tarka and Radosław Wolniak investigate the advancement of the transforming emerging economies of Central and Eastern Europe after they became new members of the European Union. The authors argue that, among other factors impacting on country internationalization and its stage in the investment development path, economy and firm augmented international competitiveness can play a key role.

In Chapter 5, based on his research findings, Marjan Svetličič expresses the notion that there is no a unique strategy suitable for all emerging economies that can facilitate the promotion of FDI as an inward source of internationalization and stimulate their economic development. He argues that FDI promotion programmes can be regarded as exceedingly particular, adapted to the unambiguous circumstances and requirements of emerging economy contexts as well as the motives and goals of foreign investors.

In Chapter 8, Andrei Panibratov brings evidence confirming that the Russian state assists the outward internationalization of domestic firms through limiting foreign firms' opportunities, thus enforcing ownership restrictions. This fact allows Russian internationalizing firms to gain profits permitting them to self-finance their acquisitions overseas. Furthermore,

Panibratov holds that, considering the host country government's perspectives, when investments are made in the emerging economies of the Commonwealth of Independent States their governments usually support investments by Russian firms and assist the implementation of Russian government policy for international expansion within their economies.

Chapter 6, by Siv Marina Flø Karlsen, Youzhen Zhao and Randi Lunnan, reconfirms that one key cause for the speedy development of Chinese SMEs and their well-built export shares is the proactive role played by the Chinese government in funding and supporting the internationalization of Chinese SMEs.

Development of firm-specific advantages and their role in firm internationalization

The theory of comparative advantage, initiated by David Ricardo (1817), suggests that there should be international specialization in which nations and their firms should not engage in business activities for which they do not possess any comparative advantages. This is reinforced by the capability notion (Peters and Waterman, 1987) bringing forward firm capabilities that are associated with and reinforce firm competitive advantages. Such a line of argument would support the concept that emerging economies and their firms should focus on low value-added activities, such as the production of labour intensive products, as they possess advantages in the manufacturing of such products not requiring advanced technology and involving low labour cost. Similarly, the conventional view in the international business literature argues that emerging economy FDI in developed countries is small and will stay as such in comparison to IFDI from developed countries because firms from emerging economies lack ownership-specific advantages. Furthermore, according to the Investment Development Path (IDP) (see for example, Dunning and Narula, 1996) the OFDI from emerging economies will become more significant only in the latter stages of their IDP development. Similarly, the product life-cycle theory, introduced by Raymond Vernon (1966), relating to FDI, presupposes that emerging economies will become outward investors when products and technologies used in developed countries mature and their product life-cycle is extended by more efficient production originating from emerging economies that generally may have advantages associated with lower labour and material costs. Such an extension of the product life-cycle can be achieved by imitation and diffusion, and it applies mostly to technologically less-advanced industries, referred to as mature mid-technologies, which are not of strategic importance to developed countries and in which developed country firms can be no longer internationally competitive. Examples of such industries include garment production or widely used consumer electronics. Such a position is supported by the perspective on country-specific advantages (CSAs), introduced by Rugman (1981), whereby the CSAs of emerging economies supposedly may stem from natural resource availability and low labour cost, whereas Western economies' CSAs are mainly based on proprietary technology, advanced knowledge and management know-how.

Despite the above arguments, the rapid globalization coupled with major changes in emerging economies has had an enormous positive effect on the volume of FDI from emerging economies. Thus, FDI originating from emerging economies has grown much faster than expected. Corroborating the evidence, the latecomer perspective regarding firm internationalization (see for instance, Child and Rodrigues, 2005; Mathews, 2006; Cuervo-Cazurra and Genc, 2008; Ramamurti and Singh, 2009; Marinova et al., 2011) has supported the notion that emerging economies and their firms internationalize to compensate for competitive disadvantages at the country and firm level, thus often engaging in accelerated internationalization into technologically advanced industries. Emerging economy firms successfully compensating for their disadvantages (Curevo-Cazurra and Genc, 2008) engage in accelerated internationalization by investing successfully into developed countries and/or high value-added activities in the global value chain using learning, leveraging and linkage capabilities (Mathews, 2002). They may also benefit, among others, from the institutional support of home country governments, and from considerable firm flexibility, speedy innovation processes, a large highly qualified and inexpensive labour force, and favourable cost structures.

In line with the above, in Chapter 16, Michael W. Hansen, Jens Erik Torp and Henrik Schaumburg-Müller present evidence that Indian and Chinese firms have engaged in strategic asset-seeking investments in technological frontier industries in Denmark, aiming at augmenting capabilities upstream or downstream of the investing firm's value chain. However, in some of these cases the realization of the strategic intent was hampered by problems inherent to a lack of or inappropriate management know-how for global business integration.

The findings of Elaine Y. T. Chew, Lee Peng Ng and Chin Kian Low in Chapter 11 confirm that firms can adopt growth patterns as a result of strategic change and thus accumulate technological capabilities. It is also interesting to note that firms from less advanced emerging economies have found it beneficial to seek greater exposure to more advanced emerging economy markets, such as China, because of their greater business dynamics and sustainable economic growth (which is more advanced than in other emerging economy technologies) and their significant latent needs for products and services. Such an approach has assisted the internationalization of the Malaysian firms, analysed in Chapter 11, to leapfrog stages in the development of technological and marketing capabilities in the process of their internationalization.

Along this line of argument, the global value chain literature claims that firms will benefit more from higher value-added activities than from low value-added operations. Therefore firms from emerging economies have also started to attempt functional upgrading in order to ensure long term sustainable development. Thus, in Chapter 10, Bent Petersen and Song-Hanh Pham found that, in exporting furniture, Vietnamese firms should gain control over pricing, as well as have greater engagement in product adaptation. Moreover, promotion and better market intelligence have contributed significantly to the export success of firms from emerging economies, which increases their bargaining power and economic return. Thus, Claude Chailan and Francis Ille's analysis, conducted in Chapter 15, supports the notion that firms from emerging economies will move up the value chain more rapidly through developing their own or acquiring well-established brands from developed economy firms. There are some good examples that warrant attention, such as the acquisition of the famous Godiva chocolate brand by the Turkish firm Üllker, the independent development of the Chinese white goods brand Haier, the creation via acquisition and independent development of the Chinese computer brand Lenovo, or the acquisition of the iconic Swedish brand Volvo by the Chinese firm Cherry, to name just a few. The current state is that firms from emerging economies still need to develop marketing competences in the international arena and upgrade their design capabilities so that their brands can contain greater chances to compete successfully in the global marketplace.

The role of entrepreneurship in firm internationalization

A key driver in the internationalization of firms from emerging economies is entrepreneurship at the firm and state level. Firm entrepreneurship is embedded in the entrepreneurial cognition, as well as in the perception of the nature, drivers and process specifics of firm internationalization. Zahra et al. (2005) argue that there is a greater need for developing an understanding of how born global entrepreneurs perceive and interpret firm internationalization. It seems that the focus on the relationship between meanings and understandings associated with entrepreneurial interpretation of firm internationalization activities drawing upon the understanding of social action (Weber, 1968), can offer a better understanding of the meanings informing international action in the interpretations of entrepreneurs. Moreover, such reasoning can shed light on the early consolidation of a born global venture and on the conditions under which entrepreneurs form the relevant meanings and understandings of internationalization. The findings from the analysis of the case of Trikke, in Chapter 13 by René Eugenio Seifert and Bruno Henrique Rocha Fernandes, suggest that the inauguration of the firm as a born global has been informed by the entrepreneurs' understanding that the firm's innovative product has an intrinsic value and potential for commercialization and by the realization that entrepreneurial success requires persistence and risk acceptance. The understandings and interpretations of entrepreneurship have been critical in orienting the firm towards international activities. More importantly, the Trikke case suggests that entrepreneurs did not perceive foreign market entry mode as a sequential commitment of resources and a process of incremental learning, rather the use of alternative governance structures, global dispersion of activities along the value chain and the subsequent international actions in multiple countries were not antecedents to the firm's inception but emerged from the entrepreneurs' attempt to venture internationally, set up the business and grow its operations, not within, but across national borders. Thus, international entrepreneurial development could be equated to international enterprising.

Motives for internationalization

Based on the matrix suggested by Ramamurti (2009) and on the content of the chapters in this volume, we can summarize the key motives for FDI flow from and to emerging economies in the matrix below (see Figure 17.1). The

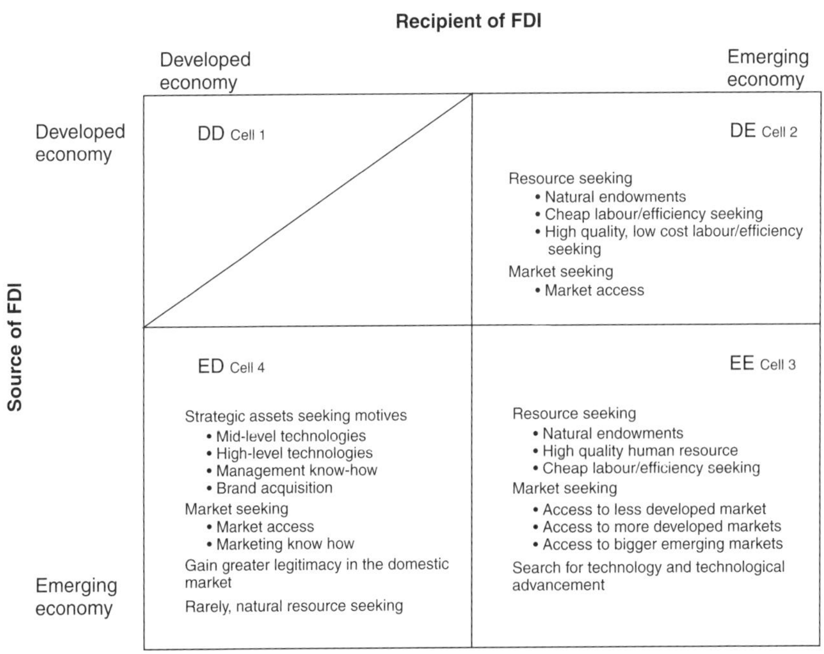

Figure 17.1 Motives behind the internationalization of emerging economies and firms

position represented by Cell 1 in Figure 17.1 is beyond the scope of our interest, as it refers to investment flows between developed economies. Cell 2 of the matrix illustrates the passive or inward internationalization of emerging economies and refers to the motives by which investing firms from the developed world go to emerging economy markets. These investments have exposed emerging economies among others to technological upgrading, more advanced methods of production and management processes, market exchanges, and greater competitive pressures. However, most of these investments are made by foreign firms with the intention of exploiting firm-specific advantages and recipient country-specific advantages. Such firms come from a more advanced technological and management position, and usually have significant experience of international operations. The most attractive assets of emerging economies are their natural endowments: their inexpensive, occasionally high quality, labour forces and their sometimes large pool of consumers, combined with high market growth potential.

Cells 3 and 4 represent two varieties of proactive or outward internationalization of emerging economy firms in which FDI originates from emerging economy contexts targeting either other emerging economies (Cell 3) or developed economies (Cell 4).

Regarding Cell 3, resource- and market-seeking motives drive emerging economy firms investing in other emerging economies. Lack of or insufficiently available natural endowments motivate emerging market firms to look for such resources in other emerging economies which is typical, for instance, of some Chinese firms investing in Africa and Latin America. The economic growth in emerging economies has increased the need for resource inputs. This need has driven companies from emerging economies lacking some resources, such as oil, gas and/or metal containing ores, to internationalize into other emerging economies that possess such natural endowments. Thus resource-seeking motives account for the internationalization of firms from some emerging economies to natural resource-rich emerging economies. For example, Chapter 12 by Diego Quer, Enrique Claver and Laura Rienda brings evidence that the search for natural resources has been a traditional objective of Chinese OFDI with an increasing emphasis on fuel and industrial raw materials.

Firms from less advanced emerging economies seek to establish themselves in more advanced ones, such as China, because of slow domestic growth potential, weak home-country government support and difficulties in securing large domestic projects. Deficiency of high quality labour brings investments from less advanced emerging economies into more advanced ones, for example Indonesian investments into China. In some emerging economies the labour cost advantage has been eroded as is the case of manufacturing production in Mexico, which is being relocated to lower cost production destinations such as other Latin American countries or even countries in South East Asia.

Market-seeking motives explain FDI flows from both more developed towards less developed emerging economies such as some Russian investments in Africa and certain Chilean investments in Bolivia, or FDI flows originating from less developed emerging economies targeting more developed ones, as is the case of Ecuadorian investments in Costa Rica. Big emerging economies, such as the ones of China and India, have been focal points of many FDIs starting from other emerging economies aiming to serve markets with enormous size and excessive growth potential. Rarely quests for technological improvement and efficiency enhancement can bring investments from one emerging economy into another.

Being a relatively recent phenomenon that gains pace on a significant scale and having attracted least attention from researchers in the international business area is the situation in Cell 4 where FDI originates from emerging economies and targets developed economies. From a conventional perspective, firms from emerging economies internationalize into developed countries to seek market access in technologically slow advancing industries (for example Indian investments in the iron and steel industry in Western Europe, Mexican investments in cement industries in developed economies or Chinese white goods investments in Western Europe and North America). The latecomer perspective suggests that many of the emerging market firms establish an international presence in developed economies to gain access to strategic assets, such as advanced technology and know-how that could enable them to implement catching up strategies. Thus internationalizing firms from emerging economies are often driven by the motive to compensate for technological disadvantages. They attempt to achieve this goal via the acquisition of strategic assets that may range from knowledge about new products or production processes to innovation approaches, design and branding. These they can later couple with advantages in low cost production and advanced technical education to trigger accelerated imitative or independent innovation processes that facilitate firm and country internationalization. Consequently, emerging economy firms internationalize into countries more developed than their home country in order to engage in active learning from developed economies' market contexts, create linkages with domestic operations and leverage their competencies across foreign markets. Examples of such investments include among others Chinese FDI in Western Europe and North America, Indian FDI in Japan and Europe, Malaysian FDI in the UK and Russian investments in Western Europe. In addition, firms from emerging economies engage in internationalization motivated by opportunities to spread risk across markets, which can make the firm less dependent on a single, sometimes less predictable or stable market, and on a single currency that may be exposed to a high degree of volatility.

The market-seeking motives of emerging economy firms are related to market access combined with exposure to advanced highly competitive markets, sophisticated consumers and experience-enhanced marketing techniques. Illustrative examples are those of the Brazilian software firm, presented in Chapter 14 by Daniela Buzzulini Prioste and Cesar Akira Yokomizo, that created a subsidiary in Canada and engaged in a partnership agreement with a Portuguese firm; as well as the launch of the Trikke product in the US by another Brazilian firm. The expertise gained from such contexts helps emerging economy firms to enhance their domestic market position and increase legitimacy in home and other emerging market contexts. Seldom, FDI from emerging economy firms into developed economies is motivated by natural resource seeking, as is the case of Chinese FDI in the primary sector of Australia.

The liabilities of foreignness

The intensified participation of firms from emerging markets in the international area and the much greater involvement of firms from developed economies in business operations in emerging economies has challenged firms in their attempts to cope successfully with their liability of foreignness (Rugman and Doh; 2008). It should be recognized that all international firms, whether from developed or emerging economies, face some degree of liability of foreignness when expanding overseas. Firms from developed economies could experience lower liability of foreignness when they internationalize into other developed markets due to similarities in the institutional contexts and social organization of business activities, while their liability of foreignness could be higher when internationalizing into emerging economy environments. By contrast, firms from emerging economies might face a lower liability of foreignness when they internationalize into other emerging country contexts due to their experience in dealing with similar institutional systems characterized by a relationship-oriented cultural background, whereas in developed markets they could encounter much greater liability of foreignness because of significant dissimilarities in institutional structures.

Thus, all internationalizing firms have to use diverse mechanisms to reduce their liability of foreignness and gain legitimacy to ease their operations overseas. While in the case of Trikke, presented in Chapter 13 by René Eugenio Seifert and Bruno Henrique Rocha Fernandes, the liability of foreignness has been reduced by cross-border entrepreneurial mobility and the formation of a competence-based management team utilizing, on the one hand, complementary expertise in market knowledge and creative marketing capabilities, and, on the other hand, expertise in engineering, creativity and innovation. In Chapter 9 by Niina Nummela and Mélanie Raukko, M&As are used as a short cut to gaining local market legitimacy. In the latter case, however, cultural difference still proved to be a major hurdle in the firms' attempts to legitimize themselves in the Indian context. Thus, cross-cultural management, through learning, interaction and acculturation, has been used to reduce the liability of foreignness linked to M&As associated with specific emerging market contexts. Consequently, in cross-border acquisitions, where the national and/or organizational cultures are unfamiliar to the acquirer and the acquired, the acculturation process usually starts slowly with the acquirer and the acquired learning more about each other and from one another, getting to know and understand better each other's cultural subtleties. Thus, Chapter 9 illustrates that internationalizing firms from emerging economies engaging in M&As have to assess carefully opportunities for cultural fit and cultural distance during the pre-acquisition phase in order to plan the integration strategy and the acculturation process.

Establishing strategic partnerships is a key mechanism for reducing the liability of foreignness to ensure better resource utilization and sharing of expertise. Partnerships can leverage strengths and enable a firm to fill in the gap between what it would like to accomplish and what its resources really would allow it to do in a foreign market. For example, the Brazilian firm discussed in Chapter 14 selected a partner in Portugal because it possessed no previous knowledge of the European market and because it did not have a well-known international brand. However, it offered the European partner an advanced and sophisticated banking and information security system. Panibratov in Chapter 8 shows that partnership formations via creation of international joint ventures and strategic alliances can reduce the liability of foreignness as they have allowed internationalizing Russian hi-tech firms rapid access to the host country infrastructure in general and distribution systems in particular.

The liability of foreignness can also be reduced by participating in business networks created through continuing reinforcement of supplier–customer relationships. As Chapter 11 by Elaine Y. T. Chew, Lee Peng Ng and Chin Kian Low indicates, key buyers in overseas markets have encouraged some Malaysian firms to search for clients abroad via minimizing risks and transaction costs concerning FDI market entry modes applied by internationalizing firms.

In Chapter 12, Quer, Claver and Rienda argue that the Chinese diaspora has contributed to China's incorporation into the world economy, due to the large number of FDIs in China originating from Singapore, Hong Kong and Taiwan. Meanwhile, the Chinese have also exercised an important influence on the selection of destination countries for their OFDI.

By comparison Chapter 11 demonstrates that firms can reduce their liability of foreignness by showing greater commitment to developing production and R&D functions in host countries. Thus a Malaysian firm committed resources to production in China, further reducing its liability of foreignness in the Chinese market by developing a close collaboration with a Chinese university to conduct research and laboratory testing in order to improve the quality of its products and their suitability to the Chinese market.

Whatever the specific mechanisms used to reduce the liability of foreignness, these mechanisms reflect management interpretation and choice based on knowledge, experience in international markets and willingness to engage in a learning process where meanings and understandings are produced and reproduced, reflecting the specifics of the context. Thus Chapter 14 by Daniela Buzzulini Prioste and Cesar Akira Yokomizo suggests that when managers who are responsible for domestic sales embrace international sales as well, there might be a conflict of priorities and preference, for choice is often impacted on by the managers' comfort zone as it is embedded in domestic sales. Such an approach seems inappropriate because in a big fast growing emerging market, where market potential is high, domestic commercial business may have a higher priority, which can jeopardize the expansion into foreign markets. Such an attitude, which we would call internationalization myopia, may put an emerging economy firm in a difficult position over time as it would eventually face competitive pressure from aggressive domestic firms with a focus on ongoing innovation as well as from foreign technologically advanced firms seeking greater market presence in the fast growing big domestic market.

Accelerated internationalization of emerging economy firms

This volume brings evidence that firms from emerging economies experience accelerated internationalization and can be found simultaneously in more than one stage of the Uppsala internationalization model. For example, the Brazilian software firm discussed in Chapter 14 engaged only in exporting concerning its European internationalization in a partnership with a Portuguese firm, but it was also in a more advanced stage of its internationalization regarding its Canadian operations where it has created a subsidiary. Furthermore, the results in Chapter 11 support the view that internationalization of firms from emerging economies is not necessarily sequential, representing internationalization as a gradual process following a well established position in the domestic market. For example, one of the firms in this study (Firm A) has been involved in multinational activities since business inception, while another (Firm D) set up its subsidiaries overseas simply two years after its establishment.

Chapter 7 by Tiia Vissak and Xiaotian Zhang brings evidence that firms from emerging economies can be born global to serve exclusively foreign customers. Such firms operate in their home country and overseas without having domestic clients. Production is usually in the home country. Such born global firms may be involved simultaneously in exporting, joint ventures and wholly owned subsidiaries in various foreign markets. Some case firms discussed in Chapter 7 have ceased their initial sales in the domestic market as foreign markets have become numerous and more lucrative than the home one. All case firms had not experienced inward internationalization prior to their accelerated outward internationalization, having become born global due to their own entrepreneurial activities.

Conclusion

Concerning the key reasons for the internationalization of emerging economy firms Chapter 8 brings evidence that sustainable economic development, low cost opportunities for international expansion, government support and a numerous, high quality, cheap workforce are the key reasons that will continue to serve as drivers to the internationalization of Russian firms. The internationalization process of firms from emerging economies brings about changes in the formal and interpersonal structures and responsibilities, apart from bringing changes in the attitudes and mindsets of people. Once changes are noted as irreversible, the firm has to restructure itself, looking for new partners and opening new offices. Moreover, it is necessary to train people to acquire new skills, invest in technology, improve product/service development processes and obtain knowledge of each country where a firm intends to trade its products and brands.

The literature on international business is well-developed concerning internationalization of developed economies and firms. International business researchers are seeking new explanations for the accelerated internationalization of emerging economies and firms using existing theoretical foundations. Nevertheless, there is a need for more rigorous development of theories and approaches concerning the internationalization of emerging economies and firms. The challenge of the market–state interface in the process of internationalization of economies and firms and its impact on economic advancement has not yet been resolved, not only in the emerging economies' context, but also universally.

References

Child, J. and Rodrigues, S. (2005). The internationalization of Chinese firms: a case for theoretical extension? *Management and Organization Review*, 1(3), 381–410.

Cuervo-Cazurra, A. and Genc, M. (2008). Transforming disadvantages into advantages: developing-country MNEs in the least developed countries, *Journal of International Business Studies*, 39(3), 957–79.

Dunning, J.H. and Narula, R. (1996). The investment development path revisited: some emerging issues, in J.H. Dunning and R. Narula (eds), *Foreign Direct Investment and Governments*. London: Routledge, pp. 1–41.

Marinova, S., Child, J. and Marinov, M. (2011). Evolution of firm- and country-specific advantages and disadvantages in the process of Chinese firm internationalization, in C.G. Asmussen, T. Pedersen, T.M. Devinney and L. Tihanyi (eds), *Dynamics of Globalization: Location-Specific Advantages and Liability of Foreignness?* Bingley: Emerald.

Mathews, J.A. (2002). Competitive advantages of the latecomer firm: a resource-based account of industrial catch-up strategies, *Asia Pacific Journal of Management*, 19(4), 467–88.

Mathews, J. (2006). Catch-up strategies and the latecomer effect in industrial development, *New Political Economy*, 11(3), 313–35.

Peters, T.J. and Waterman, R.H. (1987). *In Search of Excellence*. New York: Harper & Row.

Ramamurti, R. (2009). Why study emerging market multinationals? in R. Ramamurti and J.V. Singh (eds), *Emerging Multinationals in Emerging Markets*. Cambridge: Cambridge University Press, pp. 3–22.

Ramamurti, R. and Singh, J.V. (2009). *Emerging Multinationals in Emerging Markets*. Cambridge: Cambridge University Press.

Ricardo, D. (1817). *On the Principles of Political Economy and Taxation*. London: John Murray.

Rodrik, D. (2011). *The Globalization Paradox: Why Global Markets, States, and Democracy Can't Coexist*. Oxford: Oxford University Press.

Rugman, A.M. (1981). *Inside the Multinationals: The Economics of Internal Markets*. New York: Columbia University Press.

Rugman, A.M. and Doh, J.P. (2008). *Multinationals and Development*. New Haven & London: Yale University Press.

Vernon, R. (1966). International investment and international trade in the product cycle, *Quarterly Journal of Economics*, 80, 190–207.

Weber, M. (1968). *Economy and Society: An Outline of Interpretive Sociology*. New York, NY: Bedminster Press.

Zahra, S.A., Korri, J.S. and Yu, J. (2005). Cognition and international entrepreneurship: implications for research on international opportunity recognition and exploitation, *International Business Review*, 14, 129–46.

Index

Not all authors are listed in the index, readers wanting the names of all authors and titles of all sources are advised to refer to the references following each chapter.